core concepts in

fashion

Laura Portolese Dias, Ph.D.

Shoreline Community College, Washington

McGraw-Hill Irwin

Boston   Burr Ridge, IL   Dubuque, IA   Madison, WI   New York   San Francisco   St. Louis
Bangkok   Bogotá   Caracas   Kuala Lumpur   Lisbon   London   Madrid   Mexico City
Milan   Montreal   New Delhi   Santiago   Seoul   Singapore   Sydney   Taipei   Toronto

CORE CONCEPTS IN FASHION

Published by McGraw-Hill/Irwin, a business unit of The McGraw-Hill Companies, Inc., 1221 Avenue of the Americas, New York, NY, 10020.
Copyright © 2008 by The McGraw-Hill Companies, Inc. All rights reserved. No part of this publication may be reproduced or distributed
in any form or by any means, or stored in a database or retrieval system, without the prior written consent of The McGraw-Hill Companies, Inc.,
including, but not limited to, in any network or other electronic storage or transmission, or broadcast for distance learning.

Some ancillaries, including electronic and print components, may not be available to customers outside the United States.

This book is printed on acid-free paper.

1 2 3 4 5 6 7 8 9 0 DOW/DOW 0 9 8 7 6

ISBN   978-0-07-319622-0
MHID   0-07-319622-3

Editorial director: *John E. Biernat*
Publisher: *Linda Schreiber*
Associate sponsoring editor: *Natalie J. Ruffatto*
Developmental editor: *Peter Vanaria*
Marketing manager: *Keari Bedford*
Marketing coordinator: *Megan Gates*
Media producer: *Benjamin Curless*
Lead project manager: *Christine A. Vaughan*
Production supervisor: *Janean A. Utley*
Designer: *Cara David*
Photo research coordinator: *Lori Kramer*
Photo researcher: *Teri Stratford*
Media project manager: *Lynn M. Bluhm*
Typeface: *10/12 Times New Roman*
Compositor: *GTS – New Delhi, India Campus*
Printer: *R. R. Donnelley*

Library of Congress Cataloging-in-Publication Data

Dias, Laura Portolese.
    Core concepts in fashion / Dr. Laura Portolese Dias. — 1st ed.
       p. cm.
    Includes bibliographical references and index.
    ISBN-13: 978-0-07-319622-0 (alk. paper)
    ISBN-10: 0-07-319622-3 (alk. paper)
    1. Fashion —Vocational guidance. 2. Clothing trade —Vocational guidance. I. Title.
TT507.D5287 2008
746.9'2023 —dc22
                                                    2006035092

www.mhhe.com

:: *for Alain, Mom, and Dad with love*

dr. Laura Portolese Dias is a professor at Shoreline Community College in Washington, where she teaches fashion courses, introduction to business, international business, and essentials of supervision. In addition, she has taught fashion courses for Central Washington University, The Art Institute of Seattle, and business courses for City University.

Dr. Portolese Dias is involved in development of the fashion merchandising program at Shoreline Community College, as well as various nationally recognized entrepreneurship projects.

Dr. Portolese Dias is an advisor for College DECA, where her students compete nationally on various business and fashion related role-play events. In addition to her role as advisor, she is a member of the DECA Post-Secondary Council, which is the oversight group for College DECA.

Previously, Dr. Portolese Dias was the academic director for the fashion merchandising, visual merchandising, and fashion design programs at the Art Institute of Seattle. In addition, she has many years of fashion and business experience.

Dr. Portolese Dias lives in Seattle, Washington with her husband, Alain, and two dogs, Sam and Casey. She is an avid traveler, golfer, and of course, shopper! ✳

Fashion has to be one of the most exciting industries in which to work. It's fast paced, never boring, and changes people's lives on a daily basis. Some might snicker at that and think, "Fashion doesn't really change lives." But I truly believe it does. Consider the person who has just purchased a new outfit for a job interview. The better she feels in that outfit, the more confident she will feel in the interview, and the more likely she will be to get the job. Although we know, of course, beauty is only skin deep, we also know that clothing can change the way we feel and the way we look. Clothing can reflect our moods, our hopes, and the group to which we belong. This is what makes it such an exciting industry!

Students of fashion have a keen eye for trends. Some have a knack for drawing; while others can formulate a merchandising budget in a matter of minutes; still others can build incredibly creative display windows. The directions in which a fashion career can take you are endless; and this textbook will attempt to scratch the surface of the major areas in the fashion industry.

Lastly, congratulations. It is a big step to choose a career and to commit both finances and time to make your dream become a reality. Work hard, be kind to your professors (they have a lot of contacts in the industry!), learn as much as you can, and pat yourself on the back for taking the first steps on your journey into the fashion industry!

Warmest regards, ✻

Dr. Laura Portolese Dias

Core Concepts in Fashion offers a hands-on, comprehensive approach to learning the fashion industry. The content and the style of the book describe the three major areas of fashion—research, production, and marketing—in an enjoyable and informative manner.

After reading the chapter, you should be able to:

1 • Describe the three areas in which fashion operates.
2 • Differentiate types of jobs available in the fashion industry.
3 • Write a fashion-appropriate résumé.
4 • Compose a dynamic cover letter.
5 • Understand interviewing techniques.

chapter one

fashion careers

he most important thing in finding a job is finding something you like to do. Loving a job makes it much easier to get up and go to work everyday! Because a successful career in fashion is likely your motivation for reading this textbook, it will begin with a discussion of the types of jobs available in the industry. Before trying for an entry-level job after graduation, you may consider taking a part-time job in retail to gain experience in the industry. To this end, a section on résumés, cover letters, and interviewing is included.

Unique chapter openers layout the chapter's objectives and give the student a visual overview of topics.

chapter six

consumer behavior in fashion

onsumers buy clothing for more than practical reasons. They purchase clothing to be trendy, to fit in, and to reflect a certain image. The study of consumer behavior examines these motivations for purchasing and helps fashionistas to see exactly how customers behave when buying products. By understanding the how and why of consumer behavior, fashionistas will be better able to offer customers the products they want.

After reading this chapter, you should be able to:

1 • Explain and give examples of the consumer buying process.
2 • Use reference groups in marketing as a way to understand customers.
3 • Describe the reasons people purchase fashion items.
4 • Explain the types of market segmentation and how they might be used in marketing fashion products.
5 • Identify the primary research methods for consumer behavior.

The **Fashion Model**, detailing the three major aspects of the fashion industry, provides an overview of the topics presented in the text. Visual representations of the model appear in the form of figures.

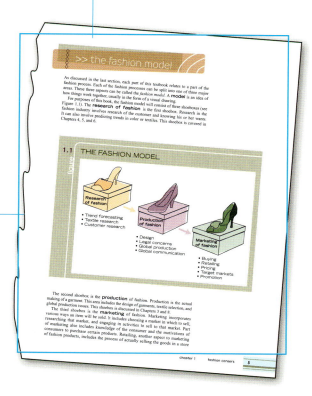

As discussed in the last section, each part of this textbook relates to a part of the fashion process. Each of the fashion processes can be split into one of three major areas. These three aspects can be called the *fashion model*. A **model** is an idea of how things work together, usually in the form of a visual drawing.

For purposes of this book, the fashion model will consist of three shoeboxes (see Figure 1.1). The **research of fashion** is the first shoebox. Research in the fashion industry involves research of the customer and knowing his or her wants. It can also involve predicting trends in color or textiles. This shoebox is covered in Chapters 4, 5, and 6.

1.1 THE FASHION MODEL

- Trend forecasting
- Textile research
- Customer research

Research of fashion

Production of fashion
- Design
- Legal concerns
- Global production
- Global communication

Marketing of fashion
- Buying
- Retailing
- Pricing
- Target markets
- Promotion

The second shoebox is the **production** of fashion. Production is the actual making of a garment. This area includes the design of garments, textile selection, and global production issues. This shoebox is discussed in Chapters 3 and 8.

The third shoebox is the **marketing** of fashion. Marketing incorporates various ways an item will be sold, to the clothes we wear; all are part of researching that market, and engaging in activities to sell to that market. Part of marketing also includes knowledge of the consumer and the motivations of consumers to purchase certain products. Retailing, another aspect to marketing of fashion products, includes the process of actually selling the goods in a store

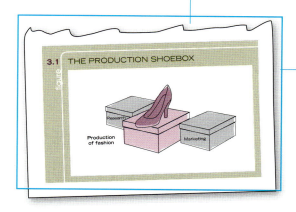

3.1 THE PRODUCTION SHOEBOX

Research

Production of fashion

Marketing

Pull quotes, numerous photos, and a unique table of contents present a magazine-like feel that immediately grabs the students' attention.

Fashion is all-encompassing. It is all around us in the products we use everyday. From the car we drive, the bed sheets we use, to the clothes we wear; all are part of fashion. The fabrics, textures, and colors used in these products are predicted far in advance, and the waves of these predictions can be seen in almost every industry. Fashion affects music, and music affects fashion. Television and movies inspire fashion. And because fashion is all-encompassing, there are many aspects of the industry that need new talent constantly.

Readers of this textbook may dream of designing beautiful garments for famous people, designing store windows on Madison Avenue in New York, or perhaps traveling to Paris and Milan to buy all of the newest fashions. Achieving one of these dreams is possible, with the right tools to make it happen. Stella McCartney, Paul Smith, and Christian Dior did not become famous designers overnight; it took extensive knowledge of the industry, hard work, and dedication to the trade. According to Webster's, a **fashionist** is a submissive follower of the modes and fashions; a **fashionista**, on the other hand, is a designer or promoter of the latest fashion. This book will provide the basic tools and overview to become a fashionista, like Betsey Johnson, Vera Wang, or Marc Jacobs.

Most people have an easier time understanding concepts from the big picture and then learning how the details fit into that big picture. Thus, this book will be structured in a similar manner. In addition, this textbook will be organized by how fashion moves from creation stages and into the hands of consumers, outlined as follows. The designer or merchandise must

1. Have a basic understanding of the industry (Chapters 1, 2, and 3).
2. Predict the trends (Chapters 4 and 5).
3. Understand the customer and market to them in the appropriate manner (Chapters 6 and 7).
4. Produce the actual goods (Chapter 8).
5. Make sure the store environment is right (Chapter 9).
6. Plan appropriately for future merchandise (Chapter 10).

> *"...because fashion is all encompassing, there are many aspects of the industry that need new talent constantly."*

The first chapter provides an explanation of the careers available in the fashion industry. Most people would not be attending college if it weren't for the hope that a better job can be obtained with a college degree. In addition, gaining some experience in the industry, while receiving formal education, is important. For this reason, Chapter 1 will also discuss résumés, cover letters, and interviewing as a means to gaining a part-time job while in school.

Chapter 2 will discuss the basics of fashion merchandising. Fashion merchandising can be considered the business side of fashion. It can include the actual selling of merchandise and the buying of merchandise to put into stores. However, any fashionista must have general knowledge of business. This chapter will discuss categories of fashion products and the process a fashion merchandiser goes through to end up with fashion products in stores.

Chapter 3 will focus on the basics of fashion design. Details within this part of the industry will be discussed. For example, the materials a fashion designer uses in his or her creations are extremely important. Therefore, textiles will be discussed from the perspective of the designer.

In Chapter 4, students will gain a historical perspective on fashion. The history of fashion is important because, as discussed in this chapter, history often helps predict future fashion trends.

Chapter 5 will discuss how a designer or merchandiser can better predict trends. Movies, television, music, and even politics are all influences that will be discussed.

Chapter 6 will cover the motivation of the customer. What makes a customer buy a particular product and the process he or she goes through when purchasing the product will be discussed in this chapter.

Chapter 7 will explain how television, radio, magazines, and other forms of marketing can be used to better sell fashion products.

Chapter 8 will cover global issues related to the fashion industry. Communication, sweatshops, and other contemporary issues will be discussed. Within the production of fashion goods, communication and working with overseas vendors is imperative to the success of a fashion product.

Chapter 9 will assume the goods have arrived within the store. Once the goods have arrived from vendors, it is up to the retail environment to make sure those goods sell. That's what this chapter will be about.

Chapter 10 will cover the importance of correctly planning the merchandise collection. Planning includes setting a budget, ordering the right merchandise at the right time, and setting the appropriate prices.

29
Ralph Lauren Fall 2006 Men's Collection

36
Women's winter outfits

REALWORLDfocus >> The Seasonal Process

Have you noticed that even before the kids go back to school, many retail shelves are already stocked with Halloween candy and Christmas cards? To be successful in this industry, retail professionals plan their product and marketing approaches months in advance.

The Retail Timeline

Laurie Karzen, a retail consultant from Emeryville, California, says retailers typically buy six months (or more) in advance for their stores. "Buyers attend trade shows in January and February, and then again in the summer," she says. "Retailers are geared up in July for what they need for the second half of the year! By early October, stores are stocked for the holidays."

Six Months to One Year in Advance

Retailers need to plan budgets and submit purchase orders to vendors long before products appear on the sales floor. Advanced planning insures that retailers have merchandise assortments targeted to their specific stores' customers. This means a clothing chain's stores in Minneapolis offer heavy sweaters in August, while its stores in Phoenix and Honolulu carry shorts in January. And when holiday merchandise appears in October, it can spur consumer demand that picks up steam in November and December.

Accurate seasonal planning leads to improved sales, higher customer satisfaction levels, less surplus stock at all levels of the supply chain, lower risk of running out of high-demand stock, and fewer markdowns. Long-range planning is tied to increased profitability.

How It's Done

Retailers navigate seasonal cycles and improve their bottom line through a process known as collaborative planning, forecasting, and replenishment (CPFR). Accurate forecasting generates initial preseason merchandise plans based on various trends, demographics, store/customer profiles, econometrics (economic factors such as income, interest rates), and so forth. Forecasting also helps generate sophisticated in-season plans based on actual versus plan results at a detailed (store or department) level.

Planning

Retail buyers have the main responsibility for seasonal merchandise plans. All year long, buyers track the trends for their product types and analyze past sales figures for their stores. Many use specialized software to build a greater understanding of consumer behavior into the merchandise planning process. They become experts in their market, its demographics and the products they buy.

Retailers commonly plan one to three seasons ahead while marketing the current season. Buyers review and modify budgets three to four months in advance. Companies that import goods plan farther ahead. Buyers help corporate and store personnel plan promotions, marketing, and advertising aligned with the seasonal plans.

But that's not all. At the chain or store level, planners, transportation, and logistics specialists and operations management personnel develop strategies for merchandise distribution and allocation. This includes in-store stocking and off-site warehousing, delivery schedules, store maintenance plans, merchandise displays, shelf setups, and shopping themes.

For the holiday shopping season, retailers must have plans in place to determine price-matching, rain-check, special order, and return policies. They need to hire and train staff before the holiday rush hits, and then they have to prepare their after-holiday clearance strategies.

Getting into the Field

When a retail company hires or promotes a planning specialist, it looks for individuals who are familiar with its merchandise as well as retailing practices. In-store experience is always valuable. A bachelor's degree in business (with emphasis on finance, marketing, or economics) or merchandising can be helpful. Visual merchandising and display professionals, who contribute to the development and execution of seasonal plans, usually have a background in graphic or fine art.

Large retail chains, such as the Federated Department Stores, have formal management-training programs for planning and merchandising specialists such as buyers. These programs typically recruit recent college graduates.

If you're interested in a career in retail planning, you need to be analytical and organized. If you're on the sales floor or in the stock room, pay attention to and ask questions about seasonal plans. Find out about opportunities to become an assistant in the corporate merchandising department.

If you're in school, check with the career services office about internships in retail management or job fairs where retailers will be recruiting. ✿

Written by Valerie Lipow. Copyright 2001, TMP Interactive Inc. All rights reserved.

>> QUESTIONS

1. What do you think it takes to be successful in retail?
2. Why is retail buying performed so far in advance?
3. Why do you think this article recommends an internship?

ANN LOOMIS
>> Director of Operations, *Helly Hanson*

Ann Loomis is the director of operations at Helly Hanson. Helly Hanson designs and produces cutting-edge clothing and textile technology for the active lifestyle. The company produces clothing for skiing, snowboarding, and outdoor work gear. With its international headquarters located in Norway, Helly Hanson has made a name for itself worldwide. The company employs 600 people and sells its products in more than 700 retailers worldwide.

>> Ann

Ann has an associate of applied arts degree in general business from Shoreline Community College in Seattle, Washington. She also studied at the University of Washington.

Prior to joining Helly Hanson, Ann did not have experience in retail, but she had extensive sales and customer service experience. Ann worked as an office manager and in sales before joining Helly Hanson.

Her job as director of operations has three major components. She is responsible for the distribution of product (how the product actually gets into the stores), customer service (management of the customer service call center), and oversight of the Helly Hanson stores (making sure sales goals are met; finding out what is selling).

Ann discusses the challenges she faced when joining the company: "I did not have experience in retail and distribution, so it required a lot of extra effort on my part to understand these areas."

An average day for Ann includes answering e-mail and voice mail and making sure staffing is at appropriate levels for the customer service department. Ann also spends much of her day reading reports on store sales, product shipments, and sales of products. She insures that the stores have the products they need today, next week, and three months from now. Much of her job includes "crisis management," in other words, being able to make decisions quickly and deal with issues and situations very quickly. Ann says because of this crisis management component, she always feels like she is running behind. In fact, the day the interview was conducted, Ann was at the office by 6:45 a.m. and didn't plan on leaving until 9 p.m., since it was the holiday season, which is their busiest time of year.

>> the fashion-design process

Now that we have discussed the major parts of a design, we will discuss the process of fashion design. The fashion-design process is a lengthy one and can have many variations, depending on the type of company. The general steps in design include:

1. Research and planning of the line.
2. Creating the design concept.
3. Development of the designs.
4. Production planning and production.
5. Distribution of the line.

:: RESEARCH AND PLANNING OF THE LINE ::

One could arguably say research is the most important part of fashion design. This is the stage during which designers research fabric trends, color trends, past sales, and goals of the organization. Some companies will produce their own merchandise, called **private label**; others may only buy designs from manufacturers. In-house design, or private-label design, occurs when retailers have their own designers create clothing for them. Many companies, such as Nordstrom, both use in-house designers for their own lines and buy outside goods. Either way, the research will be similar. Designers will review fashion magazines, look at color forecasts, and even watch celebrities to see what the new hot fashion will be. The first step sets the groundwork for the rest of the process.

:: CREATING THE DESIGN CONCEPT ::

The next step in the design phase is to create the concept. For the most part, the concept will actually be sold to in-house buyers before production even begins. In this phase, the designer will develop sketches, gather fabric samples, and develop a line, usually eight pieces, that go together. A **line board** is then presented to decision makers (buyers) in the organization, who then must approve it before the concept enters into the next steps of design.

Much of the industry is moving toward the use of computer aided design (CAD) in the development of line boards. CAD can also assist in the making and cutting of patterns. Fashion manufacturers are also experimenting with the use of CAD for everything from design to production to shipping and distribution management of the products.

:: DEVELOPMENT OF THE DESIGNS ::

After approval has been received to go ahead with the designs, the designer or patternmaker will produce a pattern for that garment. There are two ways to make a pattern. The first way is with a **flat pattern**, in which the design is made out of hand-cut pieces of heavy paper. **Draping**, the second way, consists of actually ar-

End-of-Chapter material provides reinforcement of learning and opportunities for application, research, and exploration. A list of Terms to Know is also included, with the definitions located in the book's glossary.

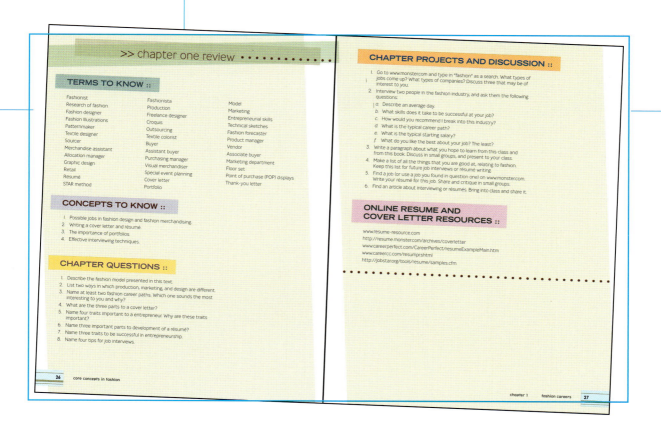

>> chapter one review

TERMS TO KNOW ::

Fashionist
Research of fashion
Fashion designer
Fashion illustrations
Patternmaker
Textile designer
Sourcer
Merchandise assistant
Allocation manager
Graphic design
Retail
Résumé
STAR method

Fashionista
Production
Freelance designer
Croquis
Outsourcing
Textile colorist
Buyer
Assistant buyer
Purchasing manager
Visual merchandiser
Special event planning
Cover letter
Portfolio

Model
Marketing
Entrepreneurial skills
Technical sketches
Fashion forecaster
Product manager
Vendor
Associate buyer
Marketing department
Floor set
Point of purchase (POP) displays
Thank-you letter

CONCEPTS TO KNOW ::

1. Possible jobs in fashion design and fashion merchandising.
2. Writing a cover letter and résumé.
3. The importance of portfolios.
4. Effective interviewing techniques.

CHAPTER QUESTIONS ::

1. Describe the fashion model presented in this text.
2. List two ways in which production, marketing, and design are different.
3. Name at least two fashion career paths. Which one sounds the most interesting to you and why?
4. What are the three parts to a cover letter?
5. Name four traits important to a entrepreneur. Why are these traits important?
6. Name three important parts to development of a résumé?
7. Name three traits to be successful in entrepreneurship.
8. Name four tips for job interviews.

CHAPTER PROJECTS AND DISCUSSION ::

1. Go to www.monster.com and type in "fashion" as a search. What types of jobs come up? What types of companies? Discuss three that may be of interest to you.
2. Interview two people in the fashion industry, and ask them the following questions:
   a. Describe an average day.
   b. What skills does it take to be successful at your job?
   c. How would you recommend I break into this industry?
   d. What is the typical career path?
   e. What is the typical starting salary?
   f. What do you like the best about your job? The least?
3. Write a paragraph about what you hope to learn from this class and from this book. Discuss in small groups, and present to your class.
4. Make a list of all the things that you are good at, relating to fashion. Keep this list for future job interviews or résumé writing.
5. Find a job (or use a job you found in question one) on www.monster.com. Write your résumé for this job. Share and critique in small groups.
6. Find an article about interviewing or résumés. Bring into class and share it.

ONLINE RESUME AND COVER LETTER RESOURCES ::

www.resume-resource.com
http://resume.monster.com/archives/coverletter
www.careerperfect.com/CareerPerfect/resumeExampleMain.htm
www.careercc.com/resumprs.html
http://jobstar.org/tools/resume/samples.cfm

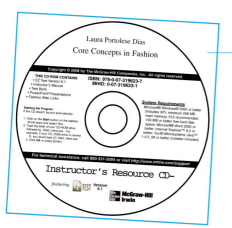

An **Instructor's Resource CD-ROM (IRCD)**, available for instructors, provides a number of instructional tools, including PowerPoint presentations for each chapter in the text, an instructor's manual with lecture notes tied to PowerPoint, projects, discussion questions, and an electronic test bank. The instructor's manual provides a "timing" matrix in each chapter for better and easier classroom instruction design and syllabus development. An answer key provides the answers to the entire end-of-chapter materials in the text. The electronic test bank will offer a variety of multiple choice, fill-in-the-blank, true/false, and essay questions, with varying levels of difficulty and tied to the chapter's learning objectives.

The Online Learning Center (OLC) is a web site that follows the text chapter-by-chapter, so students can review material or link to relevant web sites. Our Information Center features an overview of the text, Table of Contents, Preface, and background on the author. Instructors can easily access the instructor's manual, answer key, video clips, and PowerPoint presentations.

The OLC can be delivered multiple ways—professors and students can access them directly through the textbook web site, through PageOut, or within a course management system (i.e., WebCT, Blackboard, TopClass, or eCollege).

A **DVD** will also be available for instructors, which provides clips and interviews from fashion shows and industry scenarios. Two of the clips will feature the 2006 MAGIC Marketplace trade show in Las Vegas, focusing on the two major attendees of the show: buyers and designers. A third video clip will highlight the fashion industry outside the context of a trade show, integrating companies such as Patagonia and Hot Topic. These clips will also be available on the OLC.

>> acknowledgements

this book would not have been possible if it weren't for the help, support, and hard work of many individuals. I would like to thank:

✦ The entire development team at McGraw-Hill, including Linda Schreiber, Megan Gates, and Pete Vanaria for their support and professionalism.

✦ Mike Antonucci at McGraw-Hill for helping me get started.

✦ Wanda Clark-Morin, Ann Loomis, Brooke St. Sauver, and Cindi Handloff for their input and interviews, which appear in Chapter I.

✦ David and Mona Starr, colleagues at Shoreline Community College, for mentorship over the years.

✦ To my parents, Emanuele and Joann, for their constant love and encouragement throughout my childhood, education, and career. I could not have asked for more wonderful, loving parents.

✦ Lisa, my sister, and Rob, my brother-in-law, and my nieces, Victoria and Veronica. Their childhood sense of wonder always helps me remember what is important when I take things too seriously.

✦ I can't express in words how much I appreciate the support of my friends (they know who they are) during this long educational process.

✦ To my in-laws, Meme, Rosemarie, Carlos, Anne, and Ken, for their acceptance of me into their family as their granddaughter, daughter, and sister.

✦ To my husband, Alain, for so many reasons. But most of all for his patience and support (and willingness to eat frozen pizza and TV dinners while I completed this book).

✦ Many thanks to all the reviewers who helped in the development process of this text:

Alexxis Avalon
International Academy of
Design & Technology
Tampa, FL

Joan Bergholt
Academy of Art College
San Francisco, CA

Suzette Brimmer
Houston Community College
Houston, TX

Sandra K. Buckland
The University of Akron
Akron, OH

Lark F. Caldwell
Texas Christian University
Fort Worth, TX

Vivian Chesterley
The Art Institute of Seattle
Seattle, WA

Michael Discello
Pittsburgh Technical Institute
Oakdale, PA

Betty G. Etters
University of Georgia
Athens, GA

Janice M. Feldbauer
Austin Community College
Austin, TX

Marilyn Hefferon
Drexel University
Philadelphia, PA

Linda Hoffman
Sanford-Brown College
Hazelwood, MO

Soyoung Kim
University of Georgia
Athens, GA

Nancy P. McGee
International Academy of
Design & Technology
Tampa, FL

Julie Patterson
International Academy of
Design & Technology
Detroit, MI

Nancy Plummer
International Academy of
Design & Technology
Chicago, IL

Martin M. Rogoff
Philadelphia University
Philadelphia, PA

Jeremy A. Rosenau
Philadelphia University
Philadelphia, PA

Julie Schimmel
Indiana Business College
Indianapolis, IN

Dr. Laura Portolese Dias

>> brief table of contents

on the **cover:**

34

Haute couture at Christian Dior show

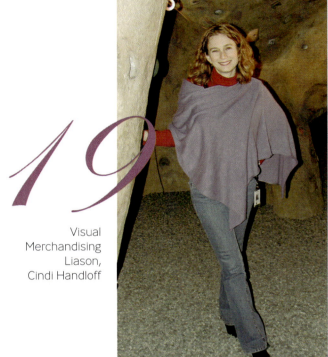

19

Visual
Merchandising
Liason,
Cindi Handloff

chapter two :: FASHION TERMINOLOGY AND THE MERCHANDISING PROCESS 28

chapter three :: TEXTILES AND DESIGN DEVELOPMENT 46

Women's winter outfits 36

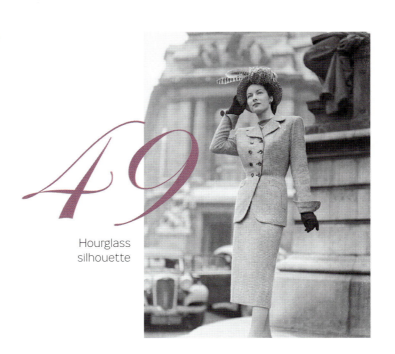

49

Hourglass
silhouette

chapter four :: HISTORICAL PERSPECTIVE 64

50

Variances in
garment colors

64

The miniskirt
of the 1960s

75

Ashton Kutcher and
Brittany Murphy
on MTV

Textiles factory

chapter nine

:: RETAILING IN A VIBRANT WORLD 170

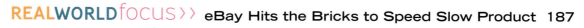

REALWORLDfocus>> **eBay Hits the Bricks to Speed Slow Product 187**

Visual
merchandising

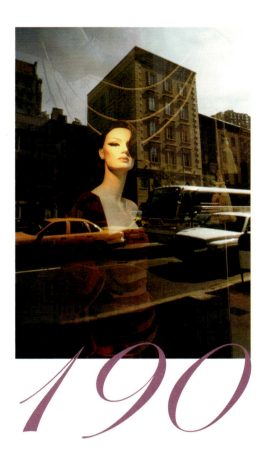

190

core concepts in

fashion careers

the most important thing in finding a job is finding something you like to do. Loving a job makes it much easier to get up and go to work everyday! Because a successful career in fashion is likely your motivation for reading this textbook, it will begin with a discussion of the types of jobs available in the industry. Before trying for an entry-level job after graduation, you may consider taking a part-time job in retail to gain experience in the industry. To this end, a section on résumés, cover letters, and interviewing is included.

After reading this chapter,
you should be able to:

1 • Describe the three areas in which fashion operates.

2 • Differentiate types of jobs available in the fashion industry.

3 • Write a fashion-appropriate résumé.

4 • Compose a dynamic cover letter.

5 • Understand interviewing techniques.

Fashion is all-encompassing. It is all around us in the products we use everyday. From the car we drive, the bed sheets we use, to the clothes we wear; all are part of fashion. The fabrics, textures, and colors used in these products are predicted far in advance, and the waves of these predictions can be seen in almost every industry. Fashion affects music, and music affects fashion. Television and movies inspire fashion. And because fashion is all-encompassing, there are many aspects of the industry that need new talent constantly.

Readers of this textbook may dream of designing beautiful garments for famous people, designing store windows on Madison Avenue in New York, or perhaps traveling to Paris and Milan to buy all of the newest fashions. Achieving one of these dreams is possible, with the right tools to make it happen. Stella McCartney, Paul Smith, and Christian Dior did not become famous designers overnight; it took extensive knowledge of the industry, hard work, and dedication to the trade. According to Webster's, a **fashionist** is a submissive follower of the modes and fashions; a **fashionista**, on the other hand, is a designer or promoter of the latest fashion. This book will provide the basic tools and overview to become a fashionista, like Betsey Johnson, Vera Wang, or Marc Jacobs.

Most people have an easier time understanding concepts from the big picture and then learning how the details fit into that big picture. Thus, this book will be structured in a similar manner. In addition, this textbook will be organized by how fashion moves from creation stages and into the hands of consumers, outlined as follows. The designer or merchandiser must

1. Have a basic understanding of the industry (Chapters 1, 2, and 3).
2. Predict the trends (Chapters 4 and 5).
3. Understand the customer and market to them in the appropriate manner (Chapters 6 and 7).
4. Produce the actual goods (Chapter 8).
5. Make sure the store environment is right (Chapter 9).
6. Plan appropriately for future merchandise (Chapter 10).

> " *...because fashion is all encompassing, there are many aspects of the industry that need new talent constantly.* "

The first chapter provides an explanation of the careers available in the fashion industry. Most people would not be attending college if it weren't for the hope that a better job can be obtained with a college degree. In addition, gaining some experience in the industry, while receiving formal education, is important. For this reason, Chapter 1 will also discuss résumés, cover letters, and interviewing as a means to gaining a part-time job while in school.

Chapter 2 will discuss the basics of fashion merchandising. Fashion merchandising can be considered the business side of fashion. It can include the actual selling of merchandise and the buying of merchandise to put into stores. However, any fashionista must have general knowledge of business. This chapter will discuss categories of fashion products and the process a fashion merchandiser goes through to end up with fashion products in stores.

Chapter 3 will focus on the basics of fashion design. Details within this part of the industry will be discussed. For example, the materials a fashion designer uses in his or her creations are extremely important. Therefore, textiles will be discussed from the perspective of the designer.

In Chapter 4, students will gain a historical perspective on fashion. The history of fashion is important because, as discussed in this chapter, history often helps predict future fashion trends.

Chapter 5 will discuss how a designer or merchandiser can better predict trends. Movies, television, music, and even politics are all influences that will be discussed.

Chapter 6 will cover the motivation of the customer. What makes a customer buy a particular product and the process he or she goes through when purchasing the product will be discussed in this chapter.

Chapter 7 will explain how television, radio, magazines, and other forms of marketing can be used to better sell fashion products.

Chapter 8 will cover global issues related to the fashion industry. Communication, sweatshops, and other contemporary issues will be discussed. Within the production of fashion goods, communication and working with overseas vendors is imperative to the success of a fashion product.

Chapter 9 will assume the goods have arrived within the store. Once the goods have arrived from vendors, it is up to the retail environment to make sure those goods sell. That's what this chapter will be about.

Chapter 10 will cover the importance of correctly planning the merchandise collection. Planning includes setting a budget, ordering the right merchandise at the right time, and setting the appropriate prices.

>> the fashion model

As discussed in the last section, each part of this textbook relates to a part of the fashion process. Each of the fashion processes can be split into one of three major areas. These three aspects can be called the *fashion model*. A **model** is an idea of how things work together, usually in the form of a visual drawing.

For purposes of this book, the fashion model will consist of three shoeboxes (see Figure 1.1). The **research of fashion** is the first shoebox. Research in the fashion industry involves research of the customer and knowing his or her wants. It can also involve predicting trends in color or textiles. This shoebox is covered in Chapters 4, 5, and 6.

1.1 figure THE FASHION MODEL

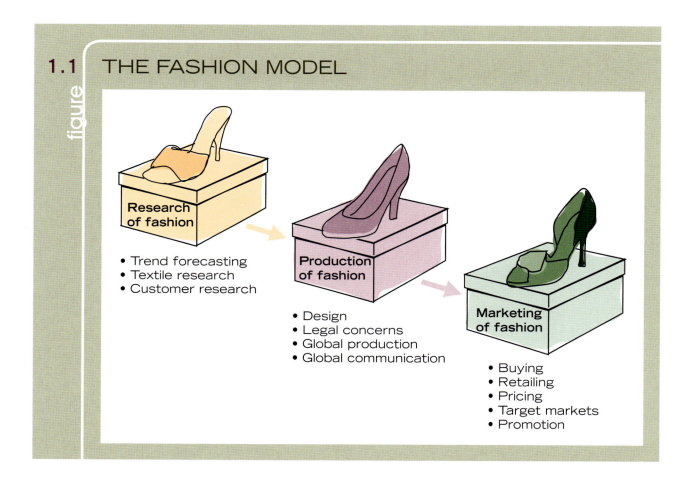

- Trend forecasting
- Textile research
- Customer research

Research of fashion

Production of fashion
- Design
- Legal concerns
- Global production
- Global communication

Marketing of fashion
- Buying
- Retailing
- Pricing
- Target markets
- Promotion

The second shoebox is the **production** of fashion. Production is the actual making of a garment. This area includes the design of garments, textile selection, and global production issues. This shoebox is discussed in Chapters 3 and 8.

The third shoebox is the **marketing** of fashion. Marketing incorporates various ways an item will be sold. It includes choosing a market in which to sell, researching that market, and engaging in activities to sell to that market. Part of marketing also includes knowledge of the consumer and the motivations of consumers to purchase certain products. Retailing, another aspect to marketing of fashion products, includes the process of actually selling the goods in a store environment. Visual merchandising, or the visual look of the store, is also an essential element of marketing and retailing. This shoebox includes material discussed in Chapters 2, 7, 9, and 10.

>> fashion career tracks

There are two main career focuses in the fashion industry: fashion design and fashion merchandising. Within each of these areas, there are many jobs available to properly motivated and educated individuals.

Each part of the fashion world is diverse; therefore, different titles tend to be used for similar positions. However, no matter where one is located, most entry-level jobs will include similar duties.

Success in a fashion design career requires the ability to conceptualize and produce clothing and accessories. Drawing, sketching, and computer skills, the ability to sew, and an understanding of the manufacturing processes are important in this career path. Besides being creative, most successful designers will have a thorough understanding of fashion trends as well as the business side of fashion. On the personal level, a successful fashion designer will have a love for fashion, be creative, and be able to work well either alone or in teams.

Types of jobs available within fashion design include designer, patternmaker, sample sewer, trend forecaster, colorist, and production. Of course, within each of these career paths are entry-level positions. It is also necessary to mention that the types of career paths and job promotions will vary greatly, depending on the company.

Fashion merchandising, fashion marketing, and business careers are all popular degrees for fashion merchandising careers. In addition to education, trend forecasting abilities and the ability to work within a budget are very important. Most fashion merchandising careers require excellent negotiation, mathematical, and budgeting skills. A fashion merchandiser must be willing to work longer than the regular nine-to-five schedule and be fashion conscious and driven.

The types of jobs available in fashion merchandising can involve buying, marketing, visual merchandising, and working in a retail environment.

In either fashion career path—design or merchandising—the importance of gaining experience before finishing school is vital to success. Obtaining an internship in the field or a part-time job is crucial. The next section will discuss specific careers in both fashion design and fashion merchandising.

>> fashion design

:: DESIGNER ::

Before discussing the jobs available within the fashion design field, it is important to note that every good fashion designer must have knowledge of clothing construction, patternmaking, draping, and fitting. Because so much production is done overseas, the ability to sew will make the designer a more effective communicator with people in a foreign country. A **fashion designer** is the person who creates new designs for clothing.

Education will provide the basic skills needed to be successful in this field. Also important is the ability and willingness to work on tight deadlines, to work overtime, or to work more than 40 hours per week.

There are many opportunities within the field of fashion design. First, many designers choose to be **freelance designers.** Freelancing means the individual works for him- or herself and accepts a variety of projects from different companies. A freelance designer can also make clothing for individuals or place the designs in his or her own store or in smaller retail boutiques. The pay scale can vary significantly, depending on the location of the freelance designer. To be successful in this field, it is important to be creative, have drawing/sketching skills, be able to communicate well with those who are actually producing the designs, and have some knowledge of business, such as how to set prices. This track can be personally difficult due to the lack of steady income. Many designers choose to freelance on the side, until they can develop enough business to leave their regular job. Freelance designers have **entrepreneurial skills.** Skills that make a business successful—such as how to keep track of income and expenses, marketing, and other business-related skills—would be considered entrepreneurial skills.

A second type of design career involves creating fashions for a particular label. Every piece of clothing purchased was designed by someone who went through the process of design, which will be covered in Chapter 3.

It would be rare for a fashionista to start with a company as a designer. Typically, the career track would include an entry-level position, such as assistant designer; a mid-level position, such as associate designer; and then a position as head designer (see Figure 1.2).

1.2 figure **CAREER PATH FOR FASHION DESIGNER**

Designer/
Director of product
development

Associate designer/
Product engineer

Assistant designer/
Product developer

It is important to note the difference between **fashion illustrations** and technical sketches, because they both require different skills. The elongated, sometimes painted, drawings used to sell ideas are called **croquis;** these illustrations are not drawn to human proportions nor actually used to produce garments. **Technical sketches** are used to actually communicate the details of the garment design. For example, they would indicate the size of buttonholes and the type of stitching to be used. To be successful at this type of design, it is imperative to have computer-aided design (CAD) skills but also to be able to work with those actually manufacturing the goods. CAD skills include the ability to design or manipulate garments using a computer.

The fashion design field, according to the U.S. Department of Labor, is expected to grow 10 to 20 percent through 2012. The Department of Labor also stated that the average earnings for a fashion designer in 2002 was $51,290. The general range for this field is $35,550 to $75,570. Of course, depending on job, company, and location, these figures can vary greatly.

:: PATTERNMAKER ::

A **patternmaker** develops the pattern used to make a particular garment. (See Figure 1.3 for a typical career path.) A designer gives the specifications of a garment to a patternmaker, and he or she then produces a pattern that can be used to actually make the garment.

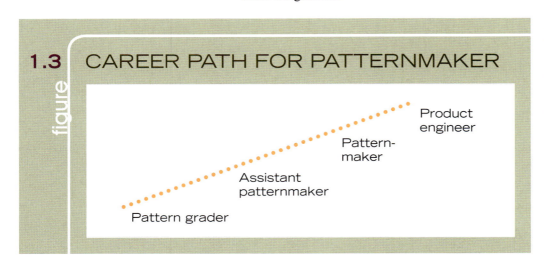

1.3 figure

CAREER PATH FOR PATTERNMAKER

Product engineer

Pattern-maker

Assistant patternmaker

Pattern grader

The patternmaking industry forecast, according to the U.S. Department of Labor, is expected to decline until 2012. In other words, there will be fewer patternmaking jobs in the United States in 2012 than there are today. It is likely that it will stabilize in 2012, but it is unlikely that patternmaking will ever be a growth field in the United States. Much of this has to do with outsourcing. **Outsourcing** is a strategy used by companies to have items produced somewhere other than the United States. Labor costs are a major factor in choosing to outsource. For example, Nordstrom outsources most of its production to China and India.

:: SAMPLE SEWER ::

Sample sewers will take the pattern given to them, cut the fabric and sew the garment. The purpose is not for this person to mass-produce the garment but rather to give the designer an idea of how the finished garment will look. (Figure 1.4 illustrates a typical career path for a sample sewer.)

Much like patternmaking, sample sewing will continue to see a decline in jobs, according to the U.S. Department of Labor. This is due to many products being produced overseas now, including samples. However, there may still be a need for tailors and people to custom-make garments. The average salary in this type of job is $14.95 per hour.

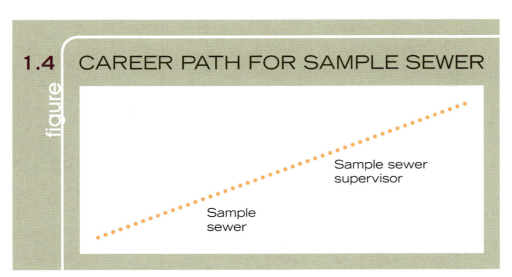

1.4 figure

CAREER PATH FOR SAMPLE SEWER

Sample sewer supervisor

Sample sewer

:: TREND FORECASTER ::

To work in trend forecasting, individuals need to have extensive experience in either fashion design or fashion merchandising. A **fashion forecaster** predicts trends two years in advance. This person must have excellent research skills and intuition to predict new trends. Forecasters look at a variety of things to predict what will be popular two years out. Music, television, history, social, and economic factors all affect new styles. Most trend forecasters are freelancers. To be successful, a trend forecaster must have experience in the field and a proven record of accurate predictions.

For a future career in trend forecasting, choosing another fashion-related career at first might be a viable option. Once the individual is well known, he or she can branch out and freelance in this area. The ability to network, research, and present this information is imperative to a successful career in forecasting.

:: TEXTILES ::

Textiles is a key area in the fashion field, because every print worn and every plaid sold was designed by an individual. The job of the **textile designer** is to design prints that will be both attractive and usable for the clothing they will eventually become. Textile designers are artists and also color experts. To be successful in this field, a degree in fine art or textile design might be required. (See Figure 1.5 for a typical career path in textiles.)

A **textile colorist** will choose the colors and patterns used in textile design. It is the responsibility of the colorist to insure the colors formulated are ones that customers will purchase.

Textile designers sometimes paint or use computers to develop new print designs.

1.5 *figure* CAREER PATH IN TEXTILES

Head textile designer

Textile designer or colorist

Textile design assistant

:: PRODUCTION ::

Due to the trend toward outsourcing, many companies are looking to **production managers** and sourcers. Although in some companies the job may be the same, a production manager generally will oversee the production process of garments, whereas a **sourcer** is responsible for research and purchasing of fabrics and trim. Either way, the purpose of these jobs to insure a trouble-free manufacturing process. A production person often comes from a design background and is responsible for the oversight of the entire production process. This

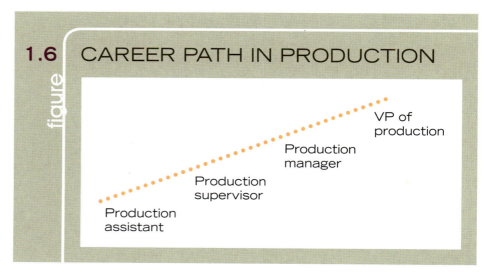

1.6 *figure* CAREER PATH IN PRODUCTION

VP of production

Production manager

Production supervisor

Production assistant

person may oversee the design of clothing and work with overseas vendors. Anyone involved in production of garments will need good communication skills, both written and verbal, have a thorough understanding of the design process, and be able to manage people to insure the production process is smooth. It is up to this person to insure all garments are manufactured with the right fit and are delivered on time. (See Figure 1.6 for production career path.)

>> fashion merchandising

:: BUYER ::

The **buyer** in a company is responsible for purchasing product to resell in stores. This person is responsible for all of the merchandise that is put into a store. Buyers research the merchandise, negotiate price, and insure the order is delivered. They can buy internally, meaning they decide which garments they want in their store from designers who work for the same company, or they work with **vendors** to purchase products. A vendor is a salesperson who represents a particular line of clothing and supplies the items to the customer. In this case, vendors represent brands that a buyer wants to carry in his or her store. It is important for the buyer to understand the needs of the company, work within a budget, and have good fashion sense. A buyer for a golf shop might work with a vendor to purchase lines of merchandise in the shop. A buyer will also work with vendors on returning merchandise that didn't sell or merchandise that is defective.

The normal career path for a buyer would be to start out as a merchandise assistant. A **merchandise assistant** is assigned to a buyer and assistant buyer. This person has an administrative role and helps the assistant buyer and buyer in day-to-day ordering and operations. A person would normally be a merchandise assistant for two or three years. Next, he or she would move to an **assistant buyer** position. An assistant buyer works with the buyer to follow trends, place orders, and track the selling of merchandise. The next step would be an **associate buyer,** depending on the type of company. This individual has seniority over assistant buyers and is the primary person helping the buyer. He or she may manage or oversee the performance of the merchandise assistant and assistant buyers. After a few years in this job, the individual would then be promoted to a buyer.

It is important to keep in mind that most retail stores have a buyer, assistant buyer, and merchandise assistant for each category they carry. For example, there may be a buying team for junior's denim and another team for misses' knits. This makes for extensive job possibilities.

Another job possibility within the buying area might be found within the field of allocation. **Allocation managers** are responsible for making sure that each store receives the proper amount of goods. An allocation manager may look at sales figures in one store and realize that the store is sold out of a product. When this occurs, he or she may have specific merchandise transferred from another store to insure highest profitability.

According to the U.S. Department of Labor, the job growth through 2012 for buyers will be from 3 to 9 percent. The median income for this job is $40,790, with a range of between $30,040 and more than $100,000.

Another job possibility is that of a **purchasing manager.** These jobs are plentiful in areas other than fashion as well. The main difference between a buyer and a purchasing agent is that buyers purchase goods for resell, whereas purchasing agents buy products and parts for use within the company. For example, a garment manufacturer may need a purchasing manager to buy buttons, thread, and other items required to complete a garment. (See Figure 1.7 for a typical career path for buyers.)

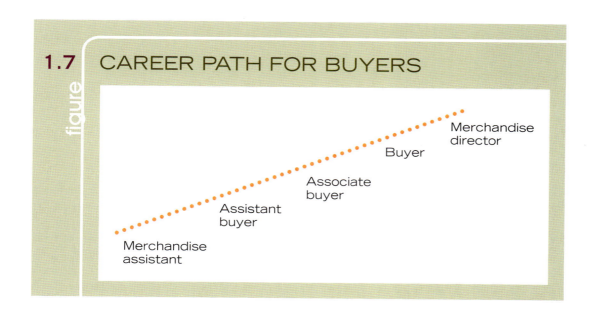

1.7 figure CAREER PATH FOR BUYERS

Merchandise director

Buyer

Associate buyer

Assistant buyer

Merchandise assistant

:: MARKETING ::

Most retail stores have **marketing departments.** This group oversees direct mailings, such as catalogs; company websites, including e-commerce sites (discussed in Chapter 9); and signage and advertising for a company. Jobs can vary greatly in

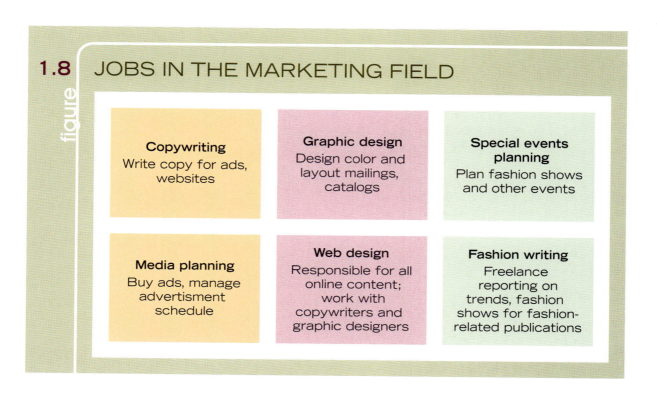

1.8 figure JOBS IN THE MARKETING FIELD

Copywriting
Write copy for ads, websites

Graphic design
Design color and layout mailings, catalogs

Special events planning
Plan fashion shows and other events

Media planning
Buy ads, manage advertisment schedule

Web design
Responsible for all online content; work with copywriters and graphic designers

Fashion writing
Freelance reporting on trends, fashion shows for fashion-related publications

the marketing department, from graphic design to copywriting. **Graphic design** would include design and choosing of colors for any published material. Copywriting would include writing of advertisements or descriptions of clothing found in a catalog. A marketing department may be responsible for special events, such as in-store fashion shows, as well.

Because of the numerous jobs in this area, salary will vary from job to job and company to company. (See Figure 1.8.)

If interested in a job within the retail marketing field, it is important to gain some experience in retail now. For example, if a student wants to work in the Nordstrom corporate office, it might be a good idea to work part-time, while in school, as a sales associate for Nordstrom. It will provide invaluable experience and get a foot in the door.

:: VISUAL MERCHANDISING ::

Visual merchandising is included within the marketing departments of retailers. Visual merchandising includes the creative aspects of design, while using many of the marketing concepts that will be discussed in Chapters 7 and 9. The job of a visual merchandiser is to insure the store presents the merchandise in the best way possible. A visual merchandiser will have several responsibilities. A visual merchandiser will choose mannequins and lighting for the store, as well as manage the displays, themes, and window designs. A person in this highly creative area of fashion works to insure that once items are purchased by buyers, they are presented beautifully, leading to successful sales of the items.

First, a visual merchandiser may be responsible for the actual store planning. This would include the layout of new stores and design of new retail space.

Second, a visual merchandiser may be responsible for putting together a floor set. A **floor set** is a general description of where merchandise and signage should be placed in the store. A floor set can describe where certain sweaters should be placed, and if they should be hung or folded. A floor set also shows the merchandise that should be placed in store windows, on mannequins, and on fixtures. This description is then sent to stores so they know specifically how to insure the store is visually pleasing.

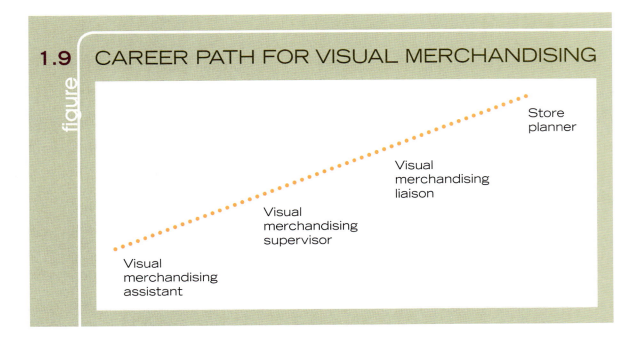

1.9 figure **CAREER PATH FOR VISUAL MERCHANDISING**

Store planner

Visual merchandising liaison

Visual merchandising supervisor

Visual merchandising assistant

Lastly, some stores have in-house visual merchandisers. These visual merchandisers might work for a company like Macy's, and they are responsible for insuring merchandise is refilled often, signed correctly, and appropriately displayed.

Growth statistics vary greatly, as do salaries in this job field, depending on the job title and region. (See Figure 1.9 for career path for visual merchandising.)

:: SALES ::

Every designer needs salespeople to sell clothing to buyers of retail stores. As a result, the sales field is growing. Examples of jobs include clothing sales representative, textile sales representative, and account representative. Each of these jobs is responsible for representing a clothing or fabric line and selling the line to customers.

As mentioned earlier, vendors are a major part of retail and fashion operations. These types of jobs are available in almost every city. For example, Union Bay has a vendor located in Seattle, Washington. This person is responsible for selling to the buyers located in this area. She is also responsible for visiting stores that carry Union Bay and gives product knowledge to the salespeople and helps with the visual merchandising of Union Bay clothing. The customers could include buyers for small boutiques, large department stores, and designers (if representing textiles).

Account representatives are also used in the field of marketing and can be responsible for selling advertising space in magazines or television. Good salespeople understand their customers and aim to please them. Sales representatives are often called *vendors* by their customers.

Jobs in this area are expected to grow, according to the U.S. Department of Labor, from 10 to 20 percent until 2012. The starting pay rate will vary greatly. However, the possibility for commission can make this a profitable career path. (See Figure 1.10 for a typical career path in sales.)

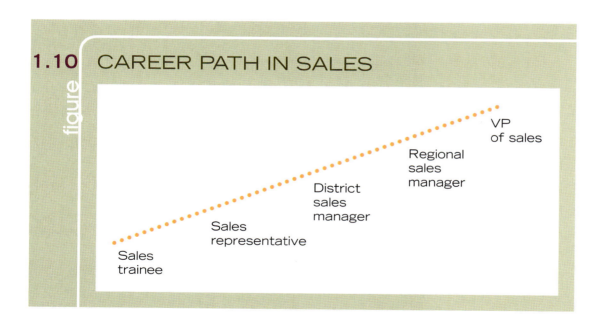

figure **1.10** CAREER PATH IN SALES

Sales trainee — Sales representative — District sales manager — Regional sales manager — VP of sales

:: RETAIL ::

Retail jobs can include store management, assistant store management, and sales associates. Managing a store requires long hours and weekend work. The advantage to any kind of retail job is the variety of skills gained. For example, a store manager must be able to hire and motivate employees, sell, handle visual merchandising, and manage day-to-day operations. After proving that he or she can be successful, a store manager may be promoted to district manager. A district manager oversees several stores and travels from store to store to insure proper visual merchandising, sales, and hiring practices. The career path would include sales associate, assistant manager, store manager, district manager, and regional manager (see Figure 1.11). Jobs in this area are expected to increase by 8 percent until 2012.

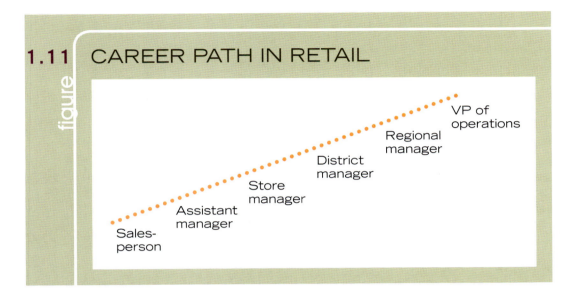

1.11 figure **CAREER PATH IN RETAIL**

- VP of operations
- Regional manager
- District manager
- Store manager
- Assistant manager
- Salesperson

:: ENTREPRENEURSHIP ::

For either fashion design or fashion merchandising, starting a retail business is also a viable option within the fashion industry. A successful entrepreneur in this business generally has enough money to purchase inventory for the store. An entrepreneur uses his or her own money, called *startup costs,* or borrows money from investors or banks. The entrepreneur must be able to survive without a salary for several months while the business is growing. When starting a new retail business, an entrepreneur must have a good business plan, be willing to work very long hours, and have general knowledge in all areas of business. Retail math, marketing, human resources, trend forecasting, and buying skills are all important when choosing this career path. Before starting a retail business, it is vital to gain some experience in retail.

:: SPECIAL EVENTS PLANNING ::

Another important area in fashion is **special events planning.** Special events planning can include planning of fashion shows and other events related to fashion. This responsibility is normally part of the marketing department and can include other duties as well. Special events are important to retailers because they give the retailer a chance to show new merchandise and bring people into the retail location. A fashion show can be informal, or formal, depending on the store and the goal of the special events planner. Success in this type of job requires the ability to deal with large amounts of stress, organizational skills, and the aptitude to see the big picture, while executing the small details to make the event a success. Special events planning can also be an entrepreneurial venture. Rather than work for a company that has special events, a planner can work for him- or herself and plan events for others. There are opportunities in this area for wedding planning, meeting planning, and fashion show or special events planning.

REALWORLDfocus >> The Seasonal Process

Have you noticed that even before the kids go back to school, many retail shelves are already stocked with Halloween candy and Christmas cards? To be successful in this industry, retail professionals plan their product and marketing approaches months in advance.

The Retail Timeline

Laurie Karzen, a retail consultant from Emeryville, California, says retailers typically buy six months (or more) in advance for their stores. "Buyers attend trade shows in January and February, and then again in the summer," she says. "Retailers are geared up in July for what they need for the second half of the year. By early October, stores are stocked for the holidays."

Six Months to One Year in Advance

Retailers need to plan budgets and submit purchase orders to vendors long before products appear on the sales floor. Advanced planning insures that retailers have merchandise assortments targeted to their specific stores' customers. This means a clothing chain's stores in Minneapolis offer heavy sweaters in August, while its stores in Phoenix and Honolulu carry shorts in January. And when holiday merchandise appears in October, it can spur consumer demand that picks up steam in November and December.

Accurate seasonal planning leads to improved sales, higher customer satisfaction levels, less surplus stock at all levels of the supply chain, lower risk of running out of high-demand stock, and fewer markdowns. Long-range planning is tied to increased profitability.

How It's Done

Retailers navigate seasonal cycles and improve their bottom line through a process known as collaborative planning, forecasting, and replenishment (CPFR). Accurate forecasting generates initial preseason merchandise plans based on various trends, demographics, store/customer profiles, econometrics (economic factors such as income, interest rates), and so forth. Forecasting also helps generate sophisticated in-season plans based on actual versus plan results at a detailed (store or department) level.

Planning

Retail buyers have the main responsibility for seasonal merchandise plans. All year long, buyers track the trends for their product types and analyze past sales figures for their stores. Many use specialized software to build a greater understanding of consumer behavior into the merchandise planning process. They become experts in their market, its demographics and the products they buy.

Retailers commonly plan one to three seasons ahead while marketing the current season. Buyers review and modify budgets three to four months in advance. Companies that import goods plan farther ahead. Buyers help corporate and store personnel plan promotions, marketing, and advertising aligned with the seasonal plans.

But that's not all. At the chain or store level, planners, transportation, and logistics specialists and operations management personnel develop strategies for merchandise distribution and allocation. This includes in-store stocking and off-site warehousing, delivery schedules, store maintenance plans, merchandise displays, shelf setups, and shopping themes.

For the holiday shopping season, retailers must have plans in place to determine price-matching, rain-check, special order, and return policies. They need to hire and train staff before the holiday rush hits, and then they have to prepare their after-holiday clearance strategies.

Getting into the Field

When a retail company hires or promotes a planning specialist, it looks for individuals who are familiar with its merchandise as well as retailing practices. In-store experience is always valuable. A bachelor's degree in business (with emphasis on finance, marketing, or economics) or merchandising can be helpful. Visual merchandising and display professionals, who contribute to the development and execution of seasonal plans, usually have a background in graphic or fine art.

Large retail chains, such as the Federated Department Stores, have formal management-training programs for planning and merchandising specialists such as buyers. These programs typically recruit recent college graduates.

If you're interested in a career in retail planning, you need to be analytical and organized. If you're on the sales floor or in the stock room, pay attention to and ask questions about seasonal plans. Find out about opportunities to become an assistant in the corporate merchandising department.

If you're in school, check with the career services office about internships in retail management or job fairs where retailers will be recruiting. ✱

Written by Valerie Lipow. Copyright 2001, TMP Interactive Inc. All rights reserved.

>> QUESTIONS

1. What do you think it takes to be successful in retail?

2. Why is retail buying performed so far in advance?

3. Why do you think this article recommends an internship?

the trade. A **Fashionist**, according ... Webster's is a submissive follower of the
modes and fashions. A **Fashionist** ... Webster's
is a designer or promoter of the latest fashion, like Betsey Johnson, Vera Wang, or

WANDA CLARK-MORIN
>> Manager of Product Engineering, *Cutter and Buck*

As a manager of product engineering, it is Wanda Clark-Morin's job to make sure the designs her designers create are effectively followed through by the garment manufacturers. Wanda works for Cutter and Buck, an upscale sportswear company. Cutter and Buck originally designed only golf wear for men, but the company has expanded its market in recent years to women's golf wear and casual sportswear for both men and women. The company's success depends on its ability to develop and manufacture high-quality garments with appealing colors. Cutter and Buck sells its clothing to resorts, golf shops, and other higher-end retailers.

Wanda holds a bachelor of fine arts degree from Virginia Commonwealth University and has spent almost 30 years in the fashion business. She started her fashion career in Los Angeles, where she worked in design production and garment manufacturing. She then moved to Seattle and joined Nordstrom, where she was the technical designer for children's wear.

Wanda sums up her job in one sentence, "It is my job to communicate what I want a garment to look like, so the overseas manufacturers can do their job properly." It is Wanda's job to oversee six people and their new designs. She oversees associate product engineers, product engineers, and senior product engineers. These engineers will develop designs (normally using computer-aided design) and develop all of the specifications necessary for creation of the design. Specifications can include buttons, sleeves, lining, and other details of a garment.

Wanda says, "there really is no average day." However, similar to people in other positions, Wanda must check e-mail every morning, to see the types of questions her overseas manufacturers may have about a garment. She explains the process, "My team and I design the garments and e-mail pictures and specifications packages for a garment. Then, the manufacturer sends samples, or photos of the sample garments. It is then the team's responsibility to make sure the fit and detailing are correct. The manufacturers often speak English as a second language, so they have many questions about how exactly a garment should be produced." Besides spending time checking e-mail and working with the manufacturers, as a manager, she is responsible for developing a timeline for all of the designs. Her department is working on several seasons at once, and each step of the design process must be completed on time in order to move to the next step. Wanda says there are constant deadlines and timelines that must be met. Unfortunately, if a

>> Wanda

deadline is not met, it holds up the entire manufacturing process, thereby delaying the arrival of merchandise into the stores.

When asked what it takes to be successful in fashion, Wanda replied, "passion." She says that a designer must love what he or she does; otherwise, it can be too hard. She also cites the ability to be flexible as an important factor for success in this industry. Wanda says you must, "eat it, love it, and breathe it" to be successful in this type of career.

The possibilities for salary in this field are endless. Wanda feels earning her bachelor's degree gave her critical thinking and research skills needed for this type of job.

She offers several bits of advice to new people entering this field: "First, practice lifelong learning. Just because you are finished with school does not mean you are finished learning." She encourages constant reading of newspapers and magazines, both fashion and nonfashion related. Wanda also recommends someone in this industry be flexible and adaptable to new and different situations. In other words, when searching for that first job, "think about where the first job can lead you." The ability to use computers and relate to others are important aspects to getting a job in this field.

Most of all, Wanda says it is important to be determined to be the best in your field, and if you have passion, you will have the drive to be the best: "If you love it, you will always love it and you won't mind coming in early, leaving late, and working on a Saturday because of a deadline. Loving it is the key."❖

CINDI HANDLOFF
>> Visual Merchandising Liaison, *REI*

Cindi Handloff is a true fashionista! As visual merchandising liaison at REI (Recreational Equipment Incorporated), it is her job to insure signage and store plans are met with precision at the corporate level.

Cindi talks about how she grew up pricing notebooks at her parents' store in Delaware. She then went to the University of Delaware and obtained a bachelor of science degree in fashion merchandising. From there, Cindi worked as an assistant manager at Kid's R Us. Cindy joined Coldwater Creek several years later as assistant manager for visual merchandising. At this job, she was able to hone her skills in the visual part of retailing. While at Coldwater Creek, Cindi had her eye on the job at REI. She met people, networked, and finally landed the job she had wanted.

Cindi says an average day for her includes development of the corporate floor set. A floor set is an overall diagram of where merchandise should be placed and how it should be placed in a store. This is done on a seasonal basis, although daily work is required. Cindi is also responsible for the development of the sales floor guide. This guide goes to all of the REI stores to help them to understand where signage should be placed. Cindi also helps vendors develop new point of purchase displays. **Point of purchase (POP) displays** provide information about the product and are located right next to the product. A POP display can include the price and information on the benefits and features of the product. For example, in the freeze-dried food section, REI's POP display includes information about how much freeze-dried food one might need to bring on a weeklong camping trip.

Cindi also trains store managers on visual merchandising as well. She says that the most important part of her job is communication. "I work with other divisions, such as buyers, and it is my job to help them figure out the assortment of merchandise they want to offer and develop signage for the key product offerings." Cindi also talks about the ability to sell ideas to others and to provide excellent internal customer service as big parts of her job too. Because she has so many projects happening at once, time management is also an important skill to have.

Cindi talks about the different departments in REI: "There is the retail side of REI. This would include the retail directors, store managers, and assistant managers, as well as sales associates. Then, there is the marketing department. This department is where I am located. Included within this department are catalog and promotional materials. Project coordinator would be the entry-level title within this department. Next, there is the buying department. To be a buyer, one would start out as a merchandise assistant. Within the buying department, there are also inventory allocations and market planners."

Cindi says the biggest challenges she faces result from the constant changing dynamics of the industry. Another challenge is that people now want to be entertained when shopping. Consumers are savvy, smarter, and already overstimulated. REI offers them the experience of entertainment while trying their products. For example, every REI store has a rock-climbing wall.

When asked what advice she would give someone entering the field, she offers the following: "Attitude is everything. Persistence pays off. Don't forget to ask for the job when interviewing. Have self-confidence. Have self-awareness (know what you are good at), and don't forget, you have more skills than you might realize."

Cindi's favorite quote is, "Treat others as if they are what they ought to be and help them become what they are capable of being." ■

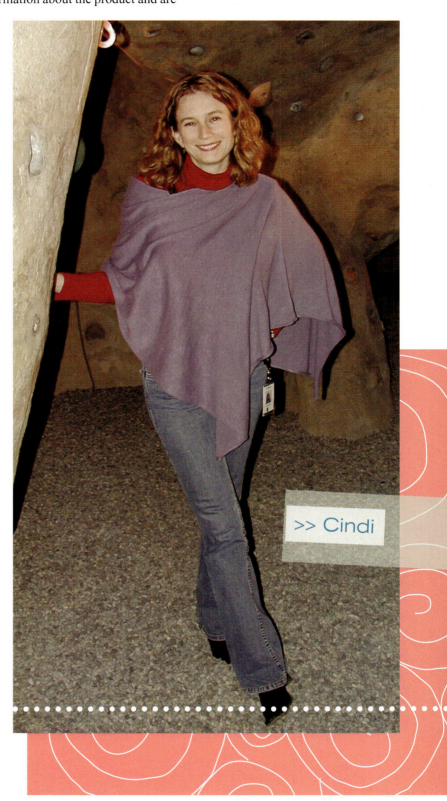

>> Cindi

ANN LOOMIS
>> Director of Operations, *Helly Hanson*

Ann Loomis is the director of operations at Helly Hanson. Helly Hanson designs and produces cutting-edge clothing and textile technology for the active lifestyle. The company produces clothing for skiing, snowboarding, and outdoor work gear. With its international headquarters located in Norway, Helly Hanson has made a name for itself worldwide. The company employs 600 people and sells its products in more than 700 retailers worldwide.

>> Ann

Ann has an associate of applied arts degree in general business from Shoreline Community College in Seattle, Washington. She also studied at the University of Washington.

Prior to joining Helly Hanson, Ann did not have experience in retail, but she had extensive sales and customer service experience. Ann worked as an office manager and in sales before joining Helly Hanson.

Her job as director of operations has three major components. She is responsible for the distribution of product (how the product actually gets into the stores), customer service of products (management of the customer service call center), and oversight of the Helly Hanson stores (making sure sales goals are met; finding out what is selling).

Ann discusses the challenges she faced when joining the company: "I did not have experience in retail and distribution, so it required a lot of extra effort on my part to understand these areas."

An average day for Ann includes answering e-mail and voice mail and making sure staffing is at appropriate levels for the customer service department. Ann also spends much of her day reading reports on store sales, product shipments, and sales of products. She insures that the stores have the products they need today, next week, and three months from now. Much of her job includes "crisis management," in other words, being able to make decisions quickly and deal with issues and situations very quickly. Ann says because of this crisis management component, she always feels like she is running behind. In fact, the day the interview was conducted; Ann was at the office by 6:45 a.m. and didn't plan on leaving until 9 p.m., since it was the holiday season, which is their busiest time of year.

"To be successful at this job, or any job for that matter, listening skills are key," says Ann. In addition, "the ability to multitask, delegate, and train people are high on the list. The ability to communicate both verbally and nonverbally is extremely important."

According to Ann, marketing coordinator, accounting assistant, and in-store jobs would be good starting positions at Helly Hanson. Ann says that entry-level jobs pay anywhere from $30,000 to $36,000, depending on experience and location. To get a job in the field, Ann recommends working while in school, to get a feel for the retail industry. She also suggests gathering background information related to the company in which you might want to seek employment.

Ann says the biggest challenges in the industry came after 9/11. Most businesses faced big challenges after this disaster and have taken quite some time to recover. She also says that knowing and understanding why sales go up and down can be a challenge: "Some of it is economy, some is product placement or the products themselves. You also have to understand the shoppers."

Ann's favorite quote is from a Serengeti proverb: "Every morning in Africa, a gazelle wakes up and knows it must run faster than the fastest lion, or it will be killed. Every morning a lion wakes up. It knows that it must outrun the slowest gazelle or it will starve to death. It doesn't matter whether you are a lion or a gazelle, when the sun comes up, you'd better be running."

>> Brooke

BROOKE ST. SAUVER
>> Associate Buyer, *Macy's*

Patience, willingness to work hard, and goal driven are all characteristics of Brooke St. Sauver. As a student, Brooke not only worked hard for good grades, but her goal was to learn and retain information. From the time she started school, she knew she wanted to be a buyer, and she has been working toward that goal with tenacity ever since.

Brooke St. Sauver, at 22 years old, is the associate buyer for junior street wear and Tommy Hilfiger at Macy's Western Region office. Brooke feels that her ability to figure out what customers want, give them the value they want, and figure out how to buy merchandise that sells well are skills that make her superior at what she does. Brooke's career track with Macy's has required patience and initiative. She started as a merchant office assistant right out of school. This job was a clerical position, but after a year, Brooke was promoted to assistant buyer of moderate sportswear. After being in that position for a year, Brooke was then promoted to assistant buyer for better sportswear, where she stayed for a year. Then, in December 2004, Brooke was promoted to her current position.

Brooke earned her associate of applied arts degree in fashion marketing at the Art Institute of Seattle in 2000. Her education there included business classes, as well as buying classes. She says that while the education she earned enabled her to get the job, there is no substitute for "real-world" training. Brooke did have retail experience prior to obtaining her job at Macy's, which, she says, helped her earn her position.

Brooke describes an average day as looking at sales and sales trends in the stores. For those items selling well, she may place reorders. For items that are not selling well, she may mark them down. She also works with vendors daily and writes orders. Brooke says being good with numbers and good communication skills are very important in her job. She also notes that having strong negotiation skills is an important trait, as well as having self-confidence and understanding trends in products. Her boss tells her, "As a buyer, you must be decent as a product person and a numbers person." In other words, only having one or the other won't be enough, you must have both.

The salary in this field can start at $30,000 per year and go up into the $100,000 range.

Brooke offers some good advice: "Do not be complacent. You must put your time in. Take every opportunity to show your skills. Always ask the boss for more. Be persistent. Go for it and don't give up. Set goals and figure out a plan to achieve them. Your own drive and determination will help you succeed."

As discussed in the last section, it is vital to gain experience in the fashion industry while in school. This section will provide tips for writing résumés, composing cover letters, and interviewing to make the task of finding a job easier. The best way to start looking for a part-time job is to develop a résumé, then go to the local mall and ask to speak with the store managers. Another option is to look at classified ads in local newspapers, or check job-hunting websites, such as monster.com. The résumé should always be tailored for a specific job. In fact, if a job description is available, the key words on the job description should be used in the résumé. Because many résumés are submitted online, this is a helpful tactic in insuring that a résumé is selected for review from the computer database.

Another way to gain experience in the industry is through internships. Many schools offer internship opportunities, and you should take advantage of them. These opportunities help students gain experience, but they also help in making valuable contacts within the industry. Some internships are paid, and many likely will allow the student to work around his or her schedule.

There are also numerous books and online resources about résumé writing. For example, *Résumés That Knock 'Em Dead* by Martin Yate gives excellent examples of résumés and cover letters and also provides techniques for writing a résumé.

:: RÉSUMÉS ::

The intention of this section is to provide information to make a résumé stand out in the fashion area. A **résumé** is a short, concise list of a job applicant's experience.

Most word processing programs provide a template in which to develop résumés in a nice, well laid out format. In Microsoft Word, go to the File menu, then click on New; in the New Document task pane that appears, click On my computer ... under Templates; in the tab called Other Documents, a Résumé Wizard can be found. (Instructions given are for Word 2003. But various versions of Word exist, so the path to the résumé template will be slightly different.)

The first section of a résumé should include a bulleted list of skills. This allows the potential employer to see the skills possessed at one quick glance. This is also good for companies that use automated or computer searches or key word searches. In automated searches, the computer program will look for key words that the company hopes the applicant possesses. These key word searches are often based on the actual job description. As a result, the qualifications listed on the résumé should match the skills requested in the job description. A key word could be a job title or job duties listed. For example, a bulleted list may look like this:

- Team player
- Motivating to others
- Consistently exceeds sales targets
- Creative
- Merchandise displays
- Excel and Word skills
- Marketing plans

The second section should include past employment. It is important to list those things that prove the applicant goes above and beyond normal job duties while at work. Rather than listing only job duties, try to show how goals were accomplished, using statements such as, "exceeded sales goals by 10 percent on a consistent basis" or "improved in-store shrinkage by 1 percent over one year due to excellent customer service." Another example might be "trained several salespeople who were eventually promoted into management." Any volunteer experience would be included in this section as well.

The third section normally lists education. A good grade-point average and classes taken should be listed in this area. Any activities relating to school should be listed here, such as involvement in DECA/DEC (Delta Epilson Chi, a student marketing organization), student government, or any on-campus clubs.

Résumés should always be tailored for a specific job. For example, the bulleted skills list could include words listed on the job posting. If the company requests a team player in its job posting, this should be one of the skills listed.

:: COVER LETTERS ::

In many ways, the **cover letter** is equally important as the résumé. Since many résumés are sent electronically, the cover letter may take the form of an e-mail. A cover letter is a short, concise introduction of the person applying for the job. It allows the applicant to highlight items listed on his or her résumé.

This is the part where the applicant can show personality and explain why he or she is the perfect person for the job. The first part of a cover letter has a short introduction. The introduction should describe the job for which the applicant is applying.

The second part is the body. The most important thing to remember about cover letters is that the company wants to know how the applicant's skills can help it do business. Don't say, "I really need this job and think I am perfect for it." It is better to say, "My experience with your type of computer system will enable me to quickly be productive in your department." This example shows that the applicant will save the company time as a result of skills already possessed.

Finally the third part is the closing. Cover letters should always end by asking for the job and making it known how excited you are to work for the company. Contact information should be included again, under the signature.

The cover letter and résumé should use the same heading and same font, so they appear as if they go together. If a reference page is required, it should have the same heading as well.

:: THANK-YOU LETTERS ::

One of the most important forms of written communication a potential employee may offer is the **thank-you letter.** After interviewing, discussed in the next section, it is imperative a follow-up letter be sent. This letter should be on professional stationery and handwritten. Another, more formal option is to type the thank-you letter. It can say something as simple as, "thank you for taking the time to interview me on Tuesday. I am looking forward to the opportunity to work with you and your company." Not only does the follow-up letter show appreciation for the potential employer's time, it also shows professionalism and again reminds the potential employer of your candidacy.

:: TYPES OF INTERVIEWS ::

There are three main types of interviews that can be administered. To save time and money, many will first perform a phone interview. A phone interview is usually conducted by the human resources department to narrow the choices. Many times the interviewer will call in the evening, to catch the applicant at home. It is not inappropriate for an applicant to ask for a minute before beginning the interview, to gather his or her thoughts. Preparing a phone script before sending out any résumés, one for each company, might assist in this preparation. The phone script should include a few main points that you would like to make to the interviewer. An applicant should always have his or her résumé and cover letter handy in case a potential employer calls.

The second type of interview is the case study or logic interview. This interview might include such questions as, "Why are manhole covers round?" or "How much pizza sells in the United States every year?" The interviewer is not looking for specific answers, rather, he or she wants to see the logic the applicant uses to answer those questions. A case study might include a situation or an issue, and the applicant would be asked what he or she would do in a given situation.

Finally, the third type of interview is the behavioral interview. In this type of interview, the applicant is asked to demonstrate particular skills that the employer has determined are necessary for the job. As the interviewee, the best way to respond to this type of question is to use the **STAR method.** That is, talk about a particular situation that relates to the question and describe what you did specifically and the positive results, using the following steps:

Situation: Describe a situation you have faced.

Task: Name a task you had to complete.

Action: Describe the action you took.

Results: Discuss the results from your action.

The best advice for a person being interviewed is to show excitement about the job. No one wants to offer a job to someone who doesn't seem excited to work there. Finally, it is extremely important to send a follow-up letter after an interview. It should be a short, handwritten note that thanks the interviewer for his or her time. Online examples are provided at the end of this chapter.

:: PORTFOLIO ::

Many employers will ask to see a portfolio at the interview. The designer's **portfolio** should show a collection of designs, both technical sketches and fashion illustrations. It should show a wide variety of design abilities, such as the ability to design a dress, as well as a polo shirt. The design portfolio should be organized in a professional manner, such as in a leather bound book. Even if the employer does not ask a candidate to bring his or her portfolio, it is still recommended as it will set this candidate apart from those who do not have anything to show.

A portfolio for merchandising students should include any store layouts, photos of any store design performed, and any samples of work done for school. This can include trend research papers, letters of recommendation from other employers, or anything that sheds light on the candidate's capabilities. For example, if you helped organize your school's fashion show, be sure to take pictures at the show and include them in your portfolio.

Because of the electronic nature of our world, it may be valuable to put portfolios on CD or DVD, or even have a website with examples of designs.

:: CLOTHING ::

A fashion book would not be complete without discussing the type of clothing that should be worn to an interview. Using common sense is the most important point; however, here are some general guidelines:

- Do not wear excessive jewelry.
- Dress "one step up" from the dress at that company. In other words, if the company dresses in jeans, wear slacks.
- Go easy on the makeup.
- Try to dress similar to the place in which you are applying. For example, if interviewing at Abercrombie and Fitch, try to wear their clothing. If interviewing at The Gap, try to dress in their style.
- Have natural or natural-looking haircolor.
- Shine those shoes!
- Don't smoke before an interview (unless something is used, other than perfume, to cover the smell).

Some final tips to landing that job include:

- Be prepared. Do research on the company.
- Be prepared to discuss salary requirements (but don't bring it up yourself!).
- Dress appropriately.
- Smile.
- STAR: Show the company why you are right for the job based on your past accomplishments.
- Have at least three good questions to ask them.
- Develop a good handshake.
- Develop networking skills. Join fashion-related organizations in your area.

>> conclusion •

This chapter has provided an overview of the textbook's content and described how it is organized. In addition, jobs available in fashion were discussed. It is important to remember with fashion design and fashion merchandising jobs, most professionals will need to be driven, have a love for the industry, and work longer hours than other types of careers. An education is also important for success in both fashion design and fashion merchandising. It is imperative to consider taking a part-time job in the fashion industry while in school. Because of this, résumés, cover letters, interviewing and thank-you notes were discussed. This chapter will allow us to move further into the textbook and discuss specific components that must be known to have a career in this industry.

TERMS TO KNOW ::

Fashionist
Fashionista
Model
Research of fashion
Production
Marketing
Fashion designer
Freelance designer
Entrepreneurial skills
Fashion illustrations
Croquis
Technical sketches
Patternmaker

Outsourcing
Fashion forecaster
Textile designer
Textile colorist
Product manager
Sourcer
Buyer
Vendor
Merchandise assistant
Assistant buyer
Associate buyer
Allocation manager
Purchasing manager

Marketing department
Graphic design
Visual merchandiser
Floor set
Retail
Special event planning
Point of purchase (POP) displays
Résumé
Cover letter
Thank-you letter
STAR method
Portfolio

CONCEPTS TO KNOW ::

1. Possible jobs in fashion design and fashion merchandising.
2. Writing a cover letter and résumé.
3. The importance of portfolios.
4. Effective interviewing techniques.

CHAPTER QUESTIONS ::

1. Describe the fashion model presented in this text.
2. List two ways in which production, marketing, and design are different.
3. Name at least two fashion career paths. Which one sounds the most interesting to you and why?
4. What are the three parts to a cover letter?
5. Name four traits important to a entrepreneur. Why are these traits important?
6. Name three important parts to development of a résumé?
7. Name three traits to be successful in entrepreneurship.
8. Name four tips for job interviews.

CHAPTER PROJECTS AND DISCUSSION ::

1. Go to www.monster.com and type in "fashion" as a search. What types of jobs come up? What types of companies? Discuss three that may be of interest to you.

2. Interview two people in the fashion industry, and ask them the following questions:

    a. Describe an average day.

    b. What skills does it take to be successful at your job?

    c. How would you recommend I break into this industry?

    d. What is the typical career path?

    e. What is the typical starting salary?

    f. What do you like the best about your job? The least?

3. Write a paragraph about what you hope to learn from this class and from this book. Discuss in small groups, and present to your class.

4. Make a list of all the things that you are good at, relating to fashion. Keep this list for future job interviews or résumé writing.

5. Find a job (or use a job you found in question one) on www.monster.com. Write your résumé for this job. Share and critique in small groups.

6. Find an article about interviewing or résumés. Bring into class and share it.

ONLINE RESUME AND COVER LETTER RESOURCES ::

www.resume-resource.com

http://resume.monster.com/archives/coverletter

www.careerperfect.com/CareerPerfect/resumeExampleMain.htm

www.careercc.com/resumpr.shtml

http://jobstar.org/tools/resume/samples.cfm

chapter two

Fashion Terminology and the Merchandising Process

the purpose of this chapter is to provide a baseline for some fashion terminology and to discuss the way fashion is accepted within the cycle of new styles. The ways in which fashion can be categorized will be discussed. Once gaining an understanding of these concepts, readers will be able to explain the process of buying and merchandising.

After reading this chapter, you should be able to:

1 • Identify the difference between a fad, a classic, and a trend.

2 • Explain categories and characteristics of women's wear, men's wear, and children's wear.

3 • Identify the pricing structure for fashions.

4 • Explain the fashion cycle and give examples of products in each phase of the cycle.

5 • Demonstrate knowledge of the merchandising process.

The total market for clothing exceeded $183 billion for retail sales in 2000, and that number appears to be growing. In a market this large, things need to change constantly in order to meet the needs and wants of consumers.

A misconception of fashion is the idea that it is dictated by fashion designers and fashion merchandisers. This is not the case. In fact, the opposite is true. To be successful, fashion designers and merchandisers must meet the demand of the consumers and understand what they are willing to buy. In the business of fashion, consumers drive product development and new styles, not the other way around.

These concepts fit into the research shoebox of fashion (see Figure 2.1) because the fashionistas who carefully follow the cycles of fashion, the length of cycles, and the trendsetters in these cycles will be the most successful in their field.

> **"To be successful, fashion designers and merchandisers must meet the demand of the consumers, and understand what they are willing to buy."**

Fashion acceptance refers to the extent to which consumers are willing to purchase and wear a particular fashion.

:: FASHION LEADERS ::

Fashion leaders are the first group to accept a new style. They will wear a style before it becomes generally accepted by the public. Fashion leaders can be regular people who follow fashion closely, or they can be movie or television stars, supermodels, and rock stars. They are confident in their taste, have a desire to express themselves through clothing, and have the funds to purchase new fashions on a regular basis. In addition, the majority of fashion leaders can afford to purchase clothing at a higher price point.

An example of the fashion leader might be the girl at school who is the first to have all of the new styles.

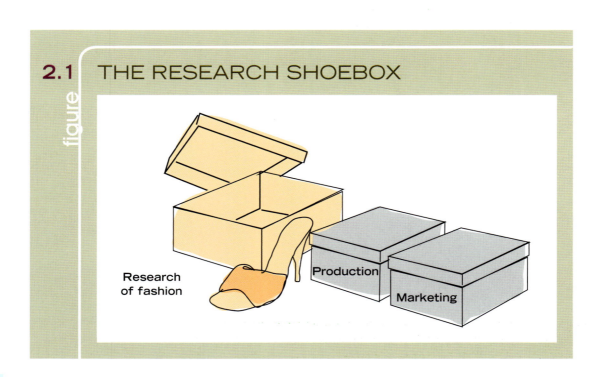

2.1 figure THE RESEARCH SHOEBOX

Research of fashion

Production

Marketing

:: FASHION FOLLOWERS ::

Fashion followers do not take risks and will purchase a fashion only after it has been generally accepted by the public. There are many reasons fashion followers choose not to lead or innovate trends. First, they simply may not have enough interest in fashion to follow trends. Second, they may not have the time or money required to follow new trends. Third, they may have established their own personal styles and are unwilling to adjust to constantly changing fashions.

Fashion followers are important to the fashion industry, as this group tends to purchase fashions that have been mass-produced, normally from stores such as Target or The Gap. **Mass-produced fashion,** sometimes called *volume fashion*, includes styles that are widely accepted. Because they are widely accepted they are produced to appeal to the largest amount of consumers possible; and they are produced in large quantities at lower prices.

Before discussing the length of fashion cycles in the next section, it is necessary to differentiate between the words *style* and *fashion*. Although some people may use them interchangeably, they actually have different meanings. **Style** is the combination of garment characteristics that makes it different from other garments. **Fashion** is a style that has been accepted and used by the majority of people in any one group, at any one time. A specific style, for example, might include peasant blouses. However, it is only when that peasant blouse becomes well accepted that it also becomes a fashion.

:: LENGTH OF FASHION CYCLE ::

A **trend** is a general direction for clothing design. For example, a trend might be three-quarter-length shirts or cocktail-length skirts. Normally, during the initial stages of a trend, a few leading designers show the specific type of garment, which is only worn by fashion leaders at this point.

A **fad,** on the other hand, is an item that comes into popularity very quickly, often with exaggerated detailing. Fads do not affect the whole market, only one part of the population such as the junior market. Fads in 2004–2005 included the "trucker hat" and accessories monogrammed with initials. A fad in the 2006–2007 season included long, flowing skirts and lots of embellished designs on tops and bottoms.

Sometimes an item of clothing that is a trend becomes a **classic.** However, a garment that is a fad will never become a classic item. A classic can be described as an item that is considered in good taste over a long period of time. It is generally a style that meets a basic need and retains characteristics and details that have appeal over an extended period. Some examples of classics are the pearl necklace, the little black dress, and the basic black jacket. These items are considered to be in good taste and have remained in style over long periods.

>> the fashion cycle

The fashion cycle relates to fashion acceptance in two main ways. First, the speed in which an item goes through the cycle relates directly to whether it is a fad, classic, or trend. The speed of movement through the fashion cycle will also depend on the initial acceptance of the clothing by fashion leaders and the subsequent acceptance by fashion followers.

To the fashion designer and merchandiser, the **fashion cycle** is one of the most significant components of fashion. Through accurate research and observation, the designer and merchandiser can determine at any given point in time where fashions exist in the fashion cycle. In doing so, they are able to design, produce, and price the products that consumers demand for any given period.

:: INTRODUCTION ::

The **introduction phase** is when clothing is introduced at a high price level. High-end fashion designers normally introduce the clothing. Clothing, in the introductory stage, may be loaned to fashion leaders, such as film stars, who are then seen wearing them to important events. Because the clothing is new, it is often introduced at a high price level, a price that most people cannot afford. However, once the general public observes the stars in the loaned clothing, excitement may be generated for the item, and the clothing might then be manufactured for the mass market.

For example, say Jennifer Lopez wears a peasant shirt by Marc Jacobs to the MTV music awards. This product is new and not yet in stores. If customers really like the shirt, it makes sense that the demand for that item will increase.

:: INCREASE IN POPULARITY OR GROWTH ::

Once designers have introduced a specific garment and fashion leaders have accepted it, the garment will enter into the second phase, referred to as the **growth phase.** In the growth phase, fashion followers will accept the garment worn by fashion leaders. Once that acceptance has occurred, manufacturers will then copy the garment and sell it for a less expensive price. During this phase, the fashion gains popularity among fashion followers. Garments in this phase can be found at stores such as Nordstrom or Macy's.

In continuation of the above example, after Jennifer Lopez wears the peasant shirt, they will no longer be manufactured only by couture or designer lines; instead, similar, less expensive shirts will be readily found in most department stores.

:: PEAK ::

In the **peak phase,** the garment can be found at almost any retailer and it is accepted by the mass market. In this phase, garments can be purchased at mass-merchandisers, such as Target, and they may be available in a large variety of colors and many variations. In addition, prices are often reduced in many retail stores. At this point, many of those who wanted a peasant shirt would have already bought one.

:: DECLINE ::

Eventually, consumers tire of the garment and start to look for something new. During the **decline phase,** fashion leaders have already moved on to new styles. Consumers still wear the fashion in decline, but retailers will likely have to mark down the garments, as consumers are no longer willing to purchase them at the regular price. These items are put on clearance for quick sale or sometimes moved to outlet stores.

At the decline phase, Jennifer Lopez has likely appeared wearing a new, trendy outfit, and the fashion leaders will be in search of that particular garment. Meanwhile, consumers are still enjoying their peasant shirts, which can likely be found on many retailers' sale racks.

:: REJECTION ::

The **rejection phase** is when most consumers will no longer buy the product, even on sale, and have moved on to new styles. There will be extreme markdowns in the rejection stage, such as 70 or 80 percent off. If the items don't sell for extreme markdowns, they may be transferred to outlet stores or sold to stores like Marshalls and Ross. It is important to note that there are many consumers, called *laggards,* who are willing to buy clothing that is considered out of date. While these consumers are not considered stylish, they do provide income for retailers.

At the rejection phase, consumers are demanding the newest fashion worn by Jennifer Lopez, or other fashion leaders, and are no longer interested in the peasant shirt. The leftover shirts will be moved off the retail floor and transferred to outlets or discount stores.

An **interrupted cycle** is one in which consumers did not necessarily stop buying the product, but it became unavailable. For example, searching for swimsuits in August can be difficult, as retailers bring in "back to school" or fall clothing. This is done to make more room on their sales floor for new seasonal merchandise, while getting rid of older merchandise.

Figure 2.2 illustrates the complete fashion cycle.

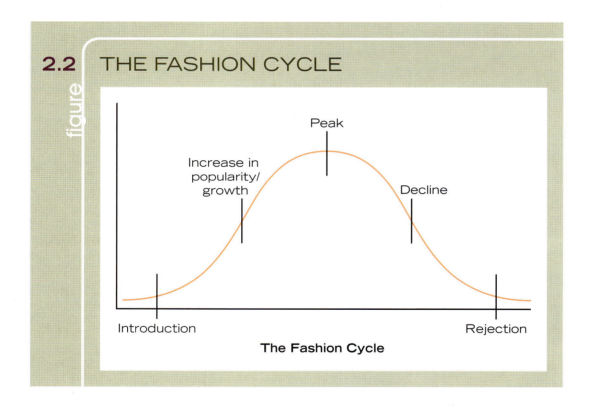

2.2 THE FASHION CYCLE

figure

The Fashion Cycle

>> categories of fashion products

Within the total market for clothing, there are three main categories: women's wear, men's wear, and children's wear. Each of these categories is important because the fashion cycle moves at a different pace for each. Men's clothing, for example, moves at a much slower pace through the fashion cycle then does women's clothing.

This section will discuss each of the three categories of fashion products, along with considerations when selling products to each of these groups. The first section will offer information on pricing for fashion products.

:: PRICING ::

Pricing is perhaps the most important factor in design and merchandising. Price is the actual price charged to the customer. Knowing the market in which the merchandiser is selling will assist that person in developing appropriate pricing strategies for the product.

Information on major price zones for women's wear, men's wear, and children's wear is included in the next section.

Couture design

These are one-of-a-kind items, made by famous designers. The clientele is small, and the garment is custom-fit to the buyer. Sometimes this type of design is called **haute couture.**

Couture design can cost $5,000 to $50,000 for one garment, and the price can be even more for evening wear or wedding gowns. Couture is obviously reserved for the very rich. Not only is the purchaser buying the designer name, but he or she also receives extremely personal service, top-of-the-line workmanship, and originality in the design. Of course, the materials, such as the fabric, are of the highest quality. In addition, a lot of time is required to produce such garments, perhaps 100 to 150 hours for a suit and up to 1,000 hours for evening wear.

Only a few thousand people in the world can afford to buy couture designs. Couture design houses may sell only 1,500 garments per year. However, couture houses gain a name for themselves through fashion shows and media publicity. Through all of this publicity, they are able to sell products like perfume at a high price, but one that more consumers will be able to afford. For men's clothing, couture is sometimes called **custom tailored** or **bespoke tailored.**

Many couture houses must design branded items like perfume, leather goods, and luggage to help offset some of the development cost for the couture lines.

Well-known couture designers include Christian Lacroix, Yves St Laurent, Valentino, and Christian Dior.

Christian Dior dress, Spring 2006.

Designer signature

Designer signature is the next highest price zone, after couture. These garments are very high in price, ranging to above $1,000 for one garment. Nordstrom, for example, has a Chanel department. Garments in this department are not couture, because they are not custom-made, but they are still expensive and exclusive. The garments are made from very fine materials. Sometimes these designs are called **ready-to-wear,** or **prêt-à-porter.** They get this name because they can be bought directly off the hanger and are not custom-made for an individual person. Prada and Versace are examples of designer signature clothing.

It is important to keep in mind that some designers may have a couture line but also a designer line. Again, the difference is that couture is custom-made for the person, whereas designer signature is not.

Examples of designer signature are Donna Karan, Bill Blass, and Calvin Klein.

Bridge

Bridge lines are high-quality garments sold at a less expensive price, priced between designer and better. Bridge lines offer less quality than designer but at about half the price. Most bridge prices range between $500 to $1,000. DKNY, Tahari, and Eileen Fisher are examples.

Better **Better** garments are usually priced below $500, but they are of better quality than what might be found at Wal-Mart or Target. This category appeals to an upper or middle-class market. Jones New York and Nautica are examples.

Moderate The **moderate** zone would include garments found at The Gap and The Limited. Clothing in this price range is generally sold in chain stores and retails for $100 or less. The quality is slightly better than budget items, and there may be more unique features in a moderate-priced product, compared to budget products.

DKNY offers designer signature and bridge lines.

It is essential to note that many designers are now entering this market as well. For example, Vera Wang designs stem wear, such as wine glasses. Ralph Lauren designs bedding and towels. The advantage that this market offers designers is that while their clothing may be priced out of range for many people, those same customers can purchase less expensive items made by them, such as bath towels or bedding.

Budget The **budget** category includes clothing aimed at the mass market. Budget items retail for less than $50 and can be found at retailers such as Old Navy, Wal-Mart, and Target.

Many designers offer items in several of the pricing categories discussed. Ralph Lauren, for example, has a couture-type line called Purple Label Custom Collection but also produces designer signature, bridge, and moderate lines. The advantage for designers to produce at many different prices levels is profit and visibility. For example, a woman just starting her career in her 20s may purchase moderate clothing made by Ralph Lauren; and by doing so, she may become loyal to the designer. As she is more successful in her career, she is able to afford the higher-end Ralph Lauren garments. Thus, by having clothing at different price levels, the designer gained the loyalty from the customer at the very beginning of her career.

:: WOMEN'S WEAR ::

The women's wear market is larger than men's wear and children's wear combined, producing more than $96 billion per year in retail sales. Besides price, women's wear can be further segmented by function, size, and season.

Mother and daughter looking for back-to-school outfits at Old Navy.

Function Women's wear is broken down into nine main functions, then further broken down within those categories, and still further by size and season. **Function** refers to how the garment will actual be used. The categories of women's clothing include dresses, formal, suits, outerwear, sportswear, active wear, swimwear, lingerie, and accessories.

Dresses include any single garment or two-piece garment that is sold as a unit. Formal apparel includes wedding dresses, special occasion gowns, such as prom dresses, and cocktail dresses. The third category is suits, which includes pantsuits and jackets or skirts and jackets. Outerwear includes jackets, coats, and ski or snowboarding outfits. Sportswear is any combination of tops and bottoms used for casual dressing, such as jeans, T-shirts, blouses, and khaki pants or shorts. Active wear is clothing used for exercise or sports; items like jogging suits would fit in this category, as would shirts used for golf and tennis skirts. Swimwear includes one-piece or two-piece swimsuits and swimsuit cover-ups. Lingerie includes sleepwear, bras, underwear, and body slimmers. Finally, accessories are scarves, hats, purses, jewelery, hosiery, and belts.

Sizes In addition to the main categories of women's wear, size can be a category. There are no required sizing standards that manufacturers need to meet; however, an organization does exist to provide voluntary standards to manufacturers. The American Society for Testing and Materials (ASTM) provides voluntary standards. These standards are based on measurements of thousands of women. The database the ASTM uses to record these standards is referred to as WK5703. Although the database has been updated since the 1940s, it is still based on the hourglass figure, of 36–26–36. The hourglass figure is one with the same size bust and hips, not necessarily 36; however, only about 8 percent of the American female population would likely have such proportions. In 2004, several major retailers participated in a study called Size USA. This study gave body scans to more than 10,000 women throughout the United States. Although this study provided good data, it is unclear if manufacturers are actually using this data when sizing their clothing. Another issue with the most recent size survey was the lack of diverse body types, which skewed the data.

The various sizes for women's clothing include

- *Junior:* includes odd-numbered sizes 1–15.
- *Junior plus:* same styles as junior, but in sizes 16–24.
- *Misses:* includes even-numbered sizes 0–20.
- *Petite:* includes those items made for smaller/shorter women, sizes 2P–16P.
- *Women's, sometimes called Plus:* includes even-numbered sizes 12–52; tends to have less fad merchandise and more classic styles.
- *Maternity:* available in misses and women's sizes, but accommodations are made for breast and midriff size.

Women's winter outfits.

A discussion on sizing would not be appropriate without mentioning that the average size for women is 14. Despite this, designers and retailers still tend to use fit models of size 6; most experts agree they should instead concentrate on designing clothing that fits the larger, average size.

Another interesting practice is the use of **vanity sizing.** Vanity sizing is marking a size smaller than it actually is, with the hope women will buy it because they feel smaller. For example, a retailer might use size 10 proportions but size the garment as an 8.

Season The last way to classify women's fashion goods is by the **season.** Garments for fall and winter, or conversely spring and summer, are usually introduced together. Spring goods will differ from summer goods in a couple of ways. First, spring items may include lighter fabrics than winter items, but they may be long sleeve. Spring items also tend to use a layered look, so customers will be better prepared for changing weather.

Region may affect the types of garments in each classification. Miami, for example, may carry very different winter garments than New York.

:: MEN'S WEAR ::

The men's wear market is large as well, with more than $69 billion in retail sales. This market is growing as a result of men becoming more concerned with their appearance. For example, many companies have developed men's-only skincare lines, such as Zirh. Men are becoming more interested in plastic surgery, weight loss, and other treatments or products typically reserved for women.

Function Besides price, men's wear is broken down into six main functions and can further be divided by size and season.

The function categories for men's clothing include tailored clothing, furnishings, sportswear, active wear, work clothing, and accessories. Tailored clothing includes suits, overcoats, tuxes, and sportcoats. Furnishings are dress shirts, ties, underwear, and shoes. Sportswear includes casual pants, jeans, sweaters, or items that are purchased separately. Active wear includes any garments used for exercise, such as bike or running shorts, and items used for sports, such as golf shirts. Work clothes include overalls, work boots, and any garment necessary to do a particular job. Accessories are wallets, belts, cuff links, and scarves.

Sizes In addition to the main categories of men's wear, size can also be a specialty. Sizes are based on the chest measurement, neck size, and sleeve length of the man:

- *Short:* 36–44
- *Regular:* 35–46
- *Long:* 37–48
- *Extra long:* 38–50
- *Portly short:* 39–48
- *Large:* 46, 48, and 50

The sizing of men's clothing presents greater difficulty than women's clothing for retailers. Since men's clothing is based not only on chest measurements but also on waist and length measurements, retailers must stock a very large range of sizes. For example, retail stores generally carry men's pants in lengths of 28, 30, 32, 34, and 36, which is called the **inseam.** These numbers represent the length of the pant in inches. In addition to stocking different lengths, the retailer must carry a range of waist sizes as well. Generally, waist sizes are the same as length: 28, 30, 32, 34, and 36. The different length and waist sizes represent many possible combinations just in pants. Dress shirts typically come in different neck sizes and arm lengths, for example, 32 (arm) by 16 1/2 (neck). Again, this creates many combinations of possible sizes a retailer must carry. This concept is called *dual sizing*. One way to control the number of sizes that must be carried is to give free alterations.

Season The last way to classify men's fashion goods, like women's fashion, is by season. Again, fall and winter, or conversely spring and summer, are usually introduced together. Straw hats and sleeveless or short-sleeve shirts are examples for summer; flannel shirts and coats are winter products.

Function, such as these outfits, is a way to divide the men's wear market.

:: CHILDREN'S WEAR ::

The children's wear market accounts for more than $21 billion in sales. Children's wear has a larger secondhand market, which is why it would appear there are fewer purchases in this category. Children's wear has some special attributes, different from men's and women's wear. For example, children's clothing might include special snaps, velcro, or buttons. In addition, the type of fabric used is important in children's wear, because of washability and durability. There are also legal issues to consider during development of children's clothing. For example, the following laws apply to outerwear for children:

- Outerwear should not have hood or neck drawstrings.
- It should not have waist strings that extended beyond 7.4 cm.
- The waist strings should be sewn down at the midpoint.
- There should not be toggles or knots on the ends of strings.

These laws are designed to protect children from strangulation. There have been several cases in which a child's neck drawstrings were caught in some sort of machinery or vehicle, such as a bus or tractor, causing asphyxiation of the child. As a result, the Consumer Product Safety Commission now oversees and implements laws to protect children from dangerous clothing.

Another legal consideration in the development of clothing for children is flammability. Sleepwear has special standards it must meet regarding flammability. These standards were implemented though the Flammable Fabrics Act.

An example of another legal issue is that of companies recalling thousands of items of clothing due to snaps or zippers that are easily removed and swallowed by children. In 2000, Nordstrom recalled 2,250 jackets for this reason. Anyone designing children's wear must be familiar with product safety issues and laws before moving forward with their designs.

Unlike women's and men's wear, classifications for children's wear are based not on function but rather on the size and the age of the child. Size and price are the main categories of children's wear. Function has less of an impact in children's wear than it does for women's or men's wear.

Size As discussed for men's and women's wear, there are several categories in the children's wear market, including toddlers and children. It is vital to note that toddler's and children's wear may sometimes overlap on sizes. Toddler's wear is different than children's in that it may have more snaps to accommodate diaper changing. Children's wear tends to have regular zippers and buttons for the more physically developed child. The age ranges for children's clothing is as follows:

- *Infants:* newborn–1 year
- *Toddlers:* 2–3 years
- *Children:* 3–6 years
- *Girls:* 7–14 years
- *Preteen:* 7–14 years (more sophisticated styling than girls, although the same age range)
- *Boys:* 7–14 years
- *Young men:* 14–20

Season Children's wear can also be classified by season. As in women's and men's clothing, fall/winter and spring/summer are the seasons used for classification. Children's wear also experiences fads, as in women's and men's wear. Both Sponge Bob and Dora the Explorer T-shirts are examples

There are many considerations for children's wear, such as flammability laws.

of fads in children's wear. Much like adult clothing, these fads can change rapidly, depending on the types of television programs children are watching.

Price   Price ranges in children's wear include budget, moderate, better, and designer. Because children outgrow clothing so quickly, most clothing in children's wear is in the budget to moderate range. However, Versace and Olily would be considered designer children's wear.

REAL WORLD focus >> Hispanic Men's Market Potential Could Redefine Ethnic Grooming Sets

The Hispanic market is hot as such celebrities as Antonio Banderas, Jennifer Lopez, and Salma Hayek become the epitome of beauty in the eyes of America. Response to this cultural shift is becoming increasingly evident in how companies go to market with women's beauty care products, but when it comes to catering to Hispanic men, a great deal of untapped opportunities remain.

"The Latina has been an incredible focus and force [in the beauty industry], and the man certainly is going to bring that same kind of sexiness," said David Wolfe, creative director for the Doneger Group. Despite the increased focus on the Hispanic community and its immense buying power, most of the ethnic grooming products still found at drugstores are geared toward African Americans, in large part because they tend to have more specific skin and hair care needs versus other ethnic groups. However, research suggests that lucrative opportunities exist for those retailers and manufacturers that can overcome the cautionary mantra of "so many options, so little demand" and effectively reach this growing consumer group.

Marketers should be encouraged to know that Hispanic men—who ascended to the rank of the most numerous U.S. minority as of 2003—are expected to have a spending power of $271 billion to $361 billion in 2004. By 2008, that spending range is predicted to climb to between $450 billion and $600 billion, according to a research report by Packaged Facts.

Furthermore, the research predicts that the men's ethnic HBC market, driven in part by Hispanic men, will be valued at more than $1.7 billion at retail as of 2008—a total gain of nearly 20 percent between 2003 and 2008.

Many industry observers agree that Hispanic men have long been known for taking great pride in their hair, skin, and clothes. So, as the men's grooming segment continues to grow, it would seem that catering to Hispanic men would be a natural fit.

[Hispanic men] were metrosexuals ahead of their time. "It is not like they are becoming metrosexuals—there was just never a word for it before," said Rochelle Newman-Carrasco, chief executive officer of Los Angeles-based Hispanic marketing firm Enlace Communications. She noted that much of Hispanic men's interest in personal grooming stems from the cultural belief that how a person presents himself to society says something about his family.

However, that is not to say that targeting the Hispanic consumer—whether male or female—is not complex. Issues that tend to tangle the web include cultural differences, language preferences, and understanding the specific needs of a customer whether they are Mexican, Puerto Rican, Cuban, or South American.

Newman-Carrasco suggests that because the Hispanic community is a collective culture—versus Caucasians, who are more individualistic—marketers should find ways to get involved in community events to get the word out, such as promoting their products at a local baseball game.

"Hispanics are community-oriented, and there are a lot of events and opportunities to integrate products into the community," Newman-Carrasco said. "What sports are Hispanics interested in? What events are they at? There are a lot of innovative ways to speak to the community."

Looking to target the Hispanic consumer in general, not necessarily just men for personal grooming, several drug chains, such as Longs Drug Stores, Walgreens, Rite Aid, and CVS, have ramped up targeted merchandising efforts to reach Hispanic shoppers.

Being based in New York, Ricky's Urban Groove—the eclectic and extremely fashion-forward chain of HBA stores—is in the heart of an ethnic melting pot and for years has merchandised its stores to reflect that diversity.

Ricky Kenig, the founder of the 22-store retail outlet, said that about 30 percent of its customers are Hispanic, and as a result, Ricky's always has offered in its ethnic section some grooming products geared toward Hispanics—male and female.

At Newark, Delaware-based Happy Harry's, Kathy Ross, HBC category manager, said she has seen very little activity from vendors looking to target Hispanic men specifically.

"It seems like [men's grooming] started leaning toward the Hispanics, and then it became more about men in general," Ross said.

However, there are indications that perhaps the Hispanic male's time is about to come.

Manufacturer Combe rolled out in 2003 a new shade of Just For Men hair color designed specifically for Hispanic men. Known as Castano Negro Oscuro, or Darkest Brown Black, the new shade is available in a shampoo-in hair color, as well as in a brush-in gel for mustaches, beards, and sideburns.

Meanwhile, Dana Classic Fragrances recently introduced in the United States four Hispanic scents for men: Musk by Dana, Vetiver by Dana, Herbissimo Mejorana, and Herbissimo Te Verde. For years, the fragrances have been hot sellers in Europe, and now the company is hoping to generate the same buzz in the U.S. market. The fragrances, which retail for $9.99 each, are being sold now in select Rite Aid and Kmart locations and likely will expand to other retailers.

"We analyzed the market, and the Hispanic market is growing very fast. It only makes sense to market to them," said Sean-Patrick Hillman of Corbin & Associates, which represents Dana Classic Fragrances. He noted that the company eventually plans to introduce ancillary products like aftershave to the U.S. market.

Patricia Bailey of the PBailey Group said that in the spring, manufacturer Global Cosmetics Co. will launch a new Hispanic line for both men and women under its Radical brand. In addition, Global Cosmetics Co. currently is targeting retailers with value sections and dollar stores with its new styling gel under the New York Style brand. The product, which has bilingual labeling, targets ethnic consumers and will retail for about $1 each.

"Now that the [term] *metrosexual* exists in the marketing segment, the next logical step is to say 'Who is the metrosexual?' and [see] that they are Hispanics," Newman-Carrasco said. ❈

Source: Antoinette Alexander Drug Store News, November 22, 2004. Copyright 2004, Gale Group.

›› QUESTIONS

1. Why are men's grooming products an important part of fashion?

2. Have you noticed a difference in the use of products by men you know? Discuss.

3. Why are the Hispanic market and African American market important markets for retailers to consider?

>> merchandising process

Basic knowledge about how fashions are accepted and go through the fashion cycle and how clothing is actually categorized assists buyers and merchandisers in making sure they have the right mix of merchandise, prices, sizes, and seasons in their store. Once they have awareness in each of these areas, they can go through the process to actually purchase clothing for their retailer.

There are several steps a buyer must go though to create a good, sellable mix of merchandise and ensure the maximization of sales. The steps in merchandising and buying process are as follows:

1. Set buying plan.
2. Buy and order.
3. Receive orders and provide information to sales staff.
4. Monitor inventory levels and sales.
5. Negotiate with vendors on buybacks.

:: BUYING PLAN ::

The first step in merchandising is the buying plan (see Figure 2.3). Because the merchandiser is responsible for providing an inventory that reflects consumer demand, sizing, and season, while staying within a set budget, a buying plan is essential. Predicting needs, demand, and sizing is called **fashion forecasting.** The buying plan is normally done on a six-month basis and is called a **six-month buying plan.** The buying plan lists expected sales and last year's sales for each classification. A **classification** is a type of good, for example, knit tops or denim bottoms. In addition, it also lists an **open-to-buy** figure. The open-to-buy is the dollar amount of merchandise the buyer may purchase during a given period. For all practical purposes, the open-to-buy figure is the money a buyer has been allocated to spend on purchases. This figure is based on expected sales figures, desired

2.3 figure A SAMPLE SIX-MONTH MERCHANDISING (BUYING) PLAN

**Casey's
Six-Month Merchandising Plan
Women's Knits**

Winter/Spring		Jan	Feb	Mar	Apr	May	Jun	Season Totals
Sales	Last Year							
	Plan							
	% of Increase							
	Revised							
	Actual							
Retail Stock (BOM)	Last Year							
	Plan							
	Revised							
	Actual							
Reductions	Last Year							
	Plan (dollars)							
	Plan (percent)							
	Revised							
	Actual							
Retail Purchases/ OTB	Planned Purchases							
	Merchandise Received							
	Goods on Order							
	Open to Buy							

Courtesy of mona starr, Shoreline Community College

inventory levels, and items already on order. Open-to-buy provides a guideline for buyers by making sure they do not overpurchase or underpurchase. Calculation of open-to-buy will be discussed in Chapter 10.

:: BUY AND ORDER ::

Once knowing what he or she has to spend, the buyer will then work with in-house designers, depending on the type of company, or attend trade shows to place orders for new fashions. It is imperative that the buyer has an accurate plan so that he or she doesn't overbuy or underbuy during the trips.

Most buyers will make at least two trips a year, one for fall/winter and one for spring/summer. There are two types of places buyers can go to purchase goods. They can attend **trade shows,** normally located in **fashion centers.** A fashion center is a city known as place in which many trade shows or showrooms are located. The major trade show is called MAGIC (Men's Apparel Guild in California), which started out as a men's-only trade show. It takes place in Las Vegas every February and August. Today, MAGIC shows men's, children's, young fashion, and women's wear. The AmericasMart Atlanta, held in Atlanta several times a year, has shows that sell sports-related products and apparel, gifts, and home furnishings. There are also specialty trade shows, such as for wedding apparel. The most popular trade show for wedding apparel takes place in Chicago and is called the National Bridal Market. There is also a Super Show, normally held in January, for sports clothing and accessories. This show is held in Orlando, Florida.

A **showroom** is the second place a buyer can go to order merchandise. Showrooms are normally run either by designers or sales representatives of the clothing line. Showrooms are located throughout the country, but the most well known are in New York City. The showrooms in New York are grouped together by price and merchandise classification. They are located in the garment district of New York, sometimes known as Seventh Avenue. Other regional showroom markets include Los Angeles, Dallas, Chicago, Atlanta, and Miami.

Buyers may also have sales representatives from various manufacturers visit them with line boards and catalogs. The buyer, as expected, has performed extensive research on trends, knows the image the company is trying to portray, and knows the price range of goods sold within his or her store. As a result, when buying and ordering, the buyer will keep these things in mind.

This designer presents his merchandise in a showroom.

:: RECEIVE ORDERS AND PROVIDE INFORMATION TO STAFF ::

Depending on the type of company, the buyer or the merchandise planner will be responsible for making sure the items arrive at the store. The items that end up in the stores should be appropriate to climate and size of the store. In addition, the buyer will communicate information about new items coming in to the visual merchandising team as well as to the people on the sales floor. This can be performed informally or formally by new product meetings with salespeople.

:: MONITOR INVENTORY LEVELS AND SALES ::

Depending on the company, monitoring of inventory might be the job of the merchandise planner. Stores use sophisticated scanning devices and inventory software to take inventory in their stores, and usually it is ongoing. This software can prevent theft, but it also provides real-time information to buyers about inventory levels. In any size company it is important for the buyer to know how well items are selling in the stores. For items that are selling very well, the buyer may want to reorder the merchandise. For those that are not selling well, the buyer may want to transfer the merchandise to a different store or markdown the merchandise. Most retailers have sophisticated computer systems to monitor inventory levels.

:: NEGOTIATE BUYBACKS OR ADVERTISING WITH VENDORS ::

The final responsibility of the merchandiser is to negotiate with **vendors.** It is important to note, though, that negotiation will occur throughout the fashion buying process. The buyer will negotiate price during the buying and ordering process, but there are a couple of other things he or she will negotiate as well. First, for companies that advertise, the buyer may work with the marketing department to negotiate with the vendor to split the cost of the advertisement, if it is featuring the garment of the manufacturer. Another negotiation might be to buyback goods that did not sell. An example might be a selection of lime-colored shirts that the vendor promised would be "hot" then didn't sell.

In addition, a merchandiser may negotiate use of point-of-purchase displays provided by the vendor at no cost or a reduced cost.

>> conclusion •

This chapter discussed concepts that can be used to effectively buy and merchandise products. Understanding how consumers actually accept garments, the cycle garments go through, and the possible categories of fashion products will assist the merchandiser in the process of buying. In order to effectively buy, one must understand not only the concepts in buying but also the process and duties a fashion merchandiser must perform.

TERMS TO KNOW ::

Fashion acceptance
Fashion leader
Fashion follower
Mass-produced fashion
Style
Fashion
Trend
Fad
Classic
Fashion cycle
Introduction phase
Growth phase
Peak phase

Decline phase
Rejection phase
Interrupted cycle
Pricing
Haute couture
Custom tailored
Bespoke tailored
Designer signature
Ready-to-wear
Prêt-à-porter
Bridge
Better
Moderate

Budget
Function
Vanity sizing
Season
Inseam
Fashion forecasting
Six-month buying plan
Classification
Open-to-buy
Trade shows
Fashion centers
Showroom
Vendor

CONCEPTS TO KNOW ::

1. The fashion cycle.
2. Pricing categories of fashion products.
3. Function classifications of women's wear and men's wear.
4. Size ranges for women's wear, men's wear, and children's wear.
5. The process of fashion merchandising.
6. Components of a six-month plan.

CHAPTER QUESTIONS ::

1. What are some garments in your closet you would consider classics? Fads? Describe each garment. What specifics about the item encouraged you to purchase it?
2. What are fashion followers? How important do you think their role is within the fashion cycle?
3. What causes fashion acceptance in fashion? What can cause fashion rejection? Discuss.
4. Why do you think children's wear does not classify by function? Name two reasons.
5. Describe two issues related to women's clothing. Do you find it difficult to find clothing that fits properly?

6. Some people think that buying is all about "shopping on other people's money." Discuss three other components to merchandising that are important.

CHAPTER PROJECTS AND DISCUSSION ::

1. Pick out five items of clothing from your closet. Either bring the garments into class or describe them to your group. Get into small groups and discuss if the items are fad, classic, or trend. What about the garment motivated you to buy it?
2. How do you think income influences the choice of fad, classic, or trend?
3. Research the fashion centers mentioned in this chapter. What do they have in common? How are they different? Are there new and upcoming places that could be considered "fashion centers"?
4. Bring in two garments you would consider to be no longer in good taste? What makes them not in good taste? Are the garments a fad, a classic, or a trend? Where does it fit in the fashion cycle?

FOR FURTHER READING ::

www.badfads.com/pages/fashion.html
www.dallasmarketcenter.com
www.magiconline.com
www.vault.com/nr/main_article_detail.jsp?article_id=1670896&cat_
   id=0&ht_type=1

Textiles *and* Design Development

Chapter Three will provide information on fashion design, including a discussion on the materials used in fashion design. Textiles are one of the major components of fashion design and affect the entire fashion a designer creates. This chapter will also discuss the process of creating new fashions.

After reading this chapter, you should be able to:

1 • Identify the four design principles in fashion.

2 • Identify types of silhouettes and give examples of each.

3 • Recognize and explain the four performance factors in natural fibers.

4 • Explain characteristics of each type of textile.

5 • Describe the process of fashion design.

>> fashion-design terminology

Fashion design is a changing, dynamic field. Because of this, designers need to be aware of the world around them in order to design clothing people will want to buy. Fashion design fits in the production shoebox (see Figure 3.1). Design includes the choosing of the elements that make the design unique, the textile used, and the actual production of the garment.

The four main principles of fashion design are silhouette, details, texture, and color. **Silhouette** is the overall outline or contour of a garment. The silhouette is normally what is first noticed about a garment, because it can be identified from a long distance away. The main types of silhouettes include A-line, hourglass, wedge, tubular, and bouffant.

The **A-line** silhouette is smaller at one point in the garment and large at another point. The A-line dress is a good example. The dress is more fitted at the top, with a slight flare at the bottom.

An **hourglass** silhouette is fitted to the female body, which makes it fitted smaller at the waist with equal size on top and bottom. A jacket and skirt that tapers in at the waist is an example.

A **wedge** is fitted larger at the top and smaller at the bottom, for example, an off-the-shoulder sweater.

A **tubular** silhouette has a straight cut throughout the garment. In other words, it is a full, straight form.

A **bouffant** silhouette flares out in fullness from the hip. Dresses in movies such as *Gone with the Wind* are examples of bouffant. Another example is a prom or wedding dress that has fullness at the bottom.

Another design word for silhouette is *shape*. **Shape** is a basic design element used not only in fashion design but also in any art form such as painting or sculpture.

Silhouettes and fashion in general tend to be cyclical in nature. **Cyclical** means they come into style and go out of style then back into style over time. In other words, what is popular today will likely not be popular in 10 years, but it may come back into fashion in 20 years.

> **"***Designers need to be aware of the world around them in order to design clothing people will want to buy.***"**

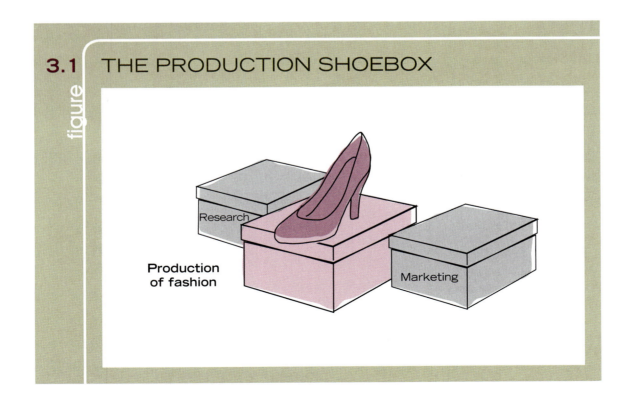

3.1 figure **THE PRODUCTION SHOEBOX**

Research

Production of fashion

Marketing

Figure 3.2 illustrates each type of silhouette.

A-line

Hourglass

Wedge

Tubular

Bouffant

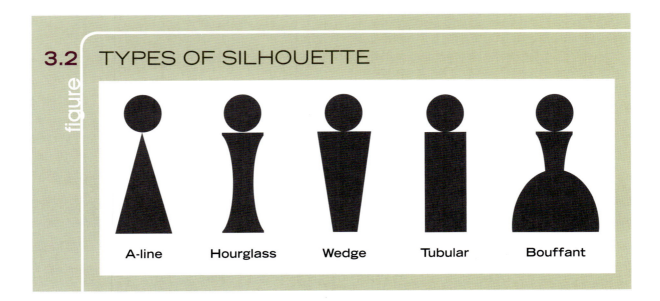

3.2 TYPES OF SILHOUETTE

figure

A-line   Hourglass   Wedge   Tubular   Bouffant

The second design principle has to do with **details.** These are the individual, unique elements of a garment. Examples of details could include trimmings, such as the types of buttons and closures, type of sleeve, neckline, and collars. Other examples of details are pleats or seams. Shoulder padding, or lack of shoulder padding, would be another example. Consider the popular peasant shirt with unique beading or embroidery. Although the basic silhouette and color of the shirt may be the same, the beading or embroidery on the shirt are details that make the garment unique.

The third design principle concerns **texture.** Texture is the look and feel of the material. Texture includes how soft or rough and light or heavy the garment appears to be.

Color is the fourth major principle in design. The color palette changes every season, and the designer must be aware of these changes. A **color palette** includes the selection of colors used in a given season. Neutrals include beige, brown, white, and black, colors almost always included in designer lines. Warm colors include red, orange, and yellow. Cool colors include blues, greens, and purple. The intensity, meaning the brightness or paleness of the garment, changes every season.

Color is a major aspect to design.

>> the materials of fashion design

:: THE TEXTILE INDUSTRY ::

Obviously, clothing cannot be made without textiles or fabrics, which makes textiles the key ingredient in fashion design. Designers and merchandisers that have knowledge of textiles will be better able to design, buy, and market clothing.

Many books have been written about the textile industry; thus, this section will only attempt to give a basic overview. **Textiles** are the cloth from which clothing and household goods are made. Textiles start as **fibers,** are then made into **yarns,** and are either woven or knit together to form the actual fabric. The steps in actual development of a new textile are listed below.

1. *Fiber development.* New fibers are being developed all the time, as well as new uses for textiles. In addition, blending various textiles can result in new fabrics. This industry is very scientific and normally requires a degree in polymer chemistry.

2. *Fiber distribution.* After the new fibers have been developed and made, the producers will sell them to fabric manufacturers. The selling of new fibers is an ongoing process. For example, manufacturers of cotton continually advertise the unique proprieties of that fiber to the general public.

3. *Textile development and design.* Once the fabric manufacturers have the fibers, they can focus on the actual development of the fabric, as well as the end use of it. This includes things like development of a printed pattern and color selection.

4. *Marketing of textiles.* Once the fabric has been developed, the textile company will market the fabric collection to design houses and studios.

One of the ways companies market their textiles is through **fabric markets,** many of which that take place twice a year. Some examples of fabric markets are Premiere Vision in Paris, the Dallas Fabric Show, and the World Fabric Show in Hong Kong. Another method of marketing fabric is through sales representatives. Fabric companies have representatives who meet with manufacturers and designers to show new fabrics. Textile manufacturers have many types of customers, which affects how the textiles will be marketed.

There are five primary types of companies that work with textiles:

1. **Producers** of natural or man-made fibers and filament yarns are those companies that actually develop new fibers.

2. **Processors** and converters of yarn include companies that actually buy the fibers and make them into usable yarn.

3. Some firms specialize in the **dyeing,** or coloring, of fibers and yarns. **Fiber dyeing** refers to the process of coloring the fiber before it is turned into yarn. **Yarn dyeing** is the coloring of yarn before it is actually made into a fabric. **Piece dyeing,** a less expensive process, is the coloring of the yarn after it has been woven or knitted into a fabric. In **garment dyeing,** yet another prevalent coloring technique, fibers and yarns are not dyed until the fabric is put together to form the piece of clothing.

4. Some firms specialize in the **finishing and coating** and printing of fabrics. For example, companies may put special wrinkle-resistant coating on garments or add a coating that makes the garment flame retardant, as is done with children's sleepwear, discussed in Chapter 2.

5. Firms may specialize in the **postprocessing** of finished fabrics. Postprocessing includes actually making the finished textile into a usable good. This process could involve the addition of any beadwork, sequins, or additional items not part of the original fibers.

Of course, many companies will specialize in two or three of these areas.

:: TYPES OF TEXTILES ::

There are two main types of fibers, **natural** and **manufactured.** Sometimes, manufactured textiles are called **man-made** or **synthetic.** An example of a natural fiber is cotton; manufactured fibers include rayon or polyester.

Natural fibers, as the name suggests, are grown or developed in nature. They normally come from plants, such as cotton, or from animal sources, such as silk or fur. Manufactured fibers are invented in a laboratory, made from chemical compounds. Extensive research in chemistry is required in the ongoing effort to invent new man-made fibers to meet the needs of the fashion industry. Currently, there are about 26 types of manufactured fibers available. Because they are man-made, they tend to be more readily available and sometimes cheaper than natural fibers.

There are specific names given to fabrics as they enter the process of production. A **filament fiber** refers to a fiber that is extremely long; a **staple fiber** is one that is short. However, as the fibers, be they natural or man-made, enter the production process, they are not yet in a usable form to make a garment.

Once the manufacturer has the fibers, it can make them into yarns. Natural fibers are cleaned and blended together. The fibers are then drawn out to form single strands of yarn. The yarns are then knitted or woven to form the textile. Manufactured fibers are processed into yarn in much the same way. For blended textiles, such as cotton and polyester blends, the fibers are combined together at this point and then are spun into the fabric or textile.

There are two ways in which the yarns can be put together to form the fabric. A **knit** is put together by using one continuous yarn, with the exception of warp knits, which is several yarns looped around each other. A **weave** interlaces individual pieces of yarn together.

There are several types of weaves, including plain, twill, satin, pile, and jacquard.

Example of a weave.

Plain weaves are tight and the most common. They do not create a design, which makes it easy for them to be printed on. A **twill** creates a design within the weave. For example, a houndstooth jacket is a twill weave. A **satin weave** has a smooth luster, but it snags easily. A **pile weave** means the yarn is interlaced or looped on both sides, such as a terry cloth bathrobe. However, velvet is also a pile weave, which has much tighter loopings than terry cloth. Similar to twill, a **jacquard weave** creates intricate designs within the weave itself. Several colors and textures may be used to create a design. Unlike the twill weave, which can create only straight designs (such as diagonal), the jacquard weave can create designs in many different directions.

The last way to put yarns together is by **engineering** them. This can be done by heating the yarns so they bond together or adding chemicals that force them to bond. A textile processor might choose to piece dye the garment at this point. If applicable, a textile producer might also add any coatings, such as wrinkle resistance. Figure 3.3 illustrates the process of textile manufacturing.

Another consideration in textiles is the aesthetic, comfort, and appearance retention of fabric. These factors can make a fabric attractive to use for a particular item, or make it unattractive to use. **Aesthetic** properties are a fabric's luster, drape, and hand. **Luster** refers to the way the light reflects from the textile. A high luster means a lot of light reflects from the garment, making it appear shiny. **Drape** refers to how the textile falls or hangs over a body. **Hand** is the way a textile feels to the touch. It can be soft, such as cashmere, or rough, such as wool.

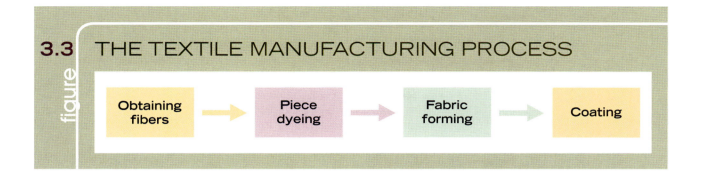

Obtaining fibers → Piece dyeing → Fabric forming → Coating

Comfort qualities relate to how well the garment can pull moisture from the body or how well it can hold heat. The latter quality is known as **thermal retention.** Wool, for example, has excellent thermal retention, which is why the fabric is often used in winter clothing such as sweaters.

Appearance retention refers to how much or little the garment wrinkles, called **resiliency,** and the type of care needed for the garment. Cotton, for example, has low resiliency, meaning it wrinkles easily.

:: NATURAL FIBERS ::

Cotton **Cotton** is a substance that is attached to the seed of a cotton plant. It is grown in 80 countries. Characteristics of cotton include pleasing appearance, high comfort, easy care, durability, and low cost. Prior to 1793, cotton had to be separated from the seeds by hand. In 1793, however, Eli Whitney invented the saw-tooth cotton gin, which made the processing much faster. Recently, cotton has been mixed with other manufactured textiles, such as spandex, to give the fabric stretch.

Cotton has excellent aesthetic qualities. Its luster is matte, its drape is soft, and its hand is smooth. Cotton is high in comfort in that it has excellent moisture absorbency. Appearance retention factors include low resiliency, which means that it has the tendency to wrinkle. One way to deal with this is to give the fabric a durable press finish or coating, or blend it with polyester. As most people find when washing clothing, cotton also has a tendency to shrink, unless it has undergone the durable-press finish or a shrinkage resistant finish during the manufacturing process. Washing cotton clothing in cold water results in less shrinkage.

A cotton plant.

Cotton does come in different qualities. Grading and classifying cotton is done by standards set within the U.S. Department of Agriculture. Fiber length and grade are ways to classify cotton. Grade refers to the amount of dirt and other matter in the cotton; length refers to how long the fiber is. There are 39 grades of cotton, and the predominant grade produced in the United States is classified as "better than," or better than average. For example, a 100 percent cotton T-shirt from Old Navy might be lower-grade cotton, hence the lower price, than a Polo T-shirt.

Wool **Wool** was one of the first fibers to be woven into cloth. In recent times, wool has been used in place of less expensive substitutions such as acrylic and polyester. There are several types of sheep that produce wool, and there are also several kinds of wool. We will not discuss this in detail here as textile courses will cover many of the details. Australia is a major producer of wool, as is Eastern Europe. South Africa and Great Britain also produce wool.

Sheep are normally sheered once a year, in the spring. Another way to get wool is to take it from the pelts of animals (called *pulled wool*); the animals are also used as meat. Although most clothing labels identify *wool* only in general, the term actually implies fiber from sheep, goats, camel, alpaca, or llama. Most labels do not specify from which type of animal the wool came.

Wool has a matte luster. It is high in moisture absorbency and high in thermal retention. It is more difficult to clean than cotton; most wool garments require dry cleaning. Home products made from wool, such as carpet, require steam cleaning.

Besides wool from sheep, other types come from goats, rabbits, and camel. For example, **mohair** is the hair from the Angora goat. Major producers of mohair include South Africa and Texas. Mohair has good resiliency and a natural insulation. It is a very soft fiber and often is used for sweaters. Mohair is also used to produce human hair substitute wigs.

Angora is another type of wool, which comes from the Angora rabbit. These rabbits can be found in Chile, China, and parts of Europe. The hair is fine, fluffy, and very soft. Angora is usually blended with sheep wool because the fiber tends to be slick, which makes it difficult to spin into garments. Angora can be found in many types of sweaters.

Cashmere comes from goats raised in Tibet, Mongolia, New Zealand, and China. It is used for very high quality garments, usually sweaters. It has a soft hand and good draping qualities.

Camel hair, also a type of wool, comes from the two-hump Bactrian camel. These camels can be found in Turkey and China. The hair is collected by a **trailer,** a person who follows the herd of camels and picks up the hair the animals have lost.

Silk **Silk** is a natural protein fiber. It comes from the cocoon of the silk worm. Two very fine threads come out of an opening in the silkworm's head, and when they are exposed to air, they harden. The four major producers of silk are China, India, Italy, and Japan.

Silk is known for its soft feel, luster, and excellent draping qualities. It is high in comfort because it has high absorbency. Silk wrinkles easily, therefore it has low resiliency. Previously, silk had to be dry-cleaned, but in the last 30 years, Chinese manufacturers have developed ways to produce cheaper, machine-washable silk. The quality is high, and it's also easier to care for.

Silk worms.

Acetate **Acetate** was first developed in Europe, and production in the United States began in 1924. Acetate was the second manufactured fiber in the United States, after rayon. It is used in evening wear such as prom dresses. Acetate has high luster, good draping qualities, and a very smooth hand. It has moderate absorbency. Acetate is a weak fiber, and therefore it has poor durability. It generally needs to be dry-cleaned.

Linen **Flax** is the plant from which **linen** is made. Flax is twice as strong as cotton. Linen is one of the oldest textiles; in fact, mummies were wrapped in linen.

Aesthetic qualities of linen include a stiff hand. Linen has a low luster and an irregular appearance (which is part of the charm) due to the large variation of thick and thin yarns used to make the fabric. It is high in comfort because of its high moisture absorbency. It has low resiliency, therefore it requires ironing. Generally, linen must be dry-cleaned.

Many of the clothing items we see today are made from linen, especially summer clothing. Linen is also used for household products, such as drapes, napkins, and tablecloths.

Ramie **Ramie,** another natural fiber, comes from a tall perennial shrub. This shrub requires a hot, humid climate to grow. It is rare to see 100 percent ramie products; normally they are mixed with other natural fibers.

Ramie fibers are separated from the plant stock. In the past, this was a high-labor task, but increased use of machines has made production easier. Ramie is a relatively inexpensive fiber, as the crops grow quickly and can be harvested every 60 days. Ramie is used in a variety of goods, including apparel and home goods. It is one of the strongest natural fibers and is actually stronger when wet.

Linen yarn being spun.

Ramie has a matte luster and a stiff hand. It has high absorbency, making it comfortable. However, ramie has low resiliency, which can cause wrinkling. Ramie can be dry-cleaned or machine-washed, depending on the garment.

Hemp Finally, the last natural fiber we will discuss is **hemp.** The Declaration of Independence was written on hemp paper! The crop was very important during that time in our history; however, it is now illegal to raise it in the United States, with two exceptions. Hawaii was given permission in 1999 to grow hemp as a means of testing the plant, under the auspices of the Hawaii Industrial Hemp Project. The other place in the United States where hemp is grown is the water gardens in Epcot Center at Walt Disney World. Hemp for clothing and industrial uses mostly comes from Europe, where there are no legal issues in regard to growing the plant.

Hemp has a similar appearance of marijuana, although it does not have the hallucinatory properties. Lawmakers are afraid that the illegal kind of hemp would be grown with industrial hemp, and that the hallucinatory hemp would be difficult to detect in fields.

Hemp is a weed, and therefore growing it does not require the use of pesticides. In addition, hemp does not require as much water to grow, whereas many of the other natural fibers already discussed require

Hemp clothing.

extreme amounts of water to properly grow. Hemp is extremely strong and is used to make rope and thread. It is also becoming popular for apparel items.

:: MANUFACTURED FIBERS ::

Because there are 26 man-made fibers, we will cover only the most popular. Some examples of man-made, or manufactured, fibers include rayon, nylon, polyester, acrylic, and spandex.

Rayon **Rayon** was the first man-made fiber to be developed, in Paris in the late 1800s. It was first called artificial silk. In 1924, Rayon was officially adopted by the textile industry. One of the major downsides to rayon is the high water and energy use required in processing. Rayon is made from wood pulp and vegetable matter. Due to the high cost of wood, rayon has become more expensive to make.

Rayon's aesthetic qualities include very good draping and a high luster. Rayon has high absorbency but poor thermal retention. It has low resiliency. Pure rayon should be dry-cleaned; but some garments made with rayon combined with other textiles may be machine washed. Rayon's ability to blend well with many other fibers has made it popular.

Nylon **Nylon,** another man-made fiber, is extremely strong. DuPont developed nylon in 1930. Nylon's first commercial use was in parachutes in World War II, and it was the first fully manufactured fiber, not using natural products for production. It is used for seat belts and carpeting as well as for clothing products.

There is a widely held belief that nylon was named for New York (ny) and London (lon); however, while interesting, this is not true. "Nyl," according to DuPont, was arbitrary, and "on" came from the endings of the words *cotton* and *rayon*.

The aesthetic qualities, including luster, of nylon can vary greatly, depending on the end use. For example, some tights made from nylon are matte in finish, whereas others might have high luster. Nylon has low moisture absorbency but very good resiliency and elastic recovery. This is part of the reason why a small amount of nylon may sometimes be blended with other fabrics. Nylon can generally be washed in a machine, but some garments made with a nylon blend must be dry-cleaned.

Polyester This fiber is a popular textile for clothing. It washes well, has high resiliency, and is relativity cheap to make. **Polyester** is also used to make plastic soda bottles, ropes, and threads. A British company, Imperial Chemical Industries, first produced polyester while working on its nylon development. In 1945, DuPont purchased rights to develop polyester in the United States.

Polyester uses many chemicals during processing. As a result, polyester is widely recycled. Recycled polyester produces less environmental pollution. In fact, it has been suggested that used recycled polyester results in 85 percent less air pollution than making new polyester.

Polyester can lack in appearance qualities if not mixed with other textiles. It has low absorbency and thermal retention. However, polyester is easy to care for and has very good appearance retention.

Acrylic **Acrylic** is often used for knitwear and activewear, due to its light weight, soft hand, and resilient nature. It was first produced in the 1950s, with the goal of mimicking the hand, texture, and warmth of wool. Acrylic also tends to draw moisture away from the body, a characteristic called **wicking,** making it popular for sweaters or to blend with other textiles.

Acrylic has many of the same aesthetic qualities of wool; however, unlike wool, acrylic can be washed in a machine.

Spandex This fiber makes some people shudder, as they remember the 100 percent spandex garments from the 1980s. Today, however, **spandex** is added to many fabrics, in part because it can stretch 400 percent without breaking. In addition, adding spandex can give a garment a nice drape. Moreover, adding spandex to garments can enhance not only the look but the durability and shelf life. Spandex is often used in swimwear and active sportswear. It has a high luster and a soft hand.

The first manufacturer of spandex initially called it *Lycra*. Lycra is a trade name still owned by DuPont. A **trade name** means that no other company can use the name.

Microfibers One of the most recent trends in textiles has been the development of microfibers. A **microfiber** is very tight fabric made from polyester yarns or nylon yarns. Microfibers are 100 times smaller than a human hair and have revolutionized fashion products. For example, the use of microfibers has allowed excellent moisture retention properties for performance wear such as ski jackets.

Microfibers have high aesthetic qualities, including a very soft hand and good drape. They are also high in comfort due to wicking. Microfibers are almost always blended with another fiber; thus, care of microfiber items vary from product to product.

In recent years, popular fabric mixes have included cotton mixed with a small amount of spandex to give it stretch, polyester mixed with cotton to make it less wrinkled, and a variety of others.

Some garments are made entirely of microfibers, which make them great for travel because they resist wrinkling. In fact, Chico's even offers a product line of such clothing called "Travelers."

REALWORLD focus >> Textiles and the Environment

Mohawk Industries

Mohawk Industries was formed in 1878 and currently employees 34,000 people. Randy Waskul is the company's vice president of environmental services. It is Randy's job to oversee the process by which Mohawk products are made.

Mohawk produces throw rugs, carpet, and tile that can be found in your neighborhood store. It produces all of its yarns in the United States, expect for one factory that is located in Mexico.

Mohawk buys 2 billion pounds of recycled bottles per year to make its yarns and is the leading recycler of plastic bottles. These yarns are eventually made into polyester carpeting.

The process is done in the United States, and people like Randy oversee the process. Plastic beverage bottles are made with top-quality PET (polyethylene terephthalate) resins as required by the U.S. Food & Drug Administration; the recycled product is superior to lower grades of synthetic fibers used in making other brands of carpet yarns. PET bottles are sorted, ground into fine chips, and then cleaned. These chips are then melted and extruded into fiber and spun into carpet yarn.

Mohawk's environmentally friendly process does not end with recycling; it has also developed processes to recycle all water in process, thereby wasting little water in manufacturing. It is companies like Mohawk that realize the value of being socially responsible and environmentally friendly that motivate other companies to do the same.

The process of making recycled bottles into yarn:

1. The used bottles arrive in the compressed bales.
2. The bottles are separated by color and type.
3. The bottles are ground into PET chips and washed.
4. The chips are melted and extruded into fiber.
5. The carpet fiber bales are used to make yarn.
6. The yarn is then manufactured into strong, luxurious carpet for homes.

Step 1

Step 2

Step 3

Step 5

Step 6

Wearing Your Values: Eco-Fashions Are on Today's Runways

During New York's famed Fashion Week last February, there was one show that drew environmentalists along with the trendy regulars and entertainment celebrities. Such well-known designers as Diane von Furstenberg, Halston, and Oscar de la Renta participated in FutureFashion, a show featuring outfits made from eco-friendly fabrics and materials. It was an unusual marriage of upscale elegance with sustainability.

The New York-based Earth Pledge sponsored Future-Fashion with some fashion muscle provided by Barneys New York, the clothing store that epitomizes what's in style. Although it may take some time for eco-friendly couture to go mainstream, FutureFashion may have been a watershed moment.

Barneys was very involved in FutureFashion and helped convince the top designers to participate. The store featured the eco-outfits in its windows for several weeks after the show was over. How far Barneys will go with eco-fashion is unclear, but Barneys' vice president and fashion director Julie Gilhart has an open mind. "We're a high-end specialty store but it's starting," she says. "I was quite surprised that the designs were so sophisticated for using sustainable fabrics, because usually we associate that with not-so-stylish clothing. This FutureFashion show proves that there's definitely a future for environmentally friendly fashion."

Richie Rich, a co-designer at Heatherette, one of the hottest labels in the fashion world, created a silver recycled polyester bustier and a pink-and-yellow skirt out of corn fiber, and he was exuberant after the show about the experience with eco-materials. ❧

Source: "Wearing Your Values" was written by Joel Gershon, The Environmental Magazine, July–August 2005.

›› QUESTIONS

1. What are the advantages for designers to be concerned with the environment?

2. Discuss other environmental issues addressed in this chapter that can harm and protect the environment.

>> the fashion-design process

Now that we have discussed the major parts of a design, we will discuss the process of fashion design. The fashion-design process is a lengthy one and can have many variations, depending on the type of company. The general steps in design include:

1. Research and planning of the line.
2. Creating the design concept.
3. Development of the designs.
4. Production planning and production.
5. Distribution of the line.

:: RESEARCH AND PLANNING OF THE LINE ::

One could arguably say research is the most important part of fashion design. This is the stage during which designers research fabric trends, color trends, past sales, and goals of the organization. Some companies will produce their own merchandise, called **private label;** others may only buy designs from manufacturers. In-house design, or private-label design, occurs when retailers have their own designers create clothing for them. Many companies, such as Nordstrom, both use in-house designers for their own lines and buy outside goods. Either way, the research will be similar. Designers will review fashion magazines, look at color forecasts, and even watch celebrities to see what the new hot fashion will be. The first step sets the groundwork for the rest of the process.

:: CREATING THE DESIGN CONCEPT ::

The next step in the design phase is to create the concept. For the most part, the concept will actually be sold to in-house buyers before production even begins. In this phase, the designer will develop sketches, gather fabric samples, and develop a line, usually eight pieces, that go together. A **line board** is then presented to decision makers (buyers) in the organization, who then must approve it before the concept enters into the next steps of design.

Much of the industry is moving toward the use of computer aided design (CAD) in the development of line boards. CAD can also assist in the making and cutting of patterns. Fashion manufacturers are also experimenting with the use of CAD for everything from design to production to shipping and distribution management of the products.

:: DEVELOPMENT OF THE DESIGNS ::

After approval has been received to go ahead with the designs, the designer or patternmaker will produce a pattern for that garment. There are two ways to make a pattern. The first way is with a **flat pattern,** in which the design is made out of hand-cut pieces of heavy paper. **Draping,** the second way, consists of actually arranging the fabric on a person or on a body form and pinning right on the form to make the pattern.

After the pattern has been made, a sample is generally made out of **muslin,** an inexpensive fabric to test for fit. Then, if the designer is happy with the fit, a sample sewer will then make the garment with the actual fabric. The sample sewers are

Flat pattern.

often in-house, or they can work for an overseas manufacturer. For example, Valentino employs a shop model so in-house sample sewers can fit garments to her body. During this phase, the price of the product will also be determined.

:: PRODUCTION PLANNING AND PRODUCTION ::

Due to the expansion of the global economy, most manufacturing is done overseas. Because of this, the designer will develop a **specifications package,** sometimes called a *spec package* (see Figure 3.4). A spec package includes drawings of and specific information related to the details of the garment. The details can include, for example, the type of closures used or the type of collar. Another element of the spec package is specific information as to how the garment should be put together, meaning, where the seams should actually be. Sometimes, the manufacturer will send a sample of the garment made from the spec package, to insure proper fit and expectations. An important part of this process includes the ability to communicate effectively with overseas producers. Once the spec package is sent, the manufacturer will cut, sew, and finish the product. It will then be shipped as requested.

:: DISTRIBUTION OF THE LINE ::

Distribution of the line can also be considered the marketing or actual selling of the line. This area fits into the last shoebox of marketing, which will be discussed in detail in Chapters 7, 8, and 9. **Distribution** is defined as the manner in which goods actually get to the customer. Distribution includes the process of working with overseas vendors, shipping the goods from overseas, and actually placing the goods in stores.

Draping.

Presentation of a line board.

SAMPLE SPEC PACKAGE

CONSTRUCTION SPECIFICATIONS

STYLE#	EG-530	PO#	9815
FABRICATION:	70cotton/30 polyester		
DESCRIPTION:	*Plaid Mens' Walkshort*		

FABRIC DEV. REF #:	5645
WASH REFERENCE:	*garment wash*
FINISHING	*grinding on edges of pockets, as well as along hems*
COST OVERVIEW	

SEASON: *Back to School 06*
DELIVERY *29-Jun* **TO** *7/13/2006*
SIZE SCALE: *28, 30, 32, 34, 36, 38, 40*
SAMPLE SIZE: *34*

CONSTRUCTION COMMENTS:	THREAD INFORMATION		Pattern ID#:	3341
Please note hand stitching on pocket edges.	Dyed to Match?	*Y/N*	Spec/Sample ID#:	530189
	Contrast?	*Y/N*	Engineering Approval:	4/11/2006

MATCHING INSTRUCTIONS:	THREAD SPECIFICATIONS		Garment Weight:	11oz
Short is plaid-match side seams, pockets, waistband, and back patch pocket	A: Thread # 642	*White*		
	B: Thread # 4114	*DTM*	Sewing Contractor:	Shortz

SEWING OPERATIONS

Step/ Operation	Description:	Machine Type	Stitch Type	Seam Type	Seam Allowance	S.P.I.	Thread A	B	C
1	merrow front/back	serge	504	SR-01	0.125	8	x		
2	merrow st. side of pocket	serge	504	SR-01	0.125	8	x		
3	merrow pkts together	serge	504	SR-01	0.5	8	x		
4	sew pktss to f/b	flat sewing	301	SS-1	0.5	8		x	
5	sew zipper to f crotches	flat sewing	301	SS-1	0.25	8		x	
6	sew placket together	flat sewing	301	SS-1	0.5	8		x	
7	sew placket to left zipper	flat sewing	301	SS-1	0.5	8		x	
8	sew remaining crotch	flat sewing	301	SS-1	0.5	8		x	
9	sew f/b crotch	flat sewing	301	SS-1	0.5	8		x	
10	sew side seams	flat sewing	301	SS-1	0.125	8		x	
11	merrow waistband	flat sewing	301	SS-1	0.5	8		x	
12	sew waistband	flat sewing	301	SS-1	~	8		x	
13	buttonhole the left fly	buttonhole	401	BH-1	~	36		x	
14	buttonhole placket	buttonhole	401	BH-1	~	36		x	
15	set l/sm buttons	hand			~	~		x	

Courtesy of Elizabeth A. Gastner

>> conclusion •

A thorough knowledge of the fabrics and processes in design is extremely important to having a successful career in fashion. A grasp of the concepts presented in this chapter—such as silhouette, details, texture, and color—will help you better understand the industry as a whole. And although you may never actually sew samples or make patterns, an understanding of the characteristics of design and textiles and the process of design will make you a better designer or buyer in the future.

TERMS TO KNOW ::

Silhouette	Natural	Angora
A-line	Manufactured	Cashmere
Hourglass	Man-made	Camel hair
Wedge	Synthetic	Trailer
Tubular	Filament fiber	Silk
Bouffant	Staple fiber	Acetate
Shape	Knit	Flax
Cyclical	Weave	Linen
Details	Plain weave	Ramie
Texture	Twill	Hemp
Color	Satin weave	Rayon
Color pallet	Pile weave	Nylon
Textiles	Jacquard weave	Polyester
Fiber	Engineering	Acrylic
Yarn	Aesthetic	Wicking
Fabric markets	Luster	Spandex
Producers	Drape	Trade name Microfiber
Processors	Hand	Private label
Dyeing	Comfort	Line board
Fiber dyeing	Thermal retention	Flat pattern
Yarn dyeing	Appearance retention	Draping
Piece dyeing	Resiliency	Muslin
Garment dyeing	Cotton	Specifications package
Finishing and coating	Wool	Distribution
Postprocessing	Mohair	

CONCEPTS TO KNOW ::

1. The types of companies involved in textiles.
2. The four basic fashion design principles.
3. Fabric properties.
4. Natural and manufactured fabrics and their characteristics.
5. The process of fashion design.

1. Describe the four principles of design.
2. What are the four types of silhouettes? Which type of silhouette do you like the best and why?
3. What is the difference between a fiber, yarn, and textile?
4. Why would a designer choose to blend polyester and cotton rather than make a 100 percent cotton garment?
5. Discuss at least four reasons the performance factors might be important to a fashion designer.
6. Name two fabric properties of both natural and manufactured textiles.
7. Discuss the process in making fabric.
8. Name two reasons for mixing other fabrics with polyester.
9. Why would a designer choose to add nylon to casual garments?
10. Discuss two environmental factors in the production of textiles.
11. Describe each step in fashion design. Which interests you the most and why?
12. Describe the components in a specifications package.

CHAPTER PROJECTS AND DISCUSSION ::

1. Choose pictures from a magazine that depict the three types of silhouette. Discuss your findings with classmates.
2. Research the uses for CAD in fashion design. Name at least three uses and two companies that provide CAD software.
3. Research the possible uses for hemp. Do you think hemp should be used in garments? Why or why not? What are the advantages of using hemp for clothing? The disadvantages?
4. What colors do you select when purchasing clothing for yourself? Why?
5. Which types of fabric do you prefer when selecting clothing? Why? Which types of fabrics do you prefer when selecting bedding? Why? How does one's occupation impact the types of fabrics they might choose?

chapter four

Historical Perspective

althought he was not speaking of fashion during a speech given in 1839, Abraham Lincoln said "What has once happened will invariably happen again, when the same circumstances which combined to produce it, shall again combine in the same way."

History repeats itself, not only with world events, but with fashion. This insight helps fashionistas recognize that fashions will recycle themselves, based on similar societal events in history. "Fashion is evolutionary, not revolutionary." In other words, fashion changes over time and is not necessarily new, but a basic design is changed to form new fashions.

This chapter will examine past fashion and discuss social, cultural, and economic forces that made fashions popular during their time. Thus, it will provide a starting point for understanding how fashion history offers inspiration for fashions created today.

After reading this chapter,
you should be able to:

1 • Compare past fashions
with fashions popular
today.

2 • Explain the nature of
cyclical fashion and use
examples.

3 • Describe how war and
economics have in-
fluenced the fashion
industry.

4 • Explain how changes in
societal norms, such as
feminism, have influ-
enced fashion trends.

5 • Name designers impor-
tant over decades of
fashion history.

History is an important aspect in fashion design and fashion merchandising because fashion is **cyclical,** which means that styles popular in one time period will likely become popular again. Bell-bottoms are a good example of the cyclic nature of fashion. They were popular in the 1960s and again in the late 1990s. Although the bell-bottoms popular in the late 1990s did not look exactly the same as those in the 1960s, the inspiration was taken from that period.

This chapter will discuss the major events that occurred during various time periods that caused significant changes in fashion. Major factors influencing fashion in the last century have been war, economics, youth rebellion, music, and movies.

The chapter discusses fashion history by decade from 1900 to today, highlighting significant fashion designers in each period. Fashion history fits into the research shoebox of fashion, in that it can provide tools to help predict fashion trends (see Figure 4.1).

> *"History is an important aspect in fashion design and merchandising because fashion is cyclical."*

:: 1900–1914 ::

The early part of the twentieth century was full of change, both in the economic and social sense. Two main factors affected fashion during this period: industrialization and the perception of women in society. **Industrialization** had an impact because clothing no longer had to be made by hand; it could be made by machines that produced clothing faster and less expensively.

But industrialization changed fashion in several other ways as well. As many people started to work in factories, a middle class emerged. Prior to this, there was a greater separation between the rich and the poor. However, because factory workers earned a higher wage than farmers, a middle class subsequently developed. People in the emerging middle class could not afford haute couture designs, but they looked for something nicer than the clothing that farmers wore. As a result of the new demand by the emerging middle class, the fashion industry began to develop ready-to-wear clothing (as opposed to haute couture introduced in Chapter 2). Ready-to-wear clothing, sometimes called *off-the-rack clothing*, is not tailored to a specific individual. Ready-to-wear is also called *prêt-à-porter* in French.

The workers who filled the many new factory jobs created during the industrialization era found they needed durable as well as comfortable clothing

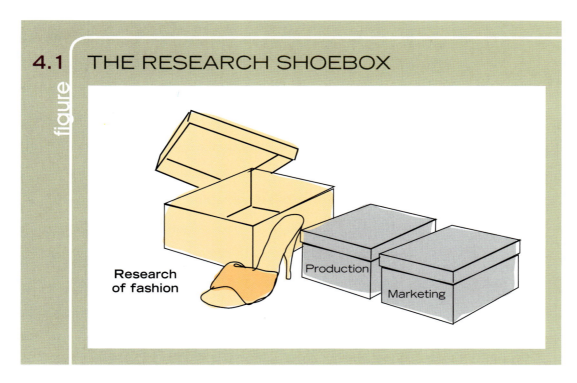

4.1 THE RESEARCH SHOEBOX

figure

Research of fashion

Production

Marketing

to wear. In the late 1800s, Levi Strauss and Jacob Davis developed what we now know as a fashion staple: jeans. Observing that many men ripped their pants in factory jobs, mainly at the pockets, Davis invented the rivet, which was applied to points of strain on pants. Although denim pants had been around before Strauss and Davis, the use of rivets made the jeans more suited to the needs of workers in the industrialization era.

Second, the changing view of women during this time impacted fashion. Women were not treated as equals; in the United States and throughout most of Europe, they were not allowed to vote until late in the second decade of the twentieth century. Women's clothing during this first part of the century reflected their lack of power. Corsets are a specific example of fashion reflecting society. Corsets, which are very tight and binding, made it difficult to move and were popular during the 1800s and early 1900s when women were not allowed to exercise much power.

A man's clothing during this period also marked his status, as did the clothing his wife wore. If a woman was dressed in expensive clothing, it implied that her husband was successful.

The clothing worn during this time was extremely feminine. Exquisite detail such as embroidery, beading, and lace were extensively used, touches that are popular even today, highlighting the cyclic nature of fashion. In the early 1900s, dresses and suits were the norm. Men even wore sportcoats while playing sports such as polo. Currently, sportcoats are worn for dressy occasions and work and would not likely be worn to play sports.

Another important societal consideration was the role fashion magazines played in guiding public taste. It was not until 1890 that photographs were included in fashion magazines, but they were common by the first decade of the twentieth century and continue to be today.

Jacques Doucet

This French designer was born in 1853 to a wealthy family that owned a lingerie business. Reflecting the influence of his family's business, he designed dresses that consisted of sheer, drapery fabric. His designs were extremely feminine through his use of ribbons, flowers, and lace. Doucet's designs were known for their dignity and luxury.

An example of a princess cut dress.

Inspirations from the early twentieth century can be seen today.

Examples of Doucet's designs in the early twentieth century.

Charles Frederick Worth

Worth is considered to be the first person to be a true fashion designer rather than a dressmaker. He was the first designer to convince customers to wear what he thought they should wear rather than the

An emerging middle class caused new demands on the fashion industry in the early 1900s.

other way around. Following his death, the House of Worth continued through 1952, when his grandson decided to close the house. Worth's former apprentice was Paul Poiret, discussed later.

:: 1914–1919 ::

During this period, World War I had a large effect on fashion. In addition, voting rights for women also affected what they wore.

Because so many men were off fighting the war, women took on many of the tasks that men performed prior to the conflict, such as factory work. But doing this "men's work" required that they change the way they dressed. Overalls and pants, even for women, were more practical for factory work. This was a major change to women's fashion, with repercussions throughout the century. As a result, in later years women were reluctant to go back to the uncomfortable and unpractical clothing of the past.

Social events were no longer a priority; in fact, they were postponed. Besides working during the day, many women were responsible for taking care of men injured during the war.

Darker colors were the norm, as is often found during periods that tend to be difficult for society. In addition, because women were responsible for much of the dirty work, darker colors showed less dirt and therefore required less washing, making them very practical. Coloring agents were not yet created, which also accounts for use of darker clothing during this time.

In the late part of this second decade, women in many countries were granted the right to vote and the suffrage movement called for voting

Example of Poiret's designs, which raised the waist of dresses.

We can see, even today, the affect Poiret's designs had on fashion.

reform in the United States. In 1920, the Nineteenth Amendment to the U.S. Constitution was ratified, giving American women the right to vote As a result of independence exercised during the war, and the equal treatment demanded by the suffrage movement, the clothing women wore changed dramatically. By 1915, skirts rose above the ankle as longer dresses no longer represented the women of that day.

When the war ended in 1918, sportswear started to become popular. U.S. Rubber developed the first sneaker, called Keds, in 1917. The word *sneaker* was coined quite literally because the rubber sole made the shoe quiet, making it easy to sneak up on someone, unlike noisy shoes of the past.

Keds

Today's fashions offer many reminders of fashion in the second decade of the twentieth century. The use of sportswear and casual clothing can be attributed to that earlier period.

Paul Poiret
Poriet was born and lived in Paris. He studied under Doucet in the early 1900s and opened his own design house in 1904. He is well known for raising the waist of dresses in his designs, to right below the bust. Poiret was considered a revolutionary designer because of his view that women should not be "bound." He may have ushered women into the twentieth century because he did not design clothing that required a corset. In his own words, he "freed the breasts." He was also the first designer to market his name on perfume.

Romain de Tirtoff (Erté)
Romain de Tirtoff, known as Erté— a pseudonym from the French pronunciation of his initials R.T.—is perhaps most famous for his elegant fashion designs that perfectly captured the art deco period in which he worked. He used delicate features while designing glamorous clothing. By far his most famous image is "Symphony in Black," depicting a tall, slender woman draped in black holding a thin black dog. This influential image has been reproduced and copied countless times and has become almost the last word in decadent grace.

:: 1920s ::

The 1920s, also called the Roaring Twenties, saw many changes to fashion. This is due to several influences. First, the war was over and economic prosperity had begun. **Economic prosperity** can be defined as a state of low unemployment, high profits, and growth in a country. Second, youth was an important influence in fashion during the 1920s. Third, women continued to celebrate their newfound freedom through the clothing they wore.

Economic influences affected the Roaring Twenties as well. After war, prosperity often occurs. The same was true after World War I. People had more money than ever before, and they spent much of it on fashion.

Because a great number of men were lost during the war, appreciation for youth became popular. It has been said that many women wanted to look seductive to compete with other women, due to lack of men available for marriage. As a result, feather boas and showy accessories were the norm. These young women were called *flappers*.

Many women behaved in what used to be considered "men's behavior." Women showed their newfound freedom through wearing makeup, smoking, swearing, and frequenting bars and nightclubs.

In the early part of the 1920s, waistlines were loose. In 1923, waistlines began to drop between the waist and hips. Two years later, in 1925, waistlines became nonexistent, and hemlines rose to the knee. The variety of waistlines used in garments in the 1920s can be seen in many of today's fashions.

Flappers in the 1920s wearing dresses with dropped waistlines.

A recent example of a dropped waistline.

Jeanne Lanvin Lanvin was a French-born fashion designer. She attracted attention because of the beautiful clothing she made for her daughter. Her empire included a textile dye factory. She had a love of fine craftsmanship and always incorporated this into her designs. She used velvet and satin in many of her designs and also preferred fine embroidery.

Madeline Vionnet Vionnet was a French fashion designer. She first designed for Doucet, but she opened her own fashion house in 1912. In the 1920s, she introduced the **bias cut,** a type of design that is cut diagonally across the grain of a fabric. It is used to create garments that closely follow the body curves.

She also designed draped garments that were inspired by Greek and Roman styles. Her style included the cowl neck and halter top. The cowl neck is a type of neckline that has a soft, draped feature.

:: 1930s ::

In the 1930s, the major economic issue was the Great Depression that followed the stock market crash of 1929. This crash brought the free feeling of the 1920s to a halt, greatly affecting fashion. Other major influences on fashion were the growth of the film industry and the acceptance of a more casual form of dress.

Many people feel that crises are not times for experimenting; those living through the Depression were no different. As a result, fashion for women in this period reverted to feminine styles. Hairstyles were grown long and softly waved, and waists and bust lines on clothing were restored to a "proper" fit.

In the 1930s, the influence of the American film industry greatly impacted fashion. Actresses like Audrey Hepburn and Greta Garbo could influence millions through the movies, whereas fashion magazines would only be seen by a few thousands.

Casual dressing also became more accepted during this time. There was a general mood of informality, which reflected the youthfulness and desire for relaxation of the 1920s. In American culture, wearing the

Audrey Hepburn in *Breakfast at Tiffany's*.

same outfit all day, rather than several different *appropriate* outfits during the day, became more accepted. Of course, this was frowned upon by many in the upper class.

This trend toward informality is also seen by the rise of the zoot suit in the late 1930s. The zoot suit was an overexaggerated version of the man's suit during this time. Large shoulder pads, longer jacket, and vivid colors were all attributes of the zoot suit.

The zoot suit was first popular with urban African American men, particularly jazz enthusiasts, and was also widely accepted by Mexican American men. Designers never dreamed this look would be adopted by the general group of young people in America. This might be one of the earliest examples of **trickle-up fashion,** which is when the general public dictates the fashion. By the early 1940s, however, as war had begun again, the zoot suit was ruled "unpatriotic" because wool production had to be reduced by 26 percent to prepare for World War II.

Licensing began to become popular for designers in the 1930s. **Licensing** is when a designer allows another to use its name to manufacture products. The designer is given a payment for each item sold that bears its name.

Many of the fashions we see today can be attributed to the trends of the 1930s. For example, colored clothes, other than black or gray, are popular in men's wear, reflecting the use of vivid colors in zoot suits. Also, casual dressing is the norm today; the need to have the right outfit for the right time of day has greatly diminished.

The zoot suit.

Cristobal Balenciaga
A Spanish designer, Balenciaga reintroduced the use of padded hips and a bustle silhouette from the nineteenth century. He also designed a short skirt that emphasized a tiny waistline.

Elsa Schiaparelli
Schiaparelli became famous for her use of the bolero jacket. Bolero jackets are shorter jackets, fit above the waist. A bolero jacket would likely be worn over a dress. She also designed a collarless coat. When compared to other fashions of that time, such as those by Chanel, her designs were considered shocking. Schiaparelli also had a perfume called Shocking, which was named after the new color, hot pink, she developed.

Gabrielle Chanel
Chanel (Coco) is still a well-known name in fashion today. She was born in 1883 and made many contributions to fashion. Chanel pioneered the use of the jersey knit (previously reserved for men's underwear) and has been called the inventor of poor chic. **Poor chic** is defined as a style that represented what a person of lower economic status might wear. An example of trendy poor chic in today's clothing might be torn jeans. Her designs combined the use of masculine power, quite unusual for women of this period. It has also been said that Coco was a genius when it came to actually "selling" to the public. In fact, she popularized the short haircut in the 1920s. Coco has also been credited with creating the "little black dress" in 1926 and popularizing costume jewelry.

Coco Chanel.

The "New Look" by Dior included nipped waists and wide skirts.

Christian Dior.

:: 1940s ::

World War II had the greatest impact on fashion in the 1940s. The war brought about many restrictions on clothing. A law named L-85 restricted the amount of fabric that could be used in clothing. In addition, there was a low supply of nylon fabric, due to the need for parachutes and other materials for WWII. The war also affected fashion because Paris, a primary design center, was occupied by the Nazi forces. Because of the occupation, many of the city's design houses and magazines were unable to do business. This forced many people to look for new designers outside of Paris.

The "New Look" by Dior symbolized the late 1940s. It included rounded shoulders, nipped waists, and wide skirts just below the knee. The New Look was created after the war, in 1947, and utilized large amounts of fabric in wide skirts. During the war, it was considered unpatriotic to use so much fabric for wide, full skirts. However, there still were fabric restrictions in place after the war, thus the New Look was somewhat controversial. Showing off tiny waists was accomplished through padding the hips in skirts. **Girdles,** similar to corsets but not laced up the back, became popular with the New Look fashion.

The use of separates was also popularized by Dior. The war meant difficult economic times on the home front, and many women had less money to spend on clothing. The use of separates allowed women to mix and match their wardrobe, thereby creating the illusion of owning more outfits.

Unlike during World War I, color remained a mainstay in women's clothing. Journalists during this time joked that "Dior Phobia" was popular among men distressed by quick style changes and, more important, the cost of expensive new wardrobes.

The 1940s saw the arrival of the New Look, or fashion that was unfussy but tailored. The rest of clothing in this century followed the trend that women's clothing did not have to be fussy or fancy to be beautiful.

Christian Dior Dior, a French designer, is still a well-known name in fashion today. Although his fashion career only lasted 10 years, his fashion empire still lives today. Dior is credited for creating the New Look that housewives in the 1940s and 1950s wanted. He is credited for rebuilding of fashion in Paris, following occupation by the Nazis. Dior also created the use of separates in wardrobes.

Gres Madame Gres was a popular designer in the 1940s. Her house closed during the Nazi occupation in France but was allowed to reopen a year later. She used pleated silk in designs, the pleats measuring about 1 cm. wide. These pleats had the look of 3D sculptures. She used this type of design for evening wear, suits, and coats. She did not branch into ready-to-wear until 1980. But by then it was too late; she no longer had funding to continue designing and had to sell her fashion house.

Claire McCardell McCardell was most famous for her denim wrap-around dress in 1942. She is also considered a pioneer of American ready-to-wear clothing, being one of the first designers to fully embrace such garments. Many rich women admired her couture lines; but her enthusiasm for ready-to-wear made her a popular designer among the middle class, which could afford some of her those pieces. She is identified with typical American style, casual and relaxed.

:: 1950s ::

Rebellion of youth through rock and roll affected the fashions of the 1950s. Advertising on television created desires for new fashions. In addition, new technology was developed to manufacture clothing faster and better than ever.

Prior to 1950, children were to be seen and not heard. The 1950s, unlike previous decades, gave a voice to the youth. Figures such as James Dean and Elvis Presley illustrated the youth rebellion and the yearning for adventure. The youth showed this rebellion through their clothing. James Dean will forever be known in his leather jacket and denim jeans, while Elvis will be known for his colorful costumes and new, sexy style of dancing.

For the older generation, glamour through dresses and evening wear was extremely important. Most women's clothing had full skirts belted at the tiny waist. Celebrities such as Marilyn Monroe characterized glamour.

James Dean.

Much of the desire to dress glamourously can be attributed to the influence of television. Although it had been around for a decade, television was not common in the average household until the 1950s. Most consumers could now see the newest fashions on popular programs and in television advertising. *I Love Lucy* was one of the first television shows that expressed women's fashion. In addition, this program was the first to identify that maternity fashions could be colorful and trendy.

Clothing made popular in the 1950s can still be seen on

"Pedal pushers" in the 1950s.

We can see that the capris of today were born from pedal pushers.

the streets today. Pedal pushers, similar to Capri pants, remain popular. Although common for only youth during the 1950s, the wearing of denim during the day has become standard for all age groups.

Hubert de Givenchy

Givenchy is known for his continuation of Dior's use of separates in 1952. These separates could be mixed and matched with each other. Givenchy is also well known for his design of the little black dress worn by Audrey Hepburn in *Breakfast at Tiffany's*. Alexander McQueen was the head designer for Givenchy during the late 1990s.

Pierre Cardin

Cardin started his career as an apprentice for Dior. He is best known in his early career for the bubble dress. The bubble dress had fabric gathered at the bottom, making it very large. It was considered more costume and art than fashion. In fact, his first designs were actually costumes for theatrical productions. He didn't design his first ready-to-wear collection until 1953.

Bill Blass

Bill Blass, an American designer, was known for his classic and conservative clothing. Blass sold his design house in 1999, but his career spanned almost one half a century. He passed away in 2002 at age 79. Blass is said to have captured the essence of the Untied States in his charming and carefree designs. He did not look at his clothing as art, like many designers, but he viewed clothing as practical. Blass designed a red gown for Nancy Reagan in the 1980s. He was quoted as saying, "Red is the ultimate cure for sadness." Besides the design of clothing, Blass is also famous for designing a Ford Cougar in the 1970s. The head designer for the Bill Blass label is Michael Vollbracht.

Hubert de Givenchy.

:: 1960s ::

The 1960s continued the rebellious look from the 1950s. Music had a major influence on fashion during this period. Musicians like the Beatles, Bob Dylan, and Mick Jagger helped popularize the 1960s look. In addition to music, rebellion against the Vietnam War and various historic figures in the forefront of the media played a role in fashion of this time.

The term **youthquake** is frequently used to capture the feeling of youth and independence during this period. The personal freedom movement for youth began in the 1950s and manifested itself in the 1960s though youthquake.

Three main styles were popularized during this period. First came the mod look in 1963. The mod look was short for "moderns" and included suits with narrow ties.

The second trend for young people was labeled the beatnik look. This look was complete with black berets, tight black pants, and turtlenecks and came from the pop culture and art scene.

In the later 1960s, the hippie look was born in San Francisco. It was a time of demonstrations against the Vietnam War and a general rebellion against many values of Western society. This look rejected traditional dress and included long hair, tie-dyed garments, beads, and colorful styles. It was also influenced by traditional Native American dress.

The 1960s started the phenomenon of consumers developing their own looks, mixing clothing from several designers. This is attributed to a feeling of individuality and a rejection of what society expected of them. One of the complaints about this period was expressed by the fashion trade publication *The Tailor and*

Cutter: "Currently the world of fashion is one of utter confusion; there is every kind of look."

Historic figures from this time included Twiggy, a model known for her boyish haircut and stick-thin figure. She popularized the miniskirt. In addition, the sophistication of Jackie Kennedy's clothing, reminiscent of the 1930s, made many women want to dress at that level of sophistication.

Today, new, updated versions of the miniskirt can be seen, along with the maxi coat. The **maxi coat**, also called a **duster**, is a long blazer/jacket, fitted at the ankles. Beaded fashions, the bohemian look, knee-high boots, and large colorful patterns are remnants of the 1960s.

Mary Quant Quant was a British designer who took advantage of changing times and changing fashions. Although she did not invent the miniskirt, she certainly made it popular. Simple lines and bold colors were the signature of Quant. Photos of Quant in the sixties picture her with short hair, tights, and boots, along with the signature dark eye shadow. Quant also designed the maxi coat, a longer jacket that helped keep women's legs warm when wearing the miniskirt.

Yves Saint Laurent He started his career as chief designer for Dior in 1957 and then designed his own line in 1962. Laurent is famous for his smoking jackets for women and minidresses. He also is credited for the beatnik look of the 1960s.

Twiggy was known for her boyish haircut and thin figure.

The "mod" style.

Mary Quant.

Valentino Valentino has great success with an all-white collection in 1969. He designed Jackie Kennedy's dress for her wedding. It was not until 1970 that he introduced a ready-to-wear line, which is still in production. His designs were famous for complementing the sensuality of women, especially those striving to be the center of attention.

:: 1970s ::

The 1970s continued, in part, the youth rebellion of the 1960s. Besides rebellion, an economic recession, concern for the environment, and feminism charted the direction of fashion.

The two main looks for young people included punk and disco. Disco began in the late 1970s, when John Travolta's *Saturday Night Fever* was first shown. Hot pants (very short shorts) were introduced, along with the "painted-on" look. The painted-on look included any type of clothing with a shiny, stretchy, tight fit. Polyester disco shirts were a popular item for men.

Punk began with musicians such as the Sex Pistols, David Bowie, and The Clash. The look included spiked dog collars, safety pins, and chains. The punk era also saw the introduction of the mohawk haircut in 1977. Punk grew as part of an outward rebellion against high unemployment and poor economic times.

Due to difficult economic times, the fashion industry saw the decline of haute couture and tailoring. Ready-to-wear and mass-marketed designs became more important in fashion. Also, thrift store shopping became popular.

Fur was out, due to environmental concern and cost. In 1975, *Vogue* writer Georgina Howell wrote, "no women with her eyes open would walk about now in the skins of a rare animal and be the butt of raised eyebrows and uncomplimentary remarks."

Another, more mature look for women in the 1970s was taken from the movies *The Great Gatsby* and *Annie Hall*. These looks stemmed from the feminist movement and the desire for equal treatment of women. Wide ties, masculine shirts, thirties-style wide-legged pants, and waistcoats became part of one of the most distinctive female looks of the 1970s. Ralph Lauren was one of the first designers to acknowledge the creative possibilities of men's wear for women. The popularity of this style can be attributed to the eventual mass entry of women into the workforce during the 1980s.

It is easy to see the influence from the 1970s in today's fashion. Thick-soled shoes came from the platform shoes and clogs of the 1970s. Also, the use of polyester in garments began in that period. Other trends found today that came from the 1970s include wide-legged pants, minidresses, halter tops, and tube tops.

1970s punk.

Giorgio Armani Italian and known for classic style, Armani was founded in 1975 by Giorgio Armani. The line became popularized by Richard Gere's wardrobe in *American Gigolo*. Armani still enjoys success today. He offers clothing at several price points, including the less expensive Armani Exchange (AX) line and more prestigious Armani Black Label.

Stephen Burrows Burrows is an African American designer and is well known for his creation of bright knits in the 1970s. He developed lettuce hemlines. A lettuce hemline is a series of tiny ruffles that provide a flirty, feminine flair.

Betsey Johnson Betsey Johnson, along with her daughter, still designs today. She launched the punk look and made it popular. Her colorful, unique designs inspired the youth of the 1970s, just as she does today.

:: 1980s ::

The 1980s were a period of excess, greed, and money. The fashions from the period showed a backlash to those popular in the 1960s and 1970s.

The period was a time of great economic growth and prosperity. Reflecting this prosperity, the term *yuppie* was coined, an acronym for "young upwardly mobile professional person." The term was, and still is, often used negatively to refer to people who have a lot of money to spend and who tend to spend it on items that give them a sense of prestige or status; it carries the connotations selfishness and superficiality.

Women entered the business workforce in much greater numbers in this period, with many competing directly with men, which affected women's fashion. The typical clothing for women was impractical, uncomfortable, and inappropriate in the business world. Thus, men's styles became popular among women. For example, large shoulder pads and tailored suit pants were selling for both men and women, all part of the yuppie look. Many women felt that "dressing like men" subdued their femininity and enabled them to compete better in the business world.

Nancy Reagan, Princess Diana, and Margaret Thatcher (former British prime minister) were well-dressed and conservative women whom other women admired and looked to as fashion role models.

Television shows such as *Dallas,* which depicted the characters, men and women, as beautiful, rich, and glamorous, also impacted the new fashions consumers demanded.

In 1987, however, the stock market crashed and the yuppie look started to retreat. For example, while still popular, shoulder pads were not as heavy as seen in the early 1980s.

The cast of *Fame.*

Exercise gained popularity from the 1970s through the 1980s, therefore running suits and sportswear were in demand. In addition, movies like *Flashdance* and *Fame* popularized this look.

Fashion from the 1980s can be seen on the streets today. Entire sportswear outfits, including pants, top, and jacket, are popular. Practical suits for women are trends still popular today.

Donna Karan Karan is an American designer. She is known for her creation of the professional look for career women in the 1980s. Also popular in the 1980s were her sportswear designs.

Issey Miyake Miyake designed women's clothing for the shape of the garment rather than designing for the shape of the body. His long, flowing garments that hid the body beneath were popular. His designs during this time were greatly influenced by his home country, Japan.

Hugo Boss Hugo Boss is a German designer. He started his company in 1923, right after World War I. His company began by making uniforms for the Nazi army, which causes some people to boycott his lines. In 1999, Boss Orange, a sporty clothing line for men, was introduced. In 2004, Boss also introduced a new, independently run clothing line called Baldessarini. This line has separated itself as more prestigious than the other offerings. Along with Armani, Hugo Boss made it trendy for men to care about looking well groomed, wearing nice-fitting suits.

Yohji Yamamoto

Yamamota was known in the 1980s for black, navy, and white garments. The garments had an unstructured, loose fit. These garments, due to their plainness, created timeless classics. Yamamoto is quoted as saying, "People of my generation were ripped off by economic success: during our youth, the industry kept pumping out new products we couldn't believe in, because we knew, come tomorrow, they would be out of style. So we became the first generation to wear secondhand clothes."

Besides his line of clothing, Yamamoto creates opera costumes and ballet sets for important entertainment companies in the world.

:: 1990s ::

The 1990s were a time of change for society. As often seen in times of social change, the fashions can change dramatically as well.

The major social change in the early 1990s was the rejection of the greed in the 1980s. Casual dressing became appropriate for work, and music played a large role in fashion, as it had in previous decades.

The 1990s were much different from the 1980s. The grunge look was one of the fashions that rejected the ideologies of greed and excess of the 1980s. The grunge look consisted of flannel shirts, baggy jeans, and unwashed hair. This look was opposed to the power-suit look of the 1980s. Musicians like Nirvana and Pearl Jam may have started the grunge look; they certainly made it popular for young people. The grunge look is the ultimate example of trickle-up fashion. After grunge became popular through music, grunge collections from various designers started to appear on the runways.

MC Hammer.

Although rap and hip-hop music had been around since the 1980s, the influence of this type of music became important to fashion in the 1990s. Early rap musicians such MC Hammer, Bell Biv DeVoe, and Sir Mix-a-Lot started many trends through their music. Baggy pants and loose, long T-shirts are examples of clothing influenced by rap musicians.

Many of the fashions in the 1990s were popular versions of clothing from the past. Bell-bottoms, hipster jeans (jeans that sit low on the hips), miniskirts, halter tops, and tube tops were all fashions from the 1960s and 1970s.

Due partly to the dress policies at companies such as Microsoft and the dot-coms, informal clothing at work has become the norm. Although some industries still require formal dress, khaki pants are acceptable at many workplaces. Since many people were no longer required to dress up for work, they demanded more casual choices in fashion.

Dolce and Gabbana

They opened their own studio in 1982 and presented their first collection in 1986, calling it "Real Women." They developed the legendary animal prints collections and designed a special collection for Madonna. In 1994, they introduced a line called D&G, aimed primarily at young people and at a lower price point.

Calvin Klein In the early 1990s he developed the layered look, which is still popular today. He is also well known for his provocative advertising, particularly for underwear. In addition, he is known for popularization of the pea coat in the 1970s. Klein is now retired.

Emanuel Ungaro Ungaro is an Italian designer who moved to Paris when he was 22. Ungaro is known for his design of fabric patterns, with exaggerated flowers and polka dots. He created sensual, draped garments before he sold his design house to Salvatore Ferragamo.

:: 2000s ::

It is difficult to predict what a decade will bring when one is still in the decade. Predictions have surfaced about this being the feminine decade. Rather than the baggy clothing of the grunge era, trend forecasters believe that bright colors, floral prints, and figure-clinging fashion will become the most memorable fashion for women. While much of the fashion from this decade has been inspired by the 1960s and 1970s, even those fashions have changed to better suit the needs of today.

Another interesting aspect to fashion design in this first decade of the twenty-first century is the trend for celebrities to design their own clothing. Celebrities such as J Lo, Paris Hilton, and Britney Spears all have perfume and clothing lines. Often, the celebrities do not actually design their own lines; rather, they license their famous names to sell clothing.

Another popular trend for the decade will continue to be vintage dressing. The use of secondhand haute couture clothing is a chic way to wear expensive clothing without paying the top price for it.

Jean Paul Gaultier Gaultier worked with Pierre Cardin in the early part of his career. He is known for his gender-bending styles: women in pinstripes, men in skirts. For his fashion shows, he chooses "real women," often times overweight women, to challenge the ideas about beauty.

Gaultier is famous for designing the bustier outfits worn by Madonna in the 1980s. He is currently designing for Hermes.

Gianni Versace He founded his label in 1978 and was popular for introducing his "bondage line" in 1991. He became famous for designing flashy, sexy, beautifully cut outfits in strikingly extreme colors, patterns, fabrics, and leathers.

He was killed in 1997, in front of his house in Miami. His sister, Donatella Versace, now runs his company.

Marc Jacobs Jacobs is a designer for the Louis Vuitton house (Vuitton died in 1892). Louis Vuitton is best known for design of handbags with the unmistakable LV symbol. Marc Jacobs also designs his own lines, including an haute couture and a ready-to-wear line, called Marc by Marc Jacobs. Jacobs designs are beautiful and simple, made for the girl next door.

Miuccia Prada Prada was originally started as a leather goods company by Miuccia Prada's grandfather. It introduced its ready-to-wear collection in 1989. Miuccia Prada's garments are known to be sexy and self-confident, without showing too much skin. Prada now offers a new line, targeted to younger customers, called Miu Miu. Miuccia Prada's husband is also in the business and he designs the shoes and purses for the line.

Alexander McQueen McQueen designed for Givenchy but now has his own line. McQueen's label was founded in 1994. He is known as the "bad boy" of fashion for his rave clothing and the design of a gothic collection in 1996.

Anna Sui   Starting as a freelance designer, she founded her own fashion company in 1983. She opened her first in-store boutiques at Macy's, while introducing a menswear line. Her first runway show was called Hippie Chic. Sui went on to become known for her romantic pirate collections. These included long, flowing blouses with pirate ruffles. Sui uses fashion history for inspiration. She is known to have 40 years worth of fashion magazines, which she calls "genius files," to help her with inspiration.

Stella McCartney   McCartney is best known for her designs for Chloe. Although she no longer designs for Chloe, her designs are still romantic, flowing, and refined. She currently operates stores that sell clothing under her own label.

Vera Wang   Wang was once a figure skater and editor at *Vogue*. Using her experience in the sport, she designs figure-skating costumes; but she is perhaps better known for her designs of wedding and evening apparel.

While preparing for marriage she was uninspired by the wedding dresses available on the market. As a result, she resigned from *Vogue* and began designing wedding dresses. She uses subtlety, sensuality, and elegance in all of her bridal designs.

Kenneth Cole   Kenneth Cole's designs are said to define modern fashion. The sleek lines and urban appeal make his designs popular with people of all ages. Innovation is the trademark of Kenneth Cole designs. He began his business in 1982 by setting up a trailer outside of a trade show in 1982. His main obstacle was a city ordinance that only allowed utility trucks and film crews to park in Midtown Manhattan. To get over this hurdle, Kenneth Cole Inc. became Kenneth Cole Productions Inc., and he applied for a permit to shoot a film entitled *The Birth of a Shoe Company*.

Tom Ford   Tom Ford has designed for Gucci and Yves Saint Laurent; but he has recently decided to stop designing fashion and, instead, direct movies. Ford is known to have recreated both Gucci and Yves Saint Laurent into sexy, fashionable brands. He was the first American designer to win the Designer of the Year award from the Fashion Editors Club in Japan.

Ralph Lauren   Lauren is known less for his actual designs than for his ability to effectively market his products as a lifestyle. Lauren sells a country club, golf, and tennis lifestyle though his clothing. He designs at several price points, including suits and suiting pieces at his higher-end prices.

REAL**WORLD**focus >> Isaac Hits the Target

Isaac Mizrahi: fashion maven, movie star, TV talk-show host, Broadway costume designer . . . discount retail supplier? Yes, and in a big way. In August, shoppers at Target stores across America began making fashion history by buying affordable and sporty wares in bright, splashy colors from style doyen Mizrahi. Hoping to dress women in what he calls a "Holly go lightly in a cornfield" sort of way Mizrahi is launching his signature line at Target's 1,191 outlets nationwide.

While Mizrahi's pricey couture and ready-to-wear lines of the past were inaccessible for most, the shirts, sweaters, and pants he's designing for Target customers—not to mention the shoes, accessories, and outerwear—range in price from $9.99 to $69.99 and can outfit ladies from head to toe without breaking the bank. And they can finally say they're wearing a Mizrahi.

The out designer's flair and sensibility is delivering a piece of Madison Avenue to Main Street. "I find that what is generally available at these price points is either so atrocious or so boring," says Mizrahi in his Manhattan studio. "I'm having a lot of fun doing what I always do—just a lot less expensively."

Mizrahi gushes when he talks about the clothes and the impact the line may have on the average American woman. In fact, the designs have come to life through a somewhat enigmatic inspiration—himself. "The customer is basically 'me'—it's me, the woman," Mizrahi admits. "It's meant to be worn by women. A woman can be 17 or a girl can be 50. [The line] isn't midriffs or full of hoodies. It's really good shirts and colors—it's a lot of problems being solved for a woman."

Mizrahi talks proudly about the solutions his new customers will experience but glosses over the newfound success this deal may bring him, even as his star is once again rising. Quite a change from October 1998, when Mizrahi announced the closing of his fashion house.

"The industry is really happy to have him back. There's real interest to see what he's going to come back with," says Eric Wilson, associate sportswear editor for *Women's Wear Daily*. "There's this whole movement in bringing trends down to a mass level. They're generally unattainable to the majority of the country.

In the early to mid '90s, Mizrahi was the star of the fashion world, creating fabulous clothing lines, with stars lining up to request unique frocks. In *Unzipped*, the hit documentary about life during one of Mizrahi's design seasons, Eartha Kitt purrs in a private meeting, "I want you to make me gowwwns."

However, all that changed when Chanel pulled the plug. Mizrahi hadn't had a good creative run for a few seasons, and sales had slipped. "When I closed my door, I cried a few times on the last day, but I felt more excited about my future than ever," he says. "I felt like I was 15 again, [able] to do exactly what I want and not be a slave to something."

In other words, free to design great clothes and not bother with the managerial duties that often bogged him down when he was heading up his own company. "I was happiest when I was overly busy," he says. "I was not necessarily thrilled doing personnel and management stuff and things I was not good at."

Over the past few years, Mizrahi has excelled at things he is good at—he has dabbled in theatrical costume design (*The Women*), staged a one-man off-Broadway cabaret (*Les Mizrahi*), penned a series of comic books (*The Adventures of Sandee the Supermodel*), and launched, with great success, his own talk show (*The Isaac Mizrahi Show* on the Oxygen Network). "It's like a synergy of many things that occur," he says. "I'm much happier when I'm overextended." Now, however, it's all about clothes for the mainstream.

"I'd love to design clothes for men," Mizrahi says. "I would probably make the same kind of problem-solving, witty clothes I try to make for women. I've had a lot of time to develop an opinion on what men should look like, and I'm dying for the opportunity." ❈

Source: Written by Ari Bendersky,
The Advocate, September 3, 2003.

›› QUESTIONS

1. What were the three reasons Mizrahi decided to close his fashion house?

2. Look at Mizrahi designs at Target. Compare them to designs from his haute couture and designer lines. What is similar? What is different?

3. What do you think Mizrahi meant by "solving problems for women?"

4. Many other designers, such as Nicole Miller, have decided to produce clothing for less expensive stores. Research other designers that have followed this path and discuss.

›› conclusion •

Economic times, war, and especially societal influences have influenced fashion over the last century. Understanding the events of each decade helps fashionistas to better predict trends. In addition, it is important to keep in mind that all fashion designers have careers that started with simple beginnings. They all had the drive, motivation, and willingness to work hard to become successful at their trade.

TERMS TO KNOW ::

Cyclical
Industrialization
Economic prosperity
Bias cut

Trickle-up fashion
Licensing
Poor chic
Girdles

Youthquake
Maxi coat
Duster

CONCEPTS TO KNOW ::

1. The cyclical nature of fashion.
2. How fashion trends have developed over time.
3. The relationship between fashion trends today and historical influences.

CHAPTER QUESTIONS ::

1. How have you seen fashion change over time? Cite four changes.
2. What two social issues caused major changes to fashion in the last century?
3. How do economic times and war impact fashion?
4. What was the significance of Worth in the early part of the nineteenth century?
5. What are three characteristics that all famous fashion designers have in common?
6. Go through a recent fashion magazine and compare and contrast characteristics of fashions today with fashions of past decades.

CHAPTER PROJECTS AND DISCUSSION ::

1. Research one designer not listed in this chapter. What is he or she known for? Why do you like the designer?
2. Find designs from your favorite designer. Make a collage out of magazines and newspapers.
3. What is your favorite decade of fashion? Why?

FOR FURTHER READING ::

www.fashion-era.com
www.costumegallery.com
www.vintageblues.com/history5.htm
www.lindyhopping.com/fashionhistm.html

trend Forecasting

p redicting fashion might be one of the most important aspects of the industry. As a buyer or designer, it is imperative to know that fashion changes in response to external factors in the world. It is also important to understand how these external factors influence the purchases of consumers both today and in the future.

After reading this chapter, you should be able to:

1 • Apply the trickle-up, trickle-down, and trickle-across theories to fashion trends.

2 • Identify the external factors affecting fashion trends: social, economic, political, legal, technological, and global influences.

3 • Give examples of social, economic, political, legal, technological, and global influences on fashion trends.

4 • Describe the difference between collection and trend reports.

5 • Use other resources available for predicting fashion trends.

>> introduction

As discussed in Chapter 2, the process of fashion design starts with research and planning (see Figure 5.1). Trend research is part of this process. Trend research provides a baseline or a starting point for design and merchandising. Fashion is constantly changing, therefore an understanding of how new trends start, and where they come from, is important to the fashionista. The previous chapter discussed fashion history, a grasp of which will also help in predicting future fashion trends.

Predicting fashion trends is a difficult task. The first section will discuss theories describing how fashion trends evolve. The second and third sections will discuss the two ways in which to predict fashion trends. The second section will include a discussion of the external factors that affect fashion trends. These include social, economic, political, legal, technological, and global changes, any of which can send fashion in a new direction. Trend forecasters must understand how these changes will affect fashion. In addition to using the external factors to help predict trends, designers or merchandisers can read fashion publications and watch a variety of people for new trends, as discussed at the conclusion of the third section.

> **"***Trend research provides a baseline or a starting point for design and merchandising.***"**

:: TRICKLE-DOWN THEORY ::

The **trickle-down theory** is sometimes called the *traditional fashion adoption theory*. A **theory** is a set of statements that has been devised to explain a grouping of facts that are widely accepted.

The trickle-down theory is based on the idea that fashions begin with the trendsetting design houses located in Milan, Paris, and New York. People who subscribe to this theory believe that manufacturers and designers see what fashions are happening in these major design centers and copy them. The copies are generally less expensive and mass-produced.

Near the beginning of the twentieth century, Thorstein Veblen, an American economist, discussed the idea of social classes. In 1904, George Simmel, a German sociologist, adapted Veblen's ideas to fashion. Simmel looked at the social phenomenon of the lower class emulating the upper classes.

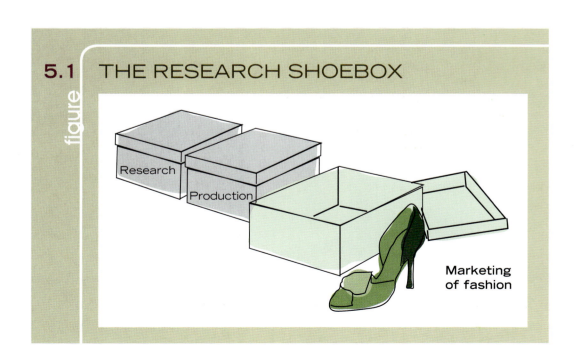

5.1 THE RESEARCH SHOEBOX

figure

Research

Production

Marketing of fashion

He believed that in order for a fashion to be accepted by the majority of people, it first had to be accepted by the upper classes in society. Further, Simmel's theory suggests that because people in the lower classes prefer to associate themselves with upper class, they would eventually adopt the fashion of upper class. Once that occurred, the upper class would then reject the fashion. The rejection would come as a result of the upper class not wanting to look like the lower class of society.

Although this theory has been supported by other fashion researchers, the social structure has changed, making the theory hard to apply today. This theory was prevalent when society was dictated by a few people with wealth and power. Now, many more everyday people have higher incomes and higher job titles, and they attain these at younger ages. As a result, there are more members of the upper class. Because of this change in social structure, the theory no longer holds true.

The theory makes the assumption that the lower-class members will follow what the upper class wear, which is no longer true. There are many different societal groups, and each has its own style and fashion sense. For example, there are soccer moms, young adults in college, teenagers who skateboard, young professional women, or retired businessmen, to name a few. These groups have their own unique characteristics, needs, likes, and dislikes, an idea related to demographics, which will be discussed in Chapter 6.

The tickle-down theory also does not take into account the power that celebrities, musicians, television, and even average people have in changing the direction of fashion.

:: TRICKLE-UP THEORY ::

The **trickle-up theory** is sometimes called the *bottom-up theory* or *reverse adoption*. This theory is the most widely used theory today. George Field created the trickle-up theory but called it *subculture leadership*. This theory proposes that fashion actually begins its development at the level of street fashion, that of the lower socioeconomic classes. **Street fashion** refers to the clothing worn by people who are considered hip or trendsetters. The Internet has also contributed to this trickle-up process of fashion in that it enables people all over the world to see fashions from other parts of the world.

Current examples of trickle-up fashion include the designs of rapper Sean "P. Diddy" Combs. His urban creations were inspired by clothing worn by African American and Latino gang members, but they have become wildly accepted by the general public. Another example of trickle-up fashion was the grunge look that took place in the early 1990s, in Seattle, Washington. The grunge look, primary components of which are jeans and flannel shirts, began as a way to be different and to rebel against society. Bands such as Nirvana and the Red Hot Chili Peppers found this type of clothing to be more practical for the hours of practice in garages, where warm clothing, such as flannel shirts, was needed. However, the look soon gained popularity, and designers were developing fashion items imitating it.

Kurt Cobain wearing the grunge look.

:: TRICKLE-ACROSS THEORY ::

The **trickle-across theory,** or sometimes called the *horizontal flow theory,* argues that fashion moves between groups rather than vertically as in the trickle-up and trickle-down theories. This theory was developed by Charles King in 1963 and served as a rebuttal to the trickle-down theory. King believed that as a result of our system of mass communication and exposure to similar social forces, fashions are generated simultaneously in various social groups. While they may vary in quality, the fashions themselves may not be very different from one another. In other words, no one social group determines the trends for everyone else. The trickle-across theory holds that while some upper-class members may accept and wear clothing from lower socioeconomic classes and vice versa, there will be some styles not accepted by each group. For example, Converse became popular again in the early 1990s as a form of rejection of expensive Nike shoes. Some groups accepted Converse as their shoe of choice, some other social groups did not.

According to the trickle-across theory, fashion will be different from social group to social group, depending on their beliefs and even where they live. For example, if Los Angeles reports that upper-class women are wearing three-inch pointed heels, lower socioeconomic classes of women in Detroit or Chicago may not necessarily accept them. In other words, when working with fashion trends, a fashion marketer must understand the trends his or her own market is adopting or not adopting.

REAL WORLD focus >> The Black Teen Explosion

African American youths have always been shapers and changers of American popular culture. But an electronic revolution and the emergence of an "electrosex" (the influence of sex in television) environment, powered by hip-hop and its offshoots, black and white, have made black youths catalysts of a new millennium pop culture that is changing the way we sing, dance, dress, talk, and buy.

Not only in rap but also in film, fashion, and love, black youths are changing the name and shape of an addictive new climate that blends fashions, sports, music, and sex, an addictive climate that powers the $164 billion youth market.

By all accounts, black teenagers in central-city areas are the pied pipers, orchestrators, and drum majors of this market.

"It starts with us," says 15-year-old Jawona Roberts of Atlanta. It starts, in other words, with the 7 million black youths between 8 and 18, who represent 7 million opportunities for new ideas and new innovations. Who are these 7 million youths? They are Southerners and Northerners, rappers and soul-stirrers, gospel singers and top students and scholars. They are, above all, innovators in music and style. They are the ones who made the chief character on *Sex in the City* think it was cool to wear gold name plates around her neck. They are the ones who taught the dictionary-makers how to spell *bootylicious.* They are the ones who were fashionably chic in velour jogging suits back in the '80s, long before Juicy Couture. They are the black youths of America, who created rap, hip-hop, and almost every other major pop development of the last 20 years and who exert major influence over the music radio stations play, the movies that get produced, the commercials that air, the fashions on the runways, the songs we sing, and the dance moves that white icons like Britney Spears make.

The provocative point here is that black youth culture has become, in a strange way, the youth mainstream, and that white youths, and white adults, are integrating into that mainstream. Author Nelson George (*Hip Hop America*) says, "We know rap music and hip hop have broken from its ghetto roots to assert a lasting influence on American clothing, magazine publishing, television, language, sexuality, and social policy." It is significant, he says, that advertisers have embraced hip-hop as a way to reach not only black youths, but all youths.

The economic consequences of all this are immense, for black teen support can mean the difference between the success or failure of a TV show, movie, or CD. In a study of the viewing habits of blacks and whites, Kevin Downey found that "although African Americans still favor shows with predominantly black actors . . . African Americans fuel ratings for certain shows, particularly those with a multiethnic cast."

The same principle operates in big-city movie houses, where long lines of black teenagers have repeatedly turned small- and medium-budget films into big moneymakers. And if Hollywood has been more responsive on some levels to black demands, it is in large part because of urban teens who speak the only language movie moguls understand, the language of big bucks at the box office.

Black teen power is especially evident in fashion, where hip-hop moguls like Jay-Z and P. Diddy have become major names in department stores and mall outlets. One reason for this, as the U.S. Urban Youth Market survey reported, is that "purchases of teen boy's and teen girl's clothing are substantially more significant among inner-city African Americans than other population groups." In fact, the study reported, inner-city African Americans are 54 percent more likely [than U.S. households in general] to have made purchases of teen boy's clothing and

46 percent more likely to have bought teen girl's apparel." The astonishing point here is that it appears that black male teens spend more money on clothes than black female teens.

The individuals in this powerful group are far from monolithic (acting as one similar large group). "I listen to R&B, pop, rap, light rock, and gospel," says 16-year-old Paige McDonald of Chicago, who lists Beyonce, Mary Mary, and Creed among her favorite artists. Pittsburgh native Cheyenne Robinson, 15, listens to, among others, Nelly, Jay-Z, and Justin Timberlake. Neesin Williams, 17, of Bellflower, California, a Los Angeles suburb, says Nas, Marvin Gaye, and Usher are among his favorites. Williams is a young entrepreneur who co-owns a record label named C. R. E. A. M. with three of his friends and is a member of a hip-hop group called Envy. But it would be a mistake to think that all black teens are defined by music and dance. In school, rap entrepreneur Neesin Williams is president of the "Young Black Scholars."

Shopping, movies, and just "hanging out" rank highly as the favorite activities of black youths. Sixteen-year-old Atlantan Amani Wimberly, a varsity cheerleader, says she, like so many other teens her age, hangs out with her friends almost every weekend. "We go shopping," she says, "and go to movies."

What do these youths want?

They want—if our nonscientific poll is any indication—the same thing black youths have always wanted—recognition, understanding, and an equal chance to fulfill themselves and to make a new world. The only difference perhaps is that they belong to a generation that has already changed one world and is in a position to make a new one.

The new generation is confronted, of course, with racism, inadequately funded schools, and high unemployment, compounded by a pervasive national drug culture and the systematic incarceration of tens of thousands of young African American males. Some critics have also complained about gangsta rap and misogynist (disrespectful to women) lyrics, but other commentators say these are individual excesses and are not representative of a generation which has, like all other black youth generations, like the blues generation, like the jazz generation, like the soul generation, transformed itself and American culture. ❖

Source: Ebony, April 2004.
Reprinted with permission.

>> QUESTIONS

1. Are there any new ethnic minorities in the forefront of fashion? Discuss.

2. Why do fashion designers need to be aware of the ethnic influence on fashion?

3. How can fashion designers and marketers better reach out to ethnic groups?

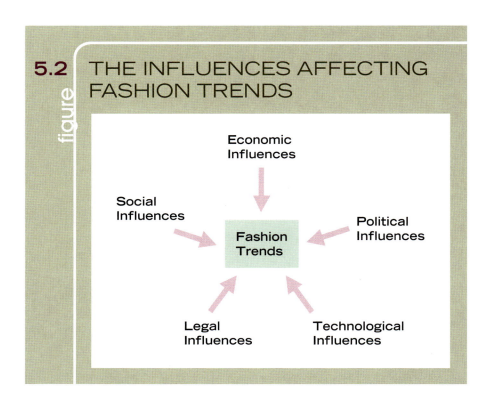

5.2 figure

THE INFLUENCES AFFECTING FASHION TRENDS

>> external factors affecting fashion

:: SOCIAL ISSUES ::

The power of youth in numbers, as the Real World Focus touched on, is one example of how societal changes can impact fashion. In her book *The End of Fashion,* Teri Agins discussed four other societal changes that have affected fashion:

1. Women no longer care about fashion, as it does not represent their lives. Women are so concerned about balancing job and family, they do not follow trends as much as they used to.

2. People started dressing down. The rise of "casual Friday" and companies that no longer require the traditional suit and tie resulted in changes to fashion. Agins also mentions the prevalence of denim and T-shirts in wardrobes.

3. Fashion started to seem too expensive for what consumers were getting. The mass production of fashion and the ability to obtain high-quality goods at affordable prices, made high-priced couture designs seem too expensive. In addition, bargain hunting, shopping in secondhand stores, and reselling clothing (such as on eBay) are widely accepted, even by the upper classes.

4. Most designers are no longer willing to take risks for fear of losing money (with the exception of haute couture designers). They now stay with safe designs they know will sell.

In any type of business, those making decisions must understand the social changes that are occurring to better develop strategy. In fashion, however, social changes are especially important. For example, during and prior to the 1950s, women had always worn dresses However, as women became more liberated, pants for women became normal, thanks to Chanel and other groundbreaking designers.

Another example can be taken from the 1960s. As discussed in Chapter 4, the 1960s saw rebellion in many garments. For example, the hippie look was counter to the culture represented by fashions of Chanel and others. Colors, such as tie-dyed designs, were very different from the feminine fashions of the earlier decade, such as the Chanel suit.

Fashion reflects societal values in many ways. Other societal changes that fashion trend forecasters must consider are related to age, women in the workforce, men's appearance, and ethnic influences.

Age   After World War II, men came home and triggered the "baby boom," a phenomenon that extended into the mid 1960s. Generations born after the boom were much smaller in size. As a result, this over-40 population, called the *baby boomers,* has been the predominant group of potential customers for marketers. The sheer size of this generation makes for a significant amount of spending power, and they have many different needs and wants for their fashion items, to which fashion merchandisers must cater.

Besides the sheer size of the baby boomer generation, an important aspect about this population is that they are over 40. Age greatly impacts the amount of money people have available to purchase clothing and fashion items. It is generally accepted that the older someone is, the more likely he or she will

The hippie look.

have money to purchase goods, such as fashion items. In addition to corresponding to the amount of money people may have to spend on fashion items, age also affects the types of clothing purchased.

Because medicine has enabled people to live longer, views on age have changed. In prior years, people of a certain age were expected to wear a specific type of clothing. For example, a 60-year-old woman would not have worn something considered trendy. However, in recent years, it has become more acceptable for people of all ages to wear what they like rather than what society expects them to wear.

Another interesting factor related to age and its impact on the merchandising of clothing is that many American women like to be thought of as younger than they in fact are. As a result, advertisements and clothing will reflect this particular need.

A soldier returns home from World War II.

Women in the workforce In the early 1900s, women could not own property, vote, or earn a living except in limited occupations. During this time, women dressed how their fathers wanted them to dress, and later how their husbands wanted them to dress. Over time, the roles of women changed, and what they wore changed, in part as a result of the women's rights movement of the 1960s. Since then, and notably in the 1980s, women entered the workforce in great numbers. Thus, fashion designers and merchandisers had to meet the demand for suits and other work-related clothing.

Some women balance work and home; other women (and men!) have decided to say at home and raise the children. This trend results in different needs for clothing. For example, easy-wear clothing such as Dockers pants (made by Levi) with stain protection and wrinkle resistance are higher in demand. This is a result of less time to spend on dry-cleaning and ironing clothing.

Along with the increase of women in the workforce came a need for different types of clothing. As discussed in Chapter 4, appropriate work-related clothing is in part worn in an effort to gain respect and equal treatment in the workforce. Clothing such as suits, slacks, and other appropriate work attire is in greater demand. The role of women in the workforce and the expectation of what should be worn in the work-place is an important social factor in trend forecasting.

Men and their appearance In recent years, plastic surgery in men has increased. Nose jobs, eyelid surgery, and liposuction are among the three most requested procedures by men. Between 2002 and 2003, plastic surgery increased 10 percent for men, and it is expected to increase every year. A recent survey reported that 78 percent of men claim their looks have a lot to do with their success at work.

In addition to surgical procedures for men, moisturizers, hair gels, and lotions are now popular products purchased by men, according to cosmetics reports. Men are also increasingly likely to use spa services like massages, facials, pedicures, and waxing. Euromonitor International, a market research firm, predicts that overall sales of male grooming products will increase 67 percent by 2008, for a total of $19.5 billion. Sales of these products and services increased 37.3 percent between 1998 and 2003, with total sales reaching $3.8 billion in 2003.

This change can be certainly be attributed to effective marketing, but it may also be a result of men getting married later in life and having to take care of themselves for a longer period of time. In the past, most shampoos and lotions were marketed to women. The market had become saturated with products for women, so manufacturers started focusing on products for men. **Saturated** means there are too many products available that serve the same purpose.

Escalating demand for surgery and personal care products for men can be attributed to the increased acceptance of the use of them; that is, more and more men feel that they can undergo cosmetic treatments and use grooming products without diminishing their manhood. The term **metrosexual** is not yet defined in Webster's, but the term refers to men who dress well, take care in their personal grooming, and exhibit sensitivity. The metrosexual man embodies heightened fashion sense. The growing acceptance, and even embrace, of well-dressed, well-groomed men means the market for men's clothing and grooming products will change in future years.

Ethnic influences The ethnic mix of the United States also affects fashion. Ethnic differences can influence the clothing a retailer must carry, but they can also serve as inspiration for new designs.

Ethnicity can affect both the type of clothing and the sizes that stores must carry. Consider, for example, the Asian influence on the market. Because Asian body types are different, a store located in Asian communities may need to carry smaller sizes in order to cater to smaller customers.

Another example is the Hispanic influence in the United States, which has brought bright colors and prints. These fashions have been readily accepted by not only the Hispanic population but the entire public. The collections of J Lo (Jennifer Lopez—singer, actress, and now designer) reflect the influence of her Hispanic heritage with the use of bright colors, flowing skirts, and femininity.

A women dancing with a Sesh or Borneo. Many fashions come from ethnic influences.

Ethnic segmentation has also become quite popular for retailers. **Ethnic segmentation** reflects the realization that because people have different values, specific products and advertisements must be used to reach specific ethnic groups. A person's ethnic background can influence his or her motivation for purchasing particular items. For example, in a 2000 study of the buying behavior of Hispanic consumers, Haegele, a research firm, found that family, formality, and status were important factors in the purchase decisions of this ethnic population, even greater than for their Caucasian counterparts.

Besides these concerns for ethnic differences from the retail point of view, ethnicity can influence fashion directly. Traditional ethic clothing can inspire new designs. For example, embroidered, silky tunics were popular in spring 2005. This design was influenced by the tura, a long, collarless tunic worn by women in India. Traditional Native American patterns have also influenced both clothing and household textiles. The poncho, popular in the 1960s and again in winter 2005, is an example of an ethnic fashion from Native Americans that became popular among women of many backgrounds.

The most successful trend forecasters and retailers are the ones that understand that the United States has always had an influx of immigrants who bring their country's style, values, and influences with them.

:: ECONOMIC FORCES ::

One of the major economic factors affecting fashion is consumer income. Consumer income tells fashion forecasters what consumers have to spend on fashion goods. Another important economic factor is the purchasing power of consumers, which is affected by layoffs, interest rates, and recessions.

Consumer income

A major concern of trend forecasters is the amount of money consumers are willing to spend on fashion goods. Personal income, disposable income, and discretionary income are names given to different types of consumer income.

Total income is the income a person makes from all sources. It could be the income earned from a full-time job plus that earned from a small business on the side.

Personal income is the total income less social security taxes. **Disposable income** is personal income minus all taxes, such as federal tax, sales tax, and property tax.

Discretionary income is disposable income minus rent and necessities. For example, if a woman makes $1,800 per paycheck and $200 consulting on weekends, her total income is $2,000 per month. Her personal income is total income less social security tax. Social security tax changes on a yearly basis, but let's assume it is 7 percent in this example. Her personal income would then be $1,860. Let's assume she pays taxes at a 20 percent rate. This would mean her disposable income is $1,860 − $372 = $1,488. Assuming her monthly necessities total $990, this leaves her with $498 of discretionary income.

Discretionary income is more important than personal income in some ways. A person may have high total income; but because of high mortgage payments and other bills, he or she may have an even smaller amount of discretionary income than someone with a lower gross income.

Many marketers focus on the teen market in the belief that teens actually have more discretionary income than their parents because they have fewer bills and financial commitments. For example, a teenager who earns $500 a month in her part-time job likely has fewer bills than her parents; as a result, she can spend most of the $500 on what she pleases. Her parents may make $4,000 per month; but after they pay the mortgage, electric bill, and car loan and buy food, they may only have $200 left for discretionary income. Therefore, the teen market is very important to fashion marketers.

Purchasing power

Purchasing power is another important economic consideration in fashion. **Purchasing power** is the amount of goods a person can buy for a given amount of money in a given time period. Interest rates, inflation, recessions, and layoffs are all phenomena that affect the purchasing power of consumers.

Interest rates are the rates charged by banks for consumers to borrow money. Interest rates are set by the Federal Reserve Bank, referred to simply as the Fed. It consists of a central board of governors in Washington, D.C., 12 regional Federal Reserve Banks throughout the United States, and other member banks. The Fed establishes interest rates and controls money supply in the United States. It also loans money to the local banks at the interest rate it has set, called a **discount rate,** and the banks in turn loan money to consumers or businesses. Large businesses and investors get a **prime rate,** and regular investors get a regular interest rate.

When interest rates are low, consumers tend to purchase more homes, cars, and other goods that are financed. Businesses tend to invest in **capital purchases,** such as new buildings and equipment, when interest rates are low. When interest rates are high, the cost to borrow money is much greater, therefore less purchasing occurs. The Fed tries to control interest rates in an effort to stimulate the economy. During the recession that began in 2000, the Fed lowered interest rates, hoping that action would encourage home buying and borrowing for capital improvements for businesses. This, in turn, creates jobs, as people are needed to manufacture the equipment and build the homes businesses and people demand.

Inflation is another occurrence that greatly affects purchasing power. **Inflation** is the normal rise of prices over time. The assumption is that consumers' income will also rise along with prices. **Deflation** is when prices actually go down. Although this may sound like a good thing, it actually means consumers can no longer afford the prices (perhaps they are out of work) so the prices must go down. Deflation normally means there are bigger problems in the economy, such as a recession or layoffs.

A **recession** is an overall decline in the **gross domestic product (GDP)** for two consecutive quarters, or six months. A **quarter** is a three-month period. The GDP is the value of all goods and services produced within the borders of a country in a given time period. It is a good measure of the overall health of the economy. If the GDP is down, it means that companies are not producing as many goods and services, which normally means that **layoffs** have occurred. A layoff is the phenomenon of a person losing his or her job as a result of low demand for the product or service he or she produces, or the shift of that job overseas. The economic impact of layoffs within a community has a domino effect. For example, if Microsoft has to lay off 5,000 people in Seattle, it is not only those 5,000 people who are affected in the community. The restaurants in the area will receive less business, because fewer people are working in the area. The restaurants then do not need as many servers, who may lose their jobs also. Consider the dry cleaners, clothing stores, and other businesses that may lose business as a result. Layoffs impact an entire community and can cause customers to search for lower price options. It is likely consumers will buy only those items of clothing they really need, or they may buy the same quantity but at a less expensive store. Thus, fashion merchandisers must understand what is happening to purchasing power now and in the future.

The last important trend in relation to economics is that Americans owe an average of $10,000 on credit cards. The total interest paid on credit cards is $50 billion. All credit card debt combined totals $1.7 trillion. This high debt can be attributed to many factors. First, credit card companies heavily market to groups, such as college students, who may not have the resources to completely pay off their balance every month. Second, many Americans embrace a "must have it now" mentality. Rather than saving and paying for goods in cash, many people prefer to have the item immediately.

Of course, such debt is making credit card companies lots of money; consumers spend an average of $1,000 in interest every year. For example, if a person carries credit card debt of $15,000 and pays $300 per month at 13 percent interest, it would take the consumer 20 years to pay off the debt, including $9,000 of interest. In other words, rather than paying $15,000, the consumer would end up paying $24,000. Because of high debts, there have been new laws introduced to make it more difficult to file for bankruptcy. It addition, higher minimum payments have recently been required and other means established to protect consumers from too much debt.

:: LEGAL FORCES ::

Legal forces guide consumers on both a personal level and a business level. Mergers, import regulations, product labeling, and advertising laws are all legal issues that affect fashion business as well as individuals.

A **merger** or an **acquisition** is a sale of one company to another. The retail world has seen an immense number of mergers over the last 20 years. For example, Federated Department Stores purchased May Department Stores in winter 2005. May owned Lord & Taylor, Filene's, Marshall Field's, and Foley's, among others. Federated already owned Bloomingdale's and Macy's, among others. This gives Federated many different major stores in a variety of markets. The most important reason to merge is competition. By acquiring another company, a retailer can better compete in markets.

A primary motivation for a merger or acquisition is revenue growth or customer growth. For example, when Nike purchased Converse in 2003, Nike did not have the same customers as Converse; the acquisition enabled Nike to gain a new stream of revenue and customers.

Sometimes mergers occur when two retailers are not doing well; the feeling is that, together; they may be able to perform better. An example of this is the recent merger between Sears and Kmart. Neither store was meeting target revenue numbers, but management believed that the merger would make the company more profitable.

On the fashion merchandising level, a merger can give the retailer greater **buying power,** meaning it may be able to negotiate better production deals with vendors, making the goods cheaper for consumers. Note, however, that there are many rules and regulations in regard to mergers and acquisitions.

A second legal concern for fashion relates to global laws and regulations for importing fashion products. **Importing** is when a company ships products into one country from another. The U.S. government has **import quotas,** which are limits on particular kinds of goods that can be shipped into the country from other, specific countries. The purpose of U.S. import quotas is to allow domestic companies to better compete. In January 2005, most import quotas on textile goods coming into the United States were eliminated. Quotas on denim jeans and T-shirts, however, were not eliminated. This created a flood of garments and textiles from China. Because of the market flooding, tariffs may be required to ensure the market does not have oversaturation of textile goods. More will be discussed on this topic in Chapter 8.

Labeling requirements also affect fashion. Examples include the requirements to list fiber content percentages, specify washing instructions, and identify country of origin. Labeling requirements may not directly affect actual fashion trends, but they can change them indirectly. For example, if enough consumers are not willing to purchase a garment because it must be dry-cleaned, as specified on its label, the manufacturer may consider using a different fabric.

Some specific examples of laws that affect fashion are the Wool Products Labeling Act, the Flammable Fabric Act, and the Care Labeling Act. Compliance to these laws is regulated by the Federal Trade Commission (FTC).

The **Wool Products Labeling Act** requires labels on all woolen products to accurately specify the fiber content, country of origin, and name of the manufacturer. It is important to note that the company selling the garments is ultimately responsible for correct labeling, even though it might be importing most of its garments. Recently, some garments have been classified as being made of pashmina. *Pashmina* is an Indian word for cashmere, but it is unclear what the fiber content of pashmina actually is. As a result, the word *pashmina* cannot be used on garment labels, as it is not recognized by the FTC.

Another act that has had a large impact on fashion is the **Flammable Fabric Act.** This act was originally passed in 1953 because of serious burn accidents involving rayon sweaters. This type of sweater became known as the "torch sweater." There are specific standards for children's clothing, as well as testing standards for clothing flammability.

The **Care Labeling Act** requires complete instructions about care for the garment. In addition, care instructions must be attached to the garment in a matter that will last the entire life of the garment. A manufacturer cannot say "dry-clean only" unless it has proof that washing a garment would be harmful to it. Any garment that is meant to cover or protect the body is included in this labeling act. This does not include items like belts, neckties, or scarves.

Care symbols, developed by the American Society for Testing and Materials (ASTM), are often used for washing instructions on garments. For example, a triangle refers to the ability to use bleach on the product; a square means the manner in which the garment should be dried; and an icon filled with water and a hand means the garment is to be hand-washed only.

Fines for noncompliance of labeling can be quite steep. For example, Jones New York was found to have an unreasonable basis for care instructions. Some of its labels required that the specific garments be dry-cleaned, but damage and fading occurred when they were dry-cleaned. The company should have labeled the garment to be hand-washed. As a result, it paid a $300,000 fine. Jones Apparel Group owns Jones New York, Evan-Picone, Norton McNaughton, Gloria Vanderbilt, Erika, l.e.i., Energie, Nine West, Easy Spirit, Enzo Angiolini, and many other well-known brands.

:: POLITICAL FORCES ::

T-shirts can support a cause.

It has been said that politics can lead to great changes in fashion. An old rule of thumb suggests, "Conservative clothing for when republicans are in office, fun clothing for when democrats are in office." Although this idea cannot be proven, trend forecasters must be acutely aware it.

In the presidential elections of 2004, T-shirts supporting a cause or a candidate were popular, motivating fashion designers to develop such garments to put in their retail stores.

Besides the obvious relation to fashion and politics, there are many other ways politics can affect fashion in more subtle ways. For example, politicians set policies on economics, laws, global policies, and even technology. These policies and laws, such as trade restrictions or requirements for product labeling, will indirectly affect retailers and all those involved in the fashion industry.

:: TECHNOLOGICAL FORCES ::

Technological forces have affected the entire fashion industry, not just fashion trends, from a communication perspective through the entire process by which the fashion business operates.

The ability to communicate quickly through e-mail and websites has enabled people to see what others are wearing throughout the world. This makes fashion more global and requires trend forecasters today to be aware of what is happening in other countries. For example, Seven Jeans have become popular throughout the world, in part through the use of blogs. A **blog** is a website on which people post their personal thoughts, an online diary of sorts. Blogs exist for almost any subject.

The Internet was only born in the early 1990s, yet most people can't imagine life without it. Companies such as eBay have allowed consumers to shop around the world, requiring trend forecasters to be keenly aware of global trends and prices.

The use of computers for designing garments, such as computer-aided design, or CAD, has impacted fashion in terms of the speed at which designs can be created. The speed allows for faster production, which allows for clothing to enter the retail stores faster. The retailers are thus able to respond to trends more timely than ever before.

Most major design firms, such as Donna Karan, have recently implemented product development management software as part of the preproduction process. Such a system allows the user to store sketches and photos of fabric samples for others to use and change. For example, the software from Gerber Technology allows fashion designers to manipulate patterns, colors, fabrics, and other aspects of a design using a computer. Another example of production software includes that by Lectra. The company's system streamlines the development process, making communication between designers and producers easier than it was prior to development of this kind of software.

Technology has also made it easier to shop online. The use of shopping carts, links to product-care information, and detailed images of each item make shopping online increasingly popular. One of the major concerns about shopping online is credit card security. New technology is entering the market to make transactions even safer.

Technology has also made is easier to track inventory. Inventory is vital in fashion, as it is the means by which retailers earn profits. Tracking inventory from the time it leaves the country of origin through the time it leaves a retail store is important. Inventory devices and software allow retailers to know exactly when an item has shipped and when it has been sold in the retail store. In knowning this, stores are able to keep real-time track of inventory, making it easier to reorder when necessary. Wal-Mart, for example, uses this kind of technology. As soon as an item has been scanned, the regional warehouse automatically knows to ship the same item to the store. Companies that produce this kind of software include Storis Management Systems, iCode, and CoreSense. By being able to replenish inventory more quickly, keep track of orders, and insure that apparel is always in stock, retailers can maintain higher profits.

:: GLOBAL FORCES ::

Due to increased competition in fashion products, global forces within the industry are a hot topic. Although Chapter 8 will go into great detail about globalization and its effect on fashion, it is important to mention some of the issues in this chapter. The use of free-trade agreements has affected fashion. A **trade agreement** is a pact between two or more countries to lower or eliminate quotas and tariffs, making it easier for businesses in those countries to trade with one another. Specific trade agreements will be covered in Chapter 8.

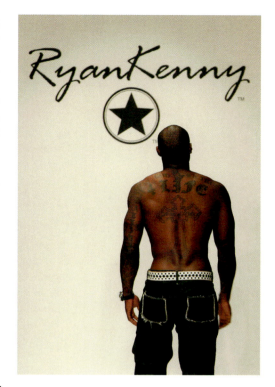

The popularization of jeans is another example of globalization.

Most U.S. clothing factories have been moved overseas, where there is cheaper labor, cheaper raw materials, like fabrics, and lower overhead costs, such as for warehouse space. This change has resulted in less expensive products for consumers but a loss of jobs for many Americans. For example, Levi Strauss had to close its last plant in San Antonio, Texas, for cost reasons. The company is moving all of its factories to China and Canada.

Besides helping companies lower costs and, ultimately, prices for products, as mentioned in the previous section, technology has played a large role in the globalization of the fashion industry. The ability to travel more rapidly and communicate in a matter of seconds through e-mail has made the actual overseas production of garments easier than ever before.

Another aspect of the increasing globalization of the fashion industry is that consumers are now able to see what the rest of the world is wearing through online fashion shows and websites. Japanese people are wearing Nike, while Americans are wearing Kimonos. The world is smaller now, and as a result, trend forecasters and designers must be aware of the industry from a global perspective rather than merely a national perspective.

Also related to globalization is the use of bar codes on garments. Bar codes are based on what is known as the **universal product code (UPC),** invented by George Laurer in 1973. This is the unique identifier of products. Because there are so many new products produced throughout the world, longer bar codes have become a necessity. A new system, which will require 14 digits instead of 8 to 12, was designed as part of the Uniform Code Council's Sunrise 2005 Initiative. This new code system will make selling products from country to country much easier both for the producers of the product and the retailers who sell the product.

New technology will slowly replace the UPC code. A new way to keep track of inventory is the **electronic product code.** It allows goods to be scanned from a remote location. For example, a customer could pick out groceries; they could be scanned remotely and automatically charged to a credit card, eliminating the need for waiting in line at the cash register.

There are many written and published sources available to assist merchandisers and forecasters in keeping abreast of all the external factors that affect fashion. Some come in the form of the written word, and many of these sources will require a fee for access; others require observation.

:: COLLECTION REPORTS ::

Collection reports are the most immediately available source of information on designer collections, but they can be expensive. These reports provide detailed sketches of new designs, including color and fabric selections, and all of them are based on a recent designer fashion show. Many companies will have these reports out two weeks after a designer's show. Among the organizations that provide collection reports are Calin International, Dominique Peclers, and ESP/Ellen Sideri Partnership.

:: TREND REPORTS ::

Several companies compile what are called **trend reports;** these sources include the Tobe Report and Block Note. One other source, Mode, provides a website that has information on all of the available trend reports. Trend reports are similar to collection reports in that they provide sketches, pictures, and fabric/color swatches to assist the fashion buyer and designer in decision making. Trend reports are written by independent companies and are not based on any one designer's collection.

Similar to trend reports, **color services** provide predictive information on popular new colors to be used for a coming season. Companies that specialize in color forecasting include the International Color Authority, The Color Box, and Concepts in Color. **Color systems** are used in color prediction. Two color systems are those provided by Pantone and SCOTDIC (Standard Color of Textile Dictionaire Internationale de la Couleur). Both of these companies keep records in the form of dyed fabric of all colors used in the past.

:: WEBSITES ::

There is a difference between a fashion forecasting website and one that provides simple trend information to designers and buyers. Fashion forecasting websites typically require fee-based subscriptions for access. An example of such a site is fashionsnoops.com, which provides long-term forecasting information and in-depth analysis on fashion trends. Another example is Worth Global Style Network (WGSN). These types of websites are geared toward buyers, which is why they charge a fee. There are also many commercial websites more geared to the consumer, but buyers will view these too. Examples of these types of websites include:

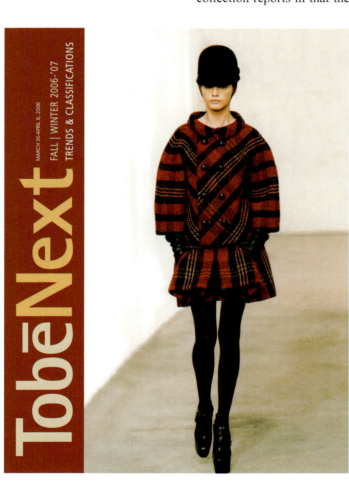

TobeNext

MARCH 30-APRIL 6, 2006
FALL | WINTER 2006-'07
TRENDS & CLASSIFICATIONS

The Tobe Report.

- www.style.com. This website shows details of garments from runway shows; it also has a section on what famous people are wearing.
- www.fashioninformation.com. This website uses creative words and pictures to describe street and retail trends in the hottest cities from around the world.
- www.snapfashun.com. This website is a fashion forecasting site that requires a subscription, but it also provides good information for free. It discusses design strategies and focuses on the top five trends of the moment.
- www.thetrendreport.com. This site discusses and provides visual examples of the top five trends.

The information provided by these available online resources, be they fee-based or free, will help fashionistas design better lines or purchase the right merchandise for their stores.

:: TRADE PUBLICATIONS ::

Trade publications can be newspapers, magazines, or journals that are written specifically with the fashion professional in mind. These publications give information on fashion trends and can be very useful. Some of the trade publications are:

Women's Wear Daily

Daily News Record (for men's wear)

Earnshaws (children's wear)

Children's Business

Sportswear International

Footwear News Magazine

Accessories Magazine

It is extremely important for people in the fashion industry to read such trade publications to learn about new trends, mergers, and other changes within the industry. Also note many of these publications offer student discounts.

Also important to read are fashion magazines, sometimes called **editorial publications** or consumer publications. These number into the hundreds, but some of the most notable are *In Style, Elle, Marie Claire, Seventeen, GQ,* and *Ebony.*

In addition to trade publications, trade associations may provide information on trends as well. A **trade association** is a professional organization of businesses or manufacturers that formed to promote their business or industry or to adopt uniform standards. Some examples of trade associations in fashion include:

Color Association of the United States

Cotton Incorporated

American Sewing Guild

:: MOVIES, MUSIC, AND TELEVISION ::

Most good trend forecasters will be aware of styles that movie and music stars are wearing. Besides providing inspiration for designers, what stars wear is useful in forecasting trends. Often, celebrities bring fashion to the mainstream, to the forefront for the mass-marketing of garments, rather than starting the actual trend.

America and much of the world is fascinated by movie, music, and television stars. These celebrities are photographed while on vacation, at home, at movie premieres, and at the Oscars on the red carpet. There is a fascination with stars, but especially with what they are wearing. Any magazine that focuses on stars, such as *US Weekly* or *People,* will write a lot about the clothing they are wearing. The fashion forecaster who takes note of what stars are wearing in these magazines may discover a new fashion trend.

A stunning example of how music and movie stars influence fashion is the "trucker hat." Ashton Kutcher began this trend in 2003 when he wore such a hat on the MTV show *Punk'd.*

Another example of how music and television has influenced fashion is the "wife beater" tank top. Musicians such as Kid Rock, Snoop Dogg, Madonna, and Britney Spears have popularized this trend. In fact, Dolce and Gabbana have offered designer wife beaters, another example of trickle-up fashion. Rapper Eve even sings about how good she looks in her "wife beater with a bangin' tan." In the movie 8 *Mile,* Eminem mocks rival rapper Papa Doc for wearing one of the shirts, calling him "Snoop Dogg in a bra." The term *wife beater* has offended some; as a result, many designers have come out with versions simply called "the beater."

In her 2003 video "Sk8er Boi," Avril Lavigne wore a green and gold Wilkesboro Elementary T-shirt. Although she purchased this T-shirt in a New York thrift store, hundreds of Lavigne fans called the school wanting to purchase the shirt.

There are numerous other examples of stars' influence on fashion. Bono, the lead singer of U2, popularized large, face-covering sunglasses. Bono, due to his popularity, has released his own clothing line (with his wife) called EUDE (suggests the word *nude*). This line supports his believe in environmentally friendly clothing. Be they the rock stars of the 1980s, with their tight leather pants, or grunge rockers of the 1990s, with their ripped jeans, or the hip-hop musicians of today—all created new trends by just being themselves. Although the public looks to the stars for entertainment, they also take on much of their fashion taste as well. Fashionistas who follow the trends of the stars are bound to find new fashions to sell to the mass market.

:: STREET FASHION ::

Finally, street fashion, or what everyday people are wearing, can be an indicator for trend forecasters. Simple observation techniques such as watching people in malls, at concerts, and at other events can discover new fashion trends. Many companies such as Zumiez send representatives to music events, skateboarding competitions, and snowboarding competitions to observe the street fashion of their target markets. Many designers will visit the streets of Los Angeles or New York to see what people are wearing and how they are putting their looks together.

Ashton Kutcher on MTV wearing his trademark trucker hat.

>> conclusion •

Fashion can take many directions, and it is up to the fashion forecaster to predict what direction that will be. When a forecaster has a good understanding of how social, economic, political, technological, and global forces affect fashion, he or she will better be able to predict future demand of clothing by the public. Also having an understanding of how past events have affected fashion will help a forecaster make more accurate predictions.

Reading fashion magazines, collection reports, and color forecasts can be tools for predicting the future. Understanding how stars and street fashion influence what people wear tomorrow will also allow the forecaster to meet demand for fashion products by consumers. Fashion forecasting requires acute awareness of the surrounding world. The awareness can come from reading, watching, and taking notes on the new trends that can occur as a result of the variety of external forces discussed in this chapter.

>> chapter five review •

TERMS TO KNOW ::

Trickle-down theory	Capital purchases	Flammable Fabric Act
Theory	Inflation	Care Labeling Act
Trickle-up theory	Deflation	Blog
Street fashion	Recession	Trade agreements
Trickle-across theory	Gross domestic product (GDP)	Universal product code (UPC)
Saturated	Quarter	Electronic product code
Metrosexual	Layoffs	Collection reports
Ethnic segmentation	Merger	Trend reports
Personal income	Acquisition	Color services
Disposable income	Buying power	Color system
Discretionary income	Importing	Trade publications
Purchasing power	Import quotas	Editorial publications
Discount rate	Wool Products Labeling Act	Trade association
Prime rate		

CONCEPTS TO KNOW ::

1. Social influences that help predict trends.
2. Economic issues and trends.
3. Political events and how they might affect trends.

4. Legal issues and their effect on trend forecasting.
5. Technological changes and their impact on fashion.
6. Components of the Wool Products Labeling Act, Flammable Fabric Act, and Care Labeling Act.

CHAPTER QUESTIONS ::

1. What are three of the tools that a fashion merchandiser can use to help predict fashion? Describe each.
2. Describe four factors a fashion merchandiser must take into consideration when reviewing trends?
3. How are economic forces important in trend prediction? Cite two reasons.
4. Name two ways in which ethnic influence can be seen in fashion today.
5. Describe three recent social changes that have occurred and how fashion might have been affected.
6. Describe two changes that occurred to fashion due to legal issues?
7. How did "casual Fridays" affect fashions? What are you allowed and not allowed to wear to work?
8. What are three characteristics you think you would need to be an effective trend forecaster?

CHAPTER PROJECTS AND DISCUSSION ::

1. Find the GDP for 1970, 1980, and 1990 (see www.bea.gov). Look through old magazines. Do you see any relation to the trends in the magazines and the GDP during these times?
2. Assemble into small groups. Discuss each of the factors affecting fashion trends. How might what you are wearing be affected by each of these factors?
3. Visit the www.polo.com and www.tommy.com. Look at the technological features of both the websites, such as the shopping cart feature. Which site is easier to search? Maneuver through? Which seems easier to shop?
4. View the Mode Info website (www.modeinfo.com). What publications might you use to predict color trends? Textile trends? Trends for teens? Trends for sportswear?
5. Visit the JLO website (www.shopjlo.com). Print three specific garments you believe to have ethnic influence and bring them to class for discussion.

FOR FURTHER READING ::

http://economictimes.indiatimes.com
www.investopedia.com
www.pantone.com/pantone.asp
www.ftc.gov

consumer behavior in fashion

Consumers buy clothing for more than practical reasons. They purchase clothing to be trendy, to fit in, and to reflect a certain image. The study of consumer behavior examines these motivations for purchasing and helps fashionistas to see exactly how customers behave when buying products. By understanding the how and why of consumer behavior, fashionistas will be better able to offer customers the products they want.

After reading this chapter, you should be able to:

1 • Explain and give examples of the consumer buying process.

2 • Use reference groups in marketing as a way to understand customers.

3 • Describe the reasons people purchase fashion items.

4 • Explain the types of market segmentation and how they might be used in marketing fashion products.

5 • Identify the primary research methods for consumer behavior.

The subject of consumer behavior is one that interests both psychologists and businesspeople alike. **Consumer behavior** refers to the way people behave when buying an item, whether it be clothing or a new car. More important to the fashion industry, studying consumer behavior can help in identifying the motivations customers have for purchasing one style over another. A designer may create what he or she considers to be an excellent new style, but if consumers do not accept the fashion, it is nothing more than a mediocre design. New research in the area of consumer behavior is performed daily because businesspeople know that the more information they have about what goes through consumers' minds when purchasing, the better they can sell to them.

This chapter will discuss the types of consumer purchases, the process by which customers purchase goods, why they purchase fashion items, and how customers can be grouped in order to sell to them more effectively. Then, information on how to research customers will be covered. All of these areas tie into the goal of fully understanding customers, making it is easier to market to them. This chapter fits in the marketing shoebox of fashion (see Figure 6.1).

> **❝***In an emotional buying motive, the consumer bases the purchase decision on his or her feelings or attitude about himself or herself or a particular product.***❞**

Before discussing the process that consumers go through when buying, it is important to know the three types of purchase decisions customers make. These are important to fashion marketing because products will be marketed differently, depending on the level of decision making the consumer makes when buying the item. For example, a customer will likely go through a different process when purchasing toothpaste than when purchasing a new pair of running shoes. The decision process will likely be much shorter for the toothpaste purchase, requiring less thought.

First, **habitual decision making** is probably the most simple of the three. These purchase decisions do not require a lot of thought. In habitual decision making, the consumer is typically loyal to the particular brand and knows what he or she wants, or the product is priced so low the consumer is not worried about making a poor decision.

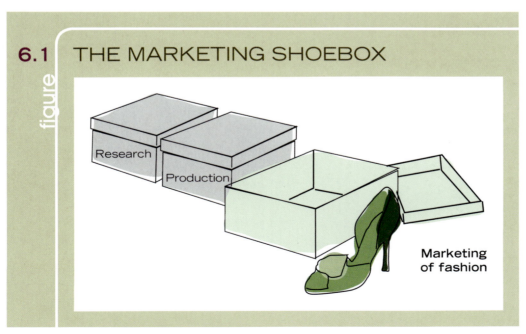

6.1 figure | **THE MARKETING SHOEBOX**

Research

Production

Marketing of fashion

It is important to note that while one consumer may use habitual decision making when purchasing a certain item, another may purchase the same type of item using a different type of decision-making process. For example, consider a man who has purchased Levis since he was 10 years old. He is now 30, and when his jeans are worn out; he goes to the store, buys Levis in the proper size, and goes home. This is an example of habitual decision making; the customer is brand-insistent. He has no motivation to try a different brand of jeans, because he likes a particular style of Levis. However, for another person, purchasing jeans can involve a day-long shopping trip. This second kind of decision making is called limited problem solving.

In **limited problem solving,** the consumer will look at many options and compare prices, features, and benefits. This is likely the type of fashion consumer who enjoys shopping and doesn't mind trying on items in several stores before making a decision. Many retailers cater to this type of customer, with salespersons who are able to point out the features and benefits of the items.

The third process, **extended problem solving,** is quite long, and the consumer may take several days, weeks, or even months to make a decision. Extended problem solving can also occur if the consumer does not have extensive knowledge about the product. Consider the purchase of a wedding dress. Most women do not go to the first wedding shop they find and buy a dress. Most will spend several weeks; they will go to different stores, taking their friends or mothers for opinions, shop online, and compare prices. This process is long, and the consumer will normally perform extensive research before buying. As another example of extended problem solving, consider the process involved in purchasing products such as snowboarding gear or ski wear. An extreme skier may shop around extensively to find the proper gear for his or her sport. Often, extended problem solving is for products that are high in price or cater to a specific kind of consumer.

Express storefront. Many customers may engage in limited problem solving when shopping there.

It is important for retailers to know what kind of purchasing decision process will be used for their products. For example, Wal-Mart caters to habitual purchases, whereas The Limited or Express cater to limited problem solving, and a small wedding boutique or Chanel section in a department store may cater to extended problem solving.

>> purchase decision process

For every type of purchase, consumers will go through a series of stages when deciding to buy. Figure 6.2 shows the stages of the consumer purchasing process. Depending on the complexity of the purchase, consumers may or may not go through each stage, or they may go through each stage quickly or slowly, depending on the type of decision they are making. For example, a consumer will likely go through this process quickly when purchasing toothpaste. In fact, he or she may even skip some of the steps. In extended problem solving, the consumer may take several months to go through this process. The purchase decision process is directly related to the type of product category.

Products that are simple and routine are called **convenience products.** A **shopping good** is a product for which it takes some shopping around before purchasing, but it does not require extensive research. For example, most consumers will try on several swimsuits before finally deciding on one. Finally, a product that takes research and extensive thought is called a **specialty good.** These are the types of products that a consumer does not purchase often.

STAGES OF THE CONSUMER PURCHASING PROCESS

figure

```
┌──────────────────┐
│     Problem      │
│   recognition    │
└──────────────────┘
         │
         ▼
┌──────────────────┐
│   Information     │
│     search       │
└──────────────────┘
         │
         ▼
┌──────────────────┐
│  Evaluation of   │
│   alternatives   │
└──────────────────┘
         │
         ▼
┌──────────────────┐
│    Purchase      │
│    decision      │
└──────────────────┘
         │
         ▼
┌──────────────────┐
│   Postpurchase   │
│    evaluation    │
└──────────────────┘
```

The first stage in the process is **problem recognition.** In this stage, a consumer recognizes that he or she has a need that is not being met.

The second stage is called **information search.** In this stage, the consumer will start looking for products to fill the need. Many times, consumers will begin on the Internet to see the choices available. The consumer may also ask for opinions of friends and family. This results in what is called an **evoked set,** which includes all of the possible alternatives the consumer may consider.

The third stage is **evaluation of alternatives.** The consumer will look at his or her evoked set and evaluate advantages and disadvantages of each possible choice. The consumer will also gauge the amount of risk involved in the purchase. For example, there is little risk in purchasing toothpaste, so this stage may go quickly for this type of convenience product. However, when shopping for a wedding dress, a consumer wants the perfect one. As a result, there is a higher risk in making the wrong decision.

In the fourth stage, the consumer will make a **purchase decision.** After evaluating all of the alternatives, the consumer decides on the best choice.

In the fifth stage, the consumer actually makes the purchase. In the last stage, **postpurchase evaluation,** the consumer will decide if purchasing the product was the right decision. If the person decides it was the wrong decision, he or she may decide to return the item.

Cognitive dissonance occurs if a customer is unsure that he or she made the right purchase choice. For example, a woman may try on several skirts to be paired with a sweater she already has at home. Cognitive dissonance would occur if the consumer gets home and realizes the skirt she bought doesn't match the sweater. To minimize cognitive dissonance, many retailers offer good return policies, warrantees, and after-sale service.

Let's look at what is involved at each stage of the purchase decision process for an item for which extended problem solving is required. Say Heidi is buying a wedding dress, a product that would be considered a specialty good.

Heidi has just started planning her wedding. After looking at many books, she realizes that she should start shopping for a wedding dress right away, to insure correct style, fit, and size. Heidi has recognized a unmet need: she must find a suitable wedding dress.

In the second stage, information search, Heidi purchases several bridal magazines and explores on the Internet to get an idea of what she wants her dress to look like. She then visits some bridal shops and tries on different styles.

In the third stage, Heidi looks at all of the alternatives. She evaluates her evoked set, in this case, the dresses she likes, to determine which one she will ultimately choose.

In the fourth and fifth stages, Heidi actually decides on a dress and goes to the bridal shop to purchase it.

Finally, in the postpurchase evaluation, Heidi decides if the dress she has purchased is the right one for her. She looks at photos of herself in the dress and get opinions from her friends on one she has chosen.

Now let's look at what is involved in the purchase decision process for an item bought through habitual decision making. Say Heidi is purchasing toothpaste, a convenience product.

Heidi is getting ready for work in the morning and realizes she is almost out of toothpaste. This is problem recognition.

She goes to a drugstore and looks at the choices available. This stage is the information search, and it usually occurs within a matter of a few seconds for habitual decision making.

Heidi prefers Mentadent, so she considers the new mint flavor and her regular flavor. This is her evoked set. She takes a few seconds to evaluate both of these alternatives.

Heidi chooses the new mint flavor. She makes the purchase decision and buys the product.

While brushing her teeth the next morning, Heidi decides that she made a good choice, as she really likes the mint flavor. This is the postpurchase evaluation.

Related to each stage of the purchase process are buying motives. The three buying motives are rational, emotional, and patronage. In **rational buying,** the consumer identifies needs and uses facts and logic to purchase a product. If purchasing because of this buying motive, a consumer will spend significant amounts of time in the information search stage. The consumer will rationally make a decision about the best product to suit his or her needs.

In **emotional buying,** the consumer bases the purchase decision on his or her feelings or attitude about him- or herself or a particular product. A consumer who has this buying motive may spend more time evaluating only the alternatives for which he or she has good feelings, or those products that made the person feel good about him- or herself.

The third buying motive, **patronage buying,** is when the consumer makes a purchase because he or she is comfortable with the product already, or the person feels comfort in purchasing from a particular company. For example, a woman who has always purchased MAC skincare and makeup products will likely purchase the brand again because she is comfortable with the products and knows they work for her. A consumer using a patronage buying motivation will likely move through the decision process quickly, since the person already knows what he or she wants.

>> reference groups

A **reference group,** sometimes called a **membership group,** is that group to which a particular person actually belongs. Members of a reference group share similar attitudes, beliefs, or ideals. For example, the reference group for most people includes their friends, their family, and perhaps co-workers or others who are part of their church or sports team.

Abercrombie & Fitch store.

Hot Topic store.

An **aspiration group** provides direction to a particular lifestyle or fashion. It is the group to which a person wishes he or she belongs. A person will normally try to dress and behave like those in his or her aspiration group. A young musician's aspiration group might be famous musicians, such as Dave Matthews or Coldplay. A 19-year-old woman who wants to be a lawyer may have older, successful lawyers as her aspiration group.

A group that a person does not want to be associated with or belong to is called a **disassociate group.** For example, many young people try to disassociate themselves from their parents. As a result, a teenage girl might not shop at the same stores at which her mother shops. In this case, "mothers" would be a disassociate group.

It is important that fashion marketers understand these three types of groups. If the aspiration group of a particular segment of people has been identified, marketers can try to manufacture clothing that will attract those consumers. On the other hand, if people disassociate themselves with a particular group, marketers will not manufacture, or advertise clothing that represents that particular group. For example, if a person's disassociate group is "punk," The Gap or Abercrombie and Fitch will not likely associate its clothing or advertisements with that particular group.

>> reasons for purchasing fashion

From a consumer behavior perspective, there are many reasons people purchase fashion items. Of course, the main reasons are practical in nature, such as to achieve warmth. However, it is well known that customers buy fashions for many other reasons, including to gain acceptance, to enhance physical attraction, to highlight self-expression, and to fill an emotional need.

:: ACCEPTANCE ::

People purchase fashions to be accepted by others, either by their reference group or by an aspiration group. This driving force is what makes people wear clothing to work that resembles the clothing their colleagues wear. Bankers or traders on the stock exchange are good examples of people who wear fashion for acceptance. Stock exchange traders all wear practically the same outfit: white shirts and black trousers. Bankers also have "uniforms." Black suits are their norm. It is a basic human need to be accepted and loved by others. **Maslow's hierarchy of needs** attempts to describe the different levels of human need.

Abraham Maslow theorized that there are five levels of human needs. He also believed that one could not move up the hierarchy to fulfill a higher need unless the needs below it were met. Maslow's hierarchy, presented as a pyramid, consists of physiological, safety, social, esteem, and self-actualization needs. Figure 6.3 illustrates this hierarchy.

The first level, the base of the pyramid, is formed by *physiological needs,* those basic needs humans must fulfill to survive. Food, water, clothing, and shelter would be considered basic needs. At

6.3 MASLOW'S HIERARCHY OF NEEDS

figure

- **Self actualization** Need to better one's self
- **Esteem** Feeling good about one's self
- **Social** Belongingness, love
- **Safety** Security
- **Physiological** Food, Water, Shelter

the second level are *safety needs*. These include the needs humans have to feel safe from harm at work, in cars, and at home. Safety also relates to financial security. *Social needs,* at the third level, include the feelings of belonging and being accepted and loved; many fashion items are purchased to fulfill these needs. *Esteem needs* include sense of self-worth and self-esteem, which lead to feelings of prestige, recognition, status, and confidence. Consumers buy many fashion items to fulfill esteem needs. Finally, at the top of the pyramid are *self-actualization needs,* those related to meeting one's life goals and continually improving oneself. Self-actualization needs are never 100 percent met, because once people have achieved goals, they establish new goals. An example of fulfilling a self-actualization need would be joining the army, volunteering for some humanitarian purpose, or going to school.

Maslow's hierarchy affects fashion on a number of levels. Clothing is really a basic need; people must have it to stay warm. However, most fashion items fill social needs (fitting in) and esteem needs (feeling good about ourselves) as well. A woman who purchases a T-shirt that she saw a friend wearing is fulfilling a social need; a woman who buys pants because she feels good in them is fulfilling an esteem need but also a social need if the pants help her feel like she fits in. Indeed, it could be argued that fashion fulfills a self-actualization need. By being able to afford, and thus purchasing, designer clothing, a women may feel that she has met her life's goal of having a successful career.

:: PHYSICAL ATTRACTION AND SELF-EXPRESSION ::

It has been said that advertising is all about sex, but it has also been said that clothing is all about sex too. In other words, clothing is worn to attract a mate; humans dress in a certain way to look better than those who may want the same mate. Throughout history people have adorned themselves with jewelry, clothing, and costumes that make them

In Hawaii a single woman wears a flower behind her right ear.

In the Middle East, many women are covered almost completely.

attractive to others. Certain colors, headdresses, or styles can mean various things. For example, according to tradition, in Hawaii a woman wears a flower behind her right ear to signify she is single, whereas a married woman wears the flower behind her left ear to show she is not available. Sometimes, however, clothing is worn to lessen physical attraction. In some parts of the Middle East, women are covered from head to toe so their physical attractiveness is not shown.

People wear clothing to express their feelings and their individuality. Although the sense of fitting in or belonging is one need fulfilled by fashion, humans still have a need to express themselves, according to Maslow. Often, this too can be done through clothing.

A person may wear fashionable items, accepted by his or her reference group, but the way fashion items are combined can create self-expression.

Self expression can also be exhibited by wearing a signature color or style. For example, Nancy Reagan always wore red, her signature color.

:: EMOTIONAL NEEDS ::

People can fulfill emotional needs, such as feeling good about one's self, by wearing new clothing or new makeup. Many people shop because they are happy, or they might feel they need to reward themselves. Some people buy fashion items because they are bored. Depression or sadness can also motivate someone to purchase fashion items. This is sometimes referred to as *retail therapy*.

>> market segmentation

Once knowing the process by which the customer buys and the reasons for buying, a fashion marketer will want to segment the market. **Market segmentation** is a term important for fashionistas to understand. It refers to the practice of breaking possible customers into smaller, **homogeneous** groups, that is, people who are similar in age, income, and other factors.

There are two main reasons to divide the market into groups. First, most marketers do not have the funds to target to all people; thus segmentation allows a marketer to focus on the needs of its specific customers. Second, to more effectively target advertising to the appropriate customers, it is necessary to know the type of people who watch or read specific media, be it television or magazines.

For an example of market segmentation, consider the strategies of two stores: The Limited and Express. Although these stores are owned by the same parent company, they cater to different market segments. The Limited targets businesswomen in their early 30s. Express markets to younger women, in high school or college. It is advantageous for this parent company to have two different stores for two market segments, as the needs of the two types of women are different.

There are six ways to segment a market, either for marketing purposes or trend forecasting purposes (which was discussed in Chapter 5): (1) demographics, (2) psychographics, (3) product parameters, (4) cohort segmentation, (5) family life cycle, and (6) geographical. Typically, a marketer would use several segmentation techniques to gain a clear picture of the customer's needs, wants, and beliefs.

:: DEMOGRAPHICS ::

The easiest way to segment a market is through demographics. **Demographics** can be defined as various statistics about characteristics within a human population. Demographics include age, income, gender, ethnic origin, education, and marital status. The U.S. Census Bureau provides useful statistics on demographics. However, using only demographics to segment a market can be problematic. For instance, a marketer might assume that married people, in a certain age and income range, will buy the same things. Of course, this is not necessarily true. Most marketers will use demographics as a starting point for segmentation but then will further divide the market using one of the several other methods.

When discussing income, rather than using actual income figures, marketers will sometimes use income categories. Figure 6.4 shows these income levels and

6.4 figure — AMERICAN SOCIAL CLASSES AND INCOMES

Upper upper (less than 1% of households)	Social elite who live on inherited wealth and have well-established family backgrounds; accustomed to wealth; buy and dress without showing wealth.
Lower upper (2% of households)	Earned high income through ability; began middle class; active in social and civic affairs; tend to purchase status symbol items.
Upper middle (12% of households)	Do not have unusual wealth; have professional jobs and keen interest in attaining the better things in life, such as a good education for children.
Middle class (32% of households)	Average-pay white-and blue-collar workers; try to do the "proper things"; concerned with trends and buy products that are popular.
Working class (38% of households)	Consists of those who depend on economic support from relatives and advice on purchases; do not have large savings; tend to live paycheck to paycheck.
Upper lowers (9% of households)	Not on welfare, but just above poverty line; lack education and perform unskilled work; they strive toward a higher class.
Lower lowers (7% of households)	Visibly poor; often do not have jobs and depend on public assistance.

Model created by Richard Colman first appeared in *Journal of Consumer Research* in 1983.

characteristics of each. Income can be an important factor when purchasing fashion products. It can indicate the types of products a customer will buy. This allows marketers to better understand their customers.

:: PSYCHOGRAPHICS ::

Psychographics represent another tool to use in segmenting markets. **Psychographic variables** are attributes that are related to lifestyles, personality, and values. The *lifestyle* variable encompasses those things that a customer does in his or her free time and cares about. It can also relate to who an individual aspires to be. Zumiez and Pac-Sun market to the lifestyle of young skateboarders and snowboarders.

Personality is the personal characteristics that make up the customer. For example, a person might have a need for high-image products. *Values* refer to the customer's overall belief system.

VALS lifestyle segmentation

VALS, short for values and lifestyle segmentation, is a system that uses psychographics to target customers. It provides a model for marketers to better understand the values and lifestyles of their customers; they will then have an idea about their customers' reasons for purchasing.

VALS was developed by SRI International in California, a market research and consulting firm. The system uses 39 psychological and demographic variables to divide adults into groups. The VALS model consists of eight main categories, each of which is based on income and personality characteristics (see Figure 6.5). The eight categories include:

1. **Innovators.** Innovators have high income levels, self-esteem, and sophistication. They look for expression of taste, individuality, and showing of independence when purchasing products.
2. **Thinkers.** These people are mature, satisfied, and comfortable. Well informed and practical, they look for function and durability when purchasing goods.
3. **Achievers.** Achievers are goal oriented and committed to family. They are interested in time-saving products and prestige products.
4. **Experiencers.** Experiencers are young, prefer self-expression, and are enthusiastic. They spend a lot of money on fashion and like having "cool stuff."
5. **Believers.** Believers follow routine and make purchases on the basis of ideals. They are loyal consumers who prefer to stay with the same product or brand.
6. **Strivers.** Strivers are concerned about the opinion of others. They favor stylish products and are motivated by achievement. They view shopping as a social activity.
7. **Makers.** Makers prefer value to luxury and value self-sufficiency. They tend to be suspicious of new ideas.
8. **Survivors.** Survivors are the lowest on the income scale. They value familiar products and prefer to purchase at discounts or sales.

The VALS model can be used in several ways. For example, if Coach identified its customers as strivers, it would market its handbags in a specific manner. Strivers care about the opinion of others; thus the company may use an advertisement suggesting that a woman will gain approval from others when she carries a Coach bag. However, if Coach had identified its customers as thinkers, it might focus on the high quality and workmanship of the handbag.

Most Resources

ACTUALIZERS

Enjoy the "finer things"
Receptive to new products,
technologies, distribution.
Skeptical of advertising.
Frequent readers of wide
variety of publications.
Light TV viewers.

Principle Oriented   **Status Oriented**   **Action Oriented**

FULFILLEDS

Little interest in image
or prestige.
Above-average consumers of
products for the home.
Like educational and public
affairs programming.
Read widely
and often.

ACHIEVERS

Attracted to
premium products.
Prime target for
variety of products.
Average TV watchers,
read business, news,
and self-help
publications.

EXPERIENCERS

Follow fashion and fad.
Spend much of disposable
income on socializing.
Buy on impulse.
Attend to advertising.
Listen to rock music.

BELIEVERS

Buy American.
Slow to change habits.
Look for bargains.
Watch TV more than average.
Read retirement, home and
garden, and
general-interest
magazines.

STRIVERS

Image conscious.
Limited discretionary
incomes, but carry credit
balances.
Spend on clothing
and personal-care
products.
Prefer TV to
reading.

MAKERS

Shop for comfort,
durability, value.
Unimpressed by luxuries.
Buy the basics, listen to radio.
Read auto, home
mechanics, fishing,
outdoor
magazines.

STRUGGLERS

Brand loyal.
Use coupons and watch
for sales.
Trust advertising.
Watch TV often.
Read tabloids and
women's
magazines.

Least Resources

Created by SRI Business Intelligence.

:: PRODUCT PARAMETERS ::

Marketers can also segment markets on the basis of product parameters, including benefits sought, frequency of use, and type of product use. When segmenting by **benefits sought,** marketers will target those customers who hope to gain a specific benefit from using the product. For example, benefits sought in exercise clothing might be that they are casual and inexpensive. New Balance understands that a primary benefit sought for walking shoes is comfort, so the company markets its shoes as being comfortable. Easy to wash and care for might be another benefit sought.

Much clothing is ultimately used for the same purpose, but the characteristics or the reasons for purchasing the products are different. Knowing this, a marketer can change its advertising and message to consumers. For example, if a fashion marketer knows a customer purchases its product for comfort, it will likely want to create advertisements that highlight the comfort that the product provides.

Frequency of use is another way to segment a market. It refers to how often the customer buys the product. For example, a man who wears jeans to work on a daily basis will likely purchase and wear jeans more often than someone who must dress up during the week. In other words, the frequency of use is much higher for the man who goes to work in jeans than for the man who doesn't.

Finally, **type of product use** can be important as well. This refers to the way the consumer will actually use the product. For example, two customers may both be looking for workout gear, but one may wear it to her yoga class, whereas the other may use it to go running. These differences of use are important to marketers when deciding how to advertise to the customer.

:: COHORT SEGMENTATION ::

Yet another way to segment markets is through generational marketing, sometimes called **cohort segmentation.** The idea behind generational marketing or cohort segmentation is that people who have shared the experience of a historical event, such as the current war in Iraq, during their formative years are somehow bound together and will tend to buy in a similar way. For example, people who grew up during World War II tend to purchase very conservatively and consider price to be a big factor.

There are five main generational segments.

Matures The **matures** were born before 1944. This group experienced World War II, and many fought in the Vietnam War. The matures are also called the *gray market.*

The fashion industry has traditionally had difficulty reaching this market. Because of aging bodies, clothing fits the mature generation differently. However, it would be incorrect to assume that as people age, they are no longer interested in fashion. In fact, this may be the opposite. This generation spends more than $60 billion per year and is willing to spend more on clothing that fits well, is easy to care for, and is styled to deemphasize the aging body. As people live longer, healthier, active lives, the demand for stylish clothing will grow in this market segment.

Baby boomers **Baby boomers** are those born between 1945 and 1965. This cohort, which resulted from the soldiers returning from World War II and having children, is extremely large in numbers as well as diverse. Many marketers will further segment this cohort into "younger" and "older" boomers, in the belief that the two groups have had different experiences.

For the fashion industry, this market is increasingly important, as the amount of discretionary income, discussed in Chapter 5, and the sheer size of this generation contribute to massive spending power. Discretionary income is the income left after paying bills and buying food. Some might call it fun money. For example, this generation spends $35 billion every year on their grandchildren! Thus, besides marketing personal clothing to this generation, those in the fashion industry should recognize boomers as a huge market for children's items, due to purchases for grandchildren.

Many retailers are cashing in on the spending power of this generation. Baby boomers care about fashion, yet as their bodies age, they require different kinds of fashion items. Glasses, for example, have become more trendy to meet the needs of this generation.

Generation X
Generation X is made up of those born between 1965 and 1976. This generation is small compared to the baby boomers, and in earlier years many characterized it as being "lazy." However, the dot-com boom in the late 1990s was in large part driven by Gen Xers, which proved they were willing to work hard, as long as it was on their own terms.

Gen Xers and their choices of fashion have always confused fashion marketers. During their teenage years, many in this cohort had body piercings and tried to look different from their peers. Marketers had a hard time trying to market to a generation that did not want to look like one another. Gen Xers looks for fashion items they can put together in an effort to create unique styles.

Because most in this cohort are now in the workplace, they have the same needs for work clothing as older generations. However, marketing to them still proves to be difficult. One reason is the focus that was put on the baby-boom generation while Generation X was growing up; as a result, they were not marketed to as heavily and do not take as well to advertising.

Generation Y
Generation Y is larger in numbers than Generation X. This generation was born between the years 1977 and 1994. Most of these people have baby-boomer parents. This is the first generation in history to not know a world without computers and the Internet, which has changed the way they shop. Gen Yers spend more than $1.8 billion a year in online stores.

More so than Generation X, Generation Y is concerned about fitting in and conformity. However, rebellion against what society views as "normal" is still a teenage trait. This makes it difficult for this generation, as they are pulled in two different ways. Still teenagers or young adults, many of these people are trying to "find themselves." This is the perfect time for retailers to sell to this age group and meet their needs throughout their lifetime.

People in this generation, much like Gen Xers, are Internet savvy and use it to find information on products or actually purchase products online. This has contributed to the demand for custom-fit clothing and shoes. For example, www.nike.com allows customers to mix 16 different color combinations of shoes to create their own unique shoes. As this generation ages, the expectations for retailers to offer custom clothing and other Internet-based services will grow. More will be covered about Internet shopping in Chapter 9.

Tweens
People younger than Generation Y, are considered **tweens,** defined as those between the ages of 8 and 12. Tweens of today are a category, but have not yet been given a name, such as Generation X.

A tween plays on her cell phone.

Tweens make up a large part of the market. At this age, kids are developing their sense of identity, especially through the clothing they wear. They are also anxious to cultivate an older self-image. Naomi Klein, author of *No Logo,* believes kids are willing to pay top dollar to be cool. For the most part, the parents are paying the high prices for brand-name clothing and shoes. However, thanks to birthday money, baby-sitting money, and generous grandparents, tweens have more of their own money to spend on cool, popular items. Besides spending money directly on fashion products, this age group has significant influence on the spending patterns of the family. What kinds of cereal to buy and where to take vacations are the types of decisions tweens help make.

The Limited Too is an example of a retailer that caters specifically to the tween market. The clothing is more adult than traditional clothing for this age group. Other retailers, such as Abercrombie Kid, also cater to this market. These retailers hope that making their clothing available to kids at a young age will create brand-loyal customers who, as they age, will eventually shop at Express, The Limited, and Abercrombie and Fitch.

:: FAMILY LIFE CYCLE ::

Focusing on the **family life cycle** is another way marketers can segment markets. This is the idea that a consumer's age does not matter as much as his or her family situation. Using this type of segmentation, marketers focus on a consumer's phase of life, for instance, the number of children the person has and the martial status of that individual. Such a life-cycle focus can be valuable to a marketer. For example, a man 60 years old with a six-year-old child is going to buy similar items as a man who is 32 with a child of six. Likewise, a divorced woman may buy similar items as a women in her 20s who has not yet been married.

Another consideration in family life cycle is **empty nesters** versus **full nesters.** Empty nesters have children who are grown and out on their own. Full nesters have children living at home. This can greatly influence the types of products purchased and also the money available for purchases.

Figure 6.6 diagrams the family life cycle.

:: GEOGRAPHICAL SEGMENTATION ::

Geographical segmentation is based on the idea that people who live in the same part of the country will want similar products, which will differ from those living in another area. Take Seattle, Washington, and Miami, Florida, for example. People who purchase in these two areas have different needs in clothing because of the different local weather patterns. In Seattle, a miniskirt may be fine for summer but not as popular in winter. However, in Miami, a miniskirt may be popular all year around. Hawaiian print shirts in Hawaii or 10-gallon hats in Texas are other examples of clothing unique to an individual area. Or geographical segmentation can focus on more general characteristics of a region. For instance, people in smaller towns may be more conservative in their dress than those in large cities.

Most marketers will use several ways to segment their markets, and geography is yet another tool to help them do so.

6.6 THE FAMILY LIFE CYCLE

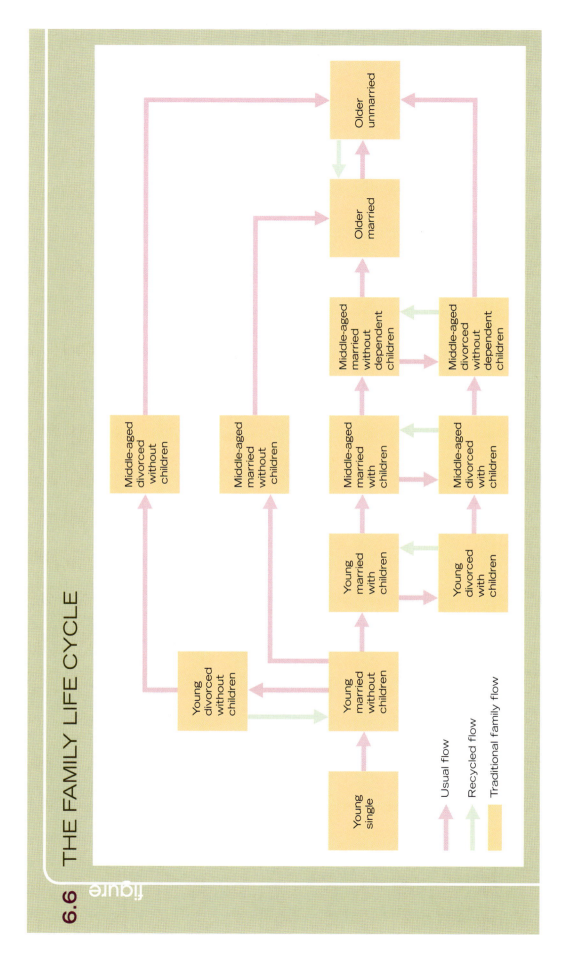

To Be about to Be, Generation Y

When Michael Piercey turned 21 last November, he celebrated the milestone like those before him have done for generations: He got mildly drunk. A part-time college student and radio engineer from Kensington, Maryland, Piercey gathered a handful of friends, ordered in pizza and Kevin Smith videos, and then drank too much booze—mostly shots of Jack Daniels chased with Coca-Cola. By midnight, he was loudly declaring his goal of becoming a radio talk-show host and toasting his newfound status as an adult.

"It's great to be able to legally do anything 24/7," says Piercey, running his fingers through a scraggly brown beard and ponytail. "I have a lot dreams and expectations."

Piercey isn't the only one with big hopes for his future. Today's businesses are eagerly courting the approximately 4 million Americans turning 21 this year as the vanguard of Generation Y, a group whose population is almost the same as the baby boomers and is expected to be every bit as powerful as a shaper of business markets. While demographers debate its size—many define Gen Yers as those 72 million Americans born between 1977 and 1994—there's little dispute about Y's spending power: an estimated $187 billion annually, destined for industries ranging from apparel to wireless tech.

Take that $187 billion, factor in the arc of career growth, household and family formation, and multiply by about another 53 years in life expectancy and you're in the $10 trillion range in consumer spending over the life span of today's 21-year-olds. The generation of echo boomers—which put Happy Meals, Lunchables, Sonic the Hedgehog, and Nickelodeon's Rugrats on the map as billion-dollar franchises—is crossing over from MTV's *The Real World* into the real world. Now that more than 20 percent of the cohort (a group with similar characteristics, such as age) has reached the age of majority, what should we make of a generation peering into adulthood whose sensibilities were shaped by years of calm followed by days like Columbine and September 11, by years of economic exuberance followed by months and months of recession, and by years of world peace followed by weeks and weeks of wars whose end is nowhere in sight?

Flash back to about 1971, when the same number (16 million or so) and percentage (about 20 percent) of baby boomers had reached their twenty-first birthday. Business, politics, careers, and culture would never be the same as young boomers emerged from a cloud of idealism to assume the responsibilities, the privileges, and the powers of adulthood.

That's where we are now with Gen Y's About-To-Be's. The attitudes of youth have begun evolving into the values that come with being a grown-up. History and culture's defining moments—Columbine, 9/11, the impeachment of President Clinton, the Dot Bust—have helped forge a sensibility that will last a lifetime in shaping expectations and entitlement, in determining what one will give to and take from society, work, one's community, etc.

As they start forming their own households, 21-year-olds will soon be shopping for their first cars, homes, and mutual funds. They'll begin developing brand loyalties that could last a lifetime. But what sounds like a no-lose scenario for marketers, however, has many of them worried. This is the most unpredictable, advertising-saturated, and marketing-skeptical group of adults America has ever seen.

Like many of his peers, Michael Piercey ignores traditional media and advertising channels. He prefers to play video games and watch DVDs than to sit down for scheduled TV shows. He'd rather read comic books than subscribe to a newspaper or magazine. And though he still crashes at his parents' house, he's more at home in a virtual world, spending six hours a day online, surfing websites of cartoon art and instant messaging his friends. "I guess I have 200 people on my buddy list," Piercey says. "One of my best friends is a guy from Milwaukee who I've never met. We both like comics."

You might think young Piercey is a consumer aberration (venturing from the normal), but marketers recognize that he looks more and more like the future. Today's 21-year-olds serve as the nation's key trendsetters, whose passion for MP3 players, camera phones, and instant messaging is transforming popular culture. More than half of all 21-year-olds still live at home, so they still hold sway over their teenage brothers' and sisters' product preferences. These echo boomers also influence the tastes of their baby boomer parents, creating such a potentially powerful phenomenon that marketers are calling it the "Boom-Boom" effect.

Companies that ignore the tastes of today's 21-year-olds do so at their peril. If a brand missed the 21-year-olds of Gen X, it could survive because that audience was relatively small. Not so with Gen Y. These newly minted adults are the bellwether (a leader of future trends) of what the nation's consumers will soon be doing, buying, and thinking. And that's what keeps marketers up at night.

As automakers have already discovered, 21-year-olds are tough to please. When Honda tried to appeal to them with its Element, a boxy vehicle that company officials described as a "dorm room on wheels," young drivers yawned. Instead, boomers latched onto the ads, which showed sexy college kids partying near the car at a beach; the average age of the Element driver is 42. The same thing happened when Chrysler unveiled its hearse-like PT Cruiser. Though the target market was the young, so many boomer moms and dads were reminded of the hot rods of their youth that there were waiting lists at dealerships. Only 4 percent of the PT Cruiser's buyers are under 25.

Toyota thought it had a better idea with Scion, its first new nameplate in 14 years. The car, introduced this spring, was for young shoppers who wouldn't want to be caught dead in their father's Camry, America's best-selling car.

Recognizing the power of the 21-year-old consumer in the marketplace, Toyota declared its audience for Scions to be thirtysomethings, although it launched an advertising campaign targeting 21-year-olds—"because they have more influence on the 30-year-olds," says James Farley, vice president of Scion. "We're going after a mind-set, the trendsetter within that group, for the heavy lifting." That meant a stealth marketing campaign: displaying the car outside coffee shops and raves, and offering test drives to the writers at hip-hop magazines like *Yellow Rat Bastard*. But early reviews of the car have been mixed—one called it "a cross between a skateboard and a toaster oven"—and even Farley admits that it's an uphill climb to move 21-year-old consumers who spend more time in the virtual world than the real one. "We started a whole new company just for Gen Yers," he says. "But we're going to have to be fluid."

In the tricky business of selling the trappings of adulthood to this particular set, no one is ready to claim victory.

Inside the Head of a 21-Year-Old

Born in 1982, today's Gen Yers are barely old enough to remember when Ronald Reagan was president. Yet in their lifetimes, American society has changed dramatically.

Immigration has made the country much more diverse: one in three 21-year-olds are not Caucasian. Family structures have also changed: one in four 21-year olds were raised by a single parent; three in four have working mothers. And while their parents are still prone to view the Internet and mobile phones as novelties, 21-year-olds have literally grown up with them and incorporated them into every aspect of their lives. "They're more sophisticated than their parents' generation," says Edward Winter, founder of Knoxville-based consulting firm U30 Group, which specializes in the under-30 market. "Boomers like to talk about being tolerant of racial diversity, but 21-year-olds live it." Winter, now the CEO of U30 owner Tracy Locke Partnership, observes that a common denominator among these ethnically diverse 21-year-olds is their urban sensibility, reflecting the influences of hip-hop and singers like Eminem and J. Lo. He recalls one focus group he conducted in which twentysomethings dismissed their ethnic heritage: "One young man said, 'My father describes himself as a fourth-generation Jamaican. I think of myself as a first-generation urban.'" ✽

Source: Written by Michael J. Weiss, American Demographics, September 1, 2003. Reprinted with permission.

›› QUESTIONS

1. Discuss how you think family structure has impacted the marketing of fashion products.

2. Discuss the events in this article, believed to have impacted Generation Y. How do you think the events have affected this generation and their buying habits?

3. Why do marketers call "selling adulthood to this set" tricky?

>> researching market segments

In order to effectively segment markets, most fashionistas will need to perform research to gather data on the customer. There are two main types of research in which marketers are interested: primary and secondary. Using these two types of research, the marketer can decide on market segments and also develop the actual product to meet the needs of the customer. For example, in the mid 1990s Express found that it was losing many of its core customers. Through research, it discovered that many customers thought that the store's merchandise was becoming too trendy and that it no longer provided the basics they wanted, such as T-shirts, dress pants, and jeans. As a result, the company, while still providing trendy merchandise, brought back some of its basics. Without research, Express would not have known this and likely would have lost money or even gone out of business.

:: PRIMARY RESEARCH ::

The first type is **primary research.** Primary research can be used in trend forecasting as well as marketing. It is research that a company actually performs itself; thus, it results in original information. However, primary research can be an expensive and time-consuming undertaking. There are many kinds of primary research that can be performed.

- **Focus groups.** In this method, 8 to 10 people together in a room are asked about their likes and dislikes in regard to products, advertisements, and so forth.
- **Mall intercept surveys.** These are surveys taken within a mall and typically include a variety of questions for the participant to answer.
- **Mail surveys.** These are surveys actually mailed out to people, who are requested to mail them back once completed. A variation of these are Internet surveys, which can be performed with much less expense because there are no mailing costs.
- **Telephone surveys.** In this type of research, people are called at home and asked questions similar to those used in mail surveys. However, there is extensive new legislation regarding telephone surveys and telephone sales, such as the Do Not Call Registry.

The challenge of primary research is the expense. It can cost from $5,000 to $25,000 for a survey and even more if an outside company provides this service. However, the advantages often outweigh the costs, because primary research can result in company-specific information.

Test marketing of products, to see if consumers will like them, is also a form of primary research.

:: SECONDARY RESEARCH ::

Secondary research is research not performed specifically for the company using it. It is data that have already been gathered by someone else. Examples of secondary research include information available in Census Bureau reports, magazines, government reports, Internet articles, trade journals, and newspapers. Although less expensive than primary research, secondary research is usually not as focused for the particular organization.

Most companies will use a variety of research, perhaps starting by gathering information from secondary research and then using focus groups, surveys, or some other form of primary research to gather more specific data.

>> conclusion •

Consumer behavior is a very important topic in fashion. If a fashionista can understand how and why consumers behave, he or she can develop products that will better suit consumer needs. In addition, this type of information can assist the marketer in developing targeted advertising and marketing campaigns. Of course, the better products a retailer can offer and marketing it can do, the more sales and profit it will enjoy. This chapter summarized the basics to understanding the customer. The next chapter will describe how to build a fashion marketing campaign.

TERMS TO KNOW ::

Consumer behavior
Habitual problem solving
Limited problem solving
Extended problem solving
Convenience product
Shopping good
Specialty good
Problem recognition
Information search
Evoked set
Evaluation of alternatives
Purchase decision
Postpurchase evaluation
Cognitive dissonance
Rational buying

Emotional buying
Patronage buying
Reference group
Membership group
Aspiration group
Disassociate group
Maslow's hierarchy of needs
Market segmentation
Homogeneous
Demographics
Psychographics
VALS
Benefits sought
Frequency of use
Type of product use

Cohort segmentation
Matures
Baby boomers
Generation X
Generation Y
Tween
Family life cycle
Empty nester
Full nester
Primary research
Focus groups
Mall intercept surveys
Telephone surveys
Mail surveys
Secondary research

CONCEPTS TO KNOW ::

1. Steps in the consumer buying process.
2. Types of problem solving.
3. The three buying motivations.
4. The types of products.
5. Levels of Maslow's hierarchy and how they relate to fashion.
6. The various ways to segment markets.
7. Advantages and disadvantages of primary and secondary research.

CHAPTER QUESTIONS ::

1. How might a fashion merchandiser use its understanding of the consumer buying process? Discuss at least two ways.
2. What are the three types of products? How does this relate to the consumer buying process?
3. Why is market segmentation important?
4. Discuss the idea of segmenting according to cohorts. How are each of the five cohort groups different? The same?
5. How might a marketer use generations as a tool to segment its market? Do you think this is an effective way of segmentation?

6. What are the differences between primary and secondary research? What are some ways you could perform each type of research?

7. Do you take mall intercept or telephone surveys? Why or why not? What would it take for you to participate in surveys?

8. How do you define *lifestyle*? What are some examples of lifestyles that might be helpful for marketers to know?

9. Why would retailers want to minimize cognitive dissonance?

CHAPTER PROJECTS AND DISCUSSION ::

1. Choose an advertisement for a fashion product that might represent each level on Maslow's hierarchy of needs.

2. Discuss your most recent fashion purchase and its relation to the consumer buying process.

3. In small groups, identify products you would consider to be habitual, limited, and extended problem solving. Are they the same for your group members?

4. In small groups, make up three different market segments using demographics, lifestyle, and benefits sought. How might you market differently to each of these groups?

5. Visit the SRI website (www.sric-bi.com/VALS/presurvey.shtml) and find out your VALS type. Discuss why or why not you think this is the correct category for you.

FOR FURTHER READING ::

www.adage.com/section.cms?sectionId=195
http://marketingtoday.com
www.consumerpsychologist.com

marketing
of fashion products

After reading this chapter, you should be able to:

1 • Name and describe each of the four Ps in marketing.

2 • Describe considerations and strategies for using the four Ps when marketing fashion products.

3 • Understand the five areas of the promotional mix: advertising, direct marketing, personal selling, pubic relations, and sales promotion.

4 • Explain how each promotional mix tool might be useful to a particular product line.

bebe

m arketing is perhaps one of the most interesting topics in fashion. *Marketing,* simply defined, means selling products to consumers, but that definition does not do the word justice. Marketing is a complicated yet exciting process that entails understanding customers, making sure products meet their needs, and designing exciting promotional techniques that will drive customers to the store.

This chapter covers the common marketing theory based on what are called the four Ps. Although the four Ps are typically examined in general terms as part of a marketing class, fashion specific examples will be given here. The four Ps are product, price, place, and promotion. After discussing the four Ps, the chapter will address five different ways fashion products can be promoted, called the *promotional mix.* (See Figure 7.1.)

>> the four Ps of marketing fashion products

The four Ps are the components used to make sure a product is successful. The four Ps are sometimes called the **marketing mix.** As discussed in Chapter 6, it is imperative for a fashion marketer to first learn about its customers and then to segment those customers into target markets. Once that has been accomplished, the marketer can focus on the four Ps. Very few fashion marketers get lucky with a product. If a product sells well, it is because the proper research was performed to determine the best mix of the four Ps. The **four Ps** consist of **product, price, place,** and **promotion.** A marketer must have all of the four Ps correct in order to make the product or product line

"The four Ps consist of product, price, place, and promotion. A marketer must have all of the four Ps correct in order to make the product or product line successful."

successful. Not having the correct mix of product, price, place, and promotion will result in lost income for the retailer.

An example of how the four Ps intermingle in fashion can be illustrated with Macy's. Assume that Macy's spends $50,000 on a sale scheduled for this Thursday (promotion), orders extra goods for the sale (product), places sale prices on garments (price), and holds the sale in all of its locations (place). If Macy's puts too high of a price on items to be included in the sale—that is, an incorrect determination of the price "P"—the sale might be unsuccessful. If it orders unpopular products for the sale, again, the sale may not be successful, due to an incorrect product "P." Or the price, place, and product may be correct, but not enough promotion was performed for the sale, resulting in low customer turnout and, again, an unsuccessful sale.

A smaller, one-store retailer might experience an unsuccessful marketing mix if it prices goods too high for its target customers to afford. The retailer may have great promotion, a great location, and attractive products, but if the price is too high, it will likely be unsuccessful. Similarly, the same retailer may have the right location, price, and product, but without proper promotion it will likely be unsuccessful.

7.1 THE MARKETING SHOEBOX

figure

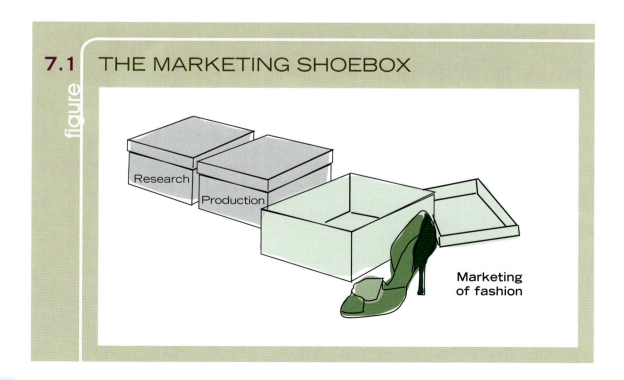

Research

Production

Marketing of fashion

Figure 7.2 illustrates how the four Ps fit into the marketing process.

>> product

The product is the actual item the customer is buying, along with several other components. A product can be a physical good, such as a sweater, or a service, such as dry cleaning. One characteristic of a product is the **variety** available to the customer. This could mean, for example, the number of colors a particular skirt comes in, or the size range available. A product also includes **features.** For example, the garment may be waterproof, or it might have a zipper. Related to features is the **design** of a product. Color, size, and dimensions of a product are included in design. Packaging, which includes the tags on the garment, could also be considered part of the design, because tags are ultimately part of the product. Good examples of well-known packages for fashion products are the famous little turquoise ring box from Tiffany's or the pink and white striped bag from Victoria's Secret.

Good research and understanding about trends and customers, as discussed in Chapters 5 and 6, will help ensure that the product is one that customers want. The process of determining the right product is where a designer, merchandiser, and marketer might work together.

Product planning is one of the most important tasks in merchandising and retailing. **Product assortment** refers to the number of different products a store carries. Product assortment can also be called the *product mix*. If a retailer carries many different types of clothing, from many different brands, it is said to have a **wide** product assortment. If a store only carries a few brands, or only one type of item, it has a **narrow** product assortment. For example, The Sock Shop has a narrow assortment; it carries only socks. Target has a wide assortment, because it carries many categories of products. In large part, the product assortment will determine a customer's expectations of the store.

In product planning, it is also imperative to consider the depth and breadth of the product assortment. The **depth** of the product assortment refers to the number of versions of each product offered. For example, The Gap offers many styles and types of jeans, representing a wide depth. The **breadth** refers to the number of product lines offered. Macy's, for example, offers a wide breadth, because it offers products from many designers.

7.2 figure **THE MARKETING PROCESS**

> Market research
>
> ↓
>
> Deciding on a market segment
>
> ↓
>
> Development of the Four P's
> Product
> Price
> Place
> Promotion
>
> ↓
>
> Development of a promotional mix
> Advertising
> Sales promotion
> Direct marketing
> Public relations
> Personal selling

>> price

A price can be defined as the amount of money asked for in exchange for something else. There are two types of price related to most products. The **wholesale price** is the price paid to the vendor; the **retail price** is the actual price the customer pays. Before setting a price, however, a retailer must consider a variety of factors. After discussing these price considerations in the following section, we will describe pricing strategies, that is, actual methods by which retail prices are set.

:: PRICE CONSIDERATIONS ::

A fashion designer or merchandiser does not simply settle on a price he or she thinks is good. When pricing products, several things are important to consider. These considerations can be external factors and internal factors. External factors are those generally out of the control of the retailer. Internal factors are those a retailer can control. Figure 7.3 shows the primary considerations in price setting.

The first external factor to consider is the **market demand** for the product. The market demand refers to the popularity of the product. If the product is popular, the retailer will likely be able to charge a higher price for it. **Competition** is another major external consideration. If two competing department stores are selling the same brand of clothing, for example, Ralph Lauren Polo shirts, they must price them similarly. For example, if one store charges $48 for a Polo shirt, while a store across the mall charges $60, it is highly unlikely the more expensive store will sell many of those shirts. In other words, when setting prices, it is imperative to know what the competing stores are charging. Another external factor to consider when setting a price is the strength of the **economy.** If the economy is doing well, it might be reasonable to charge a higher price, because consumers could likely afford it.

Some internal factors to consider in price setting include the wholesale cost of the product, the cost of marketing the product, and how a company wants to position the product.

Product **positioning** refers to how the retailer wants its customers to view the product. So, in setting prices, a successful retailer will consider the perception that it wants its customers to have of the product, or of the store itself, along with the factors mentioned above; the positioning consideration, then, goes hand in hand with external considerations. For example, Wal-Mart has positioned itself as having the lowest prices; in setting prices for the products it sells, the store weighs how factors like economy and competition affect its goal of setting the lowest prices.

7.3 CONSIDERATIONS IN PRICE SETTING

figure

Positioning

Cost considerations

Price Considerations

Economy

Market demand

Competition

Finally, there are cost considerations when setting the price of a product. These can include the actual cost for the material, labor, and shipping of the product.

Another consideration is whether or not to use **value pricing,** which requires an approach opposite to basing prices on costs. In value pricing, the company will assess the value, both tangible and intangible, of the product to the customer and price it accordingly. This is a good strategy for higher-end products, such as haute couture fashions or Rolex watches. Rolex, for instance, knows there is a perceived value to owning one of its expensive watches; so it calculates a dollar value of the desire to own the particular watch. Of course, a company selling high-end watches is unlikely to sell as many watches as, say, Timex would, which would be a consideration if choosing this strategy. An original Dior dress may be priced at $25,000, because the company knows this is the value to the customer. Also, as one might expect, the quality of the materials and labor are likely better than a shirt purchased at Wal-Mart. However, marketers using a value-based pricing strategy will know what the **intrinsic** (emotional, nontangible) **value** is to their customers. If the retailer wants to create the perception that a product is a high-status item, it may decide to sell it at a higher price. For example, because of the high value and high status of a Louis Vuitton bag, a retailer will be able to charge more. This is called **prestige pricing.**

Another pricing option is **product-line pricing.** Most fashion retailers have more than one offering of a particular type of product. As discussed in Chapter 2, to meet the needs of more consumers, many retailers will have product lines priced at different points. Product-line pricing is when there are multiple offerings of similar items, but each has different features. Nordstrom is a good example, although most retailers use some variation of this type of pricing. Nordstrom's suit department might offer a suit for $300, one for $900, and one for $1,900. By offering this assortment, the store is able to meet the needs of each customer. When using this pricing strategy, it is important to insure that customers understand the difference in quality of products at the various price points. This is where the personal selling part of the promotional mix comes in to play.

Another consideration in pricing is the use of **psychological pricing.** One such tactic is called a **twofer.** This is the pricing practice of offering a slightly lower price if the customer purchases more of the item. For example, Bloomingdale's might normally sell a particular brand of tights for $8 each. The customer can buy two pairs for $14, rather than the $16 it would cost to buy two at regular price. The advantage to using this pricing strategy is that consumers will tend to buy more if they believe they are getting a deal. Another type of psychological pricing is **multiple pricing.** This is where a product is bundled, say in threes or fours, enabling the company to charge more. Nike tube socks are normally priced this way; rather than coming in single packs, they are offered in packs of three.

Some other considerations in pricing include reference prices, promotional pricing, and geographical pricing. A **reference price** refers to the general price a customer may have in mind when buying an item. A man going to a store with the intention of buying new T-shirts may have a reference price of $15 for each. He would evaluate all of the T-shirts he looks at with this $15 price in mind.

Retailers use **promotional pricing** when products go on sale. The pricing may be for a special one-day sale, or it can be a permanent markdown. The danger of having too many sales is that consumers get conditioned to never having to pay the "list" price; instead, they wait for the sale to buy products. Related to promotional pricing is the idea of a loss leader. A **loss leader** is a heavily discounted product on which companies do not expect to make a profit; rather they use such items to entice people to the store. Old Navy has its "featured item" every week, offered at a very low price. The strategy is that people will come in to the store to purchase the product (the loss leader) but also buy additional items at the same time.

Geographical pricing has two components: pricing differently based on physical location, and pricing for shipping products purchased through the Internet or catalogs. When a merchandiser considers prices based on geographical location, it generally means that it knows a product will sell better in, say, New York than it will in Chicago. As a result, the higher prices will reflect the higher demand in New York. Some retailers offer flat-rate shipping, meaning that no matter where a customer lives, shipping will be the same. This type of pricing is called **uniform delivered pricing.**

Promotional pricing can be a special sale or permanent markdowns.

Sometimes, companies use loss leaders to drive more customers into the store.

The last consideration in pricing involve **markdowns.** Chapter 9 will discuss how to manage markdowns. A markdown is a reduction of price below the original level. There are five main reasons for markdowns:

1. To price for a special sale, such as a "half yearly sale."
2. To stimulate customer traffic.
3. To move out-of-season or obsolete merchandise.
4. To clear out slow selling goods.
5. To sell damaged or returned goods that cannot be given back to vendors.

:: PRICING STRATEGIES ::

When opening a new store, or introducing a new product, there are two broad strategies a company can use: price skimming or penetration pricing. **In price skimming,** the goal of the company is to maximize profits on a new product by attracting *early adopters,* those people who are willing to pay top dollar to be the first to own a particular item. The goal involves charging a higher price at first and then gradually lowering the price over time. This type of strategy is designed to gain higher profit margins at first but then gradually price the product so the mass public can afford it. It is often used for technology-related products, but it is also common for fashion products. When UGG boots first came out, they were very expensive, reflecting a skimming pricing strategy. As they gradually became more popular, the price was reduced, and more brands entered the market.

A second type of strategy that can be used is **penetration pricing.** This strategy, in some ways, is opposite of price skimming. This is where a retailer will mark a product very low in the hope of selling more of it and thus earning more profits through selling large quantities. This strategy is used to motivate customers to try something new. Old Navy uses this strategy on a weekly basis. Its "item of the week," maybe a T-shirt, sweater, or other seasonal item, is priced unusually low in an attempt to attract customers into the store.

After choosing to use price skimming or penetration pricing, the retailer will then decide on a specific pricing strategy. One strategy that many retailers use is **cost-based pricing.** With this strategy, a company might have a policy of marketing all shirts 50 percent above cost, all skirts 75 percent above, and so on. Of course, before the company determines these markup percentages, it must calculate its budgeted marketing costs and consider other factors as well. For example, if the retailer marked up all shirts 50 percent, one that it purchased at wholesale for $10 would be priced at $15 retail. A skirt that costs $20 would be marked up to $35, using the retailer's standard markup of 75 percent. Another store may choose to double the wholesale price (a markup of 100 percent). A pair of jeans bought at $10 then would cost the customer $20.

Keystoning is another type of pricing strategy. In keystoning, a designer would add up the cost of all the raw materials required to manufacture the garment. These might include trimming, fabric, and labor. Then, the designer might double this price and round it to the nearest dollar, if desired. For example, if buttons cost $.50, fabric costs $10, and labor costs $10, the retail price would be $40.50, or $41 if rounded up.

Another strategy often used in retail is **line-item pricing,** also called **odd pricing.** Odd pricing is a type of psychological pricing

Stores may use hangtags to indicate markdowns.

that involves setting prices that are less than round numbers, for example, $19.50 or $19.99, rather than an even $20.00. The theory is that, rather than rounding up, consumers ignore the cents digits. Odd pricing is also a consideration when using cost-based pricing.

Another strategy a retailer can use is **competitive pricing.** This is sometimes called *going-rate pricing.* In this type of pricing strategy, all companies will charge about the same price for an item. Gas stations are a perfect example of this. Gas stations across the street from each other will usually charge the exact same price. The challenge with this type of pricing is that costs of a product will vary from company to company. A large company, such as Wal-Mart, purchases thousands of items, thus it gets a lower cost for each individual product. This is called **economies of scale.** Lower cost per unit can also be achieved through mass production. Meanwhile, if a smaller store, which does not get to take advantage of economies of scale, is charging the same price for an item, it might lose money.

A final strategy in pricing is **frequency marketing.** This type of marketing rewards frequent customers. For example, Chico's offers a "passport" card, which is stamped when consumers purchase something, and the customer is rewarded with a discount. This is an excellent way to gain loyal customers.

>> place

The third P, place, refers to the number of retail locations, actual type of location, and the distribution procedure for getting the item to the proper location. There are three types of distribution strategies retailers use: intensive, selective, and exclusive. A strategy of **intensive distribution** is based on the idea that the more retail stores a product appears in, the better. The goal is to get the product in as many stores as possible, resulting in maximum exposure to customers. In a **selective distribution** strategy, the product may be found in only a few retail stores. An **exclusive strategy** means the designer will allow the clothing to appear in only one or two stores in a given region. The advantage to this strategy is to create a prestigious brand image for the product. Hanes uses an intensive strategy for its T-shirts, which can be found at Wal-Mart, Target, Sears, and higher-end department stores such as Macy's. An example of a selective strategy is the one used by Naturalizer shoes. The shoes are sold in Naturalizer stores, and a limited selection can be found at some department stores, such as Macy's. A retailer that uses an exclusive strategy is Tiffany's. Its products can be found only in Tiffany's stores, and there are not many of those locations.

:: TYPES OF RETAIL STORES ::

The types of retail stores include department stores, specialty stores, general merchandise chains, discount retailers, off-price discounters, factory outlets, and online retailers.

Department stores When most people think of the typical department store, they envision a multilevel building containing men's, women's, and children's apparel, along with perhaps a large variety of different household items, all available in a range of price levels. The assortment of goods at a department store has great depth and breadth, as discussed earlier in this chapter. Well-known department stores are Macy's, Nordstrom, and Saks Fifth Avenue. Within department stores, hard lines or soft lines might be part of the product mix. **Hard lines** include items like furniture and tools. **Soft lines** generally include clothing and bed linens.

Department stores have faced many challenges over the last few decades. Some of those challenges include:

- Lack of unique merchandise.
- Too many sales/promotions.
- Customer service issues.
- Mergers.
- Increased competition from smaller retailers.
- Increased competition from outlet stores.

An increase in competition has forced department stores to do something to differentiate themselves. As a result, many department stores offer services like special sales for credit card holders, personal shopping services, and high-end clothing, such as Chanel. A department store that sells mostly soft lines and offers a limited line (for example, clothing for a particular age range) is called a *department/specialty store*. Another way for department stores to drive business is through a concept called **lifestyle merchandising**. This is done in a store-within-a-store, sometimes called a *branded concept shop;* the customer can walk into a particular area of the store and purchase, for example, all Nautica or Kenneth Cole items. Although the approach has been popular for some time, some customers complain that merchandise, such as dresses, are spread throughout the store rather than located in one central place.

Another unique thing about department stores is their use of private labels and vendor labels. For example, one of Nordstrom's private labels is called Classiques Entier. It is developed and designed in house and sold only at Nordstrom. Besides this line of clothing, the retailer also buys clothing from vendors such as Liz Claiborne and XoXo.

Specialty store

A specialty store differs from a department store in that it has a more narrow focus of goods, from one category, maybe two. The store may focus only on young men's clothing or juniors' clothing. Good examples of specialty stores are The Limited and Express. Bed, Bath and Beyond is another, although due to its depth of merchandise, it approaches department store status. Within the category of specialty store is a type called a **single-line store,** which carries only one type of merchandise, such as The Sock Shop. Obviously, the sock shop only sells socks.

Specialty stores face many challenges. A constantly aging target market is one. A specialty store must decide if it is going to grow with its target market or if it is going to stay focused on a particular age range. For example, a 16-year-old girl might shop at Express; but at 22 she will look for a different type of merchandise and may feel that Express no longer meets her needs. The company must decide if it is going to change its focus to target such 22-year-old women or if it is going to continue to target younger women.

General merchandise chains

The major difference between department stores and general merchandise stores is that the latter tend to appeal to a broader range of target markets. A woman might never

Nordstrom, an example of a department store.

consider going to her local Sears store for clothing, but she might purchase a new television there. General merchandise stores generally use mid- to low-level pricing. For many years, JC Penney was considered this type of store, but through remodeling and selling more upscale merchandise, it is now considered a department store.

Discount retailers

A discount retailer tends to have a freestanding location with only one floor and minimal decor. Wal-Mart is an excellent example. It carries a wide range of merchandise, from hair products to digital cameras, all at low prices. Although Target started out as a discount retailer, it seems to be slowly moving into department store status, due in part to its creative designs in fashion and housewares.

Off-price discounters

T. J. Maxx, Marshalls, and Ross are examples of off-price stores. Their general strategy is to purchase merchandise at low prices, or merchandise that has not sold in department stores, and sell it deeply discounted in their own stores. Some of the merchandise sold by off-price discounters comes as a result of production overruns. Most of these stores use a pricing policy relevant to the amount of time a particular good has been on the floor. In other words, the longer an item has been there, the less expensive it will be. Some companies have introduced their own off-price stores in which they can sell their department store goods in a different location for lower prices; for example, Nordstrom has Nordstrom Rack stores. Using this strategy, an upscale retailer can protect its image by having less sale merchandise on the floor of its regular stores, while still selling the items in another location. This type of store offers little customer service and little in the way of decor. However, this strategy can be successful in that there is a large market of those who enjoy hunting through racks.

Factory outlets

Factory outlets were originally designed as places for manufacturers to sell samples, closeouts, seconds, and discontinued items. This type of store, similar to off-price discounters, does not offer much in the way of decor, but it is great for bargain hunters. Often, goods may have some sort of manufacturing flaw that prevents them from being sold in regular specialty stores. A retailer may also produce goods specifically for its outlet stores. For example, Jones New York produces garments specifically for its factory outlets, indicated by a label stating, "Jones New York, factory store."

Online stores

A large and growing retailing area is *e-tailing*, sometimes referred to as *e-commerce*. This is the practice of selling goods online, through a website. Most retailers that have a brick-and-mortar (traditional) store will also have a website for customers to shop. The advantages to having both is the visibility of the retailer and the ability to cater to markets in which there may not be a physical store. For example, Forever 21, a trendy junior store, does not have brick-and-mortar stores in Wyoming, but through its website, customers can find the products in which they are interested. Another example is www.polo.com. Ralph Lauren offers its Polo products online, but they can also be found in many retail locations. More about e-tailing and e-commerce will be covered in Chapter 9.

Gap's online store.

:: PHYSICAL DISTRIBUTION ::

Any retailer wants to receive the goods it orders as fast as possible. The process in which goods are actually ordered and shipped to stores is referred to as *physical distribution.* It relates to place, the third P, because physical distribution is the starting point for goods arriving at the right retail location. The faster the goods can be on the store shelves, the faster the stores can make money. There are four main considerations in physical distribution: order processing, managing inventory, warehousing (storing the goods), and the actual transportation of the goods (see Figure 7.4).

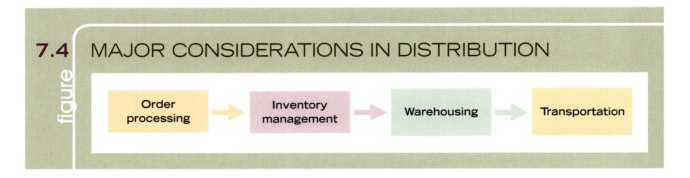

7.4 figure **MAJOR CONSIDERATIONS IN DISTRIBUTION**

Order processing → Inventory management → Warehousing → Transportation

Order processing Technology is a major factor in making this happen quickly. **Electronic data interchange (EDI)** is a system used to help companies communicate with each other. For example, using EDI, Cutter and Buck can place orders and communicate about new designs with its manufacturers in China. EDI technology can be expensive, due to the cost of maintaining the system and the fees required for a necessary telecommunications link called a **value-added network (VAN).** But new technologies are slowing replacing EDI, such as extensible markup language. **Extensible markup language** is a computer code that can be easily transferred from computer to computer, worldwide, via the Internet.

Using the EDI system and its extensible markup language, a designer in San Francisco can design an item, using technical sketches, and transfer these sketches to a manufacturer via the Internet. These systems allow manufacturers to have immediate information about the design they will be producing.

Inventory management Another type of technology is **vendor-managed inventory (VMI).** In a VMI system, the manufacturer is involved in replenishment of merchandise in a store. With this type of system, information is sent to the manufacturer when a particular size or color of an item is out of stock, or when stock is low. The vendor can then automatically send the goods needed. This type of system will generally involve extensive communication between the store and the manufacturer, such as cut-off dates for sending replenished merchandise. For example, JC Penney would not want particular items replenished if they are almost out of season. The primary benefit of such a system is ease of inventory management. The more inventory a store has on hand, the more space it takes from other merchandise that could be on the floor. As a result, a good inventory management system, such as this, is key. JC Penney, for example, knowing that it can replenish inventory quickly, has to carry less of a particular item, thereby leaving space for other items.

Another concern in physical distribution is how a retailer manages its inventory allocation if it has multiple stores. Some retailers allocate inventory according to store cluster, meaning that stores in a particular group each receives the same merchandise. Many retailers, like Gymboree, realize that to maximize store profits, they must individually allocate goods to each store. Special software that calls for several inputs such as demand, seasonality, order frequency, lead times, vendor minimums, and vendor discounts is able to statistically calculate what types of goods should go to each individual store.

Warehousing A trend in physical distribution is for retailers to have the manufacturers tag their merchandise and ship it directly to individual stores. Some retailers still have their own receiving areas, to which all goods are shipped; there they are then tagged and reshipped to individual stores. However, many retailers are finding that it is much more cost effective and timely to have manufacturers tag and ship merchandise directly to stores.

There are three main ways that merchandise can be received. The first is **centralized receiving.** Many larger stores and chain stores have centralized receiving departments. All of the goods are received in one area, allocated, tagged, and accounted for, then shipped to individual stores. The advantage to this type of system is better control of merchandise—in other words, each and every garment can be accounted for in one central location. The disadvantage is the time required to sort the goods and actually get them to the stores.

Another type of receiving system is **regional receiving.** The process involved is similar to that in centralized receiving, except there will be several receiving areas throughout the country rather than one. This type of system can reduce the travel time for goods. In addition, it can take advantage of special market needs. For example, a receiving department in Montana will likely stock more sweaters than one in Texas, simply because the weather is different.

A third type is **single-store receiving.** This is where each individual store receives goods directly from the manufacturer. The advantage to this is the speed of delivery, since goods come directly from manufacturer, but the store associates may not be as well trained in taking inventory of the goods when they arrive, unlike people in a central or a regional receiving department.

Transportation The cost and speed of delivery are major considerations when deciding how to transport goods. Since many manufacturers are located overseas, how to actually get the goods to the stores or warehouses is a big concern. Trucks account for more than 39 percent of all goods transported; railroads account for 38 percent; water carriers, 10 percent; and air carriers about 1 percent. Air is mostly used for small goods that can be easily packaged, but they tend to be costly items, such as jewelry. Water carriers can be slow, but they are cheap. Intermodal transportation, combining two or more modes, is common and can be efficient as well as cost effective. For example, the Port of Seattle accepts goods by water, but it has effective railroad systems to easily transport the goods directly off the ship onto railcars. Figure 7.5 details the advantages and disadvantages of the various types of transportation.

Transportation is a major part of marketing fashion products.

TYPES OF TRANSPORTATION

MODE	RELATIVE ADVANTAGES	RELATIVE DISADVANTAGES
Rail	• Full capability • Extensive routes • Low cost	• Some reliability, damage problems • Not always complete pickup and delivery • Sometimes slow
Truck	• Complete pickup and delivery • Extensive routes • Fairly fast	• Size and weight restrictions • Higher cost • More weather sensitive
Air	• Fast • Low damage • Frequent departures	• High cost • Limited capabilities
Pipeline	• Low cost • Very reliable • Frequent departures	• Limited routes (accessibility) • Slow
Water	• Low cost • Huge capacities	• Slow • Limited routes and schedules • More weather sensitive

>> promotion and the promotional mix

The final P in the marketing mix is promotion. Once a great product has been developed, a marketer needs to know how to promote it. This is done in five different ways: advertising, direct marketing, personal selling, public relations, and sales promotion.

:: ADVERTISING ::

Advertising is probably the type of promotion with which people are most familiar. Advertising is a one-way message to the customer; it is directed to the masses and is a method of marketing that requires payment. Advertising can be done in magazines and on television and radio. It can also include billboards and bus signs. Two terms often heard in advertising are *reach* and *frequency*. These are measurements marketers use in determining whether it is appropriate to place an ad in a particular place. **Reach** refers to the number of people who will see the ad. For example, the number of house-holds viewing the television program during which an ad will air is the reach. The **frequency** is the number of times the advertisement is shown or printed. Customers need to see things at least seven times before taking action to purchase or even consider purchasing a product. Thus, the frequency needs to be high enough to compel potential customers to take action. An example of good frequency is an advertisement to which the target market is exposed several times over the course of two weeks. The exposure could come from magazines they read, the television shows they watch, and the websites they surf. Again, the more times customers see an advertisement, the more likely they are to buy the product. Advertising, of course, can be very expensive, not necessarily because of the cost of one ad but, rather, the cost of good frequency.

There are four types of advertisements: selective demand, primary demand, institutional, and advocacy.

Selective demand advertisements create a demand for a particular product. For example, an Old Navy ad for its jeans creates a demand for a particular product.

Primary demand is created for the product in general, regardless of the brand name. For example, the Milk Commission might advertise to create demand for milk in general, but it not does not create a demand for a particular brand of milk. This type of advertising is rarely used in fashion.

Institutional advertisements are used to build the reputation of the company or the brand. For example, an advertisement for Coach may not focus on the features and benefits of the products; instead it might focus on the quality of the products Coach makes.

Advocacy advertisements are used by companies to promote a cause. In the mid 1990s, Benetton used death-row inmates in its advertisements to advocate against the death penalty. This type of advertising can be risky, because if a customer does not agree with the company's stand, he or she may decide to not buy the product.

Magazines There are two major types of magazines. The first are those primarily published for the consumer; the other type are business-to-business, or trade, publications. Consumer magazines include *Vogue* or *Harpers,* whereas a business-to-business publication would be *Women's Wear Daily.* Of course, consumers read both, as do industry people, so each is not limited to only one type of reader. There are several disadvantages to advertising fashion products (or any product, for that matter) in magazines: (1) the life of a particular issue of a magazine, hence the advertising message in it, is short; (2) magazines have special-interest audiences; (3) production costs are high, due to good-quality paper; and (4) the lead time to produce the ad is long.

This magazine ad is likely creating selective demand for Gucci eye glasses.

The main consideration in magazine advertising, as with any other marketing venture, is the target market. If a marketer wants to advertise a product to middle-class families, *Vogue* might not be the best place to do so. However, *Family Circle* or *U.S. Weekly* magazine might be good choices. Most magazines will offer a "press packet" to those interested in buying advertising space, and it will provide general target market information.

Another consideration when advertising in magazines is the circulation, which refers to the number of copies that are distributed. Although this figure will give the marketer some idea of how many members of the target market will see the publication, it does not include magazines at doctor offices, for example, where many people may view the advertisement in just one magazine.

Magazines sell their advertising space at full, one-half, one-quarter, and one-eighth page rates. Of course, the smaller the ad, the less the price. A full-page ad in a fashion magazine may run upward of $70,000 or more. Another consideration is the willingness of some magazines to offer discounts for running the ad more than once. Reach in magazine advertising generally refers to its circulation.

Newspapers Newspapers offer a less expensive alternative to magazines for advertising, but they are slowly losing readership as a result of the availability of online news. A newspaper can be a weekly, a daily, or an industry-specific publication. The turnaround time for advertisements in newpapers is much quicker than for magazines, to the point that a retailer can submit an ad just a day or two before the publication is due to go to press. Most newspapers are in black and white, which is not a particularly good format for advertising fashion products. However, newspapers can be useful if a coupon is to be used. In addition, the customer can refer back to a newpaper advertisement, unlike one on radio or television.

Television Television is an expensive form of advertising, but it very effective. It has become easier to target customers via television because of the increase of stations catering to specific audiences.

There are three considerations to the cost of television. The first is the time period in which the advertisement will be shown. The more people who are likely watching television during a particular time, the more expensive that time slot will be. The second consideration is the popularity of the program. *Desperate Housewives* or *The O.C.*, for example, will earn more ad revenue than less popular shows. Finally, the size of the viewing audience will determine the price. The larger the audience, the higher the price. For example, *American Idol* had an average reach of 38 million viewers per night in the 2003 season, and the cost of a 30-second ad was $271,360.

There are several disadvantages to television advertising. The first is the life of the message. Once the ad has been shown, it may never be seen again. In addition, thanks to TiVo and similar technology, people are now able to fast forward through commercials. However, television advertisements can allow for creativity and demonstration of a product, a major advantage of the medium.

The cost to produce a television advertisement is very expensive, up to several hundred thousand dollars. Then, of course, the cost to actually run the commercial can be expensive as well.

Related to television advertising is a relatively new phenomenon: the use of commercials in movie theaters before the movie begins. The advantage to using this type of advertising is it is shown to a captive audience; in other words, the customer will likely watch the ad because it is the only stimulus available at that time.

Radio Radio advertisements, similar to those on television, have a short life span. Because of MP3 players and other technology, many people are no longer listening to the radio. Nevertheless, radio as an advertising medium does have some advantages compared with television. For one, it is mobile; potential customers can hear it in many situations. Radio advertisements are also less expensive than television spots. Similar to television and magazine audiences, the radio audience is very specific, so a marketer will have a good idea of exactly who the radio station reaches. A radio advertisement run during drive times, or morning and afternoon commutes, will usually be much more expensive than one aired late in the evening. The cost for radio advertisements is based not only on the time of day it is heard but also on the amount of time it is run. Most radio advertisements are available in 15- and 30-second spots.

Internet A website can be an important part of any fashion designer's or marketer's promotional plan. An **e-commerce** website is one that allows customers to purchase products directly online. This is an excellent way of gaining new customers, especially in areas that may not have a bricks-and-mortar location of retailer. Banner ads are also an important part of advertising. Normally, they are paid for on a "click-through" basis, meaning that the owner of the website advertised in the banner ad will be charged according to the number of people who actually visit its site as a result of clicking on the banner.

A major advantage to websites is that they can be changed quickly. A fashionista with a website can quickly share his or her designs throughout the world, and the fee is small compared with many of the other types of advertising.

:: DIRECT MARKETING ::

Direct marketing can be defined as anything that comes "directly to the customer," typically through the mail. These include catalogs, coupons for use in the customer's favorite store, and various other forms of advertising.

Retailers can obtain mailing lists in a variety of ways. One popular method is to have a customer "guest list," which allows visitors to the retailer to provide contact information in order to receive special promotions or catalogs. This is a targeted way of gaining access to customers. Lists can also be purchased from a variety of sources. Such lists can be specifically targeted, say to "women 18 to 25 who have purchased clothing through a catalog online in the last year." And although these lists can be rather expensive, they are effective in the selling of merchandise.

Another form of direct mail is the statement enclosure, an advertisement enclosed with a monthly bill. However, many customers resist reading direct-mail advertisements, a major disadvantage for the technique.

Lands' End catalogs are a type of direct marketing.

:: PERSONAL SELLING ::

Personal selling, which will be covered in greater detail in Chapter 8, is extremely important to the promotional mix. Marketing budgets are spent to get customers in the store; but once they are in there, the retailers want them to buy. Retailers depend on their sales associates to complete this area of the promotional mix. Most stores provide tips for personal selling in their training programs, as well as continued training on product offerings. This makes personal selling a strong force in getting products in customers' hands.

:: PUBLIC RELATIONS ::

Public relations can include press releases, public service announcements, and special events,. This aspect of the promotional mix is very important in fashion.

A press release, sent to various news media, can contain information that might create excitement about a new product release. It could include unique information about a retailer or designer. A public service announcement, free on some radio and television stations, can get the word out about events in which the community might be interested. A special event could be a formal fashion show, an informal fashion show, or a trunk show. Much of the cost related to special events will involve employee time, but they too can be effective in creating excitement about a product.

Press releases Press releases can be used to get the word out about a new product, a change to a product, or an event the public might be interested in attending. Normally, a press release will be used by members of the news media only if they believe the information to be newsworthy. Press releases are a wonderful promotional tool because they are an inexpensive way to gain a wider audience. Many people who do not watch television commercials might read a newspaper article based on a press release. Generally, a press release is prepared using the "who," "what," "where," "when," and "why it is important" format. A press release can provide information about an upcoming fashion show to benefit a charity or about a company's hiring of a new CEO. It can be sent both to traditional news publications, such as local newspapers, and to television news stations. It is up to the television station or the newspaper if they want to publish it or do a story about it. If they decide to run the story, the retailer or the product has gained thousands of dollars worth of free advertising! An example of a press release appears in Figure 7.6.

7.6 SAMPLE PRESS RELEASE

figure

Cutter & Buck's Organic Cotton Integrity Pique Speaks to Corporate Customers' Values

SEATTLE, WASHINGTON January 5, 2005 – Companies that value good corporate citizenship can now express their corporate values while offering employees and business partners a smart, stylish solution. Cutter & Buck's (Nasdaq CBUK) Integrity Pique shirt is made with IOO percent organically grown cotton, and is produced at SA8OOO factories that certify fair treatment for workers.

Research shows a growing number of consumers want to purchase products that are consistent with their values, including health, the environment and fair working conditions. The Organic Trade Association's 2004 manufacturers' survey notes that sales of organic-fiber products had an annual growth rate of 22.7 percent.

Ech C&B Integrity Pique (MSRP $42.50) saves about I/3 pound of chemical fertilizers and insecticides from entering the environment. Growing cotton organically uses natural means to fertilize soil and protect crops from insects, creating healthy and sustainable farms.

According to CEO, Tom Wyatt, "At Cutter & Buck we recognize that social responsibility is a core value held by many of our corporate customers. Offering the Integrity Pique

(Continued)

for employees and business partners is a great way to put their corporate values into practice."

Every single Integrity shirt is produced at an SA8000 certified factory. SA8000 is the only international code of conduct that addresses all widely accepted labor rights, and has a global independent certification system. SA8000 sets out measurable rules that encompass child labor, forced labor, health and safety, freedom of association and collective bargaining, discrimination, discipline, working hours and compensation.

Whether spurred to purchase organic cotton clothing for health and environmental reasons, or because they want fashion with a conscience, wearing Cutter & Buck's soft and elegant organic cotton Integrity shirt "just feels right."

About Cutter & Buck

Cutter & Buck (Nasdaq: CBUK) designs, sources, markets and distributes upscale sportswear under the Cutter & Buck brand. The Company sells its products primarily to upscale specialty retail stores, golf pro shops and resorts, corporate accounts, and international distributors and licensees. Cutter & Buck products feature distinctive, comfortable designs, high-quality materials and manufacturing, and rich detailing. Additional information about Cutter & Buck is available at: http://cutterbuck.com.

Statements made in this news release that are not historical facts are forward-looking statements. Actual results may differ materially from those projected in any forward-looking statements. Specifically, there are a number of important factors that could cause actual results to differ materially from those anticipated by any forward-looking statements. Those factors include, but are not limited to our relations with and the timely performance of third parties, acceptance of new products, and competition. Additional information on these and other factors, which could affect the company's financial and operational results, are included in its Securities and Exchange Commission filings. Finally, there may be other factors not mentioned above or included in the company's SEC filings that may cause actual results to differ materially from any forward-looking statements. You should not place undue reliance on these forward-looking statements. The Company assumes no obligation to update any forward-looking statements as a result of new information, except as may be required by securities laws.

Contact: Kathleen Olson
KOKO Communications 206.979.3750

Special events/fashion shows Formal fashion shows are used to introduce new products for each season. Fashion shows by designers such as Armani or Dior are a mainstay of the industry. At a formal fashion show, the audience includes members of the press, buyers, and private customers (usually by invitation only). Apparel manufacturers also hold fashion shows, but typically without the glitz of a couture fashion show, such as one for Dior. The attendees of these shows tend to be buyers, thus such an event provides an opportunity to gain fruitful sales for the season. Formal fashion shows are generally expensive to produce, which is why many smaller designers choose not to stage them.

figure 7.7

MAJOR BUDGETARY CONSIDERATIONS FOR A FASHION SHOW

- The facility
- Invitations
- Programs
- Promotion
- Cost of hiring models
- Cost of music
- Chair or seating rentals
- Lighting
- Master of ceremonies
- Public address system
- Props
- Cost of backdrop and runway construction
- Photographers
- Food/drinks

Informal fashion shows can be inexpensive to produce. They can include those that take place in a mall or inside a department store. Or a fashion show might include several designers, who pay a fee to have their garments shown. An example of this kind of show is the Erotic Fashion Show, produced in Seattle. It features designers of leather and other fetish and gothic clothing. For some shows like this, even the attendees must pay an entry fee, which generates income for its producers.

A **trunk show** is when merchandise is brought into a store and featured for a few days. Often, customers will get special invitations to attend these events, and sometimes the designers will be on hand to answer questions. This is an inexpensive way to gain publicity and is typically used in conjunction with direct marketing to inform the customers about the show.

The major costs and budgetary items associated with a fashion show or trunk show are presented in Figure 7.7.

:: SALES PROMOTIONS ::

Sales promotions can be anything used to persuade the customer to buy "right now" or to buy more of something. It is important to note the difference between sales promotion pricing and markdowns. A markdown is a permanent price reduction; pricing for a sales promotion is temporary.

A sales promotion may be a buy-one-get-one-free offer or discounted pricing for buying in quantity. Or a retailer may simply reduce the price of an item for a limited time, such as when Victoria's Secret offers a garment for $29.50 rather than its normal price of $31.50. The idea of a sales promotion is to entice a customer to buy something he or she might otherwise not.

Express does an excellent job of sales promotion. A couple of times a year it has a sale in which customers can earn $25 certificates to use at a later date for each $100 they spend. Not only does this motivate customers to buy more at the time, but it also encourages them to come back at a later date and purchase as well. Kohl's offers senior shopper discounts on Wednesday's, another example of sales promotion.

It is important to keep in mind that all promotions must be timed correctly, reach the right audience (target audience), be within budget, and have continuity. **Continuity** refers to the idea that all promotions, advertising, or anything printed from a particular retailer, look the same. For example, Nike has excellent continuity. Every Nike commercial has a similar feeling about it and also displays the Nike swoosh. The swoosh as well as the Nike name appear on the tags of the clothing and even on the clothing itself. Besides establishing continuity, this is part of **branding,** another important consideration in any marketing mix effort. Branding is a part of the effort to establish a *corporate identity*. Nike, for example, positioned its products to be the best sporting goods available. This took time; however, by using constant advertising as part of its branding strategy, Nike succeeded in establishing the corporate identity it wanted.

Melissa Werkenthin of 360 Media offers some suggestions for branding, not only for multimillion dollar companies but for small retailers too.

- *Establish a company mission statement.* This will help define the purpose and direction of the company for its management, employees, and customers. For example, Wal-Mart's mission statement highlights the company's commitment to low prices, commitment to respecting employees, and commitment to providing good service.

- *Develop a company logo.* A strong logo can be easily obtained with the help of a professional graphic artist. For example, Old Navy has the familiar logo with the navy blue circle around the name of the store.

- *Develop a company slogan or tagline.* This can come out of the mission statement, but it should be a simple concept, targeted at the company's customers, that embodies the image the company wants to project. A retailer may change its tagline to meet the season. For example, The Gap may use "Warm up for Winter" as a tagline for winter clothing. This promotes the store's wide selection of sweaters and coats. However, it would then change the tagline when advertising spring clothes.

- *Use the logo and slogan on all internal and external communications (such as e-mail and letterhead).* People will start to associate the logo image and slogan with the business. This is especially important for small retailers and designers. It will help create a brand and an image.

- *Reinforce the mission statement through customer relationship management.* A good customer experience not only will keep that customer coming back but will help build the brand.

- *Keep the message simple.* Do not confuse the audience. Be simple and to the point when stating what the company is, what it does, and what separates it from the competition.

These tips help build the image of the fashion brand, which can increase sales and profits for a retailer, no matter how small.

REALWORLD focus >> Product, Price, and Promotion Create Sales

Vuitton Maintains Momentum amid Slump in Luxury Sector

LVMH Moet Hennessy Louis Vuitton SA, the world's largest luxury-goods company, expects monogrammed denim handbags, eyewear created with a hip-hop music star, and bags with cherry prints designed by a pop artist to help boost the company's most profitable business.

Louis Vuitton designer Marc Jacobs created LV monogrammed jeans and denim handbags trimmed with crocodile skin for his spring-summer 2005 collection, which also previewed eyewear designed with hip-hop music producer PhtuTell Williams and bags decorated with cherry prints by pop artist Takashi Murakami.

"The ready-to-wear show is a good way to bring energy to our bags and accessories businesses as well," Yves Carcelle, director of LVMH's fashion division, said in an interview after the show, held at Serre du Pare Andre Citroen in Paris.

Chairman Bernard Arnault is focusing on keeping up momentum at Louis Vuitton, which generates about 60 percent of the group's operating profit and about 25 percent of sales. A three-year slump in the $74 billion luxury-goods business has made it more difficult to turn around underperforming lines such as Fendi and Gucci. LVMH also owns the Givenchy and Donna Karan brands, among others.

The collaboration with Murakami on the cherry prints follows Louis Vuitton's first project with the Japanese artist two years ago, which produced a best-selling and widely copied line of bags with multicolored LV initials on a white background known as the "Eye Love You" collection. "Product is key, and creativity is the power behind the brand," Carcelle said. The new products haven't been priced yet.

Handbags represent one of the most profitable segments of the luxury-goods business because they have a longer shelf life and don't have the fitting and sizing requirements of clothing.

Louis Vuitton is also expanding its jewelry business, which started with a charm bracelet designed by Marc Jacobs two years ago, into a full line called "Enprise" that features luggage motifs and monogrammed flowers.

The 150-year-old brand, which already operates more directly owned stores than any other luxury brand, is keeping up its pace of opening about 15 stores each year, Carcelle said. Louis Vuitton recently opened its 335th store, in Johannesburg, South Africa. Last month, Louis Vuitton opened a 13,000-square-meter store in Shanghai, its fourteenth outlet in China. "This shows that we are rapidly penetrating new territory while continuing to grow in traditional markets such as North America," Carcelle said.

Last month, LVMH said first-half profit rose 49 percent as travelers returned to its Asian airport stores and U.S. shoppers bought more champagne and cognac. Operating profit at the fashion and leather goods unit, which includes Louis Vuitton, was unchanged at 634 million euros ($787 million). ❧

Source: Written by Sara Gay Forden. Copyright 2004, CBJ, L.P. and the Gale Group.

›› QUESTIONS

1. Why do you think the luxury-goods market went into a slump?

2. What is a directly owned store? What might the advantages be of a directly owned store?

3. Discuss why product could be the most important part of the four Ps.

>> conclusion •

This chapter has covered the four areas of the marketing mix, which assist designers and fashion merchandisers in making sure their products sell. First, a marketer must insure the products in the store have the right features to meet the needs of the customers. Next, the designer or merchandiser develops a pricing strategy that both meets the needs of the customer and reflects the value of the product. Distribution or place is key in insuring the merchandise arrives in the right place, in a timely manner. Finally, promotion encompasses all of the ways a designer or merchandiser can attract customers into the retail store. Techniques such as advertising, sales promotions, and fashion shows create a demand for the product, resulting in sales, which is the primary focus of marketing.

>> chapter seven review • • • • • • • • • • • • • •

TERMS TO KNOW ::

Marketing mix

The four Ps (product, price, place, and promotion)

terms relating to product

Variety	Design	Depth
Features	Product assortment (wide and narrow)	Breadth

terms relating to price

Wholesale price	Psychological pricing	Price skimming
Retail price	Twofer	Penetration pricing
Market demand	Multiple pricing	Cost-based pricing
Competition	Reference price	Keystoning
Economy	Promotional pricing	Line-item pricing
Positioning	Loss leader	Odd pricing
Value pricing	Geographical pricing	Competitive pricing
Intrinsic value	Uniform delivery pricing	Economies of scale
Prestige pricing	Markdowns	Frequency marketing
Product-line pricing		

terms relating to place

Intensive distribution	Lifestyle merchandising	Vendor-managed inventory (VMI)
Selective distribution	Single-line store	Centralized receiving
Exclusive strategy	Electronic data interchange (EDI)	Regional receiving
Hard lines	Value-added network (VAN)	Single-store receiving
Soft lines	Extensible markup language	

terms relating to promotion

Reach	E-commerce	Continuity
Frequency	Trunk show	Branding

CONCEPTS TO KNOW ::

1. Why the four Ps are required for successful marketing.
2. Product assortments and the importance of having a good assortment.
3. Pricing strategies and their use for different situations.
4. The three types of distribution strategies.
5. The five areas of the promotional mix and their components.

CHAPTER QUESTIONS ::

1. Discuss the importance of the proper mix of the four Ps.
2. What is the difference between depth and breadth? How does this relate to the product assortment of a retail store?
3. Explain the various ways in which to transport fashion goods. What are advantages and disadvantages of each?
4. Explain the difference between a department store and a specialty store.
5. Discuss how unreliable transportation can affect buyers and retail stores.
6. Discuss how economies of scale and the use of overseas labor impact each other.

CHAPTER PROJECTS AND DISCUSSION ::

1. Using the Internet, research the cost to advertise on your favorite television program. Bring in your research to discuss.
2. Assuming you have a small retail store and a budget of $50,000 for the promotional mix, how would you use the funds? Write down your thoughts and discuss.
3. Write a press release promoting a new product line from a store of your choice.
4. What intrinsic value do you gain from your favorite clothing item?
5. Would you consider yourself to be an early adopter? Why or why not?

FOR FURTHER READING ::

For careers in fashion marketing:
www.careerprospects.org/ briefs/P S/SummaryMarketFash.shtml
For general marketing information:
http://www.knowthis.com/
http://www.marketingpower.com/
http://www.gmarketing.com/

the fashion industry faces unique challenges as a result of globalization. This chapter will first discuss global sourcing. Then it will provide an overview of how the production process works and how to work effectively with overseas manufacturers. Legal concerns involved in importing and exporting and social responsibility in global production will also be covered. Whether you are a design or a merchandising student, the topics in this chapter are important for understanding the process of how goods are manufactured overseas.

GLOBAL SOURCING

Sourcing is one of the most interesting, and ever-changing, aspects of the fashion industry. **Sourcing** simply means to obtain materials from another country, business, or locale. In fashion, sourcing refers to the practice of allowing a company, usually overseas, to produce the goods a designer has created.

There are many reasons for sourcing overseas, also referred to as *outsourcing*. First, the abundance of workers willing to do the job makes overseas manufacturing attractive. The cheaper cost of labor is another reason for producing overseas. In addition, the requirements for working conditions are less stringent. Health care costs, social security costs, and payroll taxes are cheaper, sometimes even nonexistent overseas.

There are some disadvantages, however, to outsourcing. Loss of local jobs has a ripple effect on local communities when factories close. Closing production facilities in local areas can also cause the brand image of the company to suffer. For example, when Levi Strauss closed its plant in San Antonio, Texas, in 2003, the loss of 8,000 jobs in the area not only affected the economy but also tarnished the image of the company.

However, there are unique challenges in sourcing, many of which are involved in the production process (this chapter fits into the production shoebox; see Figure 8.1). At one time, when clothing was made locally, designers could easily stop by the factories to see samples of their garments, to test for size or quality. Because most factories are now located several thousands of miles away, this is an impossible task and results in the need for excellent communication skills.

>> product production

:: PRODUCTION FACILITIES ::

There are two types of production facilities, wholly owned factories and joint ventures. With a **wholly owned factory**, the retailer that is manufacturing the goods actually owns the factory in which they are produced. This is known as **vertical production**—the retailer owns the retail store and all of the production facilities to make the clothing that goes into the store. Vertical production allows the retailer to control the actual production process, rather than having to rely on suppliers and vendors. Many retailers do not engage in

> **"***Sourcing is one of the most interesting, and ever-changing, aspects of the fashion industry.***"**

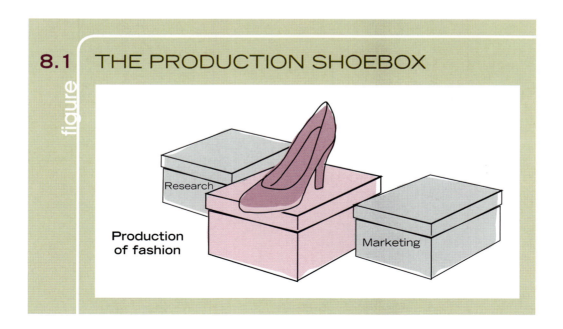

8.1 THE PRODUCTION SHOEBOX

figure

Research

Production of fashion

Marketing

vertical production, however, due to the hassles of operating a factory. The advantages to using a wholly owned factory are more control of quality and better timing of the goods. However, this option can be a lot more expensive than others.

The second type of production facility involves a **joint venture.** In this situation, a retailer or designer contracts with a factory and works with its owners to produce the product. The company producing the goods, that is, the factory owner, may also work with other retailers. For example, if Nordstrom uses a joint venture production facility, its clothing may be produced alongside clothing for Macy's or other retailers.

Once the type of production and facility have been chosen, it is up to the designers to work with the overseas manufacturers to produce the product.

:: STEPS IN THE PRODUCTION PROCESS ::

The first step in producing a new product is to estimate the production run, or the quantity that is required to meet the needs of the retail stores. At this point, a costing sheet and specifications package (see Chapter 3) are used to estimate the cost of each individual product. Once the factory and the designer/retailer agree on a price, production can begin.

First, the factory must make a pattern. Then, in a process called **pattern grading,** the factory makes the pattern to different sizes. Grading can be done either via computer or by hand but today, is normally done by computer. Once the pattern is complete, and the factory receives approval from the designer, cutting of the pattern can begin.

The factory will then cut a few samples from the agreed-upon fabric. These samples will then be sent to the designer for approval. If time is a concern, the factory may not send the actual completed garment but photos of it instead. After the factory has received approval for the finished product, it will produce the number of garments requested, usually using an assembly line that runs the full length of the factory floor. Garments are normally produced in sections. A worker would sew one or two specific sections of the garment, then pass it onto the next person to complete next section. The final processes include sewing the trimmings, buttons, and other details onto the garment.

The factory, if contracted to do so, will tag the garments with the retailer's tag, sku number, and price. At this point, the garments will be shipped to the appropriate distribution center. (Distribution centers were covered in Chapter 7.)

Figure 8.2 diagrams the steps in the production process.

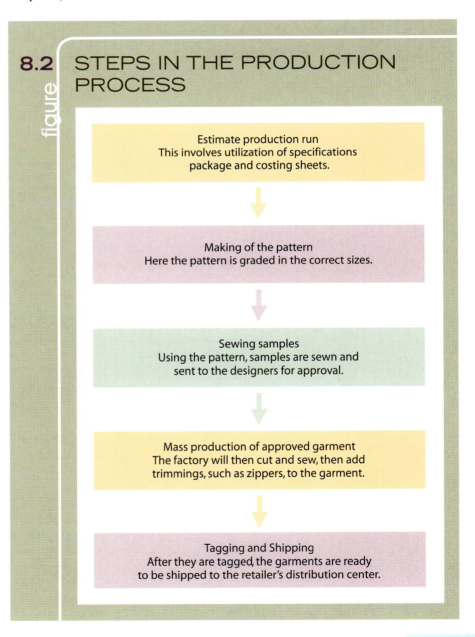

8.2 figure

STEPS IN THE PRODUCTION PROCESS

Estimate production run
This involves utilization of specifications package and costing sheets.

Making of the pattern
Here the pattern is graded in the correct sizes.

Sewing samples
Using the pattern, samples are sewn and sent to the designers for approval.

Mass production of approved garment
The factory will then cut and sew, then add trimmings, such as zippers, to the garment.

Tagging and Shipping
After they are tagged, the garments are ready to be shipped to the retailer's distribution center.

The process for reordering garments is much easier. If an item has sold well in a store, a designer or buyer may only have to call or e-mail the factory and ask for additional quantities of the garment.

To produce goods overseas, the designer would identify the origin of goods (the country that specializes in the type of goods to be produced) and locate a manufacturer. Then, the factory would see samples, at which time it would provide prices. Payment terms would be agreed upon, then the designer (or the factory) would apply for necessary licenses and arrange for the clearing of the goods through customs.

:: INTERMEDIARIES ::

Many designers and retailers rely on market intermediaries in the production process. **Market intermediaries** are sometimes called **selling agents,** or simply *agents*. An intermediary's purpose is to act as a middleman between factories and retailers.

There are several types of intermediaries. First, a **broker** brings buyers and sellers together. The broker does not carry inventory or have any involvement in payment of the inventory. The second type of intermediary is a **wholesaler.** A wholesaler is different from a broker in that the wholesaler actually takes possession of inventory, offers credit to companies, and helps in insuring delivery of the goods. A **drop shipper,** on the other hand, does not carry inventory but receives orders, selects the manufacturers, and makes sure the goods arrive at the desired location. It does not handle the products, but it does provide payment to the manufacturer and then in turn gets paid by the retailer.

The disadvantage to using an intermediary is obviously the cost. In wholesaling, the factory sells goods to the agent, and the agent in turn sells to the retailer. The retailer then sells the goods to the customer and will charge a price to obtain the desired level of profit, but it also must recoup the costs associated with product production, including payment to the agent.

A broker might be used because the person is fluent in the language of the manufacturer and can better negotiate payment terms on behalf of the retailer. The retailer pays the broker a fee to manage this process and also to insure delivery of the goods.

Because wholesalers offer credit, smaller retailers would be most likely to use them. A wholesaler can provide a one-stop-shopping experience for a retailer. The retailer can focus on running the store, leaving the worry of transporting of goods to the wholesaler.

A retailer might use a drop shipper to save time, especially if the item is relatively simple to produce, such as T-shirts. This allows the retailer to focus on other specialty items it wants to sell. A major advantage in dealing with an intermediary as opposed to the factory itself is that the designer or merchandiser can work with one person to communicate needs. In addition, often an intermediary can help in the complex process of dealing with import laws.

>> importing and exporting

One of the major challenges of working with overseas manufacturers is the process of importing goods. When goods are brought into the United States, there are several considerations, including quotas, tariffs, and customs inspections. A **quota** is a limit on the amount of goods that can be brought into a country. A **tariff,** sometimes called a **duty,** is a tax charged on imported goods. **Customs inspections** occur with every shipment of goods into a country. The inspections are to insure that no illegal goods, such as drugs, or hazardous materials enter the United States. Another reason for inspections is to accurately assess tariffs on the goods entering the country. Inspection responsibility in the United States is the domain of the U.S. Customs.

A major change happened on January 1, 2005, one that has transformed the way fashion and textile goods are brought into the country. All participating World Trade Organization (WTO) countries are allowed to import unlimited quantities of textiles and finished apparel goods into the United States. Previous quotas allowed only a specific amount of goods in each category to be imported each year. Due to this change, the amount of apparel goods imported into the United States has increased. There is a concern that large producing countries like China could flood the market with clothing. If that occurred, it would be difficult for other countries to compete, because the more of a particular item that is available in a country, the lower the price tends to be. For example, if China floods the market with millions of winter scarves, the excess supply will likely drive down the price people are willing to pay. This in turn affects the manufacturers that are dependent on obtaining a particular price for goods they sell in the United States.

Although quotas have been eliminated for WTO partners, tariffs are still charged on goods coming into the United States. Figure 8.3 shows an example of tariffs charged on some goods. Every product has a special number assigned to it. Also, for statistical reporting, they are assigned an additional number. These numbers are found in the first two columns in the chart. The third column includes a description of the article of clothing.

Every product is also placed into a specific category. The determinants of the category include the end use of the product and the materials of the product. The unit of measurement can be in kilograms (one kilogram is equal to 2.2 pounds), dozens, or actual number.

The last three columns indicate the duty or tariff charged. The rate in the "General" column is also called the *normal trade relations rate*, which is used for countries with which the United States has good relations. The "Special" column lists additional tariffs that the United States can impose on specific countries as a result of trade relations with them. Finally, the last column is an additional tariff for goods imported from countries with difficult trade relations. The fees in this last column make it difficult if not impossible, to import goods from these countries, in that the cost of the goods would be much more expensive after paying these high tariffs. The United States imposes these additional tariffs because it disagrees with the governmental policies of those countries. The intention is that by making it difficult to import here, they may someday change their behavior.

Other examples of categories and tariff charges include:

- Jar or flask, glass, produced by automatic machine, charged 2.5 percent of total value.
- Sleeping bags, containing 20 percent or more of down, charged 4.7 percent of total value.
- Ski bindings and accessories, other than cross-country, charged 2.8 percent of total value.
- Dolls, dressed or not, and stuffed are free to come in the country.

There is a long-standing argument about tariffs and quotas. Some people believe that limiting the number of goods that can be brought into a country allows local manufacturers to be more competitive. For example, because a shoe retailer will have to pay tariffs and taxes on shoes imported into the United States, it might instead buy from domestic manufacturers.

Many countries, including the United States, use tariffs and quotas to carry out what are called **protectionist policies.** In other words, they try to "protect" their own economies by making imported products more expensive. A country can also decide not to trade with another country at all. This is called an **embargo,** which typically occurs for political reasons. For example, the United States has an embargo against Cuba because it does not agree with the actions of Cuba's administration. An embargo is not a protectionist policy; rather, it is a way to try to get another government to change.

HARMONIZED TARIFF SCHEDULE

HARMONIZED TARIFF SCHEDULE OF THE UNITED STATE (2005)
Annotated for Statistical Purposes

Heading/ Sub-heading	Stat Suf-fix	Articles Description	Unit of Quantity	Rates of Duty		
				1		2
				General	Special	
6204		Women's or girls' suits, ensembles, suit-type jackets, blazers, dresses, skirts, divided skirts, trousers, bib and brace overalls, breeches and shorts (other than swimwear).				
		Suits:				
6204.11.00	00	Of wool or fine animal hair (444)	No. . . . . . kg	14%	Free (CA, CL, IL, JO, MX, SG) 12.6% (AU)	58.5%
6204.12.00		Of cotton	. . . .	14.9%	Free (CA, CL, IL, JO, MX, SG) 13.4% (AU)	90%
	10	Jackets imported as parts of suits (335)	doz. kg			
	20	Skirts and divided skirts imported as parts of suits (342)	doz. kg			
	30	Trousers, breeches and shorts imported as parts of suits (384)	doz. kg			
	40	Waistcoats imported as parts of suits (359)	doz. kg			
6204.13		Of synthetic fibers:				
6204.13.10	00	Containing 36 percent or more by weight of wool or fine animal hair (444)	No. . . . . . kg	17%	Free (CA, CL, IL, JO, MX, SG) 15.5% (AU)	58.5%
6204.13.20		Other	. . . .	35.3¢/kg + 25.9%	Free (CA, CL, IL, MX, SG) 15.5% (AU) 18.1¢/kg + 13.2% (JO)	37.5¢/kg +76%
	10	Women's (644).	No. kg			
	20	Girls' (644).	No. kg			

:: TRADE AGREEMENTS ::

A **trade agreement** is a contract signed by two or more countries and is a way of limiting protectionist policies between countries. Trade agreements allow for easier trade between countries. When signing a trade agreement, the countries agree to work together so both can benefit from trading with one another. Despite protectionist policies, there are several agreements and international organizations in place to make trade with other countries easier.

World Trade Organization The purpose of the World Trade Organization is to coordinate trade between countries. Various WTO agreements have been negotiated and signed by the bulk of the world's trading nations and ratified in the parliament or congress of each country. The goal of the organization is to help producers of goods and services, exporters, and importers conduct their business. The responsibility of the WTO is to handle trade disputes between nations, administer trade laws set forth by this agency, and provide forums for trade negotiations between countries.

Some critics view the WTO as having an unfair bias toward the big and powerful countries and multinational corporations. They believe that these large countries want to have free trade at any cost, including at the expense of the environment and workers. The WTO disputes these claims. For example, environmental laws are much more lenient (or nonexistent) in many developing nations. It costs manufacturers money to comply with environmental standards in the United States, so they may choose to manufacture in another country that has lenient standards. In addition, many people believe the WTO makes policies that encourage production of goods in countries where labor is much less expensive and where workers are not treated fairly.

A sit-down protest outside a WTO meeting.

The organization came into existence in 1995 to oversee the General Agreement on Tariffs and Trade, or GATT. Today, more than 140 countries are members of the organization.

North American Free Trade Agreement The North American Free Trade Agreement (NAFTA) eliminated all tariffs and quotas (over a period of time) on trade between Mexico, Canada, and the United States. It implementation in 1994 created a stir of both excitement and anxiety. One of the major concerns about NAFTA was that many manufacturing jobs would leave the United States and go to Mexico, where labor was much cheaper. People also had concerns about the quality of food that would flow between the countries.

Several years after its implementation, the Mexican government complained that many of the jobs that did come to Mexico were low-paying and nonmanagerial, factory type jobs. Many companies did locate their manufacturing operations in Mexico but retained their corporate offices in the United States or Canada. However, as we will discuss later in this chapter, when moving manufacturing operations to another country, a company will face issues concerning quality of products as well as communication barriers.

Central American Free Trade Agreement

The Central American Free Trade Agreement (CAFTA) is modeled after NAFTA and includes Costa Rica, the Dominican Republic, El Salvador, Guatemala, Honduras, Nicaragua, and the United States. The agreement allows for free trade of goods between member countries. It was ratified by all seven countries in 2005.

Some believe the agreement will only cause a loss of jobs for the United States, primarily textile factory jobs. Others believe CAFTA will allow the United States to export more goods, approximately $1.5 billion worth, to member countries. As with most free-trade agreements, there are strong opinions on either side. However, because this is a relatively new agreement, it is likely that its effects, be they positive or negative, won't be seen for five to ten years.

Caribbean Basin Trade Partnership Act

The Caribbean Basin Trade Partnership Act (CBTPA) is a 2000 U.S. legislative act signed by then-president Bill Clinton. It was enacted to encourage trade among the 24 countries in the Caribbean Basin, including Haiti, Belize, and Jamaica, in an effort to strengthen their economies. In 1998, hurricanes devastated this region, and the hope was that the CBPTA would help end some of the joblessness in these countries. This initiative increased certain quotas for garments like bras and underwear coming from the Caribbean Basin countries. This partnership set the groundwork for historic trade agreements such as CAFTA, discussed earlier.

The European Union

The European Union (EU) is one of the most important trade agreements ever signed. This agreement goes further than NAFTA and others in that it allows for free trade, free movement of citizens, and a single currency. The single currency of the EU is called the euro. However, not all members of the EU are required to use the euro as their currency. Britain, for example, is part of the EU, but it decided to keep its own currency, the British pound.

The streets of Hong Kong.

Although the EU is not meant to replace individual countries, it is meant to unite the member countries into one major trading power. Despite this, the EU has created similar problems as has NAFTA in terms of jobs moving to countries where it is less expensive to manufacturer goods.

At the writing of this book, the EU has 25 member countries, with four more in the process of applying for membership and others that are candidates. The long-term goal of the EU is to have one, centralized government. However, many countries are hesitant about this because they do not want to lose the individuality of their particular nation and culture.

Asian Pacific Economic Cooperation

The Asian Pacific Economic Cooperation (APEC) is different from the WTO and the EU in that it does not have any binding trade agreements. It has 21 member countries, including the United States. The purpose of the organization is to facilitate discussion to make importing easier for all countries involved.

REALWORLDfocus >> China and the Garment Trade

The Most Sweeping Reform in Industrial History Leaves China Poised to Rule the Garment Trade

John Cheh sells the shirt on his back. As chairman of Esquel China Holdings in Hong Kong, he runs a top producer of men's woven cotton shirts—or category 340Z under the World Trade Organization quota system that expired last week. "It's a high-end shirt with high yarn count. It has the feel of quality," he says, stroking his collar. Sold by Nordstrom for about $50, the label reads: made in Malaysia.

That claim complies with the quotas hammered out by trade negotiators over the decades, to be sure. But Cheh's shirt—along with millions of other garments now sold in the United States and Europe—is a camouflaged Chinese export. The cotton grew in Xinjiang, became yarn at a spinning mill in the Silk Road oasis town of Turfan, and journeyed some 3,000 kilometers by truck to be woven into fabric in China's Pearl River Delta. In local garment factories, thousands of young women cut the cloth into patterns, stitch panels together, and gather buttons, zippers, and clasps into kits that are then "finished" by workers who sew the pieces together in nations like Malaysia: Even the made in Malaysia labels are made in China.

It was this wasteful supply chain that the World Trade Organization aimed to sever back in 1994, when it resolved to abolish quotas that have contorted the global garment industry like a bonsai tree. Quotas officially expired on January 1 in what amounts to the largest simultaneous industrial rationalization in the history of, well, industry. What comes next is globalization's first great test of the new millennium. Most forecasts portend dramatic change: billions in savings on production costs, the death of an industry of middlemen who specialized in quota dodging, and falling prices for shirts, shorts, scarves, and socks as manufacturing consolidates in the nations that do it best. Nearly all analysts believe China will come out on top in a battle for control of the $350 billion industry, but not for the reasons you may think.

More than 60 countries now export garments to the West, and several dozen are likely to be driven out of the textile trade. Nations like Cambodia that bet their futures on the promise of preferential access to U.S. and European consumers have now lost that special privilege. Unions and lobbyists around the world are fighting to erect new barriers to slow the exodus of jobs and contracts to China, claiming that its current and expected future dominance is built on a system of state-run "sweatshops," implying rock-bottom wages in miserable factories.

This is a distortion, at best. China's textile advantage has little to do with its wages (which are considerably higher than those in India, Indonesia, or Vietnam) or even with labor costs more generally (which account for only about 10 percent of the cost of a shirt). Recent outbreaks of labor unrest in the Pearl River Delta are a story of worker expectations rising faster than wages—not "a race to the bottom," as some activists would have it.

What truly distinguishes China are its state-of-the-art factories, its rapidly improving transportation network—and its talent for exploiting the absurdities of the quota system. China estimates that it now turns out more than 20 billion finished garments a year, roughly four pieces of clothing for every person on Earth—the largest output by a single country ever recorded. And that figure does not even include the uncounted billions of kits that end up as clothes "made in" Malaysia, Mauritius, or the Maldives.

China's current dominance of the textile trade extends well beyond its own official quotas, and lays the basis for its future expansion. The mainland's garment industry has grown 500 percent since 1990, from $10 billion to $50 billion, and now has 40,000 clothing factories that employ some 15 million workers. In a recent Goldman Sachs poll of large American retailers, most expected China's share of the U.S. clothing market to double from 20 percent to 40 percent by 2007 and to peak at about 60 percent.

Austrian economist J. A. Schumpeter once observed that England's ascendance "can almost be resolved into the history of a single industry," namely textiles. The same might be said of China and the rest of East Asia today. The rise started in Meiji, Japan, which used cheap labor to propel itself past England to become the leading global exporter of cotton garments by 1930. In reaction to the rising prowess of Japan's mills, Washington forced Tokyo to accept "voluntary" quotas in 1955. To keep their businesses alive, Japanese companies began funding and advising garment makers in Hong Kong, Taiwan, and South Korea. This laid the roots of the "flying geese" development model, in which Japan led the Asian flock into more and more advanced technologies, and of the backlash that created the labyrinthine quota system.

Washington's response was to slap quotas on any Asian exporter that made sharp gains in the U.S. clothing market. By the early 1970s, the U.S. system had morphed into a global one, imposing complex quotas on dozens of nations in 800 categories of clothing. Though ostensibly "temporary," the system became increasingly entrenched, and illogical. Fortunes were spent on quota-filling garment factories from the United Arab Emirates to remote corners of Africa. "Mauritius? Madagascar? Who the hell would normally make garments in places so far-flung?" says industry consultant James P. Convery. "It is the ultimate case study on how intervention creates market distortions on a grand scale."

Over time the quota system became a cashless form of foreign aid. America and Europe granted needy country's preferential quotas, hoping labor-intensive garment factories would lay the seeds for broad-based industrialization. While many governments failed to capitalize on the protections, the development scheme worked in much of East Asia, though nowhere quite so spectacularly as in China after its opening in the early 1980s.

Protection seemed to have a different impact on China than on many developing nations, promoting enterprise rather than sloth. Though rules varied by country, manufacturers typically could sell to others up to half their quota

(continued)

allotment each year. Known as mothers, such sellers remained the exporters of record and kept their quotas year after year so long as none went unused. In competitive categories, quota rights sold at huge premiums; in recent years, for example, garment makers in China paid $5 per piece for quota rights to make wool sweaters, or nearly equal the cost of production. So-called matchmakers earned fortunes getting buyers and sellers together. "Several of them I know became quota millionaires," says a Western apparel buyer with decades of experience in Asia.

The system drove Chinese to make themselves hypercompetitive. Because quotas limited the number of garments China could export to the West in any single category—but not the value of those exports—local retailers strove to win upmarket clients (those who purchase higher-end goods). Better to sell $200 Hugo Boss sweaters than $20 Wal-Mart sweaters. And in the race to slash costs, cut delivery times, and raise quality, Chinese were driven to move upmarket more aggressively than their rivals in other nations, largely because they faced more domestic competition to fill their nations' limited export quota. "Retailers used to look at [just cost]: 'Your price is $3 and his is $2.90, OK, I'm going to Bangladesh,'" says Bruce Rockowitz, president of the Hong Kong-based sourcing giant Li & Fung Trading. "It's not like that anymore. They think about delivery, quality, what the selling price would be in their store after markdowns to see which one is more cost-effective. China always comes up on top."

In Gaoming, a small city in Guangdong province, Esquel produces cotton shirts for clients ranging from Wal-Mart to Nike, Hugo Boss, and Burberry. Automated assembly lines maximize each worker's output. Salaries, which have risen sharply across the Pearl River Delta in recent years, are fast approaching 90 cents an hour on average, which is 30 percent higher than in Bangladesh and more than double those in Indonesia, according to the International Labor Organization. To retain workers amid China's manufacturing boom, Esquel offers benefits like nearly free housing (line workers, mostly young women, bunk four to a room; managers get their own apartments), a gym, a library, and free Internet access. Cafeterias serve a variety of regional cuisines to suit migrant workers from across China.

Esquel estimates that because it can buy yarn and fabric from its own mills inside China, garment assembly takes 30 percent less time in Gaoming than outside the country. Proximity to Hong Kong by either barge or truck speeds up the export process; containers arriving at one of the city's state-of-the-art freight terminals are usually aboard ship and on the high seas in a few hours. According to AT Kearney, labor for a shirt made in Bangladesh runs just $1.52, compared with $2.28 in China, but after factoring in materials and transportation, the total cost of the Chinese shirt is $11.15—almost a dollar cheaper.

China continues to refine its advantages in ways that echo the ongoing revolution in the retail industry, led by Wal-Mart. Through close coordination with suppliers, tight inventory controls, and volume trade, the U.S. retailer slashed costs and passed the savings on to consumers. Trendy new fashion houses like Zara of Spain have cut the time it takes to introduce new styles from months to weeks. As the fashion seasons give way to a 24/7 cycle in which styles change constantly, China is building the high-speed factories and transport links that can meet demand. As a recent study of the quota system by the American Chamber of Commerce in Hong Kong put it: "Clothing is increasingly considered a perishable good."

Since global growth in consumption of clothing is flat, suppliers are fighting for shares of a stable pie. Rockowitz predicts that the "industry unto itself that rose up to dispense quota allotments" will die, and foreign investors will flock out of "quota countries." After Turkey gained tariff-free access to Europe in 1994, investments poured into its textile industry, "but people are exiting now because it became very expensive," says Hana ben-Shabat, a senior strategist at AT Kearney in London. "That has always been the case in the textile industry—people keep on moving from country to country."

Quotas hobbled that mobility, but no longer. With costs rising on the Pearl River Delta, the industry may push farther inland in China, or look again at rivals like Indonesia or Vietnam. One of the few nations showing some confidence in its ability to compete is India. Once the world leader in cotton-textile exports, India faded in the eighteenth century, when the British Empire created a virtual monopoly for its own—at home and in the Indian market, choking textile centers like Surat.

Today Surat is upbeat. More than one million of its 3.5 million people make their living in some way related to textiles. Even the Self-Employed Women's Association, an NGO that supports poor women, is upgrading cottage factories to meet international standards. "It's an opportunity that we don't want to let go," says Rema Nanavaty, who heads SEWA's garment venture. "We are trying to get our unit started by January to take our share in the post-quota period." One interested buyer: Wal-Mart. New Delhi hopes to boost textile exports from $11 billion last year to $50 billion by 2010, a goal analysts consider well within reach.

Yet to hit its target, analysts say, the government must copy China's massive investments in new roads and ports, and add $30 billion worth of new factory capacity. According to the Federation of Indian Chambers of Commerce and Industry, "The central theme of the developments taking place in the Indian textile industry is that players are gearing themselves up for effectively competing in the volume game" against China. Researchers at Purdue University's Global Trade Analysis Project forecast that by the end of 2005, China will capture half of the clothing market in the United States and 29 percent of Europe, and India will rank second, with 15 percent and 9 percent shares, respectively.

The most obvious winner will be consumers. In the United States, for example, clothing prices have already fallen by 8.5 percent since 2000; the elimination of quotas should drop prices further. Most analysts believe luxury prices won't come down, while retailers in the middle—like The Gap or H&M—will use the cost savings to cut prices, reinvest in better products, or both. AT Kearney predicts that the upshot of this struggle will be an 8 to 18 percent drop in retail clothing prices in the coming years. More and more of those pieces will be labeled: made in China. Or maybe India. ❁

Source: Written by George Wehrfritz and Alexandra A. Seno, Newsweek International, January 10, 2005, with Sudip Mazumdar in New Delhi. © 2005 Newsweek, Inc.

›› QUESTIONS

1. What are some of the concerns discussed in this article regarding the elimination of quotas?

2. In your opinion, who benefits the most with the elimination of quotas: the customer, the manufacturer, or the retailer?

3. Why would clothing be considered a "perishable good"?

4. How have the workers' lives changed as a result of the elimination of quotas?

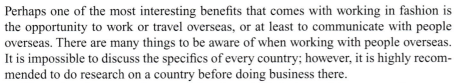

>> overseas cultural differences

Perhaps one of the most interesting benefits that comes with working in fashion is the opportunity to work or travel overseas, or at least to communicate with people overseas. There are many things to be aware of when working with people overseas. It is impossible to discuss the specifics of every country; however, it is highly recommended to do research on a country before doing business there.

The major elements of a country's culture include its social structure, language, nonverbal communication, religion, and values and attitudes.

:: SOCIAL STRUCTURE ::

Social structure is an important element, which includes the view of the family in the culture and social stratification. **Social stratification** refers to putting people in categories based on their birth, occupation, and education. The caste system in India, for example, the family one is born into determines that person's position of authority in any situation in life. India is a highly stratified country. On the other hand, there is low stratification in the United States. For example, it would not be uncommon for a manager at a retail store to give orders to her staff but yet turn around and take orders at a PTA meeting from one of her salespeople. This would not happen in a highly stratified country.

Another element of social structure is the culture's tendency toward collectivism or individualism. For example, in the United States, individual work is praised, whereas in Japan, the collective unit of the team is praised, and it would be embarrassing for someone to be praised individually.

When doing business overseas, a designer, or anyone for that matter, must understand the social stratification of the particular country and know what the people there believe his or her social status to be. Without knowing this information, the designer may speak to a highly stratified country member in an inappropriate manner.

:: LANGUAGE ::

Particularly in the fashion industry, language is a major element, and if not handled correctly, it can be a large impediment to doing business overseas. An experiment done by John Schermerhorn proved that language, even when translated well, can have entirely different meanings. He put two groups of bilingual people in a room and asked them to write an identical assignment, one in English, one in Chinese.

After making sure the translations were perfect, he found answers among the two groups to be very different. This indicated that the language itself actually changed the way the information was communicated.

Consider a hypothetical situation in which an American technical designer must work and communicate with a Mexican project manager in a manufacturing plant in Mexico. The technical designer needs to know when the samples will be ready; in addition, he must be able to make changes to the actual design. If neither party speaks the other's language well, accurate communication is lacking, and both may end up quite frustrated.

Another possible communication difference involves the use of the words *yes* and *no*. In Japanese culture, it might be considered rude to say no; by saying something such as "I understand what you are saying," the Japanese businessperson may actually be politely saying no. Meanwhile, the American has understood the agreement to be yes.

Over time, especially when the same people are working together, problems resulting from the language barrier may improve, but there are some key points that may help communication. First, ask clarifying questions, such as, "If I understand you correctly, you can send me the samples by tomorrow?" Another way to get through communication barriers is to be as short and concise as possible. Since much communication will be done via e-mail, it is important that the writing is short and easy to follow and understand. Here are some additional tips when using language overseas:

- *Speak and write using simple vocabulary.* Avoid the use of idioms, such as "flat as a pancake." Also, acronyms can also be confusing to many who speak English as a second language. A commonly used acronym such as "I need this ASAP (as soon as possible)" may cause confusion. Also avoid slang words and phrases, such as "I am really beat" or "I was really bummed after hearing the deal didn't go through."
- *Speak slowly and distinctly.* Make sure to pronounce and completely type out all words. Avoid using words like, gonna, wanna, comin', and goin'.
- *Be aware of words that have one meaning in the United States but another elsewhere.* For example, when American's say "table the discussion," they mean to set the discussion aside for awhile. When the British want to table a discussion, it means they want to talk about it right now.

:: NONVERBAL COMMUNICATION ::

Another important element of communication is nonverbal behavior. Nonverbal communication can include things like punctuality, eye contact, gestures, physical distance from the person while talking, the use of silence in conversations, speech speed and inflection, and the amount of touching. Some tips for overseas communication, offered by Roger Axtell, author of *Do's and Taboos Around the World,* include the following:

- *Watch for body language.* If you sense coolness in manner, grimace in the face, or stiffening of the body, you might have said or done something to offend the other party.
- *Be aware of the general view of punctuality in the country.* In Germany, Austria, and Switzerland, being on time is extremely important. To be even a few minutes late would be extremely offensive. In much of Southeast Asia, however, people prefer not to live their lives in measured segments, so being on time is not as important.

- *Eye contact is another imperative nonverbal consideration.* Americans tend to look people right in the eyes. In Southeast Asia and Japan, it would be rude to look directly at another person for more than a few seconds.
- *Gestures are another form of nonverbal communication.* Gestures are numerous, but some gestures acceptable in the United States may not be accepted elsewhere. For example, in Southeast Asia, the sole of the shoe should never be exposed toward another person. This is an insult because the sole of the shoe is the lowest part of the body. In Japan, the OK signal means you want your money in the form of change. Correct posture and proper seating is also extremely important in Japan.

Greetings when meeting people also vary from country to country. Because a greeting is a first impression, it is imperative to understand what is appropriate in a country. Figure 8.4 illustrates some of the differences in greetings.

:: RELIGION ::

Religion is an important aspect in most cultures. Religion most often determines social values and the relationship between people. It shapes the attitudes toward work, consumption (such as the appropriateness of drinking alcohol or not), and individual responsibility. "Appropriate" roles for women also are bound in each country's faith.

8.4 figure **GREETINGS FROM AROUND THE WORLD**

COUNTRY	GESTURE
China	Nod or bow.
Hong Kong (older Chinese)	Clasp hands together at throat level and nod.
India	Keep palms together as though praying and bend or nod; called *namaste*.
Indonesia	Say *selamat*, which means `peace'.
Japan	Bow from the waist, with palms on thighs and feet together.
Korea	Make a slight bow and shake hands.
Malaysia	Both hands touch other person's hands, then are brought back to the breast.
Philippines	Make a limp handshake.
Sri Lanka	Place palms together under chin and slightly bow.
Thailand	Place palms together, elbows down, and bow head slightly; called *wai*.
Europe	Shake hands for first meeting; at subsequent meetings, kiss on one cheek.
Jamaica	Make direct eye contact, shake hands, and smile warmly.
Australia	Shake hands and say "G'Day".

All people participating in overseas business should have an understanding of the predominant faith in the particular country, and know the differences that can occur due to the predominant faith.

:: VALUES AND ATTITUDES ::

The value and attitudes in a culture can be related to age, education, and status. All three elements can affect the way a person does business overseas. In China, for example, older executives of a firm tend to negotiate with older, more senior members of another company. Although education per se is highly valued in most countries, the type of school attended or the degree obtained can have more influence in some countries than in the United States. In addition, one's status in society can be an important factor in doing business in some countries. A businessperson's school affiliation (if it is prestigious), company affiliation, or company position may determine his or her status in the eyes of others. In India, status is determined by one's caste, and in Hinduism, one's caste reflects the virtue exhibited in a previous life.

It is vital to note that every country, even every region in a country, has different social structure, language, nonverbal communication, religion, and values and attitudes. Before working with overseas vendors, it is imperative to study these elements to gain a better understanding and appreciation of the people in that country. Those successful in doing business in another country not only research and gain an understanding of that culture, they have empathy for the culture, even though they may not agree with or understand it fully.

Worshipers inside Cao Dai Cathedral in Tay Nihn, Vietnam.

>> contemporary issues in sourcing

Social responsibility refers to the idea that businesses should not function immorally, but instead they should contribute to the welfare of their communities. In the fashion industry, this means the factories that are used overseas should not negatively impact the communities in which they operate. For example, child labor, workplace safety, environmental standards, and fair wages are all issues of concern for a socially responsible company. In Chapter 3, the Real World Focus addressed the socially responsible manner in which Mohawk Industries cares for the environment. Here we will discuss social responsibility when it comes to manufacturing.

:: CHILD LABOR ::

Concern about child labor intensified in the 1980s and 1990s. It is estimated that 120 million children between the ages of 5 and 14 work on a full-time basis; 61 percent of these children are in Asia, 32 percent in Africa, and 7 percent in Latin America.

Child labor refers to the direct use of children to produce goods made for resale. A major concern is that if children are working, they are unable to obtain an education that will help better themselves in life. Without education, they are relegated to low-paying factory-type jobs for the rest of their lives. However, some argue that many families in other countries depend on the money brought in by their children; perhaps one of the parents is ill, and the family would not eat if it weren't for the work of the child. This is a delicate issue, as some believe that Western culture is forcing its beliefs on other cultures rather than letting the society function as it always has.

In 1996, Nike found itself in serious trouble as a result of the actions of out-of-country contractors that it used in the production of its shoes. It was discovered that the contractors were providing unsafe working conditions, forcing long working hours on workers, and sexually harassing employees. Nike contended that its contractors followed all local laws, but those laws are less stringent than the labor laws in the United States. Nike eventually had a public relations campaign and hired a vice president to oversee its production facilities and contractors.

Children stitching together garments.

Another issue with child labor involves bonded or enslaved children. An agent may arrive at a small, impoverished town, promising jobs in the nearby cities for the children. The person may purchase clothing or animals for the family. Because of their intense poverty, the parents may feel it is a genuine opportunity for the child and let him or her go with the agent. The child is then sold and used as a laborer in factories or as a domestic servant. If the parents search for and find the children, they would likely be told that the child is working to pay back the money used to take care of him or her, a debt that could never be paid off.

:: WAGES AND WORKING CONDITIONS ::

Another concern that has arisen with the increase in outsourcing focuses on appropriate wages and safe, clean working conditions. A debate about these issues continues on both the international level and local levels.

A **living wage** refers to compensation for work that is enough to cover daily living expenses. There is pressure on contracting factories and firms to offer their employees an adequate wage they can live with rather than a meager wage that forces them to work many more hours to make ends meet.

Another issue in regard to wages is the idea of **fair trade,** a movement that promotes responsible social standards in the production of goods. Recently, Starbucks has had some good PR because it supports a fair trade wage in the coffee it purchases from throughout the world. The people who actually grow and harvest the coffee beans for the company are paid a percentage of what the beans are sold for rather than simply being paid a low wage. By engaging in such socially responsible behavior, Starbucks hopes to gain more loyal customers.

Other labor issues include unsafe working conditions, sexual harassment, required overtime, access to drinking water and toilets during the workday, and the ability of workers to unionize without fear of losing their jobs. For example, according to its spring 2005 corporate social responsibility report, Nike found abuses in its South Asia factories in almost all of the above mentioned areas. Workers in these factories were forced to work seven days a week, denied breaks, and sexually harassed by management.

Unfortunately, there are no international laws that govern wages, child labor, hours worked, sexual harassment, or sweatshops. A **sweatshop** is defined as a factory that employs people for low wages, who work long hours in poor working conditions. Because of the lack of international standards, companies producing goods overseas must use vendors and factories they feel meet the standards for labor they personally have set forth. Many retailers have codes of conduct for their vendors, which address such issues as working hours, working conditions, and pay in the factories. In 2005, The Gap canceled contracts with 136 factories, in Mexico, China, and Russia, citing their requirement of 80-hour workweeks and the use of bonded and child labor (discussed in the last section). Most multinational companies publish their own corporate social responsibility reports (typically available on their websites) . These will continue to set standards for companies in the developed world and help alleviate harm being caused at factories thousands of miles away.

There are several organizations that oversee working conditions and wages for overseas production. UNITE HERE is a labor union organization used to promote the rights of workers throughout the world. UNITE stands for Union of Needletrades, Textiles, and Industrial Employees, and HERE stands for Hotel Employees and Restaurant Employees International Union. The two unions merged in 2004. The organization represents workers in the traditionally low-paid hotel, food service, and apparel manufacturing industries, among others. It makes recommendations on how governmental policies can be improved to meet the needs of workers throughout the world.

The American Apparel Manufacturers Association (AAMA) represents the concerns of its members to the public and to the government. The association looks at legislative and international trade issues and lobbies for a particular point of view to the government, provides support for overseas sourcing issues, and tries to create a favorable environment for trade. **Lobbying** is when an organization hires people to advocate a certain viewpoint to the Senate and House of Representatives in Washington, D.C.

The National Retail Federation (NRF) is another organization that provides a voice for retailers with government officials. It participates in lobbying efforts, holds conferences, and collaborates on issues affecting retailing, both domestic and global.

Each of these groups assist in making labor laws fair throughout the world, but they also advocate positions on tariffs, trade agreements, and other global issues.

:: DEPENDENCE ON FACTORY JOBS ::

Many developing countries are very dependent on clothing manufacturing jobs. For example, Sri Lanka is a country of 19 million people, 450,000 of whom are employed in the textiles industry. That is more than 15 percent of the nation's population. Sri Lanka is not the only country with a dependence on this industry; China, India, and Pakistan depend on textile exports for a large portion of their economies as well.

It is important to keep in mind the domino effect this industry can have on other industries. For example, if textiles workers lose their jobs, they will no longer have money to support the grocery stores, artisans, and other businesses. As a result, the whole community suffers when jobs in the textile industry are lost. On the other hand, when the industry is performing well, the workers have more money to spend, and thus the whole region does better economically. Many scholars believe that when economic development occurs in a country, education levels rise, death rates decrease, and there is more political stability, which improves the living conditions for the people in that country.

It is important to note that the majority of the workers in the clothing manufacturing industry are women. In fact, 70 percent of the factory workers in the apparel industry are women. This makes a huge impact on communities, especially those that have lost many male breadwinners to civil wars and diseases such as HIV/AIDS. It gives mothers a way to support their children. Even unmarried women are affected by factories moving into their towns. Women who make their own money are no longer as dependent on men to provide for them.

A downside to the dependence on factory jobs is heightened by the recent elimination of quotas on textile products. Many countries are worried that the elimination of a quota system would jeopardize their textile industries. Because price is the largest factor when retailers award contracts to overseas manufacturers, workers and factories may have to take lower prices as a result of increased competition in textile trade.

:: NATURAL DISASTERS ::

When natural disasters occur, industries are affected. Tsunamis and earthquakes in developing regions have detrimental consequences, not only for the people who live there but entire industries. A large natural disaster can have obvious immediate effects such as delayed shipments or complete stoppage of production. But long-term effects may also arise, particularly in developing countries with weak infrastructures. For example, the rebuilding of factories and recruitment of new workers can take time. Often, fashion designers in the United States must build new relationships in other parts of the world to insure that future orders will be delivered on time.

>> conclusion •••••••••••••••••••••••••••••••

This chapter brought to light many issues facing retailers that produce products overseas. Trade agreements, protectionist policies, and the actual production process are all vital factors to having successful products made overseas. From trade agreements to the actual production process, the fashion marketer or designer must be aware of these new trends in global business.

>> chapter eight review •••••••••••••••••••••••••

TERMS TO KNOW ::

Sourcing	Wholesaler	Trade agreement
Wholly owned factory	Drop shipper	Social stratification
Vertical production	Quota	Social responsibility
Joint venture	Tariff	Living wage
Pattern grading	Duty	Fair trade
Market intermediaries	Customs inspections	Sweatshops
Selling agents	Protectionist policies	Lobbying
Broker	Embargo	

CONCEPTS TO KNOW ::

1. The overseas production process.
2. Trade agreements.
3. Ways to overcome communication barriers.
4. Contemporary issues in sourcing.

CHAPTER QUESTIONS ::

1. Explain what protectionist policies are.
2. Discuss the steps involved in producing goods overseas.
3. Name at least two trade agreements and discuss the implications of those agreements.
4. What would you do when preparing for an oversees trip to visit manufacturers? If you were visiting an English-speaking country, would your preparation be different. Why or why not?
5. What are the three types of intermediaries discussed in this chapter? How are they the same? How are they different?

CHAPTER PROJECTS AND DISCUSSION ::

1. Research the function of the WTO. What are the main functions of the organization? Do you think it has accomplished these functions? (See www.wto.org.)
2. Research an issue related to overseas production. Describe the issue and the long-term effects on the people of that country, as well as the fashion industry worldwide.
3. Perform an Internet search on a country of your choice. Research its normal codes of behavior, such as the culture's general view of time or gestures. Report what you have found.
4. Give an example of a company you think is socially responsible. Discuss why you believe this.
5. Look up one of the labor organizations mentioned in this chapter. Does it have a mission statement? How do you think this statement applies to global trade?
6. Do an Internet search for a fashion company's corporate social responsibility report. Describe the report's shortcomings and strengths.

FOR FURTHER READING ::

www.wto.org
http://europa.eu.int
www.cid.harvard.edu/cidtrade
www.hg.org/trade.html
www.ustr.gov/index.html

retailing in a **vibrant world**

r etailing is a very exciting part of fashion; it is where all of the hard work pays off. A designer or merchandiser will actually get to see how well his or her product is selling in a retail store.

After reading the chapter, you should be able to:

1 • Describe the four utilities in retailing, and know why they are important.

2 • Describe the important components in the process of selecting a site for a retail store.

3 • Tell a merchandise story using visual merchandising design principles.

4 • Explain human resource challenges in retail.

5 • Describe what areas should be included to make an effective retailing website.

Retailing is the process of selling goods directly to consumers through various retail channels. As a result, designers and buyers see the value of their research and marketing through sales made within the store. Retailing fits into the marketing shoebox (see Figure 9.1).

This chapter will discuss three aspects of retailing: the physical environment of a store, retail management, and electronic retailing.

Each of these areas is extremely important for maximizing sales in a retail store. First, the physical environment must meet the needs of the customer and accurately reflect the desired image of the store.

Second, employees play a major role in the retail environment. The retail manager must insure that employees complement the image the store is trying to project. This is performed through hiring, training, and reviewing the performance of employees.

Lastly, electronic retailing provides customers with more shopping options, which can result in an increase of profit for the retailer.

> **"Retailing is the process of selling goods directly to consumers through various retail channels."**

Before discussing the physical environment, retail management, and electronic retailing, we should examine the concept of **retail utility**. In economics, *utility* is a measure of the ability of a product to satisfy customer needs. Retail utility includes four components: time, place, form, and possession. To best meet the needs of customers, retailers strive to maximize all four of these components.

First, **time utility** refers to the availability of product exactly when the customer wants it. Convenience stores that are open seven days a week, 24 hours a day offer time utility. So do online stores at which consumers can shop whenever they wish. **Place utility** refers to the retailer's location, be it a bricks-and-mortar store or a website. Good place utility means the store is easily accessible. **Form utility** in retailing relates to the actual product in the store; that is, it refers to the various colors, sizes, and features of a product that are available. A retailer with a wide assortment of merchandise available has good form utility. **Possession utility** refers to the ease of ownership of a product. It can also include

9.1 figure   THE MARKETING SHOEBOX

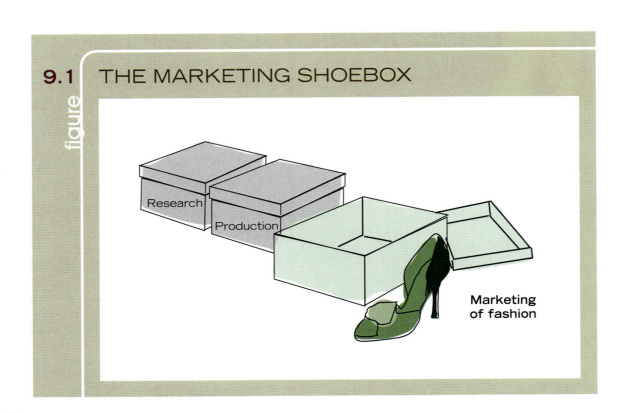

Research

Production

Marketing of fashion

the ease of transferring possession from the seller to the buyer. For example, a way to in increase possession utility is to offer a store credit card to customers. An agreeable return policy for customers is another example. If the return policy is good, customers are more likely to buy because they view purchases as being less risky.

Retailers that offer all of these utilities at high levels will be the most successful. If one or two of these utilities are missing or weak, it may be difficult for the retailer to stay in business for a long period of time. Wal-Mart, the most successful retailer in the country (maybe even the world), offers good time utility through its extended hours, especially during the holiday season. It also has good place utility by providing many locations as well as a user-friendly website. Wal-Mart enhances form utility through its wide variety of merchandise and brands. Finally, it offers possession utility by taking many forms of payment, including checks and a variety of credit cards.

The better utility retailers can offer, the more likely customers will want to shop at their store. For another illustration, consider Sephora, a beauty products retailer. Sephora has good time and place utility because its stores are typically located in malls that have longer hours for shopping. In addition, it has a website that provides 24-hour shopping. Sephora's form utility is also very good. It offers a very large assortment of beauty products, from a variety of brands. Sephora does not offer an in-store credit card, but it does have an easy return policy, which helps bolster its possession utility.

>> physical environment in retail

The physical environment of a retail store is extremely important, because it is the first impression the customer has of the store. Retailers spend valuable resources trying to entice customers into their stores, with the goal of getting them to buy something once there. If customers choose not to purchase, the marketing of a retail store or its brand is virtually useless. The next section will discuss components of a good physical environment, including site selection, store image and planning, and visual merchandising.

:: SITE SELECTION ::

The choice of a good retail location is perhaps the most important decision a retailer will make. Once a retailer has selected the type of store, covered in Chapter 7, the second step is to decide where the store should be physically located.

One type of location is the **central business district,** which is a downtown commercial area. For example, numerous retailers can be found on Chicago's Magnificent Mile, located on Michigan Avenue. The advantage to this type of location is high visibility for both businesspeople and tourists. However, the cost of the high visibility offered in a downtown area might be prohibitive for many retailers.

View of Michigan Avenue in downtown Chicago, also known as the Magnificent Mile.

A second type of location is a **freestanding store,** which is a self contained building, usually on the outskirts or in the suburbs of a city. Sometimes, a variety of freestanding stores might be located in one central area. This is called a **power node.** For example, Marshalls, Pier One Imports, and Famous Footwear located together would be considered a power node.

Retailers can also choose to locate in a strip mall or factory outlet, the latter of which was covered in Chapter 7.

When selecting a physical location, such as a central business district or a freestanding store, the retailer should consider a variety of factors.

Pedestrian traffic

Pedestrian traffic refers to the number of people who pass by a location in a given period of time. The store could be located inside a mall, strip mall, or neighborhood. When measuring pedestrian traffic, the researcher must also consider the demographics of the pedestrians. In other words, there may be 300 people who pass by a location in a given day, but a retailer needs to be sure that those passersby are within the desired target market.

Vehicular traffic

The traffic patterns in a given location are also an important consideration. Consumers must have easy driving access into and out of the possible location. Consider a Ross and Marshalls located right across the street from each other. Both stores offer similar merchandise, but customers will likely choose the one that is easiest to get to, depending on the direction they are driving, traffic lights, and traffic patterns.

Parking

The distance from the store to affordable and available parking is another important consideration. Because the cost of parking can be high in a downtown area, a retailer located there may offer discounted parking with a purchase.

Lighting and security in parking lots are also concerns. Many malls have security guards; some provide shuttles that take people from the mall door to their cars to alleviate security issues. Other options are to locate next to a major transportation hub or to offer a shuttle to the location. For example, The Gallery at Market East in downtown Philadelphia is right next to a large bus hub, making it easy for people to park and ride.

Infrastructure

Infrastructure includes the facilities and transportation systems in a particular area that promote commerce. For example, one consideration is how easy it is for delivery trucks to get to the location. Public transportation that makes it easier for customers to arrive at a particular retail location, as in The Gallery at Market East example mentioned above, is another consideration. A retailer may also consider the cost of electricity and water in the area. Other infrastructure considerations include lighted parking for customers, the availability of workers in the area, and the tax structure for the location.

Placement and visibility

The actual location on a street or in a shopping center is extremely important. Rent is generally more expensive for sites with higher visibility, such as a corner location. Many retailers will hope to gain customers who are simply walking by, such as in a mall. But a store located away from a main walkway may receive less business than one located in a major corridor. Bellevue Square Mall in Bellevue, Washington, is a large, regional shopping center. Its layout uses a "spine" approach, meaning there is a main walkway (prime space) and smaller walkways (less desirable space) leading from the bigger walkway. (This approach will be discussed in more detail in a later section on floor plans; see Figure 9.2 in that section for illustrations of various floor plans.) The amount of traffic within the smaller walkways is considerably less, resulting in less exposure; thus, rent is less expensive.

Another consideration in site selection is the type of stores around the proposed location. A high-end retailer may not want to open a store that uses the same parking lot as a discounter, such as Wal-Mart; but for another retailer, say Payless Shoes, such a location may actually drive more customers to the store.

Category killers are stores that offer a large depth of merchandise. A category killer offers such a large selection that customers may not be willing to shop at a store with a smaller selection of the same type of item. Category killers are important in determining placement and visibility. For example, Famous Footwear, a category killer, may deter people from shopping for shoes at a nearby Target. Or, if Target expects a large number of sales to come from bedding, it may choose not to be located next to Linens 'n Things.

Trading areas A trading area is another important consideration in site selection. *Trading area* refers to the geographic area in which a retailer draws its customers. The **primary trading area** is one in which a retailer expects 50 to 80 percent of its customers to live. The **secondary trading area** contains about 20 to 25 percent of the customers. The **tertiary trading area** is a wide area located outside of the primary and secondary trading areas. This can encompass 5 to 25 percent of the customers.

Depending on the type of store, a retailer may be concerned only with the primary area. For example, the owner of a convenience store knows that people will not drive 10 miles out of their way to purchase snacks. As a result, the primary area is most important to this retailer. On the other hand, a factory outlet store will depend greatly on the tertiary trading area, along with the primary and secondary areas. People will drive a great distance to shop at a factory outlet, unlike in the convenience store example above.

Buying or leasing Another consideration in site selection is whether to lease or purchase the location. The advantages to purchasing a retail space can include the following:

- The property might increase in value.
- The retailer can alter the visual look of the store without requiring permission from a landlord.
- There is no worry about a lease expiring or lease terms changing.
- Depending on the size of the space, the retailer may be able to lease some space to other retailers.

However, there are also disadvantages to purchasing a retail location:

- The cost to purchase a building can be very expensive.
- The retailer would be responsible for paying taxes and all maintenance.
- The retailer may want to focus on running the business and not on being a landlord.

Some advantages to leasing are as follows:

- The retailer can invest in inventory rather than in the purchase of a building.
- The retailer may lack capital to purchase a building.
- If a location is leased in a mall, the mall may provide advertising and marketing to draw customers.
- The retailer can focus on running the business, while the landlord handles maintenance, such as plumbing.

Inside a typical mall.

However, leasing too can have some disadvantages:

- Leasing can be very expensive.
- Some landlords, such as in a mall, may require not only the lease payment but also a percentage of sales on a monthly basis.
- Restrictions in the lease must be adhered to, such as the hours of operation and signage restrictions.

:: STORE IMAGE AND STORE PLANNING ::

Store image, sometimes called *store atmospherics,* includes all of the elements of the retail store. Retailers need a distinct identity, one that will match the type of goods they are selling. For example, at Tiffany & Co., the large doors, display cases, and salespeople in suits promote the upscale image the company is trying to achieve.

Aspects of store image can be intangible and tangible. **Intangible aspects** are those that cannot be touched or seen, such as smell. Smell can be effective in helping to create the type of ambiance a store wants. For example, Victoria's Secret stores have a distinct feminine smell (the perfume they sell). Another intangible aspect is the store's background music, not only the type of music, but the volume at which it is played. In addition, how the store is actually organized is an intangible aspect. **Tangible aspects** of a store's image are physical elements such as the types of fixtures in the store, the size of the dressing rooms, and the signage that is used to promote products.

Store planning refers to how the store will actually be laid out, for example, where the dressing rooms and **cash wrap** are located. A cash wrap is where the customers pay for their merchandise.

Physical appearance Window displays, fixtures, architectural features, and the layout of the store are all part of the physical appearance. For example, Kohl's utilizes a racetrack design in its stores (discussed later, see Figure 9.2), and the floors and restrooms of its stores are clean. To promote diversity, Kohl's has mannequins in wheelchairs.

Ambiance Ambiance is a mood evoked by the use of intangibles and tangibles. This can include the type of music played in a store, the smell of a store, and the colors used within a store. Signage, store fixtures, and use of wall space are tangible aspects of the store. Abercrombie and Fitch, for example, uses very dark lighting in its stores to create a mood for its customers. In addition, Abercrombie and Fitch brand cologne is sprayed in the stores. Nordstrom uses a variety of effects in its men's suiting department: expensive wood fixtures, large fitting rooms, soft music, and impeccable organization all work to create the desired ambiance.

Employee attitude and appearance The impressions made by the sales associates and managers affect a store's image. The way the sales associates are dressed and their overall look may help to sell the clothing. Most retailers require employees to wear its brand. Hollister, for example, requires all employees to wear Hollister clothing and to reinforce a certain image through their overall appearance, including hair and makeup.

Floor plans The floor plan of a store will help create the image the retailer wants and also encourage customers to browse longer within a retail store. There are three main types of floor plans, with variations of each. These are illustrated in Figure 9.2.

The first type of floor plan, the **grid,** is used at most supermarkets and other stores where space needs to be maximized. The grid floor plan works well for products that are smaller in size and when the products do not need to be displayed together to encourage customer purchases, unlike most fashion products. In a grid floor plan, aisles are rigid and straight. The Men's Warehouse chooses to use rigid aisles with suits lined up on large racks simply because this pattern utilizes space better for the types of products it sells.

A variation of the grid is a **spine** format, which is where there is one main aisle with smaller aisles branching off of it. This plan allows for more freedom to display merchandise than a grid, and the aisleways encourage the customers to visit the goods on the walls.

The second type of floor plan uses a **freeform,** or **freeflow,** design in which racks and shelves are strategically placed. Using a freeform approach, visual merchandisers can design pathways that lead customers toward the merchandise that they want them to see. Many smaller retail stores use some type of freeform plan because it is less rigid and thus easier to change to meet the needs of specific merchandise.

The third type of floor plan, the **racetrack,** encourages customers to span the entire space of the store from front to back. Macy's, for example, uses a combination of racetrack and freeform. The racetrack format is used for the major aisleways, while freeform is used within particular departments. The racetrack is generally used for larger stores, which have many different types of departments and many goods to display.

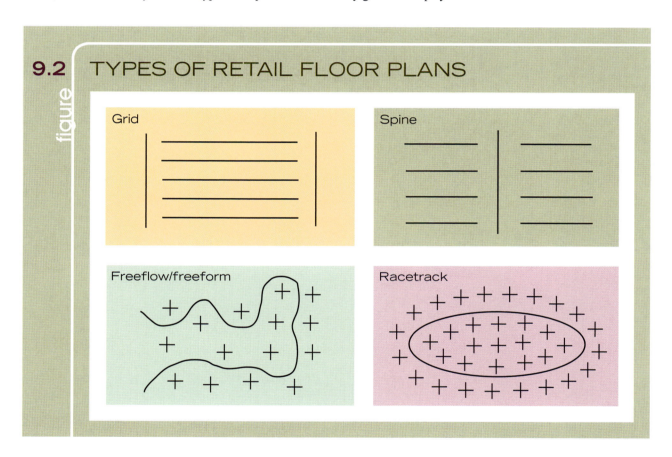

9.2 figure

TYPES OF RETAIL FLOOR PLANS

Grid

Spine

Freeflow/freeform

Racetrack

:: VISUAL MERCHANDISING ::

Visual merchandising involves the precise placement of goods, signage, window displays, and mannequins in a store.

The goal of visual merchandising is to create a story. The story can tell the consumer what tops go with what bottoms, what accessories go with a certain outfit, or how many colors are available. By creating a story, a retailer will likely see an increase in sales.

There are five main design principles involved in effective visual merchandising: color, balance, texture, line, and rhythm. Although there are many other design elements in art, these five are those most important to visual merchandisers. Each of these elements is reflected in the type of fixtures, lighting, and window displays used in the store.

COLOR SYSTEMS

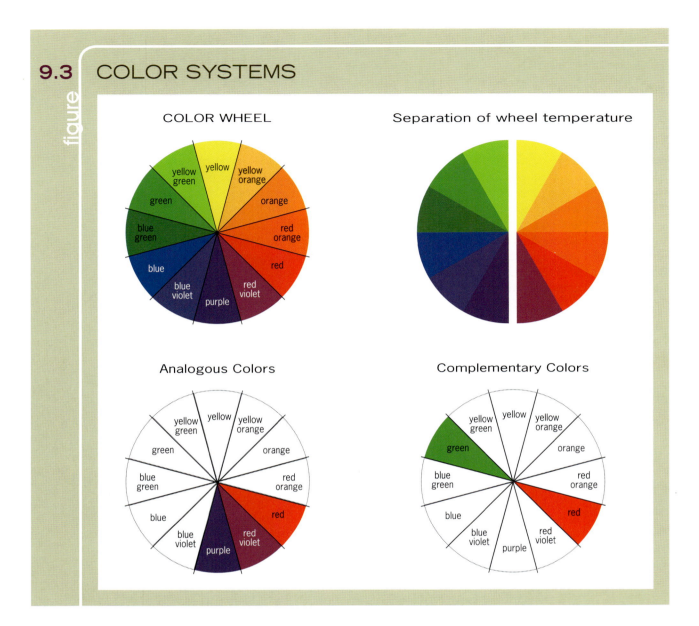

COLOR WHEEL

Separation of wheel temperature

Analogous Colors

Complementary Colors

Color There are a variety of color theories that apply to visual merchandising. A **color wheel,** based on the primary colors red, yellow, and blue, is traditional in the field of art, including fashion (see Figure 9.3). Isaac Newton developed the first circular diagram of colors in 1666. Since then, scientists and artists have studied and designed numerous variations of this concept. However, all color wheels are based on hue, brightness of the color, and saturation. *Hue* is the actual color, such as red or blue. *Brightness* refers to the amount of light that is reflected from the color. *Saturation* refers to the depth of color. For example, to paint a fashion illustration, a designer might use blue and, to saturate the color, add white to the blue. Although the color is still blue, the hue appears lighter.

Color harmony refers to how well the colors work together to produce an attractive scheme. The color wheel is an effective tool for determining color harmony. For example, **analogous colors** have color harmony; these are two or three colors next to each other on the color wheel, such as yellow and green or red and purple. **Complementary colors** are those across from each other on the color wheel, such as red and green or blue and yellow. *Monochromatic color schemes* utilize one color and its lighter and darker variations. A *warm color scheme* uses reds, yellows, and oranges, whereas a *cool color scheme* uses blues, greens, and purples. Visual merchandisers can use any of these ways, and more, to create harmony and drive sales.

Balance

Balance is a design principle that refers to the visual weighting in a composition. In visual merchandising, balance can be created by simply placing the same number of items on both sides of a display.

But balance in visual merchandising can be achieved in ways that are not strictly symmetrical. It may refer to a more general sense of order or coherence, something less formal than equal weighting. For example, a retailer may place hosiery or socks with shoes and lingerie soap in the intimates department. Also, shirts are typically placed with ties. Such order creates add-on sales, which helps the store's profitability.

Texture

Texture, the third design element in visual merchandising, can refer to a physical characteristic or a visual effect. A physical texture can be felt with the hand; for example, an item of clothing can be soft or rough. Visual texture refers to an illusion created through the use of different physical textures. All displays should have an element of texture, both physical and visual. This can be achieved by use of a variety of fabrics and different sized fixtures.

Line

Line is the appearance of a beginning and an end of a design. In visual merchandising, it refers to the start and the end of a collection of garments. Line should always appeal to the eye, and it should be used to differentiate between colors, or the particular stories being created. For example, a visual merchandiser would not place denim directly next to suits. More likely, there will be a transition between the two categories of clothing through the use of other garments, or through actual space created on the wall between the garments.

This display has excellent texture and line through the use of the hats.

Rhythm

Rhythm in visual merchandising, much like in music, is utilization of repetition that can be viewed as continuous. The visual merchandiser can create rhythm with several repetitions, perhaps with slightly different patterns and colors, to show the customer a story. On a wall display, for example, a visual merchandiser might display T-shirts paired with jackets and T-shirts alone to create a rhythm.

Each of the design elements—color, balance, texture, line, and rhythm—contribute to visually pleasing displays.

Fixtures

To help tell their story and create the desired ambiance, visual merchandisers use a variety of fixtures in their displays. Some common types of display formats are grids, gondolas, shelving, tables, two-ways (sometimes called t-stands) and four-ways.

Grids are typically placed on a wall and can be used to create a large visual story. A grid system includes various kinds of hardware, such as face-outs, hanging bars, or shelving, that allow for movement of merchandise along the wall. A **face-out** is a piece of hardware that enables merchandise to hang facing toward the customer. The advantage of using a grid fixture is the fact that pieces, such as face-outs and hanging bars, are interchangeable, allowing the retailer to display merchandise in a variety of ways.

Gondolas, usually a mixed type of fixture, can include places for small shelving and hanging items. They are ideal for creating a story in that several pieces that go together can be displayed.

This display has excellent balance, texture, line, and rhythm.

This is an example of a two-way, sometimes called a t-stand. In the background, shelving is used.

For example, a gondola can show customers how one or more T-shirts can go with a pair of pants and that those same pants can go with a jacket and skirt.

Shelving and tables might be used to display sweaters, T-shirts, or pants. The flat surface allows for a

This is an example of a four-way.

variety of options for display. The Gap is well known for its uses of tiered shelving.

Two-ways have two railings that allow for merchandise to be displayed on each side. Normally, the visual merchandiser will use one side for tops and the other for bottoms. A visual merchandiser's job is to make things look attractive so customers will want to buy the entire outfit, not just one piece.

Four-ways are similar to two-ways, except they have four rods rather than two. This allows for the visual merchandiser to place four different items on one rack. As with all displays, these items should tell a story by including pieces, say tops and bottoms, that will coordinate with each other.

Other important fixtures are the mannequins the store chooses to use. There are many different kinds. For example, Chico's uses wooden cutouts. A wooden cutout is a relativity two-dimensional figure with metal representing the head. There are also full-form mannequins, which include a body and head. There has also been an increase in the use of manneguins showing diversity in body types.

A mix of wall grids and four-ways.

An example of a gondola.

This is an example of a closed-back window.

Lighting

Lighting is another important aspect of visual merchandising. Track lighting allows the visual merchandiser to focus spotlights, and thus customer attention, on a specific item. As mentioned earlier, the lighting used can also set the mood for the store. In addition, merchandise that a visual merchandiser wants to highlight may not be highlighted as well with poor lighting.

Store windows

Another important aspect of visual merchandising is the use of store windows to attract customers into the store. There are a few types of windows. **Open-back windows** allow customers on the outside both to see the display and to see through the display to the back of the store. This creates the illusion that the store is larger than it is in reality. **Closed-back windows,** used by many department stores, do not allow the customers on the outside to see through the display into the store. A closed-back window allows for much creativity, however, because the merchandise in the window is the focus, not the merchandise behind in the store.

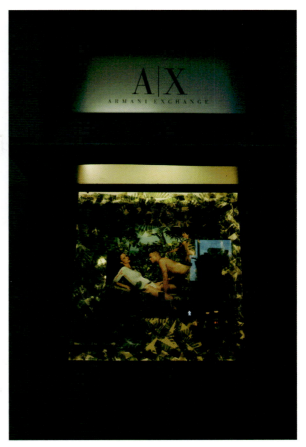

This is an example of a closed-back window.

>> retail management

So far, this chapter has focused on the overall image of a store. Because employees are elements of a store's ambiance and visual merchandising, this is good section to discuss some of the employee issues related to retailing.

A major component of retailing is the actual day-to-day operations of running a retail business. Along with managing the visual merchandising, operations include the hiring, training, and the motivating of employees.

Retailers face many challenges when hiring for retail positions. One of these challenges is irregular demand. For example, during a holiday season, demand is high for employees, but in January, demand drops. Few workers are willing to take temporary positions; therein lies the challenge. Most workers do not want to work evenings and weekends for lower wages, making long-term, loyal employees difficult to find.

In the following sections, human resource issues will be addressed, including hiring, training, motivating, and evaluating employees in retailing.

:: HIRING ::

Hiring the right person can be one of the most difficult tasks in any kind of business. The challenge of finding a customer-service-oriented person who is dependable and flexible is one that faces retailers and all other businesses. It is difficult to sit down with a person for an hour or maybe less and determine if he or she is a right fit for the company. Many companies today want to know if the potential employee has problem-solving ability, creative-thinking skills, and the ability to provide excellent customer service.

The process of hiring usually involves a resume or an application, an interview, testing, and reference checks. Many companies even offer the ability to file applications online, such as Neiman Marcus. Some online applications allow the applicant to use a code to start and stop the process, enabling the person to log back on at a later time to complete and submit the application. In many cases, the applicant can choose locations he or she might be interested in working, and the online application is then sent to those stores.

Testing for employees can include drug testing and spelling or math testing, depending on the job. Many retailers, such as Home Depot, participate in drug testing because they get lower insurance rates by doing so. Once the resume or application has been turned in and testing is complete, the retail manager will interview the candidate, perform reference checks, and then decide whether or not to make an offer to the person.

Interviews One of the best ways to assess a candidate is through an interview. The interviewer usually obtains a better feel for the person by asking open-ended questions rather than questions that can be answered with a yes or no. The following are examples of open-ended questions:

- What hours are you available?
- Tell me about your background in retail?
- Give an example of how you have provided good customer service.
- What are your strengths? Weaknesses?
- How flexible are your hours?
- Give an example of how you worked well in a team.
- What motivates you?

A relatively new type of question tests the ability of the candidate to solve problems. Questions such as, Why are manhole covers round? or How many golf balls fit in a 747 airplane? are not uncommon. In most cases, there is no right answer; it is simply a test to see how the candidate thinks, to determine creativity, and to see how the person performs when put on the spot.

Two types of interviewing techniques are role-plays and situational interviews Using the **role-play** approach, the interviewer may ask the candidate what he or she would do in a hypothetical situation, such as dealing with an irate customer. Another type of role-play technique is to actually place the candidate on the retail sales floor and see how he or she interacts with customers. In a **situational interview,** the candidate gives examples of how he or she has dealt with situations in the past. Most interviewers will also look for knowledge of the company's products as well as enthusiasm. Often, assistant managers and sales associates will also interview candidates.

Caution is advised in the interview process. There are a number of legal matters with which an interviewer should be concerned. For example, an interviewer is not allowed to ask questions about a person's age, marital status, or race or religion. The company should train its interviewers to insure that they don't ask such questions or perform illegal actions during interviews. There are many books that provide legal information for interviewing. See the "for further reading" section at the end of this chapter.

:: TRAINING ::

Training is one of the most important phases of a new employee's experience. The retailer has invested much time in finding the right person, and now the new employee must learn how to perform the job effectively. Components to retail training include orientation, sales training, and on-the-job training. In addition to retail training, many companies provide mentors to help new employees with any questions they may have during their first few weeks on the job.

Orientation   During orientation, the new employee learns more about his or her role, the company, and the policies of the company. Often, orientation is done through a series of videos and manuals. This stage is extremely important, as it helps the new employee to feel comfortable in his or her new position. Paperwork required by the Internal Revenue Service is usually completed during this period. The manager may also have the new employee "shadow," or follow around, a seasoned employee for a specific period of time. This allows the new employee in retailing to experience the company's expectations for customer service.

Sales training   In Chapter 7, personal selling was discussed as part of the promotional mix. It is important that new employees in retailing gain sales knowledge in order to better service the customer. Most retailers train their employees to use specific tactics, even steps, in personal selling, such as the following:

1. *Greet the customer.* Most retailers expect the salespeople to greet the customer within a specific time of entering the store; 15 or 30 seconds are standard for most retailers.
2. *Start a conversation with the customer.* Use open-ended questions; for example, ask "What are you shopping for today?" rather than "Can I help you?"
3. *Be helpful.* Show the customer where to find the type of item he or she wants. This may also include bringing additional items to the customer in the dressing room.
4. *Use suggestive selling.* Tell the customer about the socks that are on sale or suggest a T-shirt that looks great with the pants he or she is purchasing.
5. *Thank the customer and invite him or her back.*

In addition, product knowledge is extremely important for new employees. As a result of the Internet, many customers arrive in stores with more knowledge about products than ever before. But sales representatives should know more than the customers do about the products being sold. Important product knowledge includes details about how to wash specific garments, the size range in which they are available, and information about new product lines as they become available.

:: MOTIVATION ::

There are several ways to motivate employees to insure they are productive. Of course compensation is one way, but there are other ways as well, which we will discuss in this next section.

Compensation   There are many types of compensation plans for employees. For purposes of this section, only a few common ones will be discussed. The most common is a **straight salary** plan. This involves a set dollar amount per hour, week, or month. This is the easiest to calculate and understand, but it may not motivate employees to sell.

The other end of the spectrum is a **straight commission** plan. The employee earns a commission on what he or she actually sells. However, some employees might object to the unpredictable nature of this type of compensation; there will likely be slow days when the employee doesn't sell very much, but on other days he or she might make a lot of sales.

A common plan is **salary plus commission.** This type of plan gives the employee a salary he or she can depend on, but the person can earn more by selling well.

Another type of compensation involves what is known as **push money.** Separate from the employee's regular salary and commission, push money is a bonus for selling one item in particular. In most electronics stores, sales associates will receive push money for selling extended warranties. Also in fashion retail, a salesperson might receive more hours for high sales.

Another type of compensation uses what are called **spiffs.** These are competition-based, short-term motivational tools for employees; for example, a retailer may reward employees with money or merchandise for selling the most items in one day or for selling the most of a particular item. It could be a free lunch for the employees who meet a specific sales goal in a given day In some cases, the competition for a spiff may be between teams of employees rather than individual employees. If a retail store is near its sales goal for the day or the week, a spiff may work well in motivating employees to reach that target.

Alternative methods of motivation There are numerous books and theories about the motivation of employees. Research shows that employees are motivated by a variety of things, not just money. The following are some things that can motivate employees:

- The feeling of being part of a team.
- Good communication within the company.
- Training.
- Benevolence (attempts to make the worker happy, for example, company parties).
- Chance for upper mobility in the company.

Motivation is different from employee to employee, so it is important for the manager to know what motivates each individual person.

:: EVALUATION ::

Besides compensation and other forms of motivation, evaluation of an employee's performance can also provide motivation. Every employee should receive a formal, written performance review at least once a year. This formal review will allow the employee and employer to discuss performance issues and goals of each. If the employee needs to perform better in certain areas, a formal review will allow the manager to help the person formulate a plan for improvement.

This sort of formal communication is important. However, it is also important for the manager to give constant feedback and not wait for the performance review. If an employee has done something well, the manager should let him or her know verbally and immediately. Likewise, if an employee does something wrong, the manager should inform the person right away and not wait to discuss it at the performance review.

Two important elements of a performance review are the criteria used and the type of rating system used. The criteria will usually echo items that appear in the job description, such as "meets sales goals" or "works effectively as a team." The performance review should only rate those things relevant to the job.

The second element of the performance review is the rating system used. There are several types of systems. The review may rate the employee's performance along a numeric scale, say of 1 to10 or 1 to 5. Another option is to use a word-based rating system; for example, a criterion may be rated as being "unsatisfactory," "fair," "good," or "excellent." The company may decide to use a written essay on the performance review and give an overall rating.

Note that performance reviews must not focus on personality traits, but must be connected to the actual job description.

>> electronic retailing and nonstore retailing

Good management and hiring is imperative to the success of a retail store. But besides their bricks-and-mortar locations, more and more retailers are using electronic stores as a part of their selling strategy. Retailing on the Internet is a relatively new field, but in the last 10 years it has become an extremely popular and lucrative way for retailers to expand their sales.

E-tailing and *e-commerce* are two terms often used when discussing electronic retailing. Although they are used interchangeably, they actually have slightly different meanings. **E-commerce** refers to Internet-facilitated commerce in general, that is, the use of electronic means for promoting, selling, distributing, and servicing products. **E-tailing** has a more narrow definition. It refers to the actual process of retailing online through the use of "virtual" storefronts that serve as a catalog of products and usually include a "shopping cart" system that enables consumers to purchase online with credit cards.

Web retailers, or e-tailers, are relativity new, compared to traditional bricks-and-mortar stores. The following are five types of retailers found on the Web:

- *Pure-play retailers.* A **pure-play retailer** does not have traditional stores; it carries out its business online only. A well-known example of a pure-play retailer is Amazon.com. Amazon offers an immense variety of products, without an actual storefront. Overstock.com is another example of a pure-play retailer.

- *Dual-channel retailers.* A **dual-channel retailer** is one that primarily operates bricks-and-mortar stores but also engages in business online. Wal-Mart is an example. This type of e-tailing enables customers to shop in a store or at home. It allows those who do not live near one of the retailer's stores to still do business with the merchant. Using dual channels is also a way to gain customer loyalty.

- *Multichannel retailers.* A **multichannel retailer** sells goods in more than two places. JCPenney, for example, sells through its physical stores, catalog, and website.

- *Electronic spinoffs.* These include retailers that sold goods through means other than bricks-and-mortar stores. Examples might include QVC or The Home Shopping Network, which sell their goods on television.

- *Nontransactional sites.* These sites are meant for information purposes only and are not used to actually sell goods online. Technically, these are not actually e-tailers; instead, they are considered users of e-commerce. Express is an example. Express does not sell any clothing on its website, but it provides information to customers about new and upcoming styles. The upkeep and maintenance of this type of website is easy, but customers may become disappointed if they are unable to order products online.

Online retailers face several challenges. First, it may be difficult to duplicate a store's established image on a website. The intangible aspects that make up a store's ambiance are not easily transferred to a website. Second, driving customers to a website can be difficult. Many online retailers use combinations of the promotional mix to get customers to visit their site. A third challenge to online retailing is designing a website that is user friendly and that offers a good selection of items.

A challenge for multichannel retailers is how to structure the total business. In other words, companies have to make the choice to structure their online business as an entity separate from their retail stores or treat it as if it were a traditional bricks-and-mortar store.

An ongoing challenge in online retailing involves security and privacy issues. Security has improved through software developed over the past few years, but as hackers get more sophisticated, the software must keep pace.

Internet retailers that have been most successful are those selling products that do not require close inspection or sizing prior to purchase, such as books and music. Other retailers that have performed well online include those that sell products that people have already used and therefore know their size. For example, a woman might order a bra from the Victoria's Secret website because she knows the product and the size that works for her.

Online auction sites, such as eBay, are an effective way for smaller retailers to gain new customers. For minimal fees, a retailer can set up a virtual store that may get more than 43 million visitors monthly, giving it great visibility.

There are four main components to a good e-tailing website: usability, design, personalization, and content. *Usability* refers to how easy it is to navigate a website. The pull-down menus, shopping cart, and ability to find a specific item are all important aspects of usability. In addition, making it easy for customers to simply browse the site is important. Second, the *design* of the website is important; it should show as much ambiance as possible. The use of color and pictures should make it easy for customers to purchase the product. The third component is *personalization,* which enables the e-tailer to save information on past purchases, make recommendations to the customer, and show other items in the online store that match or complement those in the shopping cart. The fourth component is *content,* such as product reviews by other customers or relevant articles. Such information can help create loyalty.

One major concern for e-tailers is *conversion,* which is the percentage of visitors to the website who actually purchase a product. The average conversion rate is 2 percent. REI, an apparel and sporting goods retailer, has a conversion rate of 10 percent. This success is a result of the site's use of content, such as articles and tutorials to inform customers about outdoor recreation issues. The REI site also provides interactive tools; one, for instance, enables customers to select the right size ski rack.

:: OTHER NONSTORE RETAILING ::

Besides the Internet, there are other methods of retailing that don't require an actual physical store location. Avon and Mary Kay use a **direct selling** approach for retailing. Direct selling means the salespeople go to the customers' homes and offices to sell the products. Another method of direct selling is used by Pampered Chef and Home Interiors. These companies offer discounts and free merchandise to people who host parties to sell their products. The use of catalogs, as discussed in Chapter 7, is another form of nonstore retailing.

REALWORLDfocus >> eBay Hits the Bricks to Speed Slow Product

Although it might seem like a competitor, eBay wants to help traditional retailers deal with some onerous tasks in a new and less costly fashion. Working with retailers, such as Sears and Sharper Image, eBay already is acting as an off-price resource, and it is looking to expand such services to the larger retailer community, exponentially, if possible.

Much of the action selling returns, liquidations, and discontinued items takes place on eBay Home & Garden, where both vendors and retailers offer brands ranging from Kenmore to Kitchen-Aid to Sure Fit to Stanley to Disney.

The critical point people are catching on to, said John McDonald, director, eBay Home & Garden, is that eBay is a resource for essentially new products from the most popular retail and vendor names in home furnishings. Of course, eBay can be and is a resource for other categories, and new products from broadliners are available online today. Home & Garden happens to be one where retailers have built an extensive business selling goods that otherwise would move into the offprice channel.

As more people do catch on, retailers and vendors are going to discover new ways to use eBay as a way of more efficiently going to market. They can do so without having to break altogether new ground, as eBay traditionally has been successful selling refurbished and seasonal items. Obviously, a service that grew by offering used items is a ready market for refurbished goods. And eBay buyers already look for off-season bargains, McDonald said, so, again, the site itself has created favorable conditions for a class of merchandise that becomes an uglier problem in the retail environment every day past its selling period.

On returned items particularly, eBay can offer retailers better margin opportunities than do traditional off-price distribution channels, McDonald said. "We're getting the word out to take advantage of those margin opportunities," he said.

Floor models are another class of goods that move readily through eBay. "It gives retailers an available and attractive way to sell those," McDonald said.

He added that eBay could even offer better results than can retailers own websites in many cases because shoppers come looking for an item rather than an irresistible deal. In other words, the eBay shopper is more anxious and likely to bid up the item than the bargain hunter is to act on anything but the most deeply discounted piece of merchandise.

Indeed, by working through eBay, retailers have an opportunity to see how the market prices various product segments under different sales conditions, whether off season, refurbished or other.

Of course, different classes of goods come with their own challenges. Sears, for example, has to deal with scratched and dented major appliances. While most consumers who walk into Sears want appliances that are in mint condition, eBay users tend to be a bit more flexible about a little damage. So the retailer has been able to use eBay as an effective method of moving big pieces of merchandise that otherwise would take up valuable space in the bricks-and-mortar world, McDonald said.

Sharper Image found that eBay could work for them. The company had auctions on its own website, but, after being approached by eBay almost a decade ago, began to discover ways that working with the dedicated auction site could work to its advantage.

"What we were looking for was a way to transition refurbished and returned inventory, end-of-lifecycle items," said Aimee Cooper, senior VP of public and investors relations. "There is the Sharper Image customer who shops the Sharper Image website but then there is that eBay customer. We found that 70 percent of the customers on eBay were new to the file for us. They had never been Sharper Image customers."

She said the relationship between eBay has evolved over the years with technology improving and opportunities expanding.

"It has been a great distribution channel for us. It is very cost effective and provides a wide audience. It has a great brand name and great functionality, and it moves through product cost effectively and brings great customers," she said.

Today, eBay is developing programs to aid retailers who want to use the site as a resource. Already, retailers can create an eBay store for just $9.95 a month. Another initiative is eBay's effort to bring retailers and vendors together to help both use the site. Vendors, particularly with discontinued items, can work with retailers using eBay as a selling tool, gaining valuable expertise and even placement in their on-site storefronts.

A whole class of eBay sales, marketing, pricing, and related consultants has sprung up to help retailers launch and support on-line bidding projects. Service providers, such as companies that move furniture and other big items, emerged as well.

The potential for new uses is broad. For example, eBay could take some of the risk out of exclusives. Retailers want exclusive, differentiated products, but vendors want to produce items for a lot of retailers to spread out their development costs and reduce risk. As a result, so-called exclusive products aren't always strictly differentiated from one retailer to the next. With eBay available, an exclusive product that doesn't move still has a secondary sales channel, so a vendor has the opportunity to move product that doesn't have sufficient velocity on a particular sales floor.

Once, the big ideas in online retailing emerged from the pure players, but now the bond between clicks and bricks retailers are becoming closer. Much of the innovation in e-tailing is coming to the service of traditional retailers today. ✿

Source: Written by Mike Duff, *DSN Retailing Today,* October 25, 2004. Copyright 2004, Gale Group. Reproduced with permission of the copyright holder; further reproduction or distribution is prohibited without permission.

1. What is an off-price resource?

2. How has eBay changed retailing in the last 10 years?

3. What do you think eBay will need to do to stay successful in the retailing arena?

>> conclusion • • • • • • • • • • • • • • • • • • •

In this section, we covered the basics of retailing. Most fashion students will also take a retail course, but this chapter provided some basis for future courses. Retailing can include the intangible and tangible aspects of a retail store, such as the smell and the types of fixtures used. We also discussed the types of retail stores and electronic retailing, which has become popular in the last decade. Finally, our discussion ended with information a store manager might need to know, such as how to compensate employees and how to motivate them as well.

>> chapter nine review • • • • • • • • • • • • • • •

TERMS TO KNOW ::

Retailing	Grid (floor plan)	Open-back window
Retail utility	Spine	Closed-back window
Time utility	Freeform	Role-play
Place utility	Racetrack	Situational interview
Form utility	Color wheel	Straight salary
Possession utility	Color harmony	Straight commission
Central business district	Analogous colors	Salary plus commission
Freestanding store	Complementary colors	Push money
Power node	Grids	Spiffs
Category killer	Face-out	E-commerce
Primary trading area	Gondolas	E-tailing
Secondary trading area	Shelving	Pure-play retailer
Tertiary trading area	Two-ways	Dual-channel retailer
Tangible aspects	Four-ways	Multichannel retailer
Intangible aspects	Lighting	Direct selling
Cash wrap		

1. Retail utility.
2. Advantages of leasing and buying.
3. Aspects of store image.
4. Visual merchandising design principles.
5. Interviewing techniques and hiring process.
6. Types of e-tailing.
7. Nonstore retailing.

CHAPTER QUESTIONS ::

1. Discuss the five components to good visual merchandising.
2. Describe four things that can motivate employees. What motivates you the most?
3. Name the types of retail stores and describe each.
4. What are the types of layouts? Which layout do you prefer when shopping?
5. What is balance in visual merchandising? How can it be achieved?
6. Describe the meaning of analogous colors.
7. Define straight commission. Is this a type of compensation plan you would like to work for?

CHAPTER PROJECTS AND DISCUSSION ::

1. Visit three retail stores. Discuss which type of floor plan each store uses. Do you think this is the most effective layout for each store? Why or why not?
2. What are some other interview questions that can be used by retail managers? In groups, make a list of at least five other interview questions.
3. Go to www.nordstrom.com and www.thegap.com. Describe and compare the usability, design, personalization, and content of the websites.
4. What online store is your favorite place to shop? Why? What specific components discussed in this chapter make it a good place to shop?
5. Write down your favorite and least favorite store. Discuss their use of each retail utility and how they might be able to improve upon it?
6. Discuss your favorite store to shop. What store image factors make it a good place to shop? Where do you avoid shopping? What about the store makes you dislike it?

FOR FURTHER READING ::

www.dsnretailingtoday.com
www.clickz.com/stats/sectors/retailing
www.shop.org/index.asp
www.stores.org

retail Buying

this chapter will discuss the buying side of the fashion business. Buyers in the retail business are responsible for figuring out the right merchandise to sell in the stores and insuring that the right amount of inventory is available to meet customer demand. In addition, buying involves providing information that helps retailers set profitable retail prices. The buying function of the fashion business is perhaps the most crucial to know, as it provides a baseline for all other activities in the fashion industry.

The buying calculations discussed in this chapter can be applied by a wide range of retail professionals, including assistant buyers, buyers, store owners, and fashion designers.

After reading this chapter, you should be able to:

1 • Develop a profit and loss statement.

2 • Explain how profit and loss statements are used in the fashion industry.

3 • Calculate gross margin.

4 • Explain open-to-buy.

5 • Calculate planned markdowns.

6 • Explain how markdowns can stimulate sales.

7 • Calculate turnover.

8 • Explain how turnover is important for the open-to-buy calculation.

9 • Read a six-month buying plan and explain each component.

10• Explain merchandise classifications and assortment.

11 • Negotiate effectively.

Merchandising of fashion items fits in the marketing shoebox (see Figure 10.1) because it involves giving customers the right product at the right price. As discussed in Chapter 7, if customers are not offered the right prices for goods, or the right products, it is highly unlikely the retailer will be successful. However, if buyers, designers, and retailers grasp the concepts discussed in this chapter, there is a greater likelihood they will be able to meet the needs of the customer.

This chapter will present formulas that can be used to calculate components of the profit and loss statement, markups and markdowns, shrinkage and turnover rates, and other variables involved in the retail business. In addition, the chapter will discuss elements of a six-month merchandising plan.

Each formula will be presented in a separate box along with examples. The chapter will follow the activities of a buyer for Casey's, a hypothetical retail store, and take the reader through the process of preparing for a buying trip.

Although some of the information in this chapter will likely be covered in other courses, understanding the basic calculations early on will make future buying classes much more enjoyable.

> **"As in any kind of merchandising, the goal for all fashion buyers and designers is to maximize profit."**

A **profit and loss statement** is used to see the big picture in a retail environment. A profit and loss statement is generally good for a specific time period, such as one quarter (three months). As in any kind of merchandising, the goal for all fashion buyers and designers is to maximize profit, and a profit and loss statement is an essential tool for analyzing the business. Many of the numbers in a profit and loss statement are calculated not only in dollar amounts but also as a percentage of sales, which allows the retailer to know how a particular variable affected profit in the given time period.

The profit and loss statement is a formal document that lists four main components:

1. Sales.
2. Cost of merchandise (inventory) sold.
3. Operating expenses.
4. A profit or loss figure.

Figure 10.2 presents a profit and loss statement for Casey's, the store that will be used as our example throughout this chapter.

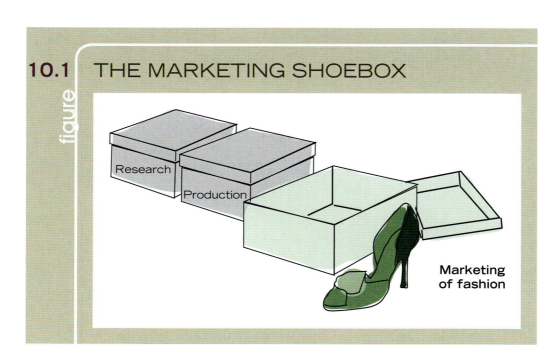

10.1 THE MARKETING SHOEBOX

figure

Research

Production

Marketing of fashion

A **balance sheet** (Figure 10.3), on the other hand, is a statement that allows the business to see the **assets** it owns. Assets include the inventory, buildings, and anything of value the company may own. The balance sheet also shows **debt,** which includes any money the retailer owes. Finally, the balance sheet lists the **owner's equity.** This is the difference between what the business has and what it owes (assets and debt). Owner's equity can be negative, if the company's debts are greater than its assets. A balance sheet is good only for a particular moment in time, because the debt and assets are constantly changing. A balance sheet is used more by accounting departments than by buyers; thus, our focus will be on profit and loss statements.

:: BUILDING A PROFIT AND LOSS STATEMENT ::

The buyer at Casey's, a small junior retail store in the trendy Buckhead neighborhood of Atlanta, wanted to know the total profit it earned in October 2007. The steps involved are as follows:

1. Determine gross sales.
2. Determine customer returns and allowances.
3. Determine net sales.
4. Determine cost of goods sold.
5. Determine gross margin.
6. Determine direct expenses.
7. Determine indirect expenses.
8. Determine total operating expenses.
9. Determine if a profit or loss exists, then calculate taxes.

figure 10.2 CASEY'S PROFIT AND LOSS STATEMENT

OCTOBER 25, 2007

Sales	
Gross sales	Step 1
Customer returns and allowances	Step 2
Net sales	Step 3
Cost of merchandise sold	
Inventory	Step 4
Transportation	Step 4
Gross margin	Step 5
Operating expenses	
Direct expenses	Step 6
Indirect expenses	Step 7
Total operating expenses	Step 8
Profit (or loss)	Step 9

figure 10.3 BALANCE SHEET

Assets

Current assets—This includes cash and any money owed to the company (accounts receiveable).

Fixed assets—These are any assets such as land, equipment, or worth of building.

Total assets—This figure is the current and fixed assets added together.

Liabilities—These include anything the company owes. For example, a bill due for shirts ordered is a liability.

Owner's equity and capital—This figure will record the amount of money initially invested in the business.

Step 1: Gross sales **Gross sales** refers to the total amount of sales, without accounting for the actual cost of items or the overhead involved to actually sell those items. Here is the formula for gross sales:

Gross Sales =	total dollar amount of sales

In October Casey's sold the following items:

15 sweaters at $49.50 each

20 skirts at $29.50 each

5 pairs of tights at $8.50 each

2 pairs of jeans at $59.50

50 t-shirts at $29.50

20 suits at $159.50

To calculate the gross sales, first multiply the unit price by the number of units sold:

$15 \times \$49.50 = \$742.50$

$20 \times \$29.50 = \$590.00$

$5 \times \$8.50 = \$42.50$

$2 \times \$59.50 = \$119.00$

$50 \times \$29.50 = \$1475.00$

$20 \times \$159.50 = \$3190.00$

Next, add up the totals from above:

Gross sales = $\$742.50 + \$590.00 + \$42.50 + \$119.00 + \$1475.00 + \$3190.00 = \$6159.00$

Gross sales is an important starting point for stores to determine their profit for a given time period, such as a day, a week, or a month.

Step 2: Customer returns and allowances Now that the buyer of Casey's knows the gross sales, she must calculate the customer returns and allowances for the day. Customer allowances account for any rebates given to customers. They can also include defective merchandise. Customer returns are subtracted from gross sales, because they are no longer sales. In other words, returns count against the sales for the day.

The formula for the dollar amount of customer returns and allowances is:

Customer Returns and Allowances =	dollar amount of returns	+	customer allowances

Casey's had the following returns during October:

2 skirts at $29.50 each

1 pair of jeans at $59.50

Casey's also had the following allowances:

A customer was given a 10 percent discount on a $29.50 skirt because its hem was loose.

Calculate the customer returns and allowances:

2 × $29.50 = $59.00

1 × $59.50 = $59.50

10% × $29.50 = $2.95

Add the totals from above:

Customer returns and allowances = $59.00 + $59.50 + $2.95 = $121.45

If the buyer at Casey's wanted to determine customer returns and allowances as a percentage of sales, she would make the following calculation:

Customer Returns and Allowances Percentage = customer returns and allowances ÷ gross sales

Customer returns and allowances = $121.45

Gross sales = $6159.00

Divide customer returns and allowances by gross sales:

Customer returns and allowances as percentage of sales = .0197 or 1.97% or 2%

Step 3: Net sales Net sales provides a picture of what was actually sold for the day, week, or month. It is the total number of sales, less returns and allowances. The formula for net sales is:

Net Sales = gross sales − customer returns and allowances

Subtract customer returns and allowances (step 2) from gross sales (step 1) to get the net sales for October:

Net sales = $6159.00 − $121.45 = $6037.55

Step 4: Cost of goods sold The next determinant of profit is the actual cost of goods sold (COGS), or what the buyer paid for the inventory sold and the transportation involved in receiving those goods. This is sometimes called *cost of inventory.*

Cost of Goods Sold (COGS) = units sold × cost of good

Casey's costs for the items sold (as listed in step 1) are as follows:

15 sweaters at $20.00 each = $300.00

20 skirts at $10.00 each = $200.00

5 pairs of tights at $3.50 each = $17.50

2 pairs of jeans at $31.00 each = $62.00

50 t-shirts at $10.00 each = $500.00

20 suits at $70.00 each = $1400.00

Add these numbers:

Cost of goods sold = $300.00 + $200.00 + $17.50 + $62.00 + $500.00 + $1400.00 = $2479.50

Transportation for these items = $20.00

Total COGS is $2479.50 + $20.00 = $2499.50

Step 5: Gross margin Besides gross sales, many buyers want to know the gross margin. **Gross margin** is useful because it provides an indication of a retailer's ability to turn sales into profit. In other words, if the gross margin is too low, it could mean that the buyer paid too much for the goods; or it could mean that customer returns and allowances were too high. Gross margin is the difference between the net sales and what the goods cost the buyer.

The formula for gross margin is:

Gross Margin = net sales − cost of goods sold

Using the totals calculated in steps 3 and 4 above, Casey's can determine its gross margin:

Net sales = $6037.55

Cost of goods sold = $2499.50

Gross margin = $3538.05

Step 6: Direct expenses Operating expenses include direct expenses and indirect expenses. **Direct expenses** can include selling salaries, advertising expenses, and rent. These are expenses that can be directly related to the items sold. **Indirect expenses** are those that are not related to the cost of items sold and would occur whether 100 items or only 2 items were sold. In other words, these expenses exist no matter how much is sold. Indirect expenses include things like insurance, electricity, and water.

The direct expenses for the day are calculated as follows:

> **Direct Expenses =** all direct expenses added together

Casey's had the following direct expenses for October:

Advertising costs = $200.00

Salaries = $1500.00

Rent = $1200.00

Add these numbers to calculate direct expenses:

Direct expenses for month = $200.00 + 1500 + 1200 = $2900 are the direct expenses for October

If Casey's wanted to calculate the direct expenses for the day (to determine the day's profit) Casey's could take the total direct expenses for the month, and divide by the number of days in the month: Direct expenses for day = $2900 ÷ 31 (days in the month) = $93.55

Step 7: Indirect expenses The next step is to calculate indirect expenses. This is normally calculated as a percentage.

> **Indirect Expenses for October =** all indirect expenses added together

Casey's had the following indirect expenses for the month of October:

Water = $100

Electricity = $125

Insurance = $25

Security system monitoring = $25

Add these numbers to calculate indirect expenses:

Indirect expenses for month = $100 + $125 + $25 + $25 = $275

If Casey's wanted to calculate the indirect expenses for the day (to determine the day's profit) Casey's could take the total indirect expenses for the month, and divide by the number of days in the month: Indirect expenses for day = $275 ÷ 31 (days in the month) = $8.87

Step 8: Total operating expenses

The next step would be to add the direct and indirect expenses. This number is the total operating expenses.

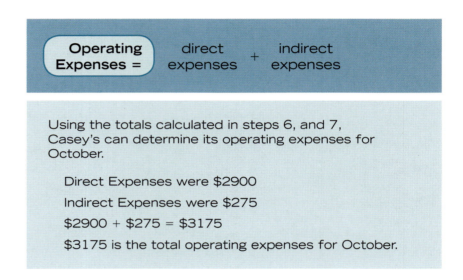

Operating Expenses = direct expenses + indirect expenses

Using the totals calculated in steps 6, and 7, Casey's can determine its operating expenses for October.

Direct Expenses were $2900

Indirect Expenses were $275

$2900 + $275 = $3175

$3175 is the total operating expenses for October.

Step 9: Profit or loss

To determine profit, the net sales are subtracted from gross margin and total operating expenses. After this task is performed, taxes must be calculated.

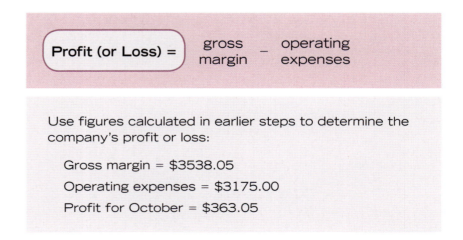

Profit (or Loss) = gross margin − operating expenses

Use figures calculated in earlier steps to determine the company's profit or loss:

Gross margin = $3538.05

Operating expenses = $3175.00

Profit for October = $363.05

Net Income =	profit − taxes owed

The profit was $363.05. If Casey's taxes were 20 percent,

Taxes = $363.05 × 20% = $72.61

Thus, Casey's profit after taxes, or net income, is as follows:

Net income = $363.05 − $72.61 = $290.44 This is the final figure, and is called net income.

Figure 10.4 presents Casey's completed profit and loss statement. Note how each calculation fits together in the statement. This allows the buyer, designer, or retailer a perspective on the total business. The buyer would not want the operating expenses to be more than net sales because that would mean it cost more to run the operations of the store than the costs of the goods sold. Also, if the cost of merchandise sold is close to the gross sales, it may mean that too many markdowns have been taken, thereby meaning the right merchandise wasn't purchased due to numerous markdowns.

10.4 figure

CASEY'S COMPLETED PROFIT AND LOSS STATEMENT

OCTOBER 1, 2007

Sales		
Gross sales		$6,159.00
Customer returns and allowances	$121.45	
Net sales		$6,037.55
Cost of goods sold		
Inventory	$2,479.50	
Transportation	$20.00	
Total COGS	$2,499.50	
Gross margin		$3,538.05
Operating expenses		
Direct expenses	$2,900.00	
Indirect expenses	$275.00	
Total operating expenses		$3,175.00
Profit (or loss)		$392.66
Taxes (20% rate)		$72.61
Net income		**290.44**

Markup is another important aspect to merchandising. **Markup** refers to the amount, above cost, that will be charged for an item. Markup is importanat to buyers, because it is a major factor as to the profit a company earns. If a buyer is able to obtain a high markup, her profit will be higher, and vice-versa. However, it is important to note that many retailers, like Wal-Mart, do not have high markups but instead rely on a large quantity of goods to be sold. It can be calculated as either a dollar amount or percentage. Chapter 7 covered the various pricing strategies and methods; this section will discuss how to actually calculate a markup.

The first step is to calculate the total dollars markup. Next, the buyer calculates the total retail cost, having these two numbers allows the buyer to know what her total markup for a purchase would be.

Markups can be performed using retail or wholesale. The markup equation is as follows:

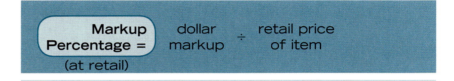

Markup Percentage = (at retail)   dollar markup   ÷   retail price of item

The buyer at Casey's may want to know the markup percentage on a skirt where the item is priced at $29.50 and the cost of the item is $10.00

First, she must calculate the dollar markup at retail, or the retail price of the item minus the cost of the item:

Dollar markup at retail = $29.50 − $10.00 = $19.50

The markup percentage then is the dollar markup divided by the retail cost of the item:

Markup percentage = $19.50 ÷ $29.50 = .66 or 66%

The buyer will more likely want to know the markup for her entire purchase of inventory, or the total dollar markup, rather than the markup for one item. To determine the total dollar markup, she would perform the following calculation:

Total Dollar Markup =   (retail price − cost) × quantity

First, the buyer would calculate the dollar markup for each individual item: (retail price − cost)

	RETAIL	COST		DOLLAR MARKUP
25 sweaters	$49.50 −	$20.00	=	$29.50
30 skirts	$29.50 −	$10.00	=	$19.50

15 pairs of tights $8.50   − $3.50   = $5.00
20 pairs of jeans $59.50 − $31.00 = $28.50

Then, the buyer would multiply the previous
figures by the quantity:

$49.50 − $20.00 = $29.50 × 25 = $737.50
$29.50 − $10.00 = $19.50 × 30 = $585.00
$8.50 − $3.50 = $5.00 x 15 = $75.00
$59.50 − $31.00 = $28.50 × 20 = $570

Adding these totals gets the total dollar markup, or
$1,967.50

Third, the buyer could calculate the total retail cost, as follows:

Total Retail Cost = each retail item cost × number of items

Sweaters $49.50 x 25 = $1,237.50

Skirts $29.50 × 30 = $885.00

Tights $8.50 × 15 = $127.50

Jeans $59.50 × 20 = $1,190.00

Total retail cost = $3,440

Then, the total dollar markup would be divided by the
total retail cost to arrive at the total markup percentage:

Total markup percentage = $1,967.50 ÷ $3,440.00
= .57 or 57%

>> markdowns

Markdowns might occur for many reasons. A **markdown** is a permanent reduction in price. This type of price reduction is different from a sales promotion, discussed in Chapter 7. A sales promotion is a temporary markdown to stimulate sales,
whereas a markdown means to lower the price of the item because it is not selling.
Markdowns provide more physical space for inventory and allow more open-to-buy
funds. As buyers become more aware of the reasons for having to markdown an item,
there should be fewer items that will need to be marked down. Reasons for markdowns can include:

I. Buying errors
   a. Overbuying of items.
   b. Buying of wrong sizes (poor form utility).

    c. Poor timing in orders.

    d. Purchasing of wrong sizes, or too many of one size.

    e. Stock becomes obsolete.

2. Pricing errors

    a. Setting the initial price too high.

    b. Not being competitive for same type of items.

3. Selling errors

    a. Careless handling that results in damaged items.

    b. Failure to display merchandise properly.

    c. Uninformed salespeople.

4. Broken assortments

    a. Merchandise has sold, leaving only a few uncoordinated miscellaneous items.

The timing of markdowns must be accurate. Here are a few determinants of when items should be marked down:

- Merchandise is slow in selling.
- Consumers are no longer interested in a particular fashion.
- A seasonal change has taken place.

Any markdown taken must be large enough to attract customers who rejected the original price. The reason for the reduction, the type of merchandise, and the quantity on hand are all considerations when deciding on the amount to mark down items. Normally, the buyer will monitor sales of items on a daily basis. In doing so, he or she will be able to take the appropriate markdowns at the appropriate time. When deciding to mark down a particular item, the buyer will generally make a price change in the point-of-sale (POS) system. This will allow the correct markdown price to ring up. The buyer will also notify the retail managers of the change. Then the retail managers will be able to inform the customers of the markdown through price changes on the tag or signage.

Another important aspect of markdowns is called markdown money. **Markdown money** involves an assurance from a vendor to take back (buy back) merchandise or refund money if the particular item does not sell well. A vendor would likely make such a agreement in an effort to build a good relationship with the buyer.

Another important concept regarding markdowns is the idea of sell-through. **Sell-through** is the percentage of merchandise that sells at the original full price. For example, if 50 percent of items were sold at full price, and 45 percent at a sale price, a buyer might say, "We had 50 percent sell-through, 45 percent at sale and 5 percent left over (or unsold).

:: DOLLAR AND PERCENTAGE MARKDOWN ::

Dollar markdown can be calculated by subtracting the original retail price from the new retail price. This formula would be used to determine the markdown on just one item:

Dollar Markdown = original retail price − new price

For example, the Casey's buyer purchased 20 pairs of jeans, and they have not been selling well. She has determined the slow sales are due to wrong purchases in sizes. All of the remaining sizes are either very small or very large. She has decided to take a markdown on these jeans to make room for items that have a better variety of sizes.

The jeans retail at $59.50, and she wants to price them at $39.50. The dollar markdown formula is:

Dollar Markdown for Multiple Items =	(original retail price − new price)	×	number of units marked down

Dollar markdown per item = $59.50 − $39.50 = $20.00

Total dollar markdown = 20 pairs × $20.00 = $400

This calculation can also be expressed as a percentage:

Percentage Markdown at Retail =	(original retail price − new price)	÷	original retail price

Of course, the numerator in the above equation is the dollar markdown. So using the figures from the previous calculation, Casey's buyer determines the markdown percentage as follows:

Dollar markdown = $59.50 − $39.50 = $20

Percentage markdown = $20 ÷ $59.50 = 34%

Casey's buyer also may want to calculate the markdown percentage after goods have been sold. This figure would show her the percentage of her total sales that resulted from markdown items. This would be done in the following manner:

Percentage Markdown After Goods have Sold =	((original retail price − new price) × number of items)	÷	net sales for the time period

Let's assume her sales for the day totaled $1,500, and she sold 14 pairs of the markdown jeans.

Percentage of goods sold that were marked down = (($59.50 − $39.50) × 14 pairs) = $280 ÷ $1,500 = 0.186 or 19% of the goods sold on this day were markdown items.

Most retail stores will track their total markdowns for a given period of time. In doing so, they are able to estimate the planned markdowns for future periods. This allows the buyers to plan on the expected number and retail cost of goods they might likely markdown in the future, based upon markdowns that happened in the past.

:: PLANNED MARKDOWNS ::

Successful buyers plan for markdowns in the coming year. This way, they can better plan their profit with the knowledge that not all products will sell at full price. Although buyers try to avoid markdowns, they are an inevitable part of retail. Because markdowns decrease profit, buyers must fully understand this aspect of the business. Usually the previous year's markdowns can provide a good starting point. The formula for planned markdowns is as follows:

$$\text{Planned Markdowns} = \text{average markdown percentage for reference year (normally the previous year)} \times \text{projected sales}$$

For example, if Casey's had the following markdown percentages in 2006, the buyer can plan the markdowns for 2007:

Month	Markdowns
January	21% markdowns
February	13% markdowns
March	15% markdowns
April	19% markdowns
May	9% markdowns
June	6% markdowns
July	18% markdowns
August	9% markdowns
September	20% markdowns
October	14% markdowns
November	4% markdowns
December	4% markdowns

She would then add all of the percentages and divide by 12 months to calculate the average markdown percentage:

$152.04 \div 12 = 13\%$ was average markdown percent.

The buyer then multiplies Casey's projected sales, $25,000, by the average markdown percentage to calculate dollar markdowns for the coming year:

Planned markdowns = $13\% \times \$25,000 = \$3,250$

In other words, the buyer knows she can plan on $3,250 of her projected sales to be markdowns.

Casey's buyer can then use this estimate when formulating her six-month merchandising plan (discussed later in chapter).

The discussion about markdowns should address the idea of **cash flow.** Cash flow is affected by the pattern of purchases the buyer makes and the amount of sales made by the store. If cash flow is too low, it could mean the buyer has purchased too many items without having enough sales. If cash flow is too high, perhaps the buyer needs to purchase more items, or reinvest the cash elsewhere to maximize the income derived from that cash. For the fashion industry, cash flow is particularly important because of seasonal fluctuations in demand. For example, a buyer may purchase many more items than usual to prepare for the holiday season, which may result in a poor cash flow if not enough items are actually sold. However, once the inventory for the holiday season is paid for and money isn't being spent on new merchandise, the retailer may find itself cash rich if it making a lot of sales. Markdowns are a good way to increase cash flow quickly in cash poor times.

REAL WORLD focus >> Using Markdowns to Drive Financial Performance

Retail executives are under more pressure than ever before to find new ways to drive better financial performance and provide attractive returns to shareholders. This pursuit has proven especially challenging in the last few years, with new competitors entering the fray and consolidation shifting the focus to mere survival.

While the boom economy of the late 1990s supported adding new stores as a strategy for growth, retailers today are faced with overstoring and an economic climate that is creating fierce competition for customer dollars. Retail executives, constrained by limited viable real estate expansion options, must focus on increasing gross margin dollars per square foot to drive comp store growth (comp store growth stands for comparative store growth; it is a way to measure how well one store is doing versus another store of similar size), Wall Street's favorite barometer of performance.

One of the quickest and most effective methods to grow comp store sales, profit, and thus earnings per share in today's complex environment is through effective markdown management. Markdowns generally take a 5 to 30 percent bite out of a retailer's revenues, but more effective management of this budget can add dollars to the bottom line. In fact, improving markdowns by 10 percent can add $20 million to the bottom line for a $1 billion retailer.

Retailers rely on merchants to manage the markdown expense. But today's merchants' responsibilities far outweigh those of their predecessors, both in terms of dollars and number of SKUs [stock keeping units] managed. The most talented merchants use their finely honed instincts to make profitable decisions about what to buy, where to allocate, and how to price thousands of SKUs at hundreds of stores. But even the best merchants can become overwhelmed with the sheer volume and velocity of these decisions, especially with regard to markdowns, which are a constant source of frustration for merchants managing that volume across several selling seasons.

Impact the Bottom Line

When merchandise is not selling well, merchants must decide when and to what extent to lower its price. They typically use spreadsheets and manual calculations with limited analytics to model consumer behavior. In other words, they rely on "gut instinct" to make decisions that have an enormous impact on profitability. Given the wild variation in demand caused by the largest economic upswing in decades, the uncertainties created by the attacks on September 11, and continuing recessionary pressures, performance is nearly impossible to benchmark. The markdown process is daunting, and each decision has a direct and dramatic impact on the company's bottom line.

The trick to marking down merchandise is to do it at the right time and, when appropriate, deeply enough to maintain or even spur demand. If merchants mark down merchandise too early, they lose margin opportunities by selling at less than full price. If they mark down merchandise too late, which is often the case, they may be faced with a scenario where no price will yield demand--out of fashion is out of fashion, regardless of the price. As a result, the retailer will have difficulty finding room for new merchandise on the selling floor and freeing up open-to-buy dollars. Add to this complexity the challenges of seasonality, regional differences, and temporary promotions, and it quickly becomes a very complicated and expensive decision. The more fashion-oriented the item, the shorter the lifecycle and the steeper the cliff.

Visionary Retailers Achieve Results

A growing number of retailers, including Best Buy, Casual Male, JCPenney, Meijer, Dillard's, and ShopKo, are profiting from the benefits of improving markdown performance through the use of markdown optimization solutions. Recent results from About.com's Markdown Optimization survey indicated that 21 percent of retailers surveyed have decided to implement markdown optimization and are in the planning/implementation phase, and 12 percent are researching their options.

An effective markdown optimization process will:

- Improve the use of capital (inventory) by increasing gross margin dollars and identifying the sales performance of each item and its response to sales drivers such as seasonality, markdowns and promotional events.
- Release money for new purchases.
- Provide input into the next season's finance, buying, assortment, and allocation plans.
- Impact store operations and customer facings.
- Create capacity for merchants to do what they love and what they were hired to do--buy merchandise.

Integrate for Success

While return on investment (ROI) has proven significant, sustainable improvement often requires integration with upstream merchandising processes and downstream retail operations. Without integration, the organization becomes mired in a perpetual pilot, the effort loses traction, and the organization moves on to the next software pilot. Markdowns are a cause (store- and distribution center–level workloads) and effect (result of poor planning and fickle customer demand) phenomenon. They impact the heart and soul of a retail organization and the relationships (vendors and customers) that give them life. Therefore, careful exploration and preparation is critical.

Capitalize on Existing Inventory Investments

In today's business climate, while collaboration with business partners is critical, retailers must not forget to look inward to drive financial performance. Successful retailers plan strategically, edit optimally, and mitigate risk. Markdown optimization enhances short-term risk mitigation by improving the return on inventory investments already made and providing input into future merchandise strategies and assortment plans. Markdowns are a practical place to quickly realize significant financial benefit.

No part of a retailer's business with such a dramatic and near-term impact on the bottom line should continue to be managed by "gut instinct." Retailers already pursuing markdown optimization should begin to integrate with other merchandising processes to capture maximum value. Those not yet on board should begin to explore markdown optimization technology and best-practice implementation.

Matthew Katz is a principal and the director of collaborative services for Kurt Salmon Associates. Katz has a broad range of experience helping clients realize dramatic improvements in supply chain performance through the adoption of next generation solutions and practices, business process re-engineering and organizational design. ✿

Source: Written by Matthew Katz, a principal and the director of collaborative services for Kurt Salmon Associates. Copyright 2003. Reproduced with permission of Kurt Salmon Associates.

›› QUESTIONS

1. What are some advantages to taking markdowns discussed in this chapter?
2. Why would a buyer be hesitant to take markdowns?
3. Name two dangers in taking markdowns too late.

>> inventory

Proper management of inventory is another important aspect of merchandise buying. The buyer must order the proper amount of merchandise for the season. If the buyer overbuys, he or she will likely not sell everything purchased, thus resulting in lost revenue through markdowns. If the buyer underbuys, he or she may not have enough merchandise in the store to make sales goals, and the retail store will look empty.

Effective inventory management requires accurate calculations of average stock, turnover, and weeks of supply or basic stock.

:: INVENTORY CALCULATIONS ::

Average stock Beginning-of-month (BOM) stock is inventory the store began with on the first day of the month. Casey's has a computerized inventory system, thus the buyer knows the stock at the beginning of every month.

Average stock is calculated by adding the BOM stock for the year and dividing it by the number of inventories taken (number of months).

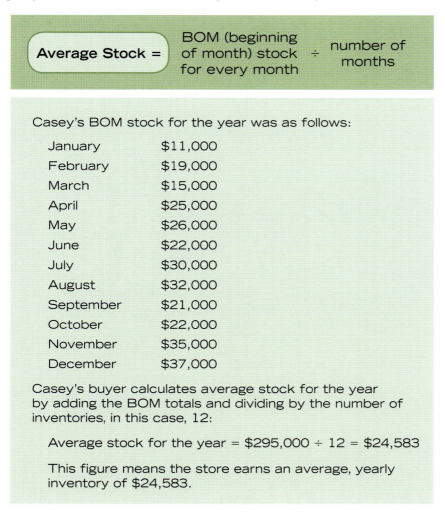

Average Stock = BOM (beginning of month) stock for every month ÷ number of months

Casey's BOM stock for the year was as follows:

January	$11,000
February	$19,000
March	$15,000
April	$25,000
May	$26,000
June	$22,000
July	$30,000
August	$32,000
September	$21,000
October	$22,000
November	$35,000
December	$37,000

Casey's buyer calculates average stock for the year by adding the BOM totals and dividing by the number of inventories, in this case, 12:

Average stock for the year = $295,000 ÷ 12 = $24,583

This figure means the store earns an average, yearly inventory of $24,583.

Some retailers may determine average stock by using only seven months of the season rather than the entire year. They would use seven months because there are six months in a season, plus the first month of the next season.

Turnover **Turnover** is another important component in merchandising. Turnover refers to how quickly all merchandise in a store sells. It is important because the faster merchandise sells, the quicker fresh merchandise can be introduced. The beginning of this chapter discussed calculation of net sales. Assume that Casey's net sales for the year totaled $126,200. Using the average stock figure she has calculated (see previous section) and net sales, Casey's buyer can calculate turnover as follows:

Turnover = net sales ÷ average stock

Turnover = $126,200 ÷ $24,583 = 5.13

This means that the average stock turned over 5.13 times during the year. Another way of looking at turnover is to say that Casey's sold all of the merchandise in the store five times during the year. This is a good number for Casey's, because it means that new merchandise was selling so fewer markdowns had to be taken. As a result, sales were stimulated because there was fresh merchandise in the store. A turnover of 2, for example, would not be a good turnover rate, because it would mean the store only sold all of its merchandise twice throughout the year. This lower turnover figure means less new merchandise could be introduced due to lack of sales.

Weeks of supply

Weeks of supply   Another important aspect in buying and merchandising is to insure there is enough inventory on hand to meet sales goals. A **weeks of supply** calculation can be performed to assist in this planning.

The buyer would use a desired turnover rate in making this calculation. Often, buyers use the turnover rate from the previous year in this planning. Planned sales, another variable in the calculation, is the dollar amount of sales the store hopes to make in a given time period. The planned sales goal is usually based on the previous year's sales figures. The formula is as follows:

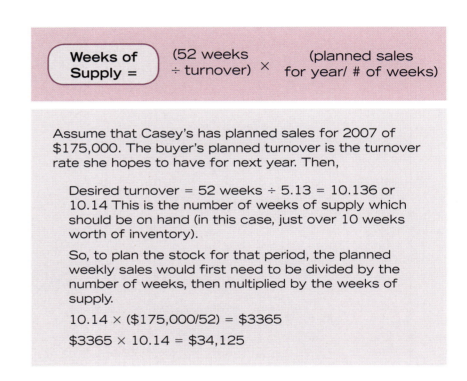

Weeks of Supply = (52 weeks ÷ turnover) × (planned sales for year/ # of weeks)

Assume that Casey's has planned sales for 2007 of $175,000. The buyer's planned turnover is the turnover rate she hopes to have for next year. Then,

Desired turnover = 52 weeks ÷ 5.13 = 10.136 or 10.14 This is the number of weeks of supply which should be on hand (in this case, just over 10 weeks worth of inventory).

So, to plan the stock for that period, the planned weekly sales would first need to be divided by the number of weeks, then multiplied by the weeks of supply.

10.14 × ($175,000/52) = $3365

$3365 × 10.14 = $34,125

In other words, $34,125 would be the estimated inventory which would need to be on hand every week in order to meet the sales goals. Of course, this is not a foolproof method, since some retailing weeks are busier than others. This method works best for retailers who have steady sales from week to week.

The average stock method may not be the best method to use if turnover or sales have not been established for the retailer. The weeks of supply method is best used by retailers that have several years of sales and turnover figures. A new retail store or one that does not have a standard track record of sales may consider using the basic stock method instead.

In determining the amount of inventories needed by using the **basic stock method,** the estimated sales for the month are added to a minimum level of stock desired. Departing from our Casey's example for a moment, assume that a buyer for a new retailer has set his sales goal to be $10,500 in one month. He has also decided that he always wants a minimum stock level of $8,700. Using the basic stock method, he would add his desired minimum stock level to what he expects to sell.

$$\text{Basic Stock Needed for the Month} = \text{minimum level of stock desired} + \text{expected sales}$$

Basic stock level needed for month = $8,700 + $10,500 = $19,200

The important thing to remember about inventory is there must be more than enough to cover the expected sales. If the inventory is not available to customers, it is unlikely that sales goals will be met. In addition, if a store looks bare (not enough stock level); a customer will not be enticed to shop there.

:: SHRINKAGE ::

Shrinkage refers to items missing when inventory is taken. It is generally due to employee or customer theft. Shrinkage in most stores is generally estimated at 2 percent of sales.

Shrinkage due to customer theft can be minimized in the following ways:

- Good customer service.
- Awareness of what a customer has in the dressing room.
- Security systems.

Shrinkage due to employee theft can be minimized by

- Offering a generous discount on merchandise.
- Checking employees and their bags or purses when they leave for lunch breaks and after shifts.
- Using skills discussed in Chapter 8 to motivate employees.
- Insuring that all cash-wrap transactions are correct.

By taking inventory often, retailers can more easily pinpoint reasons for shrinkage.

:: OPEN-TO-BUY ::

Open-to-buy (OTB) is the term used for the amount of money a buyer has available to purchase new items in a given period of time. The open-to-buy calculation is typically done in a spreadsheet in conjunction with other data, such as planned sales figures. The general calculation for OTB is

$$\text{Open-to-buy} = \text{planned purchases} - \text{merchandise received} - \text{items on order}$$

Casey's buyer needs to know her OTB for the month of October 2007. Planned purchases, or her desired level of stock, for this time period is $13,200. She is expecting a shipment of items next week worth $5,000 and has also ordered $2,000 worth of additional items. Thus,

Open-to-buy = $13,200 − $5,000 − $2,000 = $6,200

The planned purchases figure is determined by the weeks of supply method or basic stock method mentioned in the last section, depending on the retailer.

>> six-month merchandising plan

An essential tool for any buyer is the **six-month merchandising plan.** This plan tracks all pertinent information and allows the buyer to see his or her purchases from a big-picture perspective. It is important to know that such a plan will change on a monthly or even daily basis as items on order arrive. Also, as sales exceed, or do not meet, expectations, all of the numbers in the following months in the plan will likely change. Figure 10.5 shows an example of a six-month plan, with numbers corresponding to an explanation of each step in the process.

10.5 figure SIX-MONTH MERCHANDISING PLAN

Department number							
Classification number							
	January	February	March	April	May	June	July
Net sales							
LY (1)							
Planned (2)							
Actual (3)							
BOM							
LY (4)							
Planned (5)							
Actual (6)							
EOM							
LY (7)							
Planned (8)							
Actual (9)							
Reductions (markdowns + shrinkage)							
LY (10)							
Planned (11)							
Actual (12)							

The following is an explanation of the elements of the six-month merchandising plan appearing in Figure 10.5.

1. The net sales figures for last year (LY) are entered into spreadsheet; they are taken from sales reports provided to the buyer.

2. The planned sales are what the store hopes to make for the month. Most retail stores hope to increase sales over the same month from the previous year.

3. The figures for actual net sales will be entered after the month is over. The entry of these numbers will change inventory levels each month.

4. The BOM numbers from last year are entered. BOM is the inventory at the beginning of the month. The BOM inventory is carried over from the inventory at end of the previous month (EOM): for example, the EOM on December 31 becomes the January BOM.

5. Planned BOM inventory will normally be calculated using the weeks-of-supply method.

6. The actual BOM inventory amounts will be entered once the month is over.

7. The EOM figures for last year's inventory are entered into the spreadsheet.

8. The planned EOM inventory figures are calculated on the basis of the BOM figures.

9. The actual EOM inventory figures will be entered once the month is over.

10. The percentage figures for last year's markdowns and shrinkage are entered into the spreadsheet. This is useful to assist in making buying and inventory plans for this year.

11. Planned markdowns and shrinkage percentages go in this area. This is the percentage of total sales that the buyer thinks will result from expected markdowns and shrinkage throughout the year.

12. Actual markdowns and shrinkage dollar values will be entered once the month is over.

It is important to keep in mind that every store and every department is different. As a result, six-month plans will look different from store to store. It is also important to remember that the plan is only a guideline and will change as sales vary from month to month, and even week to week.

>> merchandise classifications

Yet another critical component of merchandise buying is deciding how to allocate budgets for particular types of items. This is known as **merchandise classification.** It is important to decide how dollars will be allocated to each classification. Types of classifications might include jackets, sweaters, jeans, skirts, career pants, and casual pants. Some retailers also use subclassifications. Subclassifications can be based on the type of customer who buys the product or the use of the product, for example, club-wear skirts or career-wear skirts.

The names of classifications vary greatly from store to store. **Model stock plans** are compiled, which are lists of specific, ideal stock levels for each classification during a time period. By using these models, buyers can be sure they are buying enough sweaters, tops, or jeans. Classifications are less important if a merchandising department is large and the buyer is responsible for only one classification.

The best way to determine how budgets should be allocated is to watch customer demand. Most retail stores will provide classification sales reports to the buyers. Using this report, the buyer can see, for example, how well career pants are selling versus casual pants and buy accordingly.

>> the buying trip

After all of the numbers have been calculated, the buyer from Casey's is ready to go on her buying trip. She may be attending the MAGIC show in Las Vegas or markets in New York. Either way, her trip is carefully planned so she can be assured she leaves the market having ordered the right merchandise. Assuming she has already researched trends and knows her customer, careful calculation and analysis will make the buyer better prepared to buy the right products.

First, the buyer will review her profit and loss statement. She will see what categories of clothing offered the most profit, or determine why her store or department suffered a loss. Perhaps a loss was suffered because there were too many markdowns, or maybe she did not stay within budget on her last buying trip. Whatever the reasons, knowing the bigger picture will help her make better decisions.

Second, before leaving on her trip, the buyer will know her pricing plan and how much she will mark up each item. This will put limitations on the types of products she can buy, but it will result in a positive profit and loss statement later in the year. For example, the buyer will only choose products that she can mark up high enough to make a profit.

Third, the buyer will have knowledge on her stock and turnover. She will know how much actual inventory she will need to buy based on her calculations. This gives her a clear picture regarding the number of items she will need to carry throughout the season.

Next, her open-to-buy figures will give her an exact picture of what she already has on order, so she does not duplicate items she already has. This will also provide her with a budget, based on expected sales and sales from the previous year.

Her six-month merchandising plan is perhaps one of the most important documents she will bring with her on the buying trip. This plan will allow her to see current inventory levels for particular products and expected sales for the coming months.

The classifications plan is also important to review before going on a buying trip. It will help the buyer to choose the right merchandise mix, or merchandise classifications. Because she has this plan set forth before she leaves, she knows exactly how many knit tops or casual slacks she needs to buy.

Preparation for a buying trip is very extensive.

All of these calculations are key in making the right buying decisions. Another aspect to the buying trip is to plan which vendors to visit. Perhaps the buyer has purchased from them before, or perhaps she thinks their clothing would fit in her trend, customer, and budgetary restrictions. There is a good chance the buyer will bring a laptop computer; as she makes purchases, she will enter them into her open-to-buy spreadsheet and her six-month merchandising plan spreadsheet. This gives her a clear, up-to-the-moment picture of what she has left to spend.

Before she actually makes purchases though, it is likely she will negotiate with vendors to achieve the best price, which affects the profit and loss statement.

:: NEGOTIATION ::

Successful buyers are excellent negotiators. Fortunately, negotiation is a skill that can be learned. Buyers may negotiate prices for the items. They may also negotiate buybacks for merchandise that doesn't sell. Similar to buybacks are chargebacks, which are credits refunded to a buyer's account if the merchandise is returned, defective, or doesn't sell. Of course, buybacks and chargebacks are negotiated before the purchase is completed between the buyer and the vendor. Buyers may also negotiate with vendors to assist in payment of advertising. For example, if Macy's wants to feature a Coach purse in its weekly advertisement, the buyer may negotiate with the Coach sales representative to pay for some of the advertisement. This is called **cooperative advertising.**

The following tips help when negotiating with vendors:

1. *Build trust.* Vendors will be more likely to negotiate with buyers if they know an ongoing relationship will occur.
2. *Listen.* Understand and evaluate the needs of the other party.
3. *Know the settlement range.* This is simply the range in which the price would likely fall to make the negotiation successful. An acceptable settlement range is neither at the low end or the high end of prices.
4. *Aim for a win–win agreement.* Every negotiation should be a win–win situation for both parties.
5. *Be kind to the vendor.* As the old saying goes, "You can catch more flies with honey than with vinegar." Most people do not get far by taking a hard position up front.
6. *Understand the power dynamics.* Know the position of power the other party comes from. For example, a vendor might have more power in a negotiation for the price of a trendy item than for a less popular item.

As mentioned earlier, negotiation is a skill that can be learned and developed though practice. Because of the extremely important nature of negotiation, further reading on this topic is highly recommended. Specific recommendations can be found at the end of this chapter.

>> conclusion •

To be successful, a buyer must be armed with a variety of the information. The buyer must be able to perform the basic calculations discussed in this chapter to determine what and how much of something he or she should buy. By making these calculations and analyzing them correctly, a buyer can have a successful buying trip and effectively manage the financial aspects of a retail store.

>> chapter ten review • • • • • • • • • • • •

TERMS TO KNOW ::

Profit and loss statement
Balance sheet
Assets
Debt
Owner's equity
Gross sales
Gross margin
Direct expenses

Indirect expenses
Markup
Markdown
Markdown money
Sell-through
Cash flow
Average stock
Turnover

Weeks of supply
Basic stock method
Shrinkage
Open-to-buy
Six-month merchandising plan
Merchandise classification
Model stock plan
Cooperative advertising

CONCEPTS TO KNOW ::

1. Profit and loss statements and components to a statement.
2. Balance sheets and components to a balance sheet.
3. The importance of cash flow.
4. Markdowns and their importance to inventory.
5. Reasons for shrinkage.
6. Six-month merchandising plans and open-to-buy.
7. Things negotiated in fashion merchandising.

CHAPTER QUESTIONS ::

1. Why is the profit and loss statement important? How might a manager or merchandiser use this statement to assess how the store is doing?
2. Why is a balance sheet important? How can these be used to see how a store is doing?
3. Name three reasons markdowns are taken. What can buyers do to insure that fewer markdowns need to be taken?
4. What measures can be implemented to insure that shrinkage is kept as low as possible?
5. How often should inventory be taken? What are the advantages to taking inventory as often as possible?

CHAPTER PROJECTS AND DISCUSSION ::

1. Visit a retail store. Look at its markdowns. Determine which of the reasons listed in this chapter caused the markdown for at least five different items.

2. Write two paragraphs describing your feelings about negotiation. How might this affect your skills as a buyer? What are two specific things you can do to improve this skill?

FOR FURTHER READING ::

Fisher, Roger. *Getting to Yes: Negotiating Agreements without Giving In.* New York: Penguin Books, 1991.

Harvard Business Essentials: Guide to Negotiation. Boston: Harvard Business School Press, 2003.

Miller, Lee, and Jessica Miller. *A Woman's Guide to Successful Negotiating: How to Convince, Collaborate, and Create Your Way to Agreement.* New York: McGraw-Hill, 2002.

core concepts in fashion

a

acquisition The purchasing of one firm by another.

aesthetic The visually appealing aspect of a textile; includes luster, drape, and hand.

A-line A type of silhouette that is more fitting on the top of the garment and flared at the bottom.

allocation manager A person responsible for making sure that stores receive the correct amount of goods.

analogous colors Colors that are next to each other on the color wheel.

appearance retention In textiles, refers to the stretch of the garment, the ability to retain shape, and wrinkling qualities.

aspiration group A group a consumer wishes he or she belongs to, and hopes to belong to at some point in the future.

asset Something a company owns, such as a building or cash.

assistant buyer An individual who assists a buyer in his or her daily duties; normally this position required a couple years of experience.

associate buyer An individual who assists a buyer in his or her daily duties; this position requires a few years of experience; the next step would be buyer.

average stock The average amount of inventory carried at a given time.

b

balance A concept in visual merchandising that requires equal weighting of goods on each side.

balance sheet A financial document that shows the assets, debt, and owner's equity of a company.

basic stock method A calculation that determines how much inventory is needed to meet expected sales.

benefits sought An approach to market segmentation based on defining the characteristics customers look for in a product.

bespoke tailored Couture clothing for men; also called *custom tailored*.

better A price point below $500; appeals to an upper- to middle-class market.

bias cut A type of clothing where the fabric is cut along the grain of the fabric; used to create garments that follow the curve of the body.

blog An online diary of personal thoughts.

bouffant A type of silhouette that flares out in fullness from the hip.

branding The process of developing a desired image of a product.

breadth The number of product lines offered that are in a similar assortment; for example, Macy's has excellent breadth in its shoe department because it carries more than 20 brands.

bridge A price point between designer and better garments; offers less quality than designer, but at about half the price.

broker Brings buyers and sellers together, but does not actually take possession of merchandise.

budget A price point less than $50; found at most any retailers, including discount retailers, such as Target.

buyer A person who buys goods for resale in a store.

buying power The amount of clout a company has when purchasing products from vendors; Wal-Mart, for example, has a lot of buying power.

c

CAD Computer-aided design; a computer program that allows the user to manipulate past designs, colors, and other detailing.

capital purchases Major purchase, such as machinery.

Care Labeling Act A law that requires complete instructions about care for the garment; in addition, care instructions must be attached to the garment in a matter that will last the entire life of the garment.

cash flow The amount of money coming in and out of the business; it is affected by the number of sales and expenses.

cash wrap The place where customers pay for their goods.

category killer A store that carries a large depth and breadth of products, such as Toys "R" Us.

central business district A downtown, commercial area.

central receiving A distribution strategy by which goods are received in one place and then distributed from there.

classic A garment considered in good taste over a long period of time, such as the "little black dress."

classification A category of clothing.

closed-back window A window that does not allow customers to see through it into the store.

cognitive dissonance Can occur if a customer decides he or she did not make the right choice in the consumer purchasing process.

cohort segmentation A type of segmentation that looks at the events that happened during a particular group's lifetime.

collection reports Detailed reports that include sketches of a designer's fashion show.

color harmony The visual merchandising concept that requires colors to "go together" when displayed together.

color pallet The selection of colors used in a given season.

color services Provide predictive information on popular new colors to be used for the season.

color system A record of all past colors used in previous seasons.

color wheel Developed by Newton, it is a representation of colors and derivatives of each color.

comfort In textiles, refers to how well a garment can pull moisture from the body; also refers to how well it can hold heat.

complementary colors Colors that are across from each other on the color wheel.

consumer behavior The study of how and why customers buy particular products

continuity The practice of using the same message throughout all marketing activities.

convenience product A product that is easy to get and doesn't require much thought to purchase.

cooperative advertising Occurs when a vendor provides advertising money to promote a specific item.

cost-based pricing A pricing strategy that is based on the amount of dollars a retailer wants of the percentage markdown.

cover letter Usually sent with a résumé and includes a brief introduction of the candidate.

croquis Figures used to sketch fashion illustrations; usually they are elongated rather than in normal human proportions.

custom tailored See *bespoke tailored*.

customs inspections The process every good must go through when entering the United States.

cyclical The idea that a once-popular fashion will likely come back into fashion at some point in time.

d

debt An amount a company owes to another company.

decline The fourth step of the fashion cycle; fashion leaders have moved onto new styles at this point; garments are usually marked down.

deflation A decrease in prices, due to economic downturn.

demographics Refers to sex, age, race, income, and marital status; used to segment markets.

depth The number of different products carried in the same product assortment; for example, depth might include the number of stiletto shoes carried.

design Those unique characteristic of a garment that make it different from others.

designer signature A pricing level in fashion; garments are very expensive but not custom made as in couture; also called *ready-to-wear*.

details Individual parts of a garment that make it unique; trimmings, type of sleeve, and collar are examples.

direct expenses Expenses that can be directly related to costs of selling.

direct selling A method of selling that does not involve the Internet or traditional stores.

disassociate group A group with which a consumer does not want to be associated; the consumer will likely avoid buying from the same stores at which members of the disassociate group shop.

discount rate The interest rate the Fed charges to banks.

discretionary income Money consumers have left after paying for necessities to live, such as rent, food, and basic clothing.

disposable income Money left after federal taxes, sales taxes, and property taxes have been paid.

distribution The process of how goods get from the place they are manufactured to the retail store.

drape Refers to the way the textile falls and lays on the body.

draping A way of making a pattern, by placing the fabric on the human form.

drop shipper Does not carry inventory, but receives orders, selects the manufacturers, and makes sure the goods arrive at the desired location; performs these tasks for retailers.

dual-channel retailer A retailer that uses two methods to sell its goods, such as the Internet and a storefront.

duster See *maxi coat*.

duty A tax charged on imported goods.

dyeing The coloring of a yarn or fiber.

e-commerce The practice of offering information online about products but not necessarily selling products online.

economic prosperity Refers to overall good unemployment rates and financial status.

economies of scale The ability of a store to purchase thousands of items, thereby making each individual item cheaper.

editorial publications A publication written for the general public, but usually read by fashion professionals as well.

electronic data interchange (EDI) A system used to help companies communicate with each other, usually about production of products, sizing, and other garment specifications.

electronic product code A new type of UPC that allows goods to be scanned remotely.

embargo A ban of all trade from a particular country, usually for political reasons.

emotional buying motives Reasons for purchasing that occur as a result of feelings rather than thoughts.

empty nester A person who no longer has kids living at home.

engineering A way used to put yarns together using heat or adding chemicals to form a bond.

entrepreneurial skills Skills a person needs to be successful at starting his or her own business; they include business skills such as marketing and money management.

e-tailing The practice of actually selling products online.

ethnic segmentation Market segmentation based on race.

evaluation of alternatives The third step in the consumer purchasing process; involves the consumer looking at all options.

evoked set The possible options available to a consumer.

exclusive distribution With this type of distribution strategy, goods will appear in only one or two places in a given geographic region.

extended problem solving The type of purchase decision making that requires extensive thought.

extensible markup language A set of computer code that can be easily transferred from computer to computer.

fabric market A place where textile designers and colorists show their patterns and designs for the upcoming season.

face-out A piece of hardware in visual merchandising that allows merchandise to face forward on a wall.

fad An item that comes into and goes out of fashion quickly, often with exaggerated detailing.

fair trade The practice of paying a wage that is sufficient for an individual to cover basic living expenses.

family life-cycle segmentation A way of segmenting markets based on marital status and the number of kids.

fashion A style that is accepted and worn by the majority of a population.

fashion acceptance The extent to which individuals are willing to wear a particular fashion.

fashion centers Places where buyers can go to purchase items, other than trade shows; New York's garment district is an example of a fashion center.

fashion cycle An attempt to describe the way fashion flows into and out of style.

fashion designer A person who creates new designs for clothing.

fashion follower An individual who looks to fashion leaders to find out what is in style; may not have interest in trends, or may not have the funds to keep up with trends.

fashion forecasting The process of predicting trends, usually two years in advance.

fashion illustration A drawing used to sell a line of clothing; usually painted and drawn by hand.

fashion leader An individual who sets the pace for fashion; often a celebrity; must be someone who can afford new fashions every season.

fashionist A submissive follower of fashions and modes.

fashionista Designer or promoter of the latest fashion.

features Those unique characteristics of a garment, such as zipper placement.

fiber The first step in textile manufacturing; can include raw cotton that has just been picked and is not yet usable as fabric.

filament fiber An extremely long fiber.

finishing The last step in the textile manufacturing process; includes adding any special coatings to a garment, such as wrinkle-free or stain-resistant coatings.

Flammable Fabric Act A law passed in 1953 that specified requirements for flammability of products.

flat pattern Used to make a garment.

floor set The actually design depicting where fixtures should be placed.

focus groups Used in market research; 8 to 10 are brought into a room for a discussion by a facilitator.

form utility Refers to characteristics of the actual product, such as style and color.

four Ps of marketing Also referred to as the marketing mix: product, price, place, and promotion.

four-way A type of fixture that has four different places to hang merchandise.

freeform A type of store layout that does not have an obvious path through the racks.

freelance designer A person who creates new designs but does not work for one specific company; rather, he or she accepts new designs from several different companies.

freestanding store A self-contained store, usually on the outskirts of a city.

frequency In advertising, it refers to the number of times the target market will see the ad.

frequency of use An approach to market segmentation based on defining how often customers use the product.

full nester A person who has kids living at home.

function A reference as to how the garment will be used; a way of categorizing products; sportswear and dresses are examples.

g

garment dyeing The coloring of clothing after it has already been made into a garment.

geographical price A pricing strategy in which price changes, depending on the demand in a particular geographic area.

gondolas A type of fixture that allows for hanging and folding of items.

grading The process of making a pattern in several sizes.

graphic design The process of creating unique designs using a computer or by hand; in fashion, may be part of the marketing department.

grids A type of fixture that allows hardware to be placed upon it for merchandising of products.

gross domestic product (GDP) The total amount of all goods and services produced by a country in a given period of time.

gross margin The difference between net sales and cost of goods sold.

gross sales The total amount of sales.

growth The second phase in the fashion cycle; this is when fashion followers accept the garment worn by fashion leaders.

habitual problem solving The type of purchase decision making that does not require a lot of thought.

hand Refers to how the textile feels.

hard lines A type of product that is usually for household use and tends to be big and bulky.

haute couture Custom-made garment, usually made especially for the customer; very expensive and usually referred to simply as *couture*.

homogeneous Refers to a group whose members have the same characteristics.

hourglass A type of silhouette that closely hugs the body.

hypermarket A store that carries hard lines, soft lines, and groceries.

i

import quota A limit on the amount of goods which can be brought in from a country.

importing Bringing goods from one country into another.

indirect expenses Costs that will occur regardless of the number of sales.

industrialization Refers to a time period during which society moved from individual manufacturing to manufacturing goods in a factory, in large quantities.

inflation The normal rise of prices over time.

information search The second step in the consumer purchasing process; this is where the consumer will research the product that would best meet his or her needs.

inseam The length of a pant from the rise to the hem.

intangible The attributes of a store that can not be felt, such as smell.

intensive distribution A distribution strategy based on the idea that the more retail stores a product appears in, the better.

intermediaries Individuals who act as a go-betweens for production facilities and retail buyers.

interrupted cycle A cycle in which customers didn't actually stop buying the product, but it stopped being sold; for example, retailers stop selling swimsuits in August to get ready for fall garments.

intrinsic Nontangible value gained from a product, such as "feeling good" when wearing a particular brand.

introduction The first stage in the fashion cycle; this is when a garment is new and accepted by fashion leaders; a garment is normally expensive when first introduced.

j

jacquard weave Similar to a twill weave, creates a design within the weave.

joint venture An agreement between two parties to work together; in fashion, it generally means an agreement between a retailer and a production facility to produce goods that will go into the retail store.

k

keystoning A pricing strategy that involves adding the cost of all materials and labor, and then adding the desired profit to determine the final price.

knit Fabric put together using one continuous yarn.

l

layoffs Loss of jobs due to cutbacks in a company.

licensing Agreement between two parties that allows one to manufacture a garment using the other's brand name.

lifestyle merchandising A type of visual merchandising that makes boutique-like sections within the store, with designs from the same brand in one area.

lighting One of the most important components of retail; it allows various items to be highlighted in the store.

limited problem solving The type of purchase decision making that may require some thought.

line board A flat presentation of a designers line of clothing; can include technical sketches and fashion illustrations.

line-item pricing A pricing strategy that requires all goods to end in the same number, such as $19.50 and $39.50.

living wage A wage that someone could use to pay basic expenses and purchase necessities.

lobbying The process of advocating a certain viewpoint to Senate and House of Representatives members in Washington, DC.

loss leader A product that is marked down significantly (sometimes at a loss) to drive customers into the store, with the hope they will buy more products.

luster Refers to the way the light reflects from a garment.

m

mail survey Type of primary research where people are mailed surveys and asked to respond and mail back.

mall intercept survey A type of primary research where a person is stopped in a mall and asked to answer questions.

man-made Another word for *manufactured fiber;* a fiber developed in a laboratory; also called *synthetic.*

manufactured fiber A fiber that has been developed in a laboratory; can also be called *man-made* or *synthetic.*

markdown A reduction in price due to items not selling.

markdown dollars An agreement from a vendor to take back (buy back) or refund money if a particular item does not sell well; also called *markdown money.*

market segmentation The process of breaking a group into smaller homogeneous groups.

marketing department The department responsible for the selling of garments; can include advertising and special events planning, as well as visual merchandising.

marketing of fashion Part of the fashion model; incorporates the various ways a fashion item will be sold.

markup The dollar amount or percentage above cost charged for an item.

Maslow's hierarchy of needs A theory that attempts to explain the needs of individuals; includes physiological needs, safety needs, social needs, esteem needs, and self-actualization needs.

mass-produced fashion Fashion that is made in large quantities; sometimes called *volume fashion.*

maxi coat A long blazer or jacket from the 1960s; also called a duster.

membership group The group to which someone actually belongs.

merchandise assistant One of the first steps for a career in fashion buying.

merchandise classification A category of clothing, such as girls' denim or petite knits.

merger The joining of two firms to make one.

metrosexual A term that refers to the heightened feminine senses in a male.

microfiber A type of fabric made from polyester or nylon yarns.

model Usually in the form of a visual drawing, depicts how ideas work together.

model stock plan A standard plan for the amount of goods that must be carried in a store at a given time.

moderate A price point usually $100 or less; sold in chain stores such as The Gap and The Limited.

multichannel retailer A retailer that uses several methods to sell its goods, such as the Internet, home shopping networks, and bricks-and-mortar stores.

multiple pricing A pricing strategy that offers a customer a better deal if purchasing more than one item.

muslin An inexpensive fabric used to make samples to test for fit.

n

narrow assortment A small product assortment, such as found at a store that carries only shoes.

natural fiber A fiber that can be found in nature; not man-made.

o

odd pricing The practice of ending prices in uneven numbers, such as $.99.

open-back window A window that allows customers to see past the window display into the store.

open-to-buy The amount of funds a buyer has after budgets and expenditures have been calculated.

outsourcing The practice of allowing another company to produce garments, usually overseas.

p

patronage buying motives Reasons for purchasing that involve consumer loyalty.

patternmaker A person who makes patterns to use in fashion design.

peak The third state in the fashion cycle; a fashion can be found at most retailers and the mass market has accepted the garment.

penetration pricing A pricing strategy that involves setting the price low at first, then gradually raising the price as the brand gets more recognition.

personal income Total income less social security taxes.

piece dyeing The process of coloring fabric.

pile weave A type of weave where the yarn is interlaced on both sides of the garment.

place utility Refers to the characteristics that make an item easy to get to, such as store location.

plain weave The most simple of the weaves; the yarns are woven tightly together so as to not create a design.

point of purchase (POP) A display near merchandise that provides information about the product, including price.

poor chic A style that represents what someone of lower economic status might wear.

portfolio A collection of all the work done by someone in a field; can be used to show at interviews or on a website.

positioning The image a company wants customers to have of its brand and products.

possession utility Refers to the characteristics that make an item easy to own, such as a store credit card.

postprocessing The process of taking a fabric and making it into a usable good.

postpurchase valuation The final step in the consumer purchasing process; when the consumer evaluates whether his or her decision to purchase was the right choice.

power node A variety of freestanding stores located in the same area.

prestige pricing A pricing strategy that includes pricing an item higher than it is worth to solidify the image of a prestige product in the customer's mind.

prêt-a-porter French term for *ready-to-wear* and *designer signature*.

price skimming A pricing strategy that involves setting the price high at first, then gradually lowering the price.

pricing A very important factor in fashion, it is the price charged to the consumer for a garment.

primary data Information that a researcher gathers.

primary trading area An geographic area from which 50 to 80 percent of a retailer's customers will come.

prime rate The interest rate banks offer to large businesses and investors.

private label A brand of clothing developed and manufactured exclusively for a particular store.

problem recognition The first step in the consumer purchasing process.

processors They develop new fibers and make the fibers into usable yarns.

producers Part of the textile manufacturing process; can be involved in the growing of textiles or the development of new synthetic textiles.

product assortment The number of different goods carried.

production of fashion Part of the fashion model; involves the actual making of garments, including the design, textile selection, and sourcing.

product-line pricing A pricing strategy where similar products are sold at several different price zones.

profit and loss statement A financial document that shows the sales, cost of goods sold, expenses, and the profit or loss.

protectionist policies A policy that tries to protect local manufacturers of goods.

psychographics A way of segmenting consumers based on their ideologies, views, opinions, and lifestyles.

psychological pricing A type of pricing strategy that can encompass twofers and multiple pricing.

purchase decision The fourth step in the consumer purchasing process; where the consumer actually decides what to purchase.

purchasing manager A person who buys parts for internal use in a company; in fashion, this person might buy the fabrics, buttons, and zippers for use in a garment.

purchasing power The amount of goods a person can buy for the same amount of money in a given time period.

pure-play retailer A retailer that only sells goods online.

push money Bonuses given to employees for selling one particular item, such as extended warrantees.

q

quarter A three-month period.

quota A limit on the number of goods that can be brought into a country.

r

racetrack A type of store layout that utilizes an oblong pathway through the store.

rational buying motives Reasons for purchasing that occur as a result of intelligent thought rather than feelings.

reach In advertising, it refers to the number of people in the target market who see the ad.

ready-to-wear See *designer signature*.

recession An overall decline in gross domestic product for a period of six months (two quarters).

reference group A group of people a consumer may refer to when purchasing, such as movie stars.

reference price The price a customer might expect to pay for an item.

regional receiving A distribution strategy by which goods are received in specific regions (such as West Coast) and distributed to individual stores from there.

rejection The final step of the fashion cycle; garment won't sell, even at a dramatically reduced price.

research of fashion Part of the fashion model; includes target market research as well as trend forecasting.

résumé A detailed list of education and experience.

retail The last step in the merchandising process; involves the actual selling of goods.

retailing The process of selling goods to the customer through various retail channels.

s

salary plus commission A type of compensation that offers a stable salary and additional opportunities for financial reward through selling.

satin weave A type of weave with a very smooth texture; has tendency to snag easily.

saturated The idea that things are at their limit; in fashion, a saturated market can mean too many similar products are being offered.

season Can include fall/winter and spring/summer; a way of categorizing clothing.

secondary data Information that a researcher finds already published.

secondary trading area A geographic area from which 20 to 25 percent of a retailer's customers will come.

selective distribution With this type of distribution strategy, the product may be found in a few retail stores.

selling agents Another term for *intermediaries*.

sell-through The percentage of merchandise that sells at the original full price.

shape The most basic design element used in fashion and any other type of design; shape in fashion is generally referred to as *silhouette*.

shelving A type of fixture that allows the retailer to fold items.

shopping product A product that a person would likely search for and evaluate alternatives before purchasing.

showroom Usually located in a fashion center, a place where designers can show their fashions to retail buyers.

shrinkage The amount of goods lost due to theft.

silhouette The overall contour and shape of garment.

single-line store A store that only carries one type of goods, such as socks or handbags.

single-store receiving A distribution strategy by which each store has its own receiving department and processes its own incoming goods.

site selection The process of selection a location for a store.

situational interview A type of interview in which the interviewee is asked to explain how he or she dealt with a particular scenario.

six-month buying plan Used by a buyer to plan his or her purchases.

six-month merchandising plan A plan used by a buyer that determines how many goods he or she plans to order in specific classifications.

social responsibility The idea that businesses should not function amorally, but rather should contribute to the welfare of the community, city, and world in which they operate.

social stratification The practice of putting people into social and economic categories on the basis of their birth family.

soft lines A type of product that is usually clothing or bedding items.

sourcer A person who oversees the process of outsourcing.

sourcing Obtaining goods from another source or locale.

special event planning The process of planning for events such as trunk shows or fashion shows; responsibility of the marketing department.

specialty product A product that can be difficult to find, or one for which there are few retail outlets.

specifications package A packet of information sent to production that describes details of how a garment should be made; usually includes technical sketches and specifics on type of sewing, buttons, zippers, and other detailing.

spiffs Short-term motivational tools in retail that encourage teamwork and selling in a retail store.

spine A type of store layout that uses a main aisle with other aisles branching from it.

staple fiber A very short fiber.

STAR method Situation, task, action, results— a process to follow when interviewing.

straight commission A type of compensation plan that offers money only for sales made.

straight salary A type of compensation plan that offers only salary and no extra money that may result from high sales.

street fashion Clothing worn by regular people who are considered to be trendsetters.

style The combination of characteristics that make a garment different from another.

sweatshops A factory that employs people at low wages and in unsafe working conditions.

synthetic See *manufactured fiber* and *man-made*.

t

tangible The physical attributes of a store that can be touched, such as fixtures.

tariff A tax charged on imported goods.

technical sketches Drawings, sometimes done on a computer, that depict the details of a garment.

telephone survey A type of primary research where people are called at home and asked to answer questions.

tertiary trading area An area outside the primary and secondary trading areas; can account for 5 to 25 percent of stores sales, depending on the type of store.

textile colorist Someone who chooses colors and patterns to be used in designs.

textile design The process of creating patterns on textiles; can be done by hand or by computer.

textiles Fabric used to make a garment.

texture The feel of a garment; for example, rough or smooth.

thank-you letter A message a person sends to a potential employer after an interview, thanking them for the interview; a must after any job interview.

thermal retention The ability of a garment to hold heat.

time utility Refers to the availability of a product exactly when the customer wants it.

trade agreements Agreements between two or more countries that make it easier for the two countries to trade with each other.

trade publications Magazines or newspapers written specifically with the fashion professional in mind.

trade shows Events at which designers and buyers gather to show and purchase goods; in the United States, MAGIC is a major show.

trend A general direction for clothing design.

trend reports Similar to collection reports, they provide sketches and information about new designs but are not focused on one designer's fashion show.

trickle-across theory Sometimes called the *horizontal flow theory*; says that fashion moves between groups rather than vertically as in the trickle-up and trickle-down theories.

trickle-down theory Based on the idea that fashion begins with the trendsetting design houses located in Milan, Paris, and New York; people who subscribe to this theory believe that manufacturers and designers see what is happening in these major design centers and copy them; the copies are generally less expensive and mass produced.

trickle-up fashion A fashion that begins with the masses and creates demand for haute couture garments.

trickle-up theory The opposite of trickle-down theory; says that fashion is developed by regular people then copied by design houses.

trunk show An informal fashion show; for example, a designer might bring garments to a boutique to show to customers.

tubular A type of silhouette that has the same proportions throughout.

turnover The number of times all goods in a store are sold.

twill A type of weave that creates a design within the weave, such as houndstooth.

twofer A pricing strategy that offers a lower price to the customer if buying more than one.

two-way A type of fixture that has two different places to hang merchandise.

type of product use An approach to market segmentation based on defining the way in which customers use a product.

U

uniform-delivery pricing When the same flat fee is charged for shipping, no matter where the receiver is located.

universal product code (UPC) A label attached to a garment that can be scanned to determine price.

utility The ability of a product to satisfy a customer's needs; in retail, there are time, place, form, and possession utilities.

V

VALS Stands for values and lifestyle segmentation; a way to segment markets.

value pricing A pricing strategy that takes into consideration the value of the product in the customer's mind.

value-added network (VAN) A type of network on which EDI must run in order to allow communication.

vanity sizing A retail strategy of marking the size of a garment lower than what it actually is.

variety The different characteristics of the same item; for example, a skirt coming in several colors would be considered variety.

vendor An individual who sells and provides garments to buyers.

vertical production Occurs when the retailer owns the production facility (a wholly owned factory) as well as the retail stores.

visual merchandiser A person responsible for the overall look of a retail store; responsible for fixture placement and mannequins.

W

weave Fabric made by interlacing small pieces of yarn together.

wedge A type of silhouette that fits larger at the top and smaller at the bottom.

weeks of supply A calculation that determines how much inventory is needed to meet expected sales.

wholesale Goods that are sold specifically for resale.

wholesaler A person who takes possession of merchandise for resale to retailers.

wholly owned factory A production facility that is owned by the retailer.

wicking The ability of a textile to pull moisture away from the body.

wide assortment A large product assortment, meaning many different types of products are carried.

Wool Products Labeling Act A law that requires product labels to accurately reflect the fiber content, country of origin, and the name of the manufacturer of all woolen products.

Y

yarn The second step in textile manufacturing; textiles start as fibers, then are put together.

yarn dyeing The coloring of a garment, after it has been converted from fibers.

youthquake Term used in the 1960s that refers to the feeling of youth and independence.

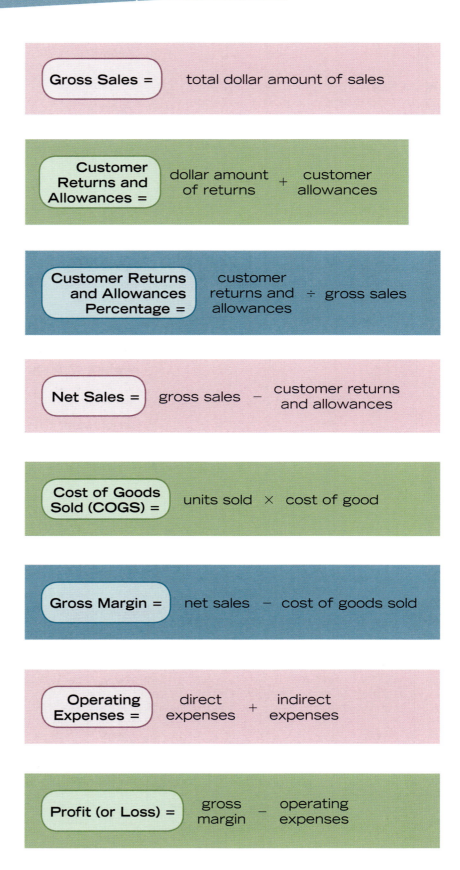

Gross Sales = total dollar amount of sales

Customer Returns and Allowances = dollar amount of returns + customer allowances

Customer Returns and Allowances Percentage = customer returns and allowances ÷ gross sales

Net Sales = gross sales − customer returns and allowances

Cost of Goods Sold (COGS) = units sold × cost of good

Gross Margin = net sales − cost of goods sold

Operating Expenses = direct expenses + indirect expenses

Profit (or Loss) = gross margin − operating expenses

Total Dollar Markup = (retail price − cost) × quantity

Dollar Markdown = original retail price − new price

Percentage Markdown at Retail = (original retail price − new price) ÷ original retail price

Percentage Markdown After Goods Have Sold = ((original retail price − new price) × number of items) ÷ net sales for the time period

Planned Markdowns = average markdown percentage for reference year (normally the previous year) × projected sales

Average Stock = BOM (Beginning of month) stock for every month ÷ number of months

Turnover = net sales ÷ average stock

Weeks of Supply = (52 weeks ÷ turnover) × (planned sales for year/ # of weeks)

Open-to-buy = planned purchases − merchandise received − items on order

1   A store sold the following items for the day: 2 sweaters at $39, 16 pairs of jeans at $59, 2 purses at $29, and 2 suits at $169. What are the gross sales for the day?

2   Besides the gross sales, the store had customer returns and allowances: 1 jean returned at $59, 2 skirts at $39. It also had to give a discount of 10 percent on a $169 suit because it was soiled. What were the customer returns and allowances for the day?

3   The store wants to calculate the customer returns and allowances as a percentage of sales. What is this percentage?

4   What were the store's gross sales for the day? The buyer wants to know her cost of goods sold. She purchased the jeans at $19, sweaters at $9, jeans at $27, and suits at $67. What was her cost of goods sold on this day?

5   What is the store's gross margin, using the numbers calculated above?

6   The direct expenses for the month included the following: $200 for advertising, $500 for salaries, and $200 in rent. What were the total direct expenses for the month? What were the direct expenses for the day, assuming a 31-day month?

7 Indirect expenses during the month were $75 for water, $89 for electricity, and $60 for insurance. What were the total indirect expenses for the month? For the day, assuming a 31-day month?

8 What are this store's total operating expenses for the day?

9 What is the profit for this store on this particular day?

10 Using the following monthly figures, calculate the store's profit (or loss) for the month.
   a. The store sold $34,600 worth of merchandise.
   b. Cost of merchandise sold (cost of goods, or inventory) was $15,890.
   c. The store had $600 in customer returns and allowances.
   d. The store's operating expenses were $6,000.

11 What is the gross margin if the store had net sales of $3,267 and cost of goods sold of $1,346?

12 A store had indirect expenses for the month of $500 for advertising, $30 for security monitoring, and $75 for insurance. What would the indirect expenses be for a day when there are 30 days in the month?

13 A buyer wants to know her markup on a purchase. She purchased 25 sweaters at $9 each and will sell them for $25. She also purchased 45 pairs of jeans at $21 each and will sell them for $45. What is her total markup in both dollars and percent for this purchase?

14 A buyer realized that several sweaters were not selling well. As a result, she marked down 30 of them from $58 to $38. What is the total dollar markdown? What is the total dollar markdown in percent?

15 A store had average markdowns last year of 21 percent. Assuming the buyer is calculating on the basis of a seven-month season, what are her planned markdowns?

16 A store had sales of $203,562 for the year. Its average stock was $57,640. What was their turnover for the year?

17 A buyer decides to use the weeks of supply method to develop her buying plan. Her planned sales are $460,000 and her desired turnover is 4. What should her weeks of supply be for the coming year?

18 A buyer has determined that the desired level of stock per month is $12,800. She plans to have sales of $5,600 for that month. What would her basic stock requirements be for the month?

19 A buyer has planned purchases (or desired inventory) of $241,571. She has already received $87,623 worth of merchandise and has ordered $46,798 more. What is her current open-to-buy?

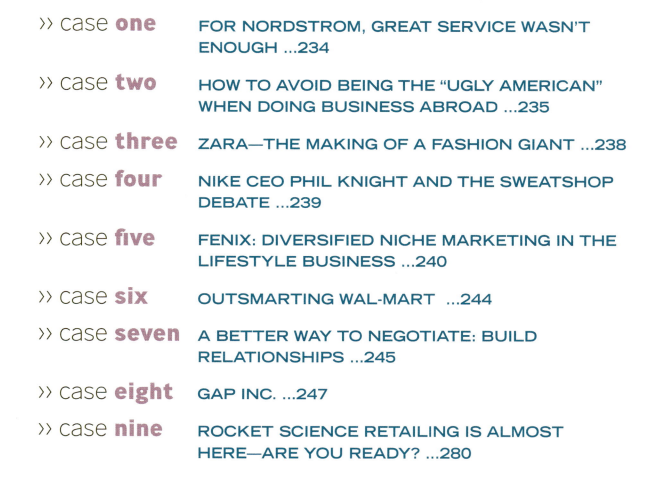

>> case studies and articles

FOR NORDSTROM, GREAT SERVICE WASN'T ENOUGH

It looked like a slam dunk. In the late 80s, Seattle-based Nordstrom Inc. set the gold standard in department store retailing. Its reputation for quality, fashion, and customer care was unparalleled, its customers among the most loyal in the industry. And while other chains were still reeling from the buyout craze of the decade, Nordstrom profits were growing by double digits. So the decision to expand beyond the West Coast seemed like a no-brainer.

It didn't quite work out as planned. After opening stores in 22 states, the company today is struggling to put its fractured brand back together. Over the past few years, Nordstrom has been battling weak sales growth, disappointing profits, and volatile stock performance. Retail experts says Nordstrom took its eye off fashion trends, sending its customers scurrying to competitors. And the 99-store chain also failed to modernize quaint systems like the handwritten notes on customer preferences that worked on a regional basis but wreaked havoc after the expansion. "We have not been able to keep up with the changing needs of the customers," concedes William E. Nordstrom, a co-president and one of six Nordstroms now in the company's executive ranks.

The damage wasn't hard to spot. Net income took a dive of 11 percent, to $147 million, in 1996. Shares, at a high of nearly $53 in 1996 plunged to a low of $34 in 1997 and have since risen only to about $40. While the income trend has improved, Nordstrom still has a lot of work ahead of it. Last year total sales rose 3 percent to just over $5 billion, but sales at stores open at least one year, the most accurate way to measure a retailer, fell 2.6 percent.

After two years of cost-cutting and modernization, management is now scrambling to woo back customers. But many of the strategies, from new ad campaigns to Internet experiments, are still works in progress, leaving the open question: Can Nordstrom reinvent its stores and marketing message? "They have a few precious moments to do this," says Peter Glen, a New York-based retail consultant.

How did one of America's premier retailers get in this fix? The problems can be traced directly to the start of the chain's expansion a decade ago. As Nordstrom grew, management failed to centralize common functions. The number of buyers chainwide ballooned to 900—compared with the lean team of 100 in charge of buying for R. H. Macy & Co. Vendors were driven to distraction by the multiple and conflicting orders. "The fragmentation of the buying organization works at cross-purpose sometimes," says Paul R. Charron, chairman of Liz Claiborne Inc.

Lost Touch

Customers were equally put off. As Nordstrom grew, the retailer became less adept at keeping up with lifestyle changes. While working women started to dress more casually for the office, for example, Nordstrom continued to stock its old, buttoned down styles. And shoppers noticed. Nita Ostlund, 54, was a loyal Nordstrom shopper for 20 years. But lately, the store has disappointed her, "I think they've lost touch with the customer," she says.

Despite signs of shopper revolt, Nordstrom execs first focused on cost-cutting in an effort to boost profits and regain the confidence of investors. In 1997, Nordstrom cut the number of buyers by 19 percent, organized itself into divisions, and made dramatic slashes in inventory. That helped boost net income 11 percent to $207 million, for the fiscal year ended January, 1999. Analysts expect earnings to rise another 16 percent to 18 percent this year.

The strategy appears to have bought the company some slack with investors. "This is a good story. The trend is positive," says Mark Grolig, principal of institutional investor Palley–Needelman Asset Management Inc. which owns 2 million Nordstrom shares. "Management has targeted doubling earnings in the next couple of years, which is very aggressive. But with these changes, hopefully they can get there."

Nordstrom has also moved to tackle its computer phobia—possibly the last major retailer to do so. Until recently, there was little centralized gathering of customer trends. Salesclerks kept notes on shoppers' likes and dislikes in looseleaf binders. "This company was in the Dark Ages," says Jennifer Black, president of Black & Co. a brokerage based in Portland, Oregon.

This year, Nordstrom built a new multimillion-dollar data center in Denver to help collect and analyze buying habits, lifestyle trends and inventory management. Even the information kept in salespeople's binders is going online. The goal, say company execs, is to back up employees' intuition with solid data to build a more consistent and on fashion merchandise mix. That should result in better same-store sales by late '99, says Michael A. Stein, the new chief financial officer Nordstrom recruited from Marriott International Inc. last year.

But other improvements are still in the experimental stage. The company is taking itself through a crash course in Internet retailing. It launched a modest e-commerce website in October that is not yet profitable. But it has also invested in online shopping services such as Streamline, which arranges a multitude of personal services, from shopping to errand running via e-mail, and Scotty's Home Market, a grocery-shopping service. Co-president Daniel Nordstrom says the partnerships will give the company insight into how upscale Yuppie shoppers—the kind Nordstrom wants to attract—are using the Internet to shop. "We don't see a lot of boundaries between different product categories on the Web," he says. Outsiders agree it's a good move. "It's a smart way to approach the

Internet," says Harry A. Ikenson, Hambrecht & Quist's senior retail analyst. "They are learning without taking incredible financial risks."

Rave Reviews

Other tactics poised for rollout include an ad campaign. It's under development now by Minneapolis ad agency Fallon McElligott. The retailer is also carving its marketing into more distinct demographic groups to lure both the traditional Nordstrom woman and the younger shopper. Youth efforts included promotions of the hot sneaker Skechers and prom dresses licensed from the hit Gen Y show Buffy the Vampire Slayer and running ads for Doc Marten boots on alternative rock stations. "They are trying to formulate a way to become not only the mom store but the young women's store," says Dean A. Ramos of Kansas City investment bank George K. Baum.

"They" is the operative word. Nordstrom has one of the more eccentric management structures in Corporate America. For four generations, it has operated under a tradition of "consensus management." Family members hold most of the top positions and public squabbling is unheard of. Currently, a group of six brothers and cousins, all in their 30s, hold the title of co-president, the biggest such group in the company's history.

To groom the new group, which attained their current title in 1995, Nordstrom has kept John J. Whitacre, 45, who also worked alongside the previous generation of Nordstrom men. Whitacre, now chairman and CEO, directs the six "with an iron hand," says retail analyst Walter Loeb of Loeb Associates Inc. And Nordstrom has opened its executive ranks to other outsiders. Stein, the new CFO, drew rave reviews from Wall Street analysts at a recent meeting. "He brings a new sophistication," says Loeb.

In part to make sure this huge office of the president functions smoothly, Nordstrom brought in Marakon Associates Inc., a Stanford (Connecticut)-based management-consulting firm, for a broad review of the company strategies. Among the recommendations: create more defined areas of responsibility for the Nordstrom six so they don't undermine one another. "While the management structure is unconventional, it can be a potential strength as long as clear decision-making and accountability are present," says Paul Favaro, managing partner at Marakon.

Still, the big unknown for Nordstrom is whether it can win back its once-loyal customers. While the retailer has struggled to regain its footing, they're being lured by everything from reinvigorated specialty chains such as Ann Taylor to new Internet shopping sites. Nordstrom may finally be on the right track. Question is, has its customer already pulled too far ahead to catch? ◎

—Seanna Browder

Source: "For Nordstrom, Great Service Wasn't Enough," by Seanna Browder, Business Week. This material is used by permission of The McGraw-Hill Companies, ©2000.

QUESTIONS

1. This case discusses how Nordstrom lost touch with its consumers. Discuss in what ways it actually lost touch. Can you think of any other retailers that have lost touch?

2. How might Nordstrom's investment in technology spur sales? Discuss at least two ways.

3. How effective do you think Nordstrom's advertising has been?

4. When loyal to a store, do you have expectations of what the store should provide? Give examples of what you would expect.

5. The article covers the idea of *consensus management*. Look up the term and define it. What are the pros and cons to this type of management?

6. Do an Internet search of Nordstrom's last company report. What were sales last year? Did sales improve over the previous year?

HOW TO AVOID BEING THE "UGLY AMERICAN" WHEN DOING BUSINESS ABROAD

As business becomes more global, don't let communications gaffes compromise your results.

You know the stereotype: They're bold, brash, and all business. They've got lots of money but little culture. They're immune to self-doubt and oblivious to cultural nuance.

They're the Ugly Americans.

The 1958 book and 1963 film adaptation gave the stereotype its name. How closely does the stereotype fit the reality of Americans doing business abroad today? How "ugly" are American businesspeople as they work with foreign partners in this our globalized world?

"Americans have a much greater willingness to adapt to other cultures than they did when that book was written," says Prabhu Guptara, director of the Executive Development Centre for UBS bank in Wolfsberg, Switzerland. "But Americans often still need to improve self-consciousness to understand that the qualities that make you win in the U.S. could as easily make you fail in Europe or Asia."

American execs need to be especially sensitive about three aspects of communications when they go abroad:

1 *The rhythm of negotiations.* Speed and directness are not necessarily qualities that foreigners appreciate, even though Americans like them.

2 *The dynamics of personal relationships.* Business in most of the developed world is people-based, not deal-based, so don't parachute in with the "lawyers and the dollars."

3 *The depth of presentation.* Slick speeches and Power-Point slide shows may not get you far in cultures that value depth. You'd better have all the numbers and know what they mean.

Why these areas in particular? "Because Americans tend to value fast and agile dealmaking, and intense and skilled marketing, while not putting much value on personal relationships in business," explains Ann McDonagh Bengtsson, a France-based international consultant specializing in change management, especially where a number of different cultures are involved. "Whereas, most Europeans and many Asians want to develop a solid personal relationship before even considering a deal, and then expect very detailed and painstaking research to have gone into the preparation of any accord," Bengtsson says.

Says Japanese intercultural expert Shinobu Kitayama: "American culture emphasizes the core cultural idea of independence by valuing attending to oneself and discovering and expressing individual qualities while neither assuming nor valuing overt connectedness. These values are reflected in educational and legal systems, employment and caretaking practices, and individual cognition, emotion, and motivation."

In contrast, Bengtsson and Kitayama argue that Asian and European cultures tend to emphasize interdependence by valuing the self and individuality within a social context, connections among persons, and attending to and harmoniously coordinating with others. When Kitayama asked 65 middle-class American and 90 Japanese students attending the same Oregon university to list situations in which they felt that they were winning or losing, the American students focused more on ways in which they won individually, while the Japanese students won when the group with which they were associated enjoyed a success.

American execs abroad have to take these differences into account. So, when abroad:

Slow Down

The rhythm of negotiations and all business discussion is much slower outside the United States, as executives from the New York–based Bankers Trust had to learn when it merged with the Frankfurt-based Deutsche Bank two years ago.

Deutsche Bank was a very large, "universal" bank, as the Germans call such an entity. The bank was active in all sectors of banking, but the area where it needed the most reinforcement was investment banking. Hence the plan to merge with investment house Bankers Trust, a dedicated merchant bank with an American, "deals-based" culture.

The American executives quickly found that they could not fathom their German partners, reports international management professor Terry Garrison of the Henley Management College (Henley-on-Thames, England). "Accustomed to making split-second decisions, and managing on a project basis in which planning rarely extended beyond a given deal, the Bankers Trust 'hot-shots' found themselves working with 'universal' bankers who planned several years at a time, for whom a given 'deal' was something they felt they could take or leave, and who operated within a corporate governance framework that looked and felt completely alien to the Americans."

Garrison ran a seminar in which he helped the American execs get in tune with Continental banking culture. "It was a matter of teaching the Americans to slow down and think in different terms," Garrison says. "Those Germans who had spent a lifetime in a credit-management culture saw themselves as needing not just a crash course in merchant banking but a whole new vocabulary rooted in American capitalism."

Deutsche Bank executive Siegfried Guterman admits that "there were a lot of unmeasurable factors that were difficult to take into account before we accomplished the merger."

It is not that Asians and European cultures do not value efficiency. Rather, business for them is more conceptual and long-term. A given transaction is only interesting if it is part of the accomplishment of a much more stable, greater objective. "Attempts to hurry your foreign interlocutors along may just make them withdraw from the discussions altogether," Bengtsson points out.

Don't Arrive with "the Lawyers and the Dollars"

Personal and business relationships are more intertwined in Europe and in Asia than they are in the United States.

"Achieving trust with European and Asian partners is a key factor in success outside the U.S.," Guptara says. "Americans may not like each other, but if there is a 'deal' on the table, they do business. Most Asians and Europeans—even the British—want to get to know you first. They want to assure themselves that you are reliable, that you will not only go the distance for them this time, but that you will be there to do it again when they call upon you."

So, take the time to go for lunch with your prospective business partners abroad. Don't talk business right away—ask them about what things are like in their country. Find something that you have in common with them. Maybe you both like a certain sport? Perhaps you share an interest in Italian wine?

During this time, you can observe your interlocutor's reactions. What makes him laugh? Does he react with hostility to certain kinds of expressions? "When you get around to dessert, bring up the subject of the business at hand in a very casual way. Get some indications from his reaction about how to proceed. But let your interlocutor lead you through it all," says Guptara.

Negotiating experts agree that forcing a conclusion with a foreign partner can only cause problems. "Don't be afraid to drop the matter and to talk about the weather," says Garrison. "Don't be too serious, especially at the outset. Show your interlocutor that you are in no hurry to conclude, and he will assume that you are serious. Insist on a conclusion, and he will assume that you are desperate."

Establishing trust is a factor that an American businessperson abroad must take into account not only in negotiations, but also in working with Europeans or Asians on a day-to-day basis.

Disney had to endure an expensive lesson of this type when it opened EuroDisney outside Paris. The management expected the French employees to conform to American expectations in their work, and did little to build up trust. A long and agonizing conflict with French labor unions was the only result of this policy. Finally, Disney gave up and hired French managers. Labor difficulties were smoothed out when managers and workers began to trust each other.

Get the Details Right

Although the British may accept a slick PR demo while negotiating, most of the cultures on the Continent and many in Asia do not.

"There is a real academic side to business in Europe and in parts of Asia," Guptara says. "A business presentation to such interlocutors is like defending a PhD thesis. They expect you to have real depth, all the numbers, and to be able to answer every question. Fail at this and they will never trust you. The word that Europeans apply to a businessman who can't answer key questions is *liar*."

It may seem useless pedantry on the part of your prospective business partners to insist on great detail, "but their view is that the details are the easy part," says Bengtsson. "And a thoroughness in knowledge of your subject means—especially to Europeans, rightly or wrongly—that the risks are being adequately managed."

One American manufacturer recently hit all the wrong buttons in discussions with a French acquisition. Arriving in Paris, the American company promptly invited the board of the French company to lunch. The French board was of the most traditional sort—all graduates of the *grandes écoles*, they perceived themselves to be fashionable, witty, and cultivated.

When the French businessmen arrived at the lunch, they were astonished to find their American colleagues wearing baseball hats and T-shirts with the name of the acquiring company on them. There was also a pile of such hats and shirts on the table, and they were bidden to put them on.

This suggestion did not go over well. But even worse was the period at lunch when the French—after what they thought was a decent delay—began asking strategic questions. It became obvious that the American executives knew little or nothing about the company they were acquiring apart from its balance sheet.

After that, the massive departure of the French businessmen from the company should not have taken the Americans by surprise.

Play by the Rules—Their Rules

When an American executive goes abroad, it's very easy for cultural assumptions to slip into her suitcase. "When negotiations are prolonged, or frustrating, these cultural assumptions tend to jump out of the suitcase, onto the negotiating table," Bengtsson points out. The point to remember at times like this is that you are in someone else's culture and, for the time being, you need to play by their rules.

Because of tighter budgets, companies are sending fewer executives abroad these days, so the executive who is sent to a foreign country has mission-critical work to do. Thus it's essential that the executive adapt to a different culture's rules: for communication, interaction, and negotiation. If he doesn't, if he acts the proverbial "Ugly American," his chances for success are small. ◎

QUESTIONS

1. How can development of personal relationships help in negotiation?
2. Why is it important to understand the culture in which you are operating? What could happen if you don't understand it?
3. What considerations should be made about verbal and nonverbal behavior when working with people overseas?
4. How does time to make a decision vary from culture to culture? How might this affect business relations?

ZARA—THE MAKING OF A FASHION GIANT

Zara [www.zara.com] has turned the fashion 'rag trade' on its head. This Spanish fashion retailing company, which doesn't use glossy images to advertise and is run by a reclusive self-made billionaire who shuns publicity, has taken on the fashion world and is winning. This retailing chain is seen as Europe's answer to Gap. Zara is the main part of the Spanish Inditex group, which in a recent Initial Public Offering [IPO] was valued at nearly 9 billion euros. So how has this multi-billion-dollar retail chain been so successful and created such a furor in the fashion industry, without spending a fortune on glossy billboards, magazines, extravagant launch parties or on highly paid supermodels to flag its wares?

Zara opened its first store in 1975 in Spain and has now become a fashion powerhouse, operating in four continents, with 449 stores located in 29 countries. Zara has become very hip with European shoppers, for its value-for-money, stylish designs. The chain is building a large number of brand devotees thanks to its fashionable designs, which are abreast of the very latest trends and which make up a very convincing price-quality offering.

Zara was started by Amancio Ortega, who built a fashion empire from scratch in little over 25 years. Ortega is now one of Spain's wealthiest individuals, if not one of Europe's. This low-key billionaire still has a very hands-on approach to the business; he is still in charge of personally approving every one of the 11,000 designs Zara produces each year. Inditex's main headquarters are located in Arteixo La Coruna, northwest Spain. Although it is far away from cosmopolitan centers such as Barcelona or Madrid, or the catwalks of Paris or Milan, this town is home to one of Europe's major fashion players.

Zara does not undertake any conventional advertising, except as a vehicle for announcing a new store opening, the start of sales or the start of seasons. The company uses the stores themselves as its main promotional strategy: to convey its image. The company is meticulous in this regard. Zara tries to locate its stores in prime commercial areas, employing the age-old adage 'location, location, location'. Deep inside the lairs of Inditex's corporate headquarters, 25 full-scale store windows are set up, whereby Zara window designers can experiment with design layouts and lighting. The approved design layouts are shipped out to all of Zara's stores, so that a Zara shop front in London will be the same as that in Lisbon and throughout the entire chain.

One of Zara's key philosophies was the realization that fashion, much like food had a 'best before' date—that fashion trends change rapidly. The style that consumers want this month may not be the same in two months time. Fashion has to adapt to what the marketplace wants here and now. CEO of Inditex, Jose Maria Castellano, believes that, "In fashion, stock is like food. It goes bad quickly.

So the key is to minimize your inventory." Zara uses it stores to find out what consumers really want, what designs are selling, what colors are in demand, which items are hot sellers or which are complete duds. Zara uses a sophisticated marketing information system to provide feedback to headquarters and allow it to respond to marketplace demands.

At the end of the each day, Zara sales assistants report to the store manager, using wireless headsets to communicate inventory levels. The Zara store managers then report back to the La Coruna design and distribution departments on what consumers are buying, asking for or avoiding. Top-selling items are requested from headquarters, low-selling designs are taken off the shelves after just a week on display. The group believes it is catering for what consumers want: disposable fashion. Holding excess inventory is a "sin" according to Zara's business philosophy. Garments are produced in comparatively small production runs, so as not to be overexposed, particularly if an item is a poor seller. Zara produces nearly 11,000 designs per year. Stock is seen as an asset that is extremely perishable, and if it is sitting on shelves or racks, it is simply not making money for the organization.

Zara's 250 designers use the market feedback when preparing their next creations. Once designs have been approved, fabrics are dyed and cut by highly automated production lines in La Coruna. These pre-cut pieces are then sent out to nearly 350 workshops in Galicia, Spain and northern Portugal. Zara does not directly own these workshops; the workshops employ nearly 11,000 grey economy workers, mainly women, who may want to supplement their incomes. Seamstresses stitch the precut pieces into garments using easy-to-follow instructions supplied by Zara. The typical seamstress's wages in Zara's workshop network are extremely competitive when compared to those in the other developing countries to which other fashion retailers outsource their production. Furthermore, the proximity of these workshops allows for greater flexibility and control.

The finished garments are sent back to the La Coruna headquarters with its colossal state-of-the-art logistics center, where they are electronically tagged, checked for quality and then sorted into distribution lots, ensuring that the items arrive at their ultimate destinations. Each item is tagged with pricing information, highlighting its price in 29 different currencies. There is no pan-European pricing for Zara's products, prices are different in each national market as Zara believes that each national market has its own particular nuances, such as higher salaries or higher taxation. Zara has to adjust the price of its garments to make it suitable for each country and to reflect these differences. Shipments leave La Coruna, bound for each one of the Zara stores in over 29 countries, twice a week every week. The company's average turnaround time from design to delivery of a new garment is 10 to 15 days, and delivery of goods takes a maximum of 21 days, which is unparalleled in an industry where lead times are usually measured in months not days. Zara's business model tries to fulfill real-time fashion retailing and does not involve second-guessing what consumers' needs will be next season, which may be six months away. ◎

Source: "Zara—the Making of a Fashion Giant," taken from Foundations of Marketing by Fahy and Jobber, ©2007. Reproduced with the kind permission of the Open University Press/ McGraw-Hill Publishing Company.

QUESTIONS

1. How does Zara manage its inventory? Is it effective?
2. How has Zara dealt with quickly changing fads?
3. Visit www.zara.com. In how many countries is Zara selling its products? Would you buy this brand?
4. What type of fashions or retail stores could be compared to Zara?
5. What types of market segmentation do you think Zara uses?

NIKE CEO PHIL KNIGHT AND THE SWEATSHOP DEBATE

The Nike swoosh is one of the world's most recognized symbols. Athletes like Tiger Woods and Michael Jordan have been paid millions of dollars to wear the swoosh when they compete. Founded by Phil Knight in 1964 outside Portland, Oregon, Nike is the number one athletic shoemaker around the globe. In recent years, Nike has come under fire from human rights groups for outsourcing production to Asian factories that maintain sweatshop conditions. Instances of physical abuse of workers have been reported. Depending on the country, wages can average about $1.84 a day. Critics have charged that workers as young as 14 are making shoes which sell for more than $100 in the United States. Some factories that produce Nike products are also making employees work mandatory overtime and subjecting them to unsafe working conditions.

Nike's problems illustrate the dilemmas faced by many firms in the apparel and footwear industry. In pursuit of lower manufacturing costs, Nike outsourced its production to factories in some of Asia's poorest economies. But paying its subcontractors less made Nike vulnerable to charges by human rights groups and the media that the company was exploiting workers. The result has been a public relations nightmare for Nike. The cartoon strip Doonesbury poked fun at the shoemaker. In his film *The Big One*, Michael Moore targeted Nike. The negative publicity has spilled over to universities where student groups have criticized Nike for paying athletes for wearing its clothing. After years of tremendous growth, sales and profits dropped and the company faces increasing financial pressure.

To address the accusations facing his firm, Nike CEO Phil Knight proposed several major changes in the firm's overseas operations:

- Employees must be at least 18 years old.
- Factories will be made safer in accordance with U.S. standards.
- Independent monitoring of factories by nongovernment organizations will be expanded.
- Free middle and high school classes will be offered at factories during off hours.

Some critics think these proposed changes are a step in the right direction, but are simply a response to pressure and should have been implemented long ago. Knight's response to these critics is that Nike has always tried to do the right thing, but in fact the criticism has sped up the firm's efforts in human rights. Knight acknowledges that mistakes have been made, but says that critics have focused on isolated instances that don't portray what the overseas factories are really like. Rather than trying to defend his company's actions, Knight believes the most constructive approach is to ask how a twenty-first century shoe factory should operate and make the changes to meet this standard. Knight also points out that workers in overseas factories are not technically Nike employees, nonetheless he accepts responsibility for the conditions under which they work. The Asian factories are more than subcontractors; they are Nike's partners, if not in a legal then in a moral sense.

Critics point out that Knight's proposal failed to address wages. Knight notes that the policy of paying no less than minimum wages in any country has not changed and wages are reviewed periodically. In all Indonesian factories, for example, a 15-percent hike brought entry-level wages to 15 percent above minimum wage. Knight cites studies indicating that Nike workers overseas not only make enough money to live on, but also enough to be able to save some.

Nike continues to be the target of critics, who ask, How can shoes made for $3 in Asia sell for over $100 in the United States? How can age requirements be enforced in foreign factories? How can athletes be paid millions to endorse Nike products when the people making them are paid so little? CEO Knight, of course, has a different view. Nike's money is made on volume—175 million pairs sold a year—not on gross profit, which at 40 percent is about the industry average. Knight says with confidence that factory age requirements are being enforced. And finally, he notes that athletes are part of an advertising campaign and are paid what the market dictates. So why is Nike the object of continued criticism? In short, Knight believes it is because his company is number one in the industry. ◉

Source: "Nike CEO Phil Knight and the Sweatshop Debate," taken from International Business, 10th edition by Donald Ball, Wendell McCulloch, Paul Frantz, Michael Geringer, and Michael Minor. This material is used by permission of The McGraw-Hill Companies, ©2005.

QUESTIONS

1. As a result of accusations, Nike now releases a social responsibility report every year. Do an Internet search on Nike. Read the company's most recent social responsibility report. Discuss the changes Nike has made in its policy after this article appeared?

2. Do you think companies like Nike have a responsibility to workers in other countries?

3. Do you think Nike should accept responsibility for factories that had terrible labor conditions? Why or why not?

4. What additional changes do you think Nike should implement to improve social responsibility in its business?

FENIX: DIVERSIFIED NICHE MARKETING IN THE LIFESTYLE BUSINESS

Background and Issues

› INTRODUCTION

In 2002, the Fenix Group celebrated its thirtieth anniversary. The commemorative booklet "Gracing Life with Style," featuring a cover decorated with velvet and pages adorned with scented, colorful dried flowers was the embodiment of the Fenix Group's business—it was about lifestyle, of the classy kind.

Mr. Anthony Keung managing director of the Fenix Group, looked back on history and reflected upon the building of Italian fashion brand Anterprima and the establishment of the lifestyle megastore City'super. Both were bold decisions supported by his belief in niche marketing. The two ventures proved to be successful and reinforced the Group's "quality lifestyle" market positioning.

Looking out from his top-floor office, as he reminisced about the Groups' challenges and achievements, Mr. Keung pondered what the future would bring and where the next niche market would be.

› COMPANY BACKGROUND

Knitwear Manufacturing and Marketing

In 1972, Mr. Anthony Keung and Mr. Masaki Ogino founded Fenix Hong Kong Limited The two were former colleagues of a Japanese yarn supplier in Hong Kong. Sharing the same vision, they decided to start their own company. Initially they exported garments made of Japanese materials to the U.S. and European markets, but later noticed that the demand for knitwear in Japan itself was underserved. They went on to set up their own factory. Within a short time, they had successfully established a foothold in Japan—a market considered to be very difficult to penetrate. Their strengths in grasping market trends and in packaging and promoting products were officially recognized when Hong Kong Trade Development Council conferred on them the Export Marketing Award in 1998.

Fashion Retailing

Building on their knowledge in the apparel business and their ability to identify market trends, Keung and Ogino took on fashion retailing in the 1980s. They started off by introducing Japanese and American brands to Hong Kong, opening boutiques in a popular department store. However, the brands were not well known in Hong Kong and were not supported by adequate promotions. The two retail outlets did not do well and were eventually closed down. The entrepreneurs were down, but not out. Undeterred by the failure, they decided to tap into the market for designer-label goods by obtaining distribution rights of several European brands. This time they found the right formula. The associated value of superior quality, designer labels, and fashion from Europe fueled the rocketing sales. Demand grew rapidly and what started off as niche markets soon became the mainstream. Encouraged by the success, Fenix started to build its own brand name in 1994.

The Birth of Anteprima

The upscale lifestyle positioning took shape during the 1980s, when Fenix started handling the then little known brand—Prada. The Prada brand included fashion, shoes, handbags, and accessories. Its funky, minimalist yet intelligent designs using alternative materials appealed to the avant-garde niche market. They spread the trend and within five years Prada became a leader in the luxury market. The most popular product line was the black nylon bag, which could fetch a few hundred U.S. dollars apiece. Prada successfully banked on people's need to make a statement about their lifestyle through what they carried and wore.[1]

Fenix gained insider know-how that was critical to building a successful high-end designer label and benefited from the superior margins that characterized value-based niche marketing. The Prada experience opened the door to the designer label world. In 1996, Fenix built its own brand, Anteprima in Milan, and successfully broke into the exclusive close-knit Milan fashion circle. Mr. Ogino's wife, who was in charge of Prada's Japan business, headed up Anteprima as creative director.

Anteprima's unique blend of Italian and Japanese creativity in fashion, knitwear, shoes, and handbags appealed to the niche market of consumers who identified with a style of "simple sophistication and seduction."[2] It was a great success in Japan, within a few years 14 Anteprima shops were opened. They were also springing up in Europe, Hong Kong, Taiwan, mainland China, and Singapore. By 2002, Anteprima became the flagship label of Fenix, representing more than 50 percent of all its fashion-retailing business.

Transforming Grocery Shopping: City'super

With the addition of Anteprima to its portfolio, Fenix Group became a truly multinational network of knitwear manufacturing and fashion retailing. The natural next step would be be to pursue other areas within the apparel business. However, Keung and Ogino had something else in mind: they had a broader vision.

As they were building Anteprima, they noticed that the quest for high-end fashion was just one aspect of people's pursuit of a stylish and modern lifestyle. The demand for classy premium products extended from fashion to other things in daily life. Keung and Ogino believed that a high-end goods and general merchandise store would fill this gap in the market. At around the same time, a group of retail professionals who had previously managed Seibu, a posh Japanses-styled department store, proposed to partner with Fenix. Sharing the same vision, the two parties came to an agreement on the concept of a new store—City'super.

City'super was a new concept in Hong Kong. The emphasis was on providing exciting high-quality products. City'super transformed what people used to call "grocery shopping" into an exciting and enjoyable experience. The target customers were advocates of a cosmopolitan lifestyle. City'super offered trendy, alternative, and stylish merchandise from around the world including food items, fashions accessories, gadgets, stationery, interior goods and kitchenware, and skincare and healthcare items. Instead of buying out of necessity, Fenix wanted to create a buying at leisure experience. Unlike supermarkets, which used bright lights and a clinically white dècor. City'super was decorated in warm earth tones using wooden floors and shelves. Dimmer and softer lighting was used in the store to create a friendly and welcoming shopping environment (see Exhibit 1). Products were new and exotic imports, choices that could not be found in local supermarkets. Innovative products and services such as the personalized wine (bottles of wine with customized labels) and gourmet-on-demand (fresh food and produce imported to order) were introduced into the store. To match the "e-lifestyle" of its clienteles, City'super offered a Super e-card, a membership and stored-value card that could be used as cash for in-store or online shopping. Value added services such as valet parking and home delivery were also available in selected locations.

Fenix leveraged its retail experience and knowledge in fashionable trends to manage City'super. The first store opened in December 1996. It proved to be a successful venture, so the second store opened in 1998. Contrary to the general view that food and merchandise retailing was an odd choice for an apparel veteran, City'super struck the same chord with Fenix's, existing businesses. The diversification and investment in City'super reinforced the group's strategy to focus on high-value-adding niche markets in lifestyle consumer products.

› THE FENIX GROUP IN 2002

By 2002, Fenix had already created its own environment of satellite companies within a diversified framework that encompassed 19 regional companies, 14 production lines and 80 retail stores worldwide with a workforce of more than 5,000 staff. The subsidiaries were launched in partnership with entrepreneurial employees who were committed and shared the same management philosophy (see Exhibit 2). Annual turnover amounted to US$230 million, of which US$80 million came from manufacturing. Fashion retailing and City'super contributed US$50 million and US$90 million respectively.

› MULTINICHE MARKETING IN THE LIFESTYLE BUSINESS

It is important to identify your competitive advantage in order to find the niche markets in which you can add value.

Mr. Anthony Keung
managing director of the Fenix Group

Over its 30-year history, Fenix evolved from a yarn material trader and knitwear manufacturer in the '70s to a fashion retailer in the '80s. In the '90s, the Group branched out to become a general merchandise retailer. The common thread that ran through these diverse business units was the strategy of "multiniche marketing in the lifestyle business."

› WHAT NEXT?

Over the years Fenix had nurtured a mix of brand names in Hong Kong and catered for different niche markets, from trendy teens to independent modern women. Together they accounted for 74 boutiques in seven countries (see Exhibit 3). On the manufacturing side, Fenix had also become one of the largest knitwear suppliers in the Japanese market, producing more than nine million pieces annually.

When asked about his management philosophy, Keung enthused about his "persistence on quality and focus on business closely tied with trendy lifestyle." Behind his pledge that "Fenix will continue to build fruitful partnerships and fill niche markets with innovative and creative products and services," Keung wondered what the next bold step Fenix should take to charter the course of the future, carrying Fenix to new heights. ◎

Source: "Fenix: Diversified Niche Marketing in the Lifestyle Business," by B. Yim. This material is used by permission of The Centre for Asian Business Cases at The University of Hong Kong (http://www.acrc.org.hk). ©2003.

[1] The 12-year collaboration with Prada ended in 1999 when Prada headquarters decided to handle worldwide distribution themselves.

[2] According to Anteprima's official website: www.anteprima.com.

QUESTIONS

1. How did the drive of the two entrepreneurs (Keung and Ogino) help with their success?

2. What is a niche market? How is it helpful in segmenting markets?

3. What does this case mean by "lifestyle business"? Define and describe. Are there any other products that abide by a lifestyle business model?

4. What is the company's formula for success? How does it tie into its mission statement?

---

exhibit 1

CITY'SUPER STORE

Four divisions of City'super Store:

Food Market	An international gourmet food market selling produce from around the world.
Cooked Deli	A cafeteria offering a variety of fast food in a comfortable environment.
The Gadget	A division that sells high-quality lifestyle products, from makeup to aromatherapy, toys, and luggage.
Page On	A bookshop that offers international literature in all categories as well as magazines and paper-based gift items.

ORGANIZATION CHART, FENIX GROUP HOLDINGS LTD.

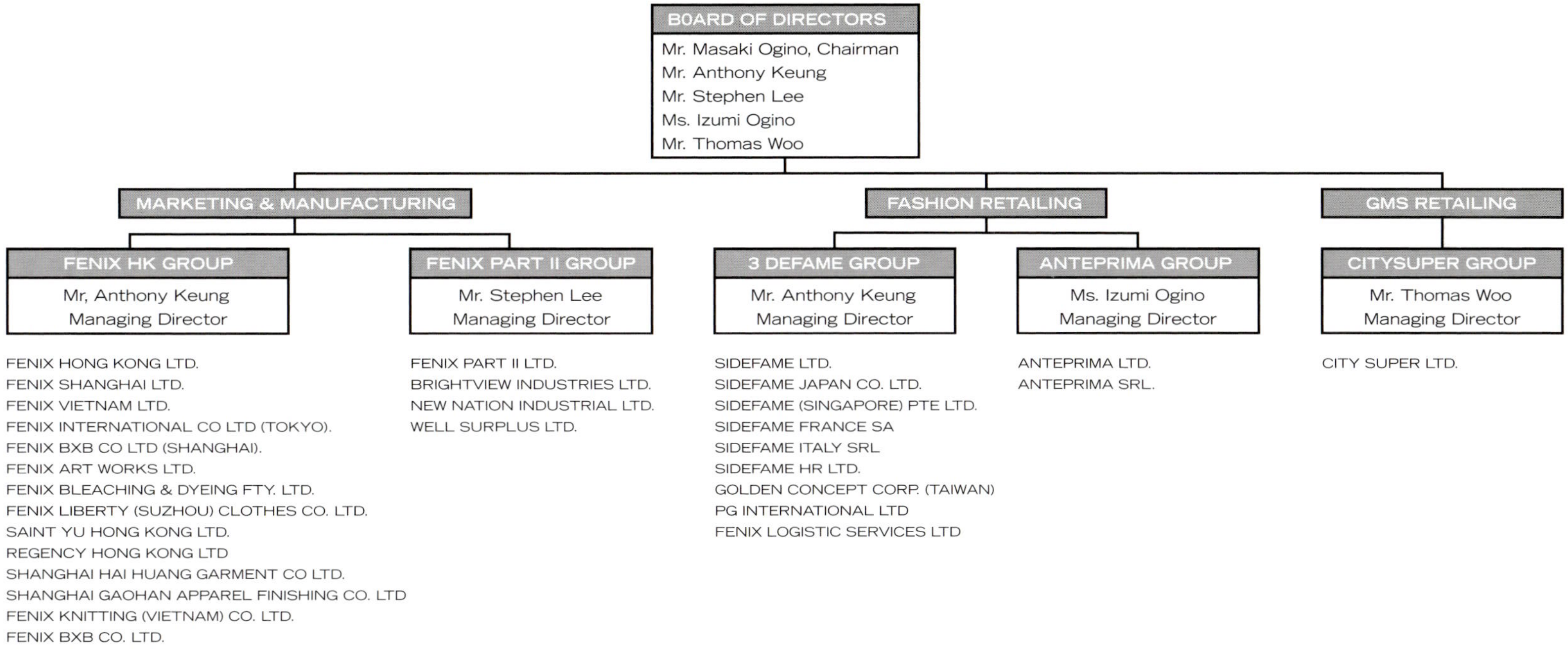

BOARD OF DIRECTORS

Mr. Masaki Ogino, Chairman
Mr. Anthony Keung
Mr. Stephen Lee
Ms. Izumi Ogino
Mr. Thomas Woo

MARKETING & MANUFACTURING

FENIX HK GROUP
Mr. Anthony Keung
Managing Director

FENIX HONG KONG LTD.
FENIX SHANGHAI LTD.
FENIX VIETNAM LTD.
FENIX INTERNATIONAL CO LTD (TOKYO).
FENIX BXB CO LTD (SHANGHAI).
FENIX ART WORKS LTD.
FENIX BLEACHING & DYEING FTY. LTD.
FENIX LIBERTY (SUZHOU) CLOTHES CO. LTD.
SAINT YU HONG KONG LTD.
REGENCY HONG KONG LTD
SHANGHAI HAI HUANG GARMENT CO LTD.
SHANGHAI GAOHAN APPAREL FINISHING CO. LTD
FENIX KNITTING (VIETNAM) CO. LTD.
FENIX BXB CO. LTD.

FENIX PART II GROUP
Mr. Stephen Lee
Managing Director

FENIX PART II LTD.
BRIGHTVIEW INDUSTRIES LTD.
NEW NATION INDUSTRIAL LTD.
WELL SURPLUS LTD.

FASHION RETAILING

3 DEFAME GROUP
Mr. Anthony Keung
Managing Director

SIDEFAME LTD.
SIDEFAME JAPAN CO. LTD.
SIDEFAME (SINGAPORE) PTE LTD.
SIDEFAME FRANCE SA
SIDEFAME ITALY SRL
SIDEFAME HR LTD.
GOLDEN CONCEPT CORP. (TAIWAN)
PG INTERNATIONAL LTD
FENIX LOGISTIC SERVICES LTD

ANTEPRIMA GROUP
Ms. Izumi Ogino
Managing Director

ANTEPRIMA LTD.
ANTEPRIMA SRL.

GMS RETAILING

CITYSUPER GROUP
Mr. Thomas Woo
Managing Director

CITY SUPER LTD.

FENIX GROUP BRAND-NAME PORTFOLIO

Brand Name	Style and Image
Anteprima	A blend of simplicity, sophistication and seductiveness
Atsuro Tayama	Japanese designer's own label with a sensuous and creative style
A/T	Atsuro Tayama's line with a younger and funkier style
Indivi	Japanese brand of innovative modern daily wear for the office
OZOC	A brand that offers sassy street-style casual wear
Heroic Rendezvous	A happy and cultural-conscious label for teenagers
Pearly Gates	Golf apparel and accessories
Furla	Luxurious leather goods from Italy
City'super	Lifestyle megastore

OUTSMARTING WAL-MART

For a lot of retailers, the notion of competing against Wal-Mart seems daunting, if not futile. Yet a few are quietly and systematically doing just that. The CEO of one successful competitor described his strategy by citing an old saw: "It's like the two outdoorsmen who wake to find a raging bear at their campsite," he said. "One camper slowly stands and backs away; the other starts to lace up his sneakers. 'You can't outrun that bear!' whispers the first. 'I don't have to,' replies the second. 'I just have to outrun you!'"

Rather than trying to outrun Wal-Mart, as it were, companies like this CEO's are both exploiting the weaknesses of other Wal-Mart competitors and simply maneuvering around the bear. Consider HEB and Publix in grocery stores, Best Buy in consumer electronics, Walgreens in pharmacy products, PETsMART in pet supplies, and Target in discount stores. All are managing to coexist and even thrive in the same forest with Wal-Mart.

The Wal-Mart threat shrinks into proper perspective when you segment the market along the lines of quality, service, convenience, selection, and price and then look closely at where the retail giant really dominates. Wal-Mart clearly wins on price and, to a lesser degree, selection—but nowhere else. Price isn't everything. Two-thirds of shoppers find Wal-Mart's assortments, middling product quality, and limited services not worth the savings. That means, regardless of Wal-Mart's proximity, there are plenty of customers looking for alternatives.

Our research shows that Wal-Mart's competitors succeed by doing four things well: First, they aggressively build local market share. Profitability in retail is strongly determined by regional share. When Wal-Mart enters the scene, a shakeout begins. Savvy retailers know that market share will change hands like never before. They add stores as competitors' sales decline—either by building new ones or by buying the assets of dying rivals. By being prepared to capture share just as rapidly as Wal-Mart does, aggressive competitors end up even stronger than before. Target has used this approach to attract and keep customers who once patronized now-defunct Ames, Bradlees, Venture, Jamesway, and Caldor.

Next, winning competitors carefully segment their customers and then wow the ones that matter most. They cater to targeted segments, expanding signature categories, customizing local assortments, and raising loyalty benefits. Because Wal-Mart seldom takes even as much as 30 percent of any regional market, 70 percent or more of the market remains for fairly priced competitors to serve in ways that Wal-Mart can't—whether it's with personal attention or ten types of tomatoes.

Winners also develop more rigorous pricing strategies. Wal-Mart's entry marks the end of hunch-based pricing, since it puts price gaps so squarely in the spotlight. Successful competitors therefore sharpen their analysis of price elasticity curves, geographic pricing zones, and the implications of everyday pricing versus high-low promotions for each product category. They expand and accelerate the gathering of competitive intelligence and train local store managers to quickly identify pricing opportunities or vulnerabilities.

Finally, because market prices generally decline as much as 10 percent when Wal-Mart enters a market, winning competitors scrutinize their supply chains, store labor deployment, marketing programs, and overhead costs to eliminate every wasted dollar. Competing against a behemoth enjoying 22 percent lower costs than an average retailer is tough. The key to survival? Play the bear's game while others become it. ◎

QUESTIONS

1. How are category killers affecting Wal-Mart?
2. How can smaller retailers benefit from the shortcomings of Wal-Mart? Discuss at least three ways.
3. What is market share? Look up and define *market share*. Why is it important?
4. What type of pricing strategies does Wal-Mart use?

A BETTER WAY TO NEGOTIATE: BUILD RELATIONSHIPS

Seven ways to strengthen your business alliances

The VP of business development—let's call him Jason—was a stickler when it came to contracts. He favored detailed documents that anticipated every conceivable problem and laid out penalties for each. Trust was a foreign concept. In his view, partnerships were built on legalese and the sure promise of reprisals if either party fails to keep up its end of the bargain. So imagine his shock over the proposed contract he encountered in his first meeting with the new partners in Japan; it consisted of two vague paragraphs. Jason was even more befuddled when his Japanese counterparts bristled at his insistence that their simple pact would not do.

Managers are beginning to appreciate the importance of relationships in their companies' dealings with employees, customers, partner companies, and even rivals. Why didn't Jason's company's Japanese partners need a long contract? Because they believed the mutual concern for the relationship would ensure good faith.

"Relationships are a long-neglected aspect of organizations," says Leonard Greenhalgh, a professor at Dartmouth College's Tuck School of Business and the author of *Managing Strategic Relationships: The Key to Business Success*. "Yet when you think about what goes on between individuals, groups, and organizations, management effectiveness depends very much on relationships."

Like Greenhalgh, business author and Cambridge, Massachusetts–based consultant Chris Turner attributes the new interest in relationships in part to the steady inflow of a new generation of young people who were weaned on the Web and have little interest in contributing their talents to organizations based on hierarchy and regimentation.

"We're definitely in a transition," says Turner, author of *All Hat and No Cattle: Tales of a Corporate Outlaw*. "People are recognizing that command-and-control isn't an effective way to run organizations."

Here are seven concepts experts recommend to managers who want to improve their ability to be more effective in their business relationships.

Recognize that transactions are hardly ever one-shot deals

Jason took pride in his reputation as someone who drove a hard bargain. In his dealings with his company's suppliers, he strove for the bargain-basement price, often pitting supplier against supplier in his quest for the best possible deal. Little did he care that his counterparts usually left with a silent vow to settle the score later. Their opportunity came when Jason's company found itself in an emergency and needed to ask for a special favor. Jason got the predictable response: "no." Had Jason and his organization treated the suppliers better—had they fostered a positive relationship—they would have stood a far better chance of finding a cooperative partner when crunch time came.

"Treat people as if you will need to deal with them again," Greenhalgh says. "One-shot deals are very hard to find. It is far better to have people regard you with a sense of trust, rapport, and good will than a desire for revenge."

What about those voluminous contracts? "A comprehensive written contract is necessary only if the relationship is bad," Greenhalgh writes. "It serves as a substitute for trust and good will—but it's not a good substitute. Managers would be better off fixing the relationship."

Negotiate from the same side of the table

Rather than approaching bargaining as a zero-sum contest, one with a winner and a loser, experts suggest putting the negotiators together on the same side of the table, in a figurative sense, united against the challenge or problem.

A competitive man by nature, Jason suffered from what Greenhalgh calls the "fixed-pie syndrome." He couldn't shake the notion that it was his loss every time the other party got something it wanted in the give-and-take. But it is often possible for negotiators to achieve agreements in which both companies end up in a better position than before. For example, if Jason's company agrees to a more generous price for the supplier's widgets, that company might be able to afford manufacturing improvements. Over the long run, Jason's company begins to receive fewer defective parts, and the supplier is better able to help when sudden spikes in demand call for rush orders.

Choose your relationships with care

As your company becomes more mindful of strategic relationships, pay special attention to the people it appoints as representatives. "When you deal with another business, it's not one abstract entity dealing with another abstract entity," Greenhalgh says. "It's one person dealing with another. You need someone who embodies the organization you represent."

According to Turner, the "Vince Lombardi type"—a chest-pumper who calls comrades to arms and sets out to beat the opponent at all costs—is not the person you want representing your organization in the new environment. Nor, says Greenhalgh, will an aggressive person—or someone with a fondness for argument and debate—be effective in forging strategic relationships. The ideal liaisons have a talent for cogent communicating and an ability to achieve and demonstrate understanding of the allies' needs.

Include the implementers in the courting

Too often, says Gene Slowinski, managing partner of Alliance Management Group (Gladstone, New Jersey) and director of strategic alliance research at Rutgers' Graduate School of Management, "The deal guy and the lawyer from Company A meet with their counterparts and do a deal. They then throw it over the wall to the implementers and say, 'Don't screw it up.' That's the model that doesn't work." Slowinski recently completed a study in which he learned that successful inter-organization alliances usually involve the "implementers"—the employees who will actually live and work the terms of the agreement—into the deal-making process. This, Slowinski says, can be accomplished by reserving space on both negotiating teams for one or two of the people who will execute the deal.

Including the implementers helps the relationships between organizations, Slowinski says. Because the deal-makers have a realistic grasp of capabilities, expectation errors are eliminated; and because the staffers on the ground are learning about the nascent alliance as it's forming, they're better prepared to begin the execution once the pact is signed.

Foster cooperation, not competition, between individuals

According to old-school thinking, the sure way to get the most from your employees is to get them to compete with one another: measure individual performance and award bonuses, raises, and promotions to those who outperform their colleagues. The problem with this approach is that when one employee's gain is another one's loss, people have a powerful disincentive to come together in the kinds of collaborations that will benefit the organization in the long term. The same holds for competition between companies. Rather than going to war with the rival that sells the same service as you, why not work together to grow the sector?

"When you encourage people to excel relative to their peers," Greenhalgh says, "they stop collaborating with one another. If I help someone and she does better as a result, then I'm at risk of losing the competition. Some companies have a rule that you won't be evaluated positively if your success comes at someone else's expense. That's a much better approach."

Another effective approach is to evaluate team, rather than individual, performance. But be careful not to stoke a kind of team-versus-team competition that will plague a company just as surely as when individuals are going at it.

Share the knowledge

Just like marriages, strategic relationships are built on good communication. Getting too crafty about managing a spouse's information—what to tell and what to keep secret—inevitably leads to a decline in the mutual confidence that the partners can count on one another. The same is true of relationships in your organization, says Turner. "Transparency increases trust, and trust strengthens relationships," she says. "The more information you can get out there the better, because information is power."

Another key to communication is a horizontal, rather than vertical, information flow. In traditional reporting relationships, knowledge travels from top to bottom—from supervisor to manager to worker—and sometimes from bottom to top, as a manager collects intelligence from people on the front lines. But in today's more complex organizations, Greenhalgh says, companies need communication from department to department and team to team. When the information is trapped in vertical "silos," Department A won't benefit from what Department B has just learned about a shift in customer behavior, for example. One effective solution: develop task forces composed of members of different functional areas.

Slowinski urges managers to confront problems with their allies while they're still at the fact level and before they've escalated to the emotional level. At quarterly meetings, he says, time should be reserved to discuss potential problems lest they become full-blown deal-wreckers by the next meeting. "Things fester," Slowinski says, "if we don't learn how to bring them up and resolve them."

Create community, not castes

As Greenhalgh reports in his book, managers at the credit card company MBNA have no special section in the parking lot or cafeteria. They dress just like the employees staffing the telephones, and they work out of cubicles like everyone else. The result, Greenhalgh says, is a conspicuous absence of the distance that often grows between managers and employees—a distance that can hurt morale, enthusiasm, and productivity. The MBNA staffers give a spirited effort because all the signals tell them they're valued members of the team.

Turner says there is enormous value in managers' getting to know team members in casual conversation; call it Management by Hanging Around. "One of the most important things a manager can do is get to know the people they're working with," she says. "Part of the work of a leader is to foster the kind of community where good things happen."

Castes, Greenhalgh says, create barriers between people. "This notion of castes is embodied in the practice of referring to the boss as your 'superior,'" he says. "It's implicit in the extra privileges you give to people who are higher up in management. It undermines the effectiveness of the whole institution. If you're doing things that make the caste distinctions more apparent, be prepared for the organization to be less effective as a result." ◎

QUESTIONS

1. What mistakes did Jason make in his business dealings?
2. In the fashion business, how might "implementers" be included, as the article suggests?
3. How do you feel about negotiation? Describe ways in which you could practice these skills.
4. Why is clear communication important in successful negotiations?

GAP INC.

Introduction

For nearly 20 years (1983–2002), Gap Inc., the leading specialist clothing retailer in the United States, was synonymous with its CEO Millard S. Drexler, the "merchant prince." However, after three years of declining like-for-like sales between 1999 and 2002, Drexler's tenure was ended, and Paul S. Pressler, formerly of The Walt Disney Company, became CEO in October 2002. Pressler closed nearly 200 underperforming stores, reduced excess inventory,[1] and conducted extensive market research to better determine customer preferences, resulting in a "spectacular turnaround" in 2003.[2] Between 2002 and 2003, net earnings more than doubled to $1.03 billion. (See Exhibits 1 and 10a–h.) At the end of 2003, the firm had a 9.5 percent market share in the $166.2 billion U.S. apparel market.[3]

The momentum slowed down somewhat at the end of 2004 and beginning of 2005. The company posted a profit of $1.14 billion on revenue of $16.3 billion in 2004, but comparable store sales were flat. In the first quarter of 2005, they decreased 4 percent compared with a 7 percent increase in the same period of 2004.[4] Additionally, industry observers raised concerns about Pressler's lack of experience in the apparel sector, the company's "near market saturation in all three of its brands,"[5] cannibalization among the brands, and the company's "fashion lapses."[6]

However, Pressler forecast a strong 2005 and identified a number of initiatives, including better buying, easy-to-shop environments, supply chain improvements, and new outlet additions.[7] The firm was also establishing a new brand, Forth & Towne. Would these moves help reestablish momentum?

Apparel Industry Overview

In 2004, apparel sales reached $172.8 billion in the U.S.,[8] a significant fraction of the $768 billion global retail apparel market.[9] (See Exhibit 2.) Industry subsectors included accessories; intimate apparel; and children's, men's, and women's clothing. In 2004, U.S. consumers spent $95 billion on women's apparel, $49 billion on men's apparel, and $29 billion on children's clothes; from 2003 to 2004, men's and women's apparel sales each increased approximately 5 percent, while sales of children's apparel remained flat.[10] In addition, women made one-third of men's apparel purchases in 2004;[11] they had made 52 percent in 1998 and 60 percent in 1985.[12]

Industry observers categorized retailers that sold clothing as discount/value (e.g., Marshalls, Old Navy, and Wal-Mart), mid-price (e.g., Gap, Limited Brands, and Macy's), or high-end/luxury (e.g., Barneys, Neiman Marcus, and Saks Fifth Avenue). They also categorized them by channel (e.g., specialty, mass, and off-price). (See Exhibit 3.) Wal-Mart, the top vendor of clothes in the U.S., had a 9.8 percent dollar market share in 2003, ahead of Gap Inc.'s 9.5 percent share. Wal-Mart's 2003 unit market share was 23.2 percent. JC Penney had a 6.1 percent dollar share; Target, 3.8 percent; Kohl's, 3.8 percent; and Gap Inc.'s Old Navy, 3.2 percent. While Wal-Mart's share of the apparel market was bolstered by its sales of underwear, socks, and children's clothing, it was striving to target more fashion-conscious consumers, and analysts believed the retail behemoth could double its share of the apparel market by 2009.[13]

Specialty clothing retailers accounted for 30 percent of total apparel sales in 2004.[14] Gap Inc. had the largest market share of this group, 31.4 percent. It was followed by Limited Brands (13 percent), Charming Shoppes (4.5 percent), Abercrombie & Fitch (3.9 percent), and American Eagle Outfitters (3.6 percent).[15] (See Exhibits 4 and 5.)

Several trends were impacting the U.S. apparel industry. To begin, consumers were spending less of their income on clothes. Clothing and accessories decreased from 12 percent of personal consumption expenditures in 1950 to 5 percent in 2003. Medical care spending, on the other hand, increased from 5 percent to 20 percent during the same time frame.[16] Other products and activities, such as home furnishings, spa treatments, and electronics, vied with apparel for consumers' discretionary dollars.[17] Regarding electronics, chairman of Saks Inc. Brad Martin commented, "Now, fashion includes iPods and high tech."[18]

Retailers of apparel were focusing on niche markets for growth opportunities. Because Americans were becoming larger, the plus-size apparel market was expanding. In 1985, the most often purchased woman's dress was a size 8; in 2005 it was a size 14, and plus-size purchases accounted for 25 percent of women's apparel sales in 2004.[19] Plus-size women who desired more fashionable clothing choices represented an underserved demographic. Some apparel retailers, such as Charming Shoppes' Lane Bryant, catered solely to the plus-size consumer, while others, such as Old Navy and Talbots, were incorporating plus-size lines into their existing collections.

The changing shape of the average American consumer was the catalyst for SizeUSA, a 2003 study sponsored by the apparel industry, U.S. government, and academic and research institutions. According to a report in *American Demographics*, "most [current] women's size systems can be traced back to a 1941 study that fielded measurements from a small sample of mostly white, young women in the military."[20] However, due to social trends and increased diversity, the size of the average American had changed significantly in 60 years. The SizeUSA study was the "first-ever statistically representative census of American body shape and size" and used body scanners to "measure[e] the complete physical dimensions of 10,000 Americans from a range of demographic segments."[21] Its purpose was to provide clothing designers, manufacturers, and retailers detailed information about their target consumers. Industry observers anticipated that the study could eventually help retailers offer betting fitting merchandise and even enable them to better match inventory demographically.

In addition to paying more attention to plus-size shoppers, retailers were also targeting older consumers. Baby boomers, the 80 million people born between 1946 and 1964, were attractive to apparel retailers. Research indicated that many did not plan to retire before age 70 and thus would continue needing work-appropriate clothes. Clothing retailers recognized the 40 million boomer women as a "powerful consumer group" that spent approximately $41 billion on clothes each year, $27 billion of it on themselves—more than younger women spent.[22] Many of these women also desired fashionable, age-appropriate clothes that fit well and felt they were underserved by an industry that catered to the young and thin. Furthermore, in March 2005 *Women's Wear Daily* proposed, "Apparel players can cater to a 55-and-up population whose ranks are projected to expand nine times faster than those 34 and younger, in the next 15 years."[23] However, the apparel industry would continue to compete with other sectors, such as the vacation, housing, and automobile industries, for boomers' money.

Department stores' significance in the U.S. apparel industry continued to decline. Department stores first appeared in the U.S. in the late 1800s; they thrived immediately after World War II and during the 1960s and early 1970s when shopping center construction accelerated.[24] In the late 1970s, however, "new off-price and discount store chains, and niche-oriented specialty stores, began to outprice and outsell department stores, drawing off their clientele."[25] Throughout the 1980s, market saturation curtailed shopping center construction considerably, and consolidation among department stores occurred, which continued into the 1990s. In 2005, department stores remained a force in apparel retailing but continued to face intense competition from discount and specialty clothing stores. By 2004, department-store chains' market share of women's apparel had decreased to less than 20 percent, while specialty retailers' share had increased to 30 percent. Furthermore, department stores' practice of holding frequent sales events had diminished profit margins by conditioning consumers not to pay full price for items.

In 2005, Federated Department Stores, which operated Bloomingdale's and Macy's, acquired The May Department Stores, operator of Filene's and Lord & Taylor, for $17 billion. This move positioned Federated as a $30 billion retailer with 950 department stores nationwide.[26] According to Merrill Lynch, "Many apparel brands view Federated as something of the 'last great hope' of the department store business, with merchandise management best equipped to reenergize the traditional department store concept."[27] Pre-merger, women's apparel sales accounted for 27 percent of Federated's $15.3 billion 2003 revenue; men's and children's apparel sales, 21 percent.[28]

Discount retailers of apparel such as Target and Wal-Mart were becoming increasingly significant in the sector, especially as they added fashionable items to their clothing lines. Morgan Stanley analysts noted, "The mass channel remains the biggest threat to apparel retailers. ... Mass can do to specialty what specialty did to department stores."[29] Discount clothing sales accounted for approximately $70 billion, or 40 percent,[30] of total apparel sales in the U.S. in 2004, up from approximately 25 percent in 1989.[31] Again, Wal-Mart was the leading vendor in this market, with a 24.6 percent share, followed by TJ Maxx/Marshalls (10.1 percent), Target (8.4 percent), Old Navy (7.8 percent) and Kmart (6.1 percent).[32] In recent years, Target had famously collaborated with designers Isaac Mizrahi and Mossimo Giannulli to offer trendy, inexpensive casual and career apparel; the Mizrahi offerings, sold at all 1,300 Target stores, included $29.99 blazers. Mossimo products generated $1 billion in sales for Target between 2001 and 2004.[33]

Wal-Mart was foraying into fashion categories as well. It acquired the U.K. retailer Asda in 1999, and through it sold the "cheap chic" George line of clothing. At the end of 2004, Asda surpassed Marks & Spencer as the leading apparel retailer in Great Britain, with a 9.4 percent market share.[34] In the U.S., Wal-Mart lagged behind Target in its sales of fashionable apparel items; however, it was striving to become trendier in consumers' eyes. In 2003, Levi Strauss partnered with Wal-Mart to create a low-priced line of Levi's jeans for the store.

The modern fast fashion business model, pioneered by Spain's Zara and Sweden's Hennes & Mauritz (H&M) was revolutionizing the sector, especially in Europe. Using this model, retailers "design[n] trendy, inexpensive clothes that mimic high-end fashion and ... are delivered to consumers at lightning speed—two to four weeks after conception. This turnaround time is a far cry from the four to nine months that U.S. mass retailers typically require."[35] Gap could produce an item in three months, but required nine months to produce the majority of its merchandise, for example.[36] A 2004 *Harvard Business Review* spotlighted Zara for its super-responsive supply chain, which enabled it to turnaround clothes so quickly.

HBR noted the chain (1) had tight communication among shoppers, store managers, designers, production staff, and distributors so it could "regular[ly] creat[e] and rapid[ly] replenis[h] ... small batches of new goods"; (2) "manage[d] all design, warehousing, distribution, and logistics functions itself" and even produced half of its own merchandise, enabling it to rhythmically order all steps in the supply chain; and (3) made capital investments allowing vertical integration (e.g., it owned its own factories, mostly located in Spain), increasing the chain's flexibility.[37]

Fast fashion retailers stocked limited numbers of each size of an item to create environments of scarcity and exclusivity in their stores, thus encouraging full-price purchases. Only 15 percent of Zara's merchandise was sold at a discount, for example, compared to 30–40 percent for the industry average.[38] Fast fashion retailers also turned over clothes quickly to encourage frequent store visits. For example, Spain's Mango added new apparel to its outlets weekly compared with once every six weeks for the "typical American clothing chain."[39] It also used a proprietary software system to match clothing styles with stores where the apparel would sell best. H&M added new items to its sales floor daily.[40] Benefits of the fast fashion business model included leaner inventories, higher profit margins, and the ability to increase production of in-demand items. The 730 Zara stores in 55 countries generated sales of $4.7 billion in 2004;[41] Zara's revenue and net income grew annually at 20 percent from 2001 to 2003.[42] In 2004, H&M operated 1,100 outlets in 20 countries and posted $8 billion in revenue;[43] it operated 65 outlets in the eastern U.S., and planned to open 35 more U.S. stores in 2005.[44] Mango was preparing to enter the U.S. in late 2005; it operated over 730 stores in 72 countries and had $782 million in sales in 2003.[45]

January 1, 2005, marked the end of the World Trade Organization's (WTO) phase-out of the Multifiber Agreement (MFA) quotas. The MFA, established in 1973, limited the number of clothing products developing markets could export to the U.S., Canada, and several European countries in order "to protect European and American producers from a flood of cheap imports."[46] The quotas "began to be phased out in 1994 as the newly formed World Trade Organization went about liberalizing global trade."[47] China stood to gain much from the cessation of the quota system. Morgan Stanley posited, "We expect China to dominate apparel manufacturing in the post-quota world. ... China's share of U.S. apparel imports could grow to 17–20 percent within one year (from 12.5 percent) and reach 50–60 percent in the longer term."[48] The quotas added approximately 20 percent to U.S. retail prices; without them, analysts and government officials estimated that retail apparel prices could eventually drop 5–11 percent.[49] Seventy percent of Gap's merchandise was subject to quotas in 2004.[50] While some lauded the end of the quota system, others decried it. Concerned about the effect on U.S. apparel and textile industry jobs, some in the sector were lobbying the government to impose safeguard measures.

Consumers were depending less on "fashionistas" to prescribe trends and were mixing and matching items from different brands, designers, and stores (discount and high-end), in order to project their personal styles.[51] Also, people were dressing up wardrobes, notably their work attire. Business casual dress became popular during the late 1990s, when many companies offered it as an employee perk; in the years after the dot-com bubble burst, however, office wear was becoming somewhat dressier. Between 2003 and 2004, sales of men's tailored clothing (e.g., suits, sports coats, and jackets) increased 24 percent.[52] Finally, apparel luxury items and accessories (e.g., jewelry, belts, purses, and scarves) were selling well. For example, women were purchasing twice the amount of handbags they bought in the late 1990s.[53]

Gap Inc. History

Gap Inc. stemmed from a negative shopping experience: real estate developer Donald Fisher was unable to return a pair of Levi's jeans that were too short. Learning from first-hand experience that there was a "need for a place that sold jeans in a comprehensive array of sizes," he and his wife Doris founded the first Gap store (named after "the generation gap") in 1969 in San Francisco, California.[54] It primarily carried Levi's jeans and the concept was popular from the start, especially among teenagers. The chain earned high margins on its sales of jeans because Levi Strauss did not allow its merchandise to be discounted. The Fishers established five more stores by the end of 1970; in 1976 Gap went public.

In 1976 the Federal Trade Commission ruled that manufacturers could no longer set prices; as a result, retailers began selling discounted Levi's. During the late 1970s, the Fishers progressively sold fewer Levi's as it became difficult to compete with discounters, and they incorporated several lines of private label active wear into the company's clothing mix. The active wear expanded Gap's customer base but since the clothing was considered "junky," it sold only at reduced prices.[55] By the early 1980s, approximately 500 Gap outlets existed.

Seeking a solution to his problems, Fisher hired Millard "Mickey" Drexler, president of women's clothier Ann Taylor, as president of the Gap division in 1983. Among other things, Fisher wanted to make the company vertically integrated. Drexler revamped Gap. First, he got rid of the low quality merchandise through promotions. He hired new designers and the company henceforth concentrated on selling basic, casual apparel: sturdy, colorful cotton clothing; jeans; and sweats under a single label, Gap (Levi's jeans were completely phased out by 1991). Drexler overhauled the stores to insure pleasant shopping experiences; e.g., white shelves and tables with neatly folded clothing replaced crowded circular clothing racks. He also replaced "executives who relied on complicated quantitative research" with "people who understood his approach

of quickly testing his fashion intuition in new products."[56] The first year of Drexler's overhaul was challenging for the company—profits dropped 43 percent due to the merchandise liquidation—but thereafter, it thrived. Initially, Drexler "oversaw every major design decision"; he kept close tabs on designs as the company grew.[57] His vision for the brand: "Everybody can wear [Gap] clothes. ... We want to provide the basic pieces for anyone's closet."[58]

In order to diversify the company, Fisher purchased Banana Republic, a two-store enterprise that sold safari-inspired clothing, in 1983. The firm also purchased Pottery Barn in 1984 but sold it two years later as it was not profitable. Banana Republic did well initially but floundered after the safari craze ended in 1987. During the next few years, Gap Inc. repositioned Banana to include a broader range of higher-priced basic apparel and expanded Gap in and outside of the United States. In 1987, the company introduced Hemisphere, which sold "expensive 'European-inspired' clothes."[59] The merchandise didn't sell well, and the company closed the nine-store chain in 1989. The Gap division opened its first international unit in England in 1987; it entered Canada in 1989 and France in 1993. Gap Inc. also added new brands to its company portfolio. Frustrated that he couldn't find desirable clothing for his young son, Drexler launched GapKids in 1986; the division generated $2 million in sales in its first year; five years later, it produced revenues of $260 million.[60] Drexler was promoted to president of Gap Inc. in 1987; in 1990 babyGap was born.

The company experienced significant growth during this period as it "revolutioniz[ed] the casual-apparel market for men, women, and children, providing dressed-down clothes at affordable prices."[61] Popular advertising campaigns (e.g., "Individuals of Style" and "For Every Generation, There's a Gap") gave the company and its products "the beginning of a brand image."[62] By 1992, the firm operated over 1,200 units, and it was located in nearly half of the 1,500 largest malls in the U.S.[63] In the early 1990s, the firm took "advantage of recessionary blues by locking up sweet lease deals, moving into downtowns and urban neighborhoods, and opening on the main streets of midsize cities."[64] It produced quality clothes at low cost because it "design[ed] its own clothes, cho[se] its own materials, and monitor[ed] manufacturing so closely."[65] It also had "200 quality-control inspectors working inside factories in 40 countries to make sure specifications [were] met right from the start."[66] New collections appeared in stores every six to eight weeks, and individual stores carried many sizes (as opposed to styles) of items to cater to Gap Inc.'s range of customers.

However, by the mid-1990s, the company's growth leveled off. Analysts declared it "mature." The casual apparel market had become increasingly competitive. Furthermore, the media (e.g., *Saturday Night Live*) parodied Gap on occasion and decried its use of "sweatshop" labor in factories throughout the world.

Drexler did not believe that the company was mature, however. His vision for Gap Inc. involved making it a ubiquitous global brand, like Coca-Cola. To achieve this goal and turn the company around, he established the company's third main brand, Old Navy, in 1994, (Drexler was named CEO of Gap Inc. the following year) and increased the rate of expansion of Gap outlets. Old Navy, which sold clothes at lower price points than the Gap division and competed with Sears and Target, was successful from the start. By 1997, Gap Inc. had opened nearly 300 Old Navy stores and the brand's sales reached $1 billion. The company revamped the image of the Gap brand, returning to basics after trying to lure teenage shoppers with trendy apparel. It received heady promotion when actress Sharon Stone wore a Gap turtleneck along with a Valentino skirt to the 1996 Academy Awards—the turtleneck sold out the following week.[67] The firm also opened stores at a rapid pace and expanded into smaller cities. Furthermore, the firm began selling products online in 1997. In the same year, Donald and Doris' son Robert became president of the Gap division.

The company also benefited from the business casual trend that exploded in the wake of the dot.com boom. Due in part to a popular advertising campaign that promoted a new line of khakis, 1998 was a very successful year for the company. Some of the campaign's television spots ("Khakis Swing") featured khaki-clad young people dancing to swing tune "Jump, Jive, an' Wail." Gap Inc. earned $825 million on $9.05 billion of sales (up from $6.5 billion in 1997), and comparable stores sales growth was 17 percent in 1998 (versus 6 percent in 1997).[68] It introduced GapBody stores, which sold intimate apparel, in 1998 as well.

Gap Inc. "misjudged fashion trends in 2000"[69] and subsequently had unsatisfactory earnings and negative comparable store sales growth for 2000, 2001, and 2002. Its trendy apparel—an attempt to appeal to the youth market—alienated core shoppers. It had $2 billion in debt in 2002, largely due to its rapid expansion of stores; lost ground to lower-priced competitors; and saw its stock price decrease from a high of $53.75 in February 2000 to $14 in May 2002.[70] By 2000, several top designers and executives left the company "disillusioned with how bureaucratic the organization had become."[71] Furthermore, while Gap had made "button-down shirts, chinos and basic cotton T-shirts the boomer uniform," it struggled to resonate as well with some members of Generation Y (those born in the late 1970s to early 1990s) who were "looking for individuality, not conformity."[72]

In 2002, Drexler retired and Paul S. Pressler became CEO of Gap Inc. Pressler had spent 15 years with the Walt Disney Company, ending his tenure there as chairman of Walt Disney Parks and Resorts. Drexler became CEO of clothier J. Crew in 2003. The press noted the difference in the two men's leadership styles. Whereas Drexler "flew by the seat of his khakis," relying on his honed intuition to direct apparel development, Pressler was research-oriented and left decisions about apparel to Gap Inc.'s designers.[73] "I had to demonstrate to everyone that the general manager is here to lead the people—not pick the buttons," he stated.[74]

After Pressler became CEO, he oversaw a major research initiative that collected insights from thousands of consumers and employees about the company's brands. Additionally, he slowed the rate of new openings and called for an IT overhaul as well as the implementation of a localization program for inventory management. In 2003, Gap Inc. issued its first social responsibility report, detailing its efforts to improve working conditions for the manufacturers of its garments in factories throughout the world; the company was lauded for its efforts and the honesty of the report.[75] In 2004, Robert Fisher replaced Donald Fisher as Gap Inc.'s chairman of the board. In the company's 2003 annual report, Donald Fisher noted that he planned to remain "on the board as a director, and … continue as an advisor and employee of the company in the role of founder and chairman emeritus."[76]

Gap Inc. in 2005 and Beyond

› THE BRANDS

Gap Inc.'s portfolio consisted of Gap, Banana Republic, and Old Navy. The firm was preparing to launch its fourth brand, Forth & Towne, in the fall of 2005. Company research revealed that consumers thought the three main divisions resembled each other too closely and differentiated them largely by price. As such, the company had been working to establish distinct "identities" for each one. At the end of 2004, Pressler admitted, "We think we have a better separation of our brands today. That's our biggest focus."[77] The company had positioned Gap as the purveyor of "fresh, casual American style," Banana Republic as an "affordable luxury" retailer with an "elevated designer expression," and Old Navy as a "formidable player in the value sector" offering basic and fashionable items in a fun shopping environment.[78] (See Exhibit 6.)

Gap

The Gap division "traditionally offered key items with a focus on casual weekend" but "broadened that offering [in 2004] and added pieces that allow customers to dress up their wardrobe for work or going out in addition to casual weekend wear."[79] In addition to offering clothing for men and women, the division included sub-brands GapBody (intimate apparel), GapKids, and babyGap. Although teenagers and adults of various ages shopped at Gap, the brand targeted 18- to 30-year-olds. Of the 4,000 women's and girl's apparel brands in the U.S. in 2004, Old Navy and Gap were the top sellers followed by Hanes/Hanes Her Way, Polo/Ralph Lauren, and Victoria's Secret.[80]

Cynthia Harriss was named president of Gap in May 2005 after initially being hired as president of the company's discount outlet stores in February 2004. She replaced Gary Muto, who had been selected to head Forth

& Towne. Harriss previously worked for the Walt Disney Company first as vice president of stores for The Disney Store and then as president of the Disneyland Resort division. Before joining Disney, she worked at Paul Harris Stores, a women's apparel retailer, for 19 years.[81]

Pressler and Muto hired Canadian Pina Ferlisi as executive vice president of product design in March 2003 to define the division's style aesthetic. Before joining Gap Inc., Ferlisi worked at Perry Ellis, Tommy Hilfiger, and Theory; she also helped launch the successful Marc by Marc Jacobs line. Her Gap design team was located in New York City and included vice president of women's design Louise Trotter, who formerly worked at Calvin Klein, and vice president of accessories design Emma Hill, who previously held a similar post at Marc Jacobs. Both Trotter and Hill hailed from the U.K.

Scores of consumer and employee insights conducted after Pressler became CEO indicated that female Gap customers felt the brand's offerings were too androgynous and boxy. Hence, Ferlisi made the women's lines more feminine and focused on fabric and fit. The unit strove to be known for its work and special occasion wear as well as its casual weekend apparel. Also, it shifted its emphasis from purveying separates to purveying outfits. For example, Hill was designing accessories to complement certain garments; corduroy bags she designed sold out in all colors. Ferlisi's task included balancing Gap's offering of basics and fashion. She explained, "We're now trying to appeal to the customer who wants to feel current and stylish but not necessarily trendy."[82] Trotter added, "Our eye is not on fast fashion or copying trends for the masses. ... Our eye is on giving style to the masses."[83]

Research also revealed differences in the ways men and women shop. Pressler explained, "Women view [shopping] as an emotional, social experience, and opportunity for self-improvement. ... A majority of men are rationally motivated to shop. It's all about the mission: stocking up and replacing."[84] Hence men's sections highlighted the "Fundamentals"—pieces that men could wear for work, going out, or the weekend. The firm learned that many men valued ease-of-care apparel and introduced stain- and wrinkle-resistant khakis in early 2004.

Another major initiative at Gap was the redesign of the stores to improve customers' shopping experiences and help maximize sales. The firm redesigned seven stores in Denver, Colorado, in early 2005; they served as prototypes for the new Gap. The company expected to upgrade its entire fleet of Gap units during the next several years. The wide-open design of the old stores, where the men's and women's sections blended together, was replaced with a "gallery of shops .... organized by occasion dressing."[85] Men and women entered their departments separately, with 60 percent of each store devoted to women's apparel, 40 percent to men's. New store features included "timeless hickory fixtures, terrazzo marble tile and dark oak floors," track lighting, and a lounge section with playing cards and reading material.[86] Fitting rooms were more cozy and personal. Further changes were implemented to help the staff be more efficient, and store managers were given more authority regarding in-store displays and work scheduling. Christopher Hufnagel, vice president, Gap brand store experience, stated, "Instead of pushing customers through the store with a campaign, we can be a store that pulls customers in with the store experience."[87]

Some industry observers believed that Old Navy was cannibalizing Gap. Old Navy's revenues surpassed those of the flagship brand in North America in 2002.[88] Furthermore, there was concern among company executives that Gap stores placed too closely together were cannibalizing each other. Most of the 158 units the company closed in 2004 were North American Gap stores; in 2005 Gap Inc. planned 135 closings, most of which would be Gap stores as well.[89] The company was conducting intense demographic research before opening an outlet and closing stores to rationalize its Gap fleet. The research was also used to determine where the company might open stand-alone babyGap and GapKids stores.

Gap's top U.S. competitors included Abercrombie & Fitch (A&F) and American Eagle Outfitters (AE). A&F sold clothes to men, women, and children through its three main brands; its flagship brand targeted college age individuals. The firm operated 790 stores and had $2 billion in sales in 2004. AE catered to 15- to 25-year-olds and earned $1.9 billion in revenue via its 850 U.S. stores in 2004.[90]

In 2004, Gap Inc. operated nearly 250 Gap brand stores in the U.K., France, and Japan, and international sales accounted for over 9 percent of the firm's total revenues. Its long-term growth strategy included further international expansion, and it expected to open 50 more stores in Europe and Japan by 2007. While Gap Inc. owned and operated its own stores as of 2005, it planned to use franchising to establish itself in new markets such as (possibly) Australia, Latin America, and the Middle East, in the next several years. According to one report, "Under a franchise arrangement Gap would source and supply product of the same style and quality as sold in its North American stores. But it would seek a local partner which understood and worked in the market it was entering."[91] At the company's April 21, 2005 investor update meeting in San Francisco, Pressler announced, "In 2006 we will begin exploring opportunities to enter China."[92]

Pressler acknowledged challenges selling Gap abroad. The firm exited the German market, where it had been for 10 years, late in 2004 because of lackluster sales; it sold its stores to H&M. It planned to localize sizing and merchandise abroad in the future. Pressler explained, "We are now building merchant teams in-country, as well as a dedicated international design team, to ensure that products are appropriately tailored for customers in Japan and Europe."[93] In June 2005, the company filled a new post, president, Europe, Gap Inc. International, with Stephen Sunnucks, a veteran of the U.K. retail industry who began his career at Marks & Spencer and most recently was CEO of fast fashion retailer New Look. Sunnucks explained, "Gap has three fantastic businesses which until now have been mostly U.S.-centric. But now Gap is putting a team behind its European business. My track record is helping build business in the clothing area, and my role here will be to look at positioning and strategy."[94] Sunnucks reported to the company's international unit president, Andrew Rolfe, a 1992 Harvard MBA and former CEO of food retailer Pret A Manger.

Banana Republic

In 2004, Banana Republic accounted for approximately $2.3 billion of Gap Inc.'s revenues and 462 of the company's total stores. For years it had a reputation for being "a purveyor of chic basics—casual office wear in black or beige"[95]—i.e., an upscale Gap. However, under the direction of president Marka Hansen, the division had recently focused on making its product assortment more fashionable and trendy in order to minimize the overlap between Gap and Banana, catering to 25- to 30-year-old professionals. Hansen explained, "What's the hook or differentiation? … It's an affordable, covetable luxury. … We're bringing fashion to a wider audience."[96]

The brand was receiving positive press for its efforts to go upscale. It began producing its own runway shows in 2003. It also added jewelry cases to all of its units in 2004 and experienced great success in the area, inspiring the company to expand the brand's jewelry and handbag offerings. Vice-president of men's product and design Michael Anderson, a former Nautica designer, and executive vice-president of design Deborah Lloyd, a former Burberry London designer, incorporated "elements of European sensibility" and "high-quality Italian piece goods" in the 2005 collections.[97] While the division was positioning itself as more fashionable, it was concomitantly "depicting ordinary, real-world settings in ads so [its] clothes [would] appear accessible and wearable."[98]

As part of the firm's growth plans, Banana Republic prepared to venture outside of North America—it was scheduled to open three to five stores in Tokyo, Japan, in fall 2005 (Gap entered Japan in 1995). In addition to including petite offerings at more of its existing stores, Banana rolled out a handful of stand-alone Banana Republic Petite stores, which catered exclusively to women 5'4" and shorter. David Moin remarked in *Women's Wear Daily*, "Banana Republic is considered a mature concept in the U.S. However, it is considered an expansion vehicle in other countries under its regular size format, and could grow under other formats because of its widely recognized brand name."[99]

Banana's competitors included J. Crew, which operated 245 stores in the U.S. and Canada and had $804 million in sales and a net income loss of $100 million in 2004, and Urban Outfitters, Inc., which had sales of $828 million, net income of $90.5 million, and 170 stores in the U.S., Canada, and the U.K.[100]

Old Navy

Old Navy strove to provide inexpensive basic and trendy clothing for entire families in fun, warehouse-type shopping environments. In 2004, sales at the division made up 41 percent of Gap Inc.'s total revenues. Among female consumers, Old Navy was the top selling brand of apparel in the U.S. in 2004.[101] Gap Inc. opened a total of 130 units in 2004 and planned to open 175 store locations in 2005—the majority of these were Old Navy stores.[102] Company capital expenditures, which were $440 million in 2004, would rise to $625 million in 2005 and $725 million in 2006, driven largely by the opening of Old Navy units.[103]

President Jenny Ming oversaw several division initiatives in recent years. In 2001, she refocused Old Navy on families (from teenagers), rolling out underwear, maternity, and infant lines to raise margins; after Pressler joined Gap Inc. he encouraged Ming to increase the rollouts.[104] The division entered Canada in the same year. It targeted Hispanics with its first Spanish television spot at the end of 2003. The company's localization strategy was tested in select Old Navy stores in 2004, and the company planned to extend the program to all Old Navy outlets in 2005.

In order to capture more of the $25 million women's plus-size apparel market, which had been growing at 3 percent to 5 percent per year,[105] Old Navy established its Women's Plus Sizes line in 50 stores and online in July of 2004; it expanded the line to over 150 locations by the beginning of 2005.[106] It also catered to plus-size children, offering a "husky" fit for boys and a "plus" fit for girls.[107]

The division introduced maternity clothing, which had previously been available only at www.oldnavy.com, in its stores in 2003 and expanded the line to approximately 350 stores in 2004.

In mid-2005 the brand's product development team relocated from New York City to company headquarters in San Francisco; the objective of the move was to "foste[r] creativity and collaboration … [among] Old Navy's design team … [and] senior staff" and to improve "'speed to market' with new products."[108]

Forth & Towne

Gap Inc. planned to establish five test stores of Forth & Towne in Chicago and New York by fall 2005. Under Gary Muto's leadership, the firm was positioning Forth & Towne to appeal to women aged 35–50, women "who want to dress appropriately without being swathed in yards of fabric, and who need outfits that can go from the office to the school soccer field to dinner."[109]

The Forth & Towne concept stemmed from research regarding the company's growth opportunities. Pressler remarked, "While Gap Inc. holds either the number one or number two specialty market share for segments under age 35, we don't yet have a significant share of segments over 35. So targeting this age group is the next natural step in expanding our portfolio."[110] He also noted that the over-35-year-old woman grew up with Gap and still shops there for her kids' clothes but "when it comes to her own wardrobe [the company has] lost touch with her."[111] Company research revealed these women felt underserved, cared about fit and versatility in their clothes, and desired an inspirational in-store experience. Pressler also noted, "Right now she's shopping more in department stores than in any other channel. Boomer women represent the only apparel segment that's still dominated by department stores."[112] The 40 million U.S. baby boomer women spent $27 million on clothes for themselves in 2004. Inspired by the success of women's clothier Chico's FAS, which catered to women over 35, the company felt it could be a formidable player in the niche.

Forth & Towne would offer clothes that were feminine and fit comfortably; it would use size 10 as its standard, as opposed to size 8 (the benchmark at Gap and Banana), and employ women over 35 as fit models.[113] Stores would be between 8,000 and 10,000 square feet and designed in "a town square format" with the fitting rooms in the middle of the store surrounded by the products.[114] Muto explained, "We created an address with the name 'Forth & Towne,' because we wanted it to evoke a sense of place—to signify a special and unique shopping destination. ... 'Forth' references our fourth brand, and 'Towne' conveys a sense of community that we want to create for our customers when they shop with us."[115] Pressler noted, "We harkened back to what we believe is the old grandeur of those great department stores, the ones that used to sit on the corner of Main and State in great cities. ... It was a romantic time when women got dressed up to go to department stores, and they felt they were treated with respect."[116] The CEO added that prices at Forth & Towne would be between those at Gap and Banana Republic.

The division's competitors would include Chico's, which had $1.1 billion in sales in 2004 via its 670 U.S. stores, and Talbots, which operated 1,050 units in the U.S., Canada, and the U.K., and had sales of $1.7 billion in 2004.[117] (See Exhibit 7.)

Gap Inc. anticipated establishing 5 more Forth & Towne stores in 2006 and 20 more in 2007, bringing the total to 30 by the end of 2007.[118] Management hoped the new concept would eventually add $1 billion to $2 billion per year in sales to the firm's total revenues.[119]

› MARKETING

For 2004, 2003, and 2002, Gap Inc.'s advertising expenses were $528 million, $509 million, and $496 million respectively.[120] Each of the firm's brands had its own in-house marketing team which created in-store posters, billboards, and television ads. In June 2005, *Women's Wear Daily* reported, "Gap Inc., already high profile and celebrity-oriented with its advertising, is getting even more marketing-driven as it builds its roster of agencies working for its brands."[121]

Under Pressler's direction, Gap Inc. was positioning its divisions as lifestyle brands. The CEO remarked, "We need to bring more theatrics, storytelling and consistency [to retail]. If you can't tell me what a Gap dinner party, Banana Republic car or Old Navy vacation looks like, then we haven't built our stories."[122] Pressler had also been focused on differentiating the brands and "upgrading the marketing functions at all of Gap's brands, including the hires of new head marketers at all three units."[123] The company was targeting particular segments (e.g., men, mothers, teens) with its advertising in response to disappointing sales. It was also incorporating consumer insights via surveys and focus groups and feedback from store managers in its marketing.

Recent Gap brand TV advertising featured actors and singers. The company paid 40-year-old actress Sarah Jessica Parker, former *Sex and the City* star, $38 million to appear in television and print ads for three seasons during 2004–2005. It replaced Parker with 17-year-old British soul singer Joss Stone as its Gap spokesmodel in the summer of 2005.[124] In an effort to tout its "vastly expanded variety of fits" in jeans, the company planned to use more nontraditional types of advertising; i.e., "guerrilla marketing and grassroots tactics," according to Jeff Jones, executive vice president of marketing at Gap.[125]

Through its campy advertising, some of which spoofed old television shows and featured eccentric spokespeople, Old Navy had established a tongue-in-cheek image. Susan Wayne, executive vice president of marketing at Old Navy explained, "The smile and wink in our brand is critical to who we are."[126] Old Navy advertising expenditures were approximately $181 million in 2003.[127] Spring and summer 2005 TV ads featured Old Navy–clad people frolicking to 1980s pop tunes. These spots accounted for four of the top 10 apparel retail TV ads with the highest amount of viewer recall in the first half of 2005, according to a media research group. A Gap brand spot accounted for one.[128]

Banana Republic relied on print and outdoor advertising to target professionals in their 20s and 30s. In conjunction with efforts to position itself as a retailer of fashionable apparel, it had been conducting an "aspirational" yet "approachable" ad campaign.[129]

› INSIDE THE ORGANIZATION

Various units at Gap Inc. were working to carry out Pressler's strategy for 2005 and beyond.

Supply Chain

Gap Inc. designed, merchandised, marketed, and retailed its own apparel, and each brand had its own team for these functions. However, buying and logistics were handled centrally. Fifteen Gap Inc. centers in the U.S., Canada, the U.K., and Japan distributed the company's merchandise to its 3,000 stores worldwide. The firm outsourced the manufacture of its apparel. (See Exhibit 8.)

Seven hundred vendors using 3,000 factories in 50 countries produced 1 billion units of clothing for Gap Inc. in 2004. In 2003, "China [was] the company's biggest sourcing market. … represent[ing] 16 percent of [its] total merchandise units purchased and 17 percent of total merchandise costs."[130] At Gap Inc.'s first conference for analysts in April 2005, chief supply chain officer Nick Cullen outlined ways the firm's supply chain would transform as a result of the end of the MFA quotas. He explained:

In the past, quota required that we spread our sourcing across more than 700 vendors in 50 countries, and in some ways our size was actually a disadvantage. We were forced to diversify and fragment our spend, and were limited [in] our ability to grow relationships with the best vendors. Our focus was diffused … Now we're free to pursue strategic long-term partnerships. And already we've reduced our vendor count by over 100. And in our first season post-quota, we've increased our spend with our top vendors by 16 percent.[131]

While the company felt its current supply chain worked well, it anticipated an even more efficient one as it forged stronger relationships with fewer vendors. It expected that as it placed larger orders with particular vendors, it would be able to receive discounts and to request that vendors invest in IT, strategically-located factories, etc. Without quota restraints, for example, the company purchased large orders of denim for its three brands from top mills, saving it 5 percent in denim fabric costs in the first part of 2005. Cullen summarized how the company would benefit from the changes, "The new ways of working, stronger relationships with our vendors and sorting by category will bring us four combined benefits—it will allow us to reduce costs, drive innovation in both our products and our processes, improve speed to market, and increase efficiency and productivity."[132]

Information Technology

One of Gap Inc.'s main objectives was to better cater to customer taste and fit by localizing the products offered in its stores. Using tracking technology, the company piloted a merchandise localization program in Old Navy stores in 2004 to place "the right sizes in the right stores for [its] customers."[133] Gap Inc. believed the strategy could significantly improve margins by decreasing the need for markdowns, and it planned to extend the program, which would utilize inventory-management software from Oracle's Retek unit, to all adult Gap and Old Navy departments in 2005. Chief financial officer Byron Pollitt termed it the company's "single most important [IT] initiative" in 2005.[134] The company allotted nearly 22 percent of its 2005 capital spending—$135 million—to IT.[135]

Calvin Hollinger, vice president of information technology, explained, "Our goal is to change and enable the customer experience with technology."[136] At the end of 2004, the company upgraded the point-of-sale systems in all of its U.S. stores and planned to extend the upgrades to Japan, the U.K., and France in 2005 and 2006. Web browsers which were added to registers allowed employees to "access store e-mail and customer information without leaving the sales floor."[137] The company aimed to facilitate customer checkout by moving all nonsales transactions away from registers—in the future, employees would use handheld devices to check sizes in stock, for example. It was also considering allowing customers to pay for merchandise in fitting rooms and via self-service kiosks.[138]

Toby Lenk, a 1987 Harvard MBA, headed the company's online division, Gap Inc. Direct. In 2004, Gap Inc. was the largest U.S. online apparel retailer with sales of over $0.5 billion. It was "redesign[ing] and rebuild[ing] all of [its] websites from the ground up" to enhance visitors' online shopping and to improve online and in-store integration.[139] Lenk noted that 35 percent of the company's website visitors were pre-shoppers preparing for store visits and 13 percent of those who entered a Gap Inc. store had visited the store's online site beforehand. The firm's new e-commerce platform would allow the sites to take back orders and preorders. Lenk explained, "This means we will never have to walk a sale on a basic item, and at the same time it will allow us to run our basic inventory much tighter."[140] The company planned to have most of the website enhancements completed by the 2005 holiday season.

Human Resources

Eva Sage-Gavin, who had been with the company since March of 2003 and was a member of the executive leadership team, headed HR. One of her first tasks was to develop a "new purpose and values philosophy for the organization"; she also centralized HR to "maximize the company's global HR potential."[141] Previously each of the 19 units ran its own HR division independently.

Gap Inc. employed over 150,000 people. Its executive leadership team, led by Pressler, consisted of 14 individuals. Ten of the 14 had been at Gap Inc. less than three years as of June 2005; six of the 14 were former Walt Disney Company employees. In March 2005 the National Association for Female Executives named Gap Inc. one of the 30 best companies for executive women. Approximately 50 percent of the company's management team and 70 percent of total employees were women.[142]

The company developed an "innovative approach" to recruit sales staff—it used "its own experienced sales associates to assess candidates' aptitude for retail work and suitability for the GAP environment."[143] The approach improved retention and productivity among associates, according to one source. Gap Inc. also administered several assessments (shop-floor, communication, self-motivation) to place prospective sales employees in positions.[144]

Each brand had its own store management organization. (See Exhibit 9.) At Gap stores, for example, a general manager oversaw sales, operations, and personnel, and all other store managers (e.g., assistant, associate, and store) reported to the general manager. District managers, who developed sales goals for stores and trained managers, reported to regional directors. Regional directors "communicate[d] brand strategy and ensure[d] consistent execution; use[d] customer feedback to identify broad band issues; [and] monitore[d] … trends to anticipate business implications."[145] They, in turn, reported to zone vice presidents, who supervised up to 300 stores in four to five regions.

Gap Inc. was investing in employee training. Sage-Gavin explained, "We have new products coming into stores 16 times a year, and our employees' ability to change and adapt is critical. … If we want to establish a consistent global brand, our customer service and training capability needs to be the same at every store worldwide."[146] Sales associates were trained to answer customers' questions about "fabric, fit and fashion"; from 2003 to 2004, the firm doubled the amount of training it offered employees.[147] It rewarded employees who met performance or company goals with bonuses.

The company "encouraged [employees at its San Francisco, California, headquarters] to take up to five hours a month of paid time off to volunteer with local organizations"; its charitable arm, the Gap Foundation, matched employee contributions to charities.[148]

Conclusion

CEO Pressler had outlined his key priorities for 2005:

1. Providing trend-right and appropriate products in easy-to-shop environments.

2. Improving the supply chain to increase cost savings and operating efficiencies via consolidating vendors and "aggregating category buys."

3. Expanding its efforts to get the right sizes in the right stores in Gap and Old Navy to improve margins.

4. Growing existing brands through two initiatives: the opening of 175 stores and the expansion of product initiatives …. such as maternity and plus sizes …. and petites.

5. Returning excess cash to shareholders via dividends and share repurchases.[149]

The opening of up to five units of its fourth brand, Forth & Towne, in the latter part of 2005 was another major priority for the year.

Pressler was confident that these initiatives would deliver strong financial performance for 2005 and build momentum for the future. However, the company's brands faced formidable competitors. Wal-Mart, the number one discount retailer, had the lead in clothing sales in the United States and was aiming to move into more fashionable merchandise. Although Abercrombie & Fitch had one-eighth of Gap Inc.'s revenues, it was planning to expand domestically and internationally. Fast fashion retailers H&M and Mango anticipated increasing their U.S. apparel market share. Additionally, Chico's was growing phenomenally. Was Gap Inc. taking the necessary steps to sustain its position against this onslaught? ◎

exhibit

1 GAP INC. FINANCIAL AND STATISTICAL DATA

Fiscal Year	1993	1994	1995	1996	1997	1998	1999	2000	2001	2002	2003	2004
Financial Results ($ in millions)												
Net sales	3,296	3,723	4,395	5,284	6,508	9,054	11,635	13,673	13,848	14,455	15,854	16,267
COGS and occupancy expenses	1,997	2,202	2,646	3,094	3,776	5,013	6,361	8,657	9,733	9,541	9,885	9,886
Operating expenses	748	854	1,004	1,270	1,635	2,403	3,043	3,629	3,806	3,901	4,068	4,296
Net interest expense	0.8	−11	−16	−19	−3	14	32	63	96	212	196	108
Net earnings (loss)	258	320	354	453	534	825	1,127	842	−25	478	1,031	1,150
Purchase of property and equipment	216	237	310	376	483	843	1,269	1,989	1,026	308	261	442
Merchandise inventory	331	371	483	579	733	1,056	1,462	1,904	1,769	2,048	1,704	1,814
Total assets	1,763	2,004	2,343	2,627	3,338	3,964	5,189	7,387	8,096	10,283	10,713	10,048
Shareholders' equity	1,126	1,375	1,640	1,640	1,584	1,574	2,233	2,816	2,880	3,526	4,648	4,936
Financial Ratios												
Gross margin (% of sales)	39.4%	40.9%	39.8%	41.4%	42.0%	44.6%	45.3%	36.7%	29.7%	34.0%	37.6%	39.2%
Expense ratio (% of sales)	22.7%	22.9%	22.8%	24.0%	25.1%	26.5%	26.2%	26.5%	27.5%	27.0%	25.7%	26.4%
Operating profit (% of sales)	16.7%	17.9%	17.0%	17.4%	16.9%	18.1%	19.2%	10.1%	2.2%	7.0%	12.0%	12.8%
Net income (% of sales)	7.8%	8.6%	8.1%	8.6%	8.2%	9.1%	9.7%	6.2%	−0.2%	3.3%	6.5%	7.1%
Stock turns per year (COGs/inventory)	6	6	5	5	5	5	4	5	6	5	6	5
ROTA (net earnings/total assets)	14.6%	16.0%	15.1%	17.2%	16.0%	20.8%	21.7%	11.4%	−0.3%	4.6%	9.6%	11.4%
ROE (net earnings/shareholders' equity)	22.9%	23.3%	21.6%	27.4%	33.7%	52.4%	50.5%	29.9%	−0.9%	13.6%	22.2%	23.3%
Dividend payout (% of net earnings)	20.5%	20.3%	18.9%	18.5%	15.0%	9.3%	6.7%	8.9%	−304%	16.3%	7.7%	6.9%

(Continued)

exhibit 1

GAP INC. FINANCIAL AND STATISTICAL DATA (CONTD.)

Fiscal Year	1993	1994	1995	1996	1997	1998	1999	2000	2001	2002	2003	2004
Statistics												
Number of new store locations opened	108	172	225	203	298	356	570	434	324	115	35	130
Number of store locations closed	45	34	53	30	22	20	18	60	75	95	130	158
Number of store locations open at year end	1,370	1,508	1,680	1,854	2,130	2,466	3,018[a]	2,848	3,097	3,117	3,022	2,994
Square footage of store space at year-end (000)	7,546	9,166	11,100	12,645	15,313	18,757	23,978	31,373	36,333	37,252	36,518	36,591
Average store size, square feet	5,508	6,078	6,607	6,820	7,189	7,606	7,945	11,106	11,732	11,951	12,084	12,221
Number of employees at year-end	44,000	55,000	60,000	66,000	81,000	111,000	140,000	166,000	165,000	169,000	153,000	152,000
Comparable store sales increase (decrease)	1%	1%	0%	5%	6%	17%	7%	-5%	-13%	-3%	7%	0%
Sales per store ($000)	2,406	2,469	2,616	2,850	3,055	3,672	3,855	4,801	4,471	4,637	5,246	5,433
Sales per employee, current $ (000)	$75	$68	$73	$80	$80	$82	$83	$82	$84	$86	$104	$107
Sales per square foot, current $	$437	$406	$396	$418	$425	$483	$485	$436	$381	$388	$434	$445
Sales per employee, real 2004 $ (000)	$92	$81	$86	$92	$91	$92	$92	$89	$89	$89	$106	$107
Sales per square foot, real 2004 $	$535	$487	$465	$482	$482	$541	$536	$472	$403	$403	$443	$445
GDP deflator (2000 = 1.000)	0.884	0.903	0.921	0.939	0.954	0.965	0.979	1.000	1.024	1.041	1.060	1.082

Sources: Gap Inc., 1999 Annual Report, (San Francisco: Gap Inc., 2000), pp. 18, 19, and 2004 Annual Report, (San Francisco: Gap Inc., 2005), p. 20, www.gapinc.com, accessed April 2005; GDP deflator nos. from U.S. Dept. of Commerce, Bureau of Economic Analysis, www.bea.doc.gov, accessed June 2005.

[a] In its 1999 Annual Report, Gap Inc. started recording the number of store concepts (e.g., babyGaps, GapKids, Gaps) separately even if housed in the same location (the pre-1999 numbers reflect store locations). It reverted back to recording store locations in 2003; the post-1999 numbers reflect total Gap Inc. store locations.

2

THE WORLD'S TOP RETAILERS OF APPAREL

Company	Total 2002 Sales (U.S.$bn)	Apparel Sales (U.S.$bn)
Wal-Mart	258.7	24.3
Gap Inc.	15.9	15.9
Federated Department Stores	15.4	10.7
TJX Cos.	13.3	9.9
JC Penney	17.8	9.8
Target	42.7	8.9
May Department Stores	13.5	8.9
Kmart	23.3	6.7
Hennes & Mauritz (H&M)	6.0	6.0
Sears	41.1	5.3
Karstadt Quelle	17.3	5.3
Inditex	5.4	5.2
Limited Brands	8.9	5.1
C&A	4.7	4.7
Dillard's	7.6	4.7
Next	3.3	3.3
Fast Retailing	3.1	3.1
Arcadia Group	2.9	2.9
Burlington Coat Factory	2.9	2.7
Charming Shoppes	2.4	2.4
Total	**519.8**	**151.9**

Source: Michael Flanagan, "How Retailers Source Apparel," *Just-Style*, January 2005, via Proquest/ABI Inform, www.proquest.com, accessed April 2005.

3

APPAREL SPENDING BY CHANNEL, 2003

Channel	Examples	Men's Wear Purchases	Women's Apparel Spend
Department Stores	Dillard's, Macy's	18.8%	20.9%
National Chains	JCPenney, Sears	15.7%	12.9%
Specialty Stores	Gap, Abercrombie & Fitch	26.4%	32.3%
Off-Price Retailers	Marshalls, Ross, TJ Maxx	9.3%	8.8%
Mass Merchants	Kmart, Target, Wal-Mart	16.0%	14.0%
Factory Outlets		2.4%	1.2%
Catalogue/Internet		5.8%	6.5%

Sources: Scott Malone, "Squeezed Consumers Spending Less on Apparel," *Women's Wear Daily*, August 25, 2004; and Ira P. Schneiderman, "Men's Wear in a Malaise in '03," *DNR*, March 29, 2004 via Proquest/ABI Inform, www.proquest. com, accessed June 2005.

exhibit 4

TOP SPECIALTY APPAREL RETAILERS IN THE U.S. IN 2004

Rank	Company	Brands/Concepts	Sales, $ millions	Change over 2003	Specialty Market Share
1.	Gap Inc.	Gap, Banana Republic, Old Navy, Forth &Towne	$16,270	2.6%	31.4%
2.	Limited Brands, Inc.[a]	Victoria's Secret, Express, Bath & Body Works, The Limited, The White Barn Candle Co., Henri Bendel	$6,720	5.3%	13.0%
3.	Charming Shoppes, Inc.	Lane Bryant, Fashion Bug, Catherines	$2,330	2.0%	4.5%
4.	Abercrombie & Fitch Co.	Abercrombie & Fitch, Hollister Co., RUEHL	$2,020	18.4%	3.9%
5.	American Eagle Outfitters, Inc.	American Eagle Outfitters	$1,880	31.1%	3.6%
6.	AnnTaylor Stores Corp.	Ann Taylor, Ann Taylor LOFT	$1,850	16.7%	3.6%
7.	The Talbots, Inc.	Talbots	$1,700	6.5%	3.3%
8.	Claire's Stores, Inc.	Claire's, Icing by Claire's	$1,280	−12.9%	2.5%
9.	Goody's Family Clothing, Inc.	Goody's	$1,270	3.3%	2.4%
10.	Pacific Sunwear of California, Inc.	PacSun, d.e.m.o.	$1,230	18.1%	2.4%
11.	New York & Company, Inc.	New York & Company	$1,040	8.1%	2.0%

(Continued)

exhibit 4

TOP SPECIALTY APPAREL RETAILERS IN THE U.S. IN 2004 (CONTD.)

Rank	Company	Brands/Concepts	Sales, $ millions	Change over 2003	Specialty Market Share
12.	Chico's FAS, Inc.	Chico's, White House/Black Market, soma by Chico's	$1,010	38.8%	1.9%
13.	Aéropostale, Inc.	Aéropostale	$964.2	31.2%	1.9%
14.	Urban Outfitters, Inc.	Urban Outfitters, Anthropologie, Free People	$827.8	50.9%	1.6%
15.	The Cato Corp.	Cato, It's Fashion!	$773.8	5.7%	1.5%
16.	Too, Inc.	Limited Too, Justice	$675.8	12.9%	1.3%
17.	Hot Topic, Inc.	Hot Topic, Torrid	$656.5	14.8%	1.3%
18.	Coldwater Creek, Inc.	Coldwater Creek	$590.3	13.8%	1.1%
19.	Guess?, Inc.	Guess?	$518.9	15.9%	1.0%
20.	Wilsons The Leather Experts Inc.	Wilsons Leather	$441.1	-15.3%	0.8%
21.	All other public and private specialty retailers		$7.8		15.0%

Sources: Cecily Hall and Meredith Derby, "The WWD List: Leaders of the Pack; Top 20 Publicly Traded Specialty Retailers Ranked by Annual Volume," *Women's Wear Daily*, May 12, 2005 via Proquest/ABI Inform, www.proquest.com, accessed June 2005; Limited Brands, Inc., 2004 Annual Report (Columbus, Limited Brands, Inc., 2005), p. 26, www.limitedbrands.com, accessed June 2005; company websites.
[a] Limited Brands, Inc.'s revenue was $9.41 billion in 2004. Sales of clothes and intimate apparel accounted for approximately 70% of total sales; bath and beauty products, the remainder.

TOP U.S. PUBLIC APPAREL COMPANIES BY 2003 PROFIT MARGIN

No.	Company	2003 Profit Margin (Net Income/ Sales)	2003 Net Income ($ mil.)	2003 Sales ($ mil.)	2002 Profit Margin	2002 Net Income ($ mil.)	2002 Sales ($ mil.)	% Change in Profit Margin 2002/ 2003	% Change in Sales 2002/ 2003
1.	Chico's Fas, Inc.	13.0	100.2	768.5	12.6	66.8	531.1	3.7	44.7
2.	Abercrombie & Fitch Co.	12.0	205.1	1,707.8	12.2	194.9	1,595.8	1.7	7.0
3.	Christopher & Banks Corp.	10.1	39.3	390.7	11.9	32.9	275.9	15.6	41.6
4.	Urban Outfitters	8.8	48.4	548.4	6.5	27.4	422.8	36.2	29.7
5.	Limited Brands, Inc.	8.0	717.0	8,934.0	5.9	502.0	8,445.0	35.0	5.8
6.	Pacific Sunwear of California, Inc.	7.7	80.2	1,040.3	5.9	49.7	846.4	31.3	22.9
7.	VF Corp.	7.6	397.9	5,207.5	-3.0	-154.5	5,083.5	351.4	2.4
8.	Jones Apparel Group	7.5	328.6	4,375.3	7.7	332.3	4,312.2	-2.5	1.5
9.	Aéropostale	7.4	54.3	734.9	5.7	31.3	550.9	30.0	33.4
10.	Liz Claiborne, Inc.	6.6	279.7	4,241.1	6.2	231.2	3,717.5	6.0	14.1
11.	Gap Inc.	6.5	1,030.0	15,854.0	3.3	477.5	14,454.7	96.7	9.7

(Continued)

TOP U.S. PUBLIC APPAREL COMPANIES BY 2003 PROFIT MARGIN (CONTD.)

No.	Company	2003 Profit Margin (Net Income/ Sales)	2003 Net Income ($ mil.)	2003 Sales ($ mil.)	2002 Profit Margin	2002 Net Income ($ mil.)	2002 Sales ($ mil.)	% Change in Profit Margin 2002/ 2003	% Change in Sales 2002/ 2003
12.	Polo Ralph Lauren	6.5	171.0	2,649.7	7.3	172.5	2,363.7	–11.6	12.1
13.	The Talbots, Inc.	6.4	104.7	1,624.3	7.6	120.8	1,595.3	–14.9	1.8
14.	Ann Taylor Stores Corp	6.4	100.9	1,587.7	5.8	80.2	1,381.0	9.4	15.0
15.	Quiksilver, Inc.	6.0	58.5	975.0	5.4	38.0	705.5	11.4	38.2
16.	Bebe Stores, Inc.	6.0	19.3	323.5	8.4	26.5	316.4	–28.8	2.2
17.	Jos. A. Bank	5.5	16.6	299.7	2.4	5.8	243.4	132.4	23.1
18.	Caché, Inc.	5.1	11.1	216.3	4.5	8.9	199.4	15.0	8.5
19.	Delta Apparel, Inc.	4.7	6.1	129.5	4.9	6.5	131.6	–4.6	–1.6
20.	Gymboree Corp.	4.4	25.7	578.0	4.0	21.8	546.8	11.5	5.7

Source: Michael D. Cole, "Facing A Brave New World," *Apparel* 45 (July 2004): 22.

GAP, BANANA REPUBLIC, AND OLD NAVY SALES AND STORES, 2004

	Gap, North America	Gap, International	Banana Republic	Old Navy
Net sales ($ million)				
Stores	5,510	1,494	2,178	6,511
Online	236	NA	91	236
Total	$5,746	$1,494	$2,269	$6,747
Change from 2003	−0.5%	−2.2%	8.6%	4.5%
No. of units	1,396	247	462	889
Square feet (in millions)	13.0	2.4	3.9	17.3
Average store size, square feet	9,312	9,717	8,442	19,460

Source: Gap Inc., 2004 Annual Report (San Francisco: Gap Inc., 2005), pp. 24, 25, www.gapinc.com, accessed April 2005.

exhibit 7

GAP INC. AND COMPETITOR DATA, 2004

	Gap Inc.	Abercrombie & Fitch Co.	Ann Taylor Stores Corp.	Chico's FAS	H&M	Inditex (2003 data)
Financial Results ($ in millions)						
Net sales	16,267	2,021	1,854	1,067	8,001	5,708
COGS	9,886	1,038	820	408	3,424	2,974
Operating expenses	4,296	562	843	398	2,988	1,944
Net earnings	1,150	216	63	141	1,084	557
Cash dividends paid	79	46	0	0	740	—
Capital expenditures	442	185	153	94	235	—
Merchandise inventory	1,814	211	229	73	766	604
Total assets	10,048	1,348	1,327	716	4,191	4,357
Shareholders' equity	4,936	669	927	561	3,309	2,614
Financial Ratios						
Gross margin (% of sales)	39.2%	48.6%	55.8%	61.8%	57.2%	47.9%
Expense ratio (% of sales)	26.4%	27.8%	45.5%	37.3%	37.3%	34.1%
Operating profit (% of sales)	12.8%	20.8%	10.3%	24.5%	19.9%	13.8%
Net income (% of sales)	7.1%	10.7%	3.4%	13.2%	13.5%	9.8%

(Continued)

GAP INC. AND COMPETITOR DATA, 2004 (CONTD.)

	Gap Inc.	Abercrombie & Fitch Co.	Ann Taylor Stores Corp.	Chico's FAS	H&M	Inditex (2003 data)
Stock turns per year (COGS/ inventory)	5	5	4	6	4	5
ROTA (net earnings/total assets)	11.4%	16.0%	4.7%	19.7%	25.9%	12.8%
ROE (net earnings/ shareholders' equity)	23.3%	32.3%	6.8%	25.1%	32.8%	21.3%
Dividend payout (% of net earnings)	6.9%	21.3%	0.0%	0.0%	68.3%	—
Statistics						
Employees at year end	152,000	62,140	14,900	8,800	31,701	39,760
Sales per employee ($000)	107	33	124	121	252	144
Shares outstanding (millions)	861	86	71	179	—	—
1-year sales growth	2.6%	18.4%	16.7%	38.8%	24.9%	32.8%
1-year net income growth	11.7%	5.5%	-37.3%	40.9%	27.8%	17.0%
Market capitalization as of June 27, 2005 ($ in millions)	17,636	5,825	1,793	5,910	—	—

Sources: Gap Inc., 2004 Annual Report, (San Francisco: Gap Inc., 2005), p. 20, www.gapinc.com, accessed April 2005; Hoover's Inc., www.hoover's.com, accessed June 2005.

Stage 1: Design and Merchandising

Designers and merchants develop product assortments; patternmakers create samples.

Stage 2: Planning and Sourcing

Planning and distribution specialists and merchandisers determine quantities to order. Factories are selected to manufacture garments.

Stage 3: Production and Marketing

Factories produce samples. The company approves the fit then production begins.

The marketing teams review samples to develop marketing strategies.

Stage 4: Distribution

The merchandise is sent to Gap Inc.'s distribution centers where audits are performed, the products are inventoried and designated for particular stores, then shipped to the stores.

Stage 5: Sales and Analysis

The Visual Merchandising team determines the floor set-up for the products. Company planners and distribution analysts review stores' sales data for replenishment and assessment purposes.

Source: Adapted from Gap Inc., "From Concept to Store Shelf: Our Product 'Lifecycle,'" Gap Inc. website, www.gapinc.com, accessed June 2005.

exhibit 9

THE BRANDS' STORE MANAGEMENT STRUCTURES

Gap	Banana Republic	Old Navy	Forth & Town
President Cynthia Harriss	President Marka Hansen	President Jenny Ming	President Gary Muto
Zone Vice President	Zone Vice President	Zone Vice President	
Senior Regional Director	Senior Regional Director	Senior Regional Director	
Regional Director	Regional Director	Regional Director	
District Manager	District Manager	District Manager	
General Manager	General Manager	General Manager	General Manager
Store Manager	Store Manager		Supervisor
Associate Manager		Operations Manager	Associate Manager
Assistant Manager	Assistant Manager	Merchandise Manager	

Source: Gap Inc., "Store Management Opportunities," Gap Inc. website, www.gapinc.com, accessed June 2005.

GAP INC. NET SALES AND NUMBER OF STORES, 1976–2004

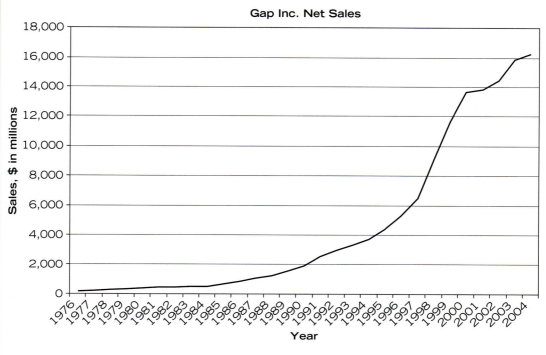

Gap Inc. Net Sales

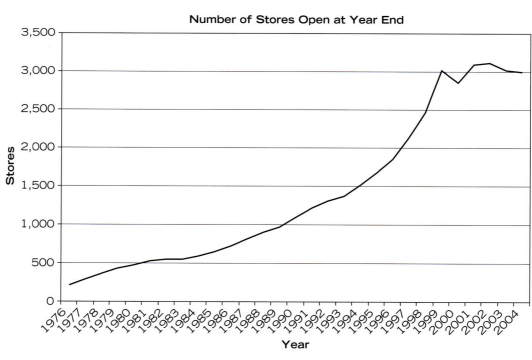

Number of Stores Open at Year End

Source: Gap Inc. 1980, 1986, 1995, 1999, and 2004 Annual Reports.

AVERAGE STORE SIZE AND SALES PER STORE, 1976–2004

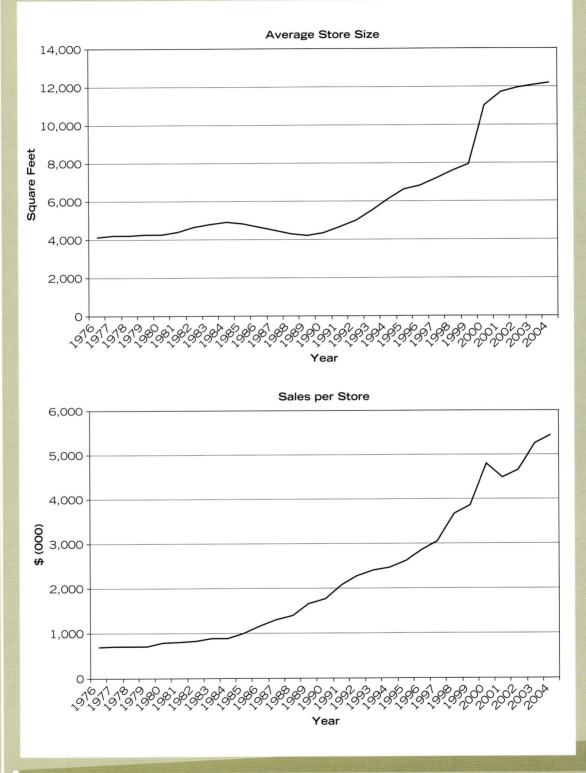

Source: Gap Inc. 1980, 1986, 1995, 1999, and 2004 Annual Reports.

SALES PER EMPLOYEE AND SALES PER SQUARE FOOT, 1976–2004

Sales per Employee

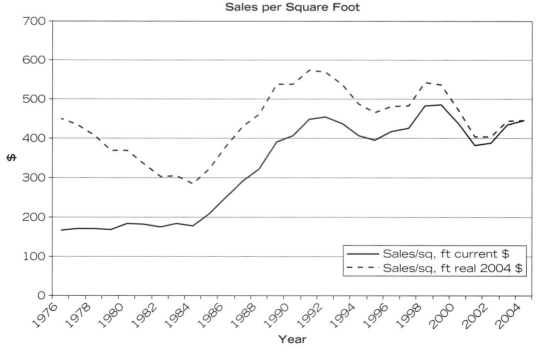

Sales per Square Foot

Source: Gap Inc. 1980, 1986, 1995, 1999, and 2004 Annual Reports.

GROSS MARGIN AND EXPENSE RATIO, 1976–2004

Gross Margin (% of Sales)

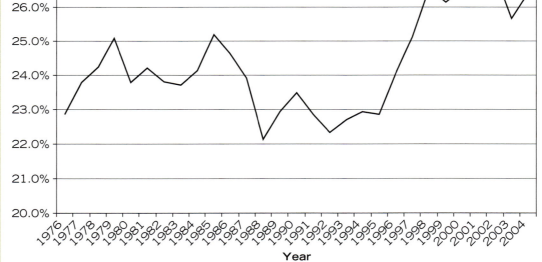

Expense Ratio (% of Sales)

Source: Gap Inc. 1980, 1986, 1995, 1999, and 2004 Annual Reports.

OPERATING PROFIT AND NET INCOME, PERCENT OF SALES, 1976–2004

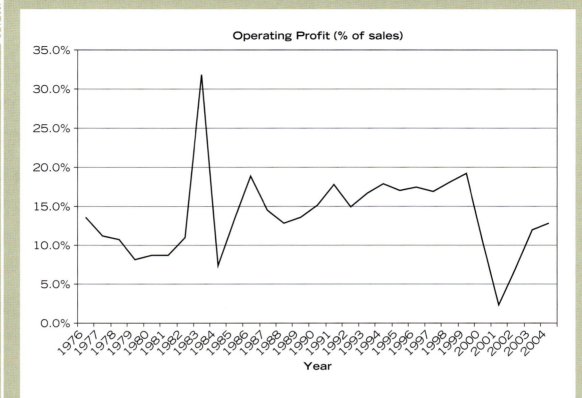

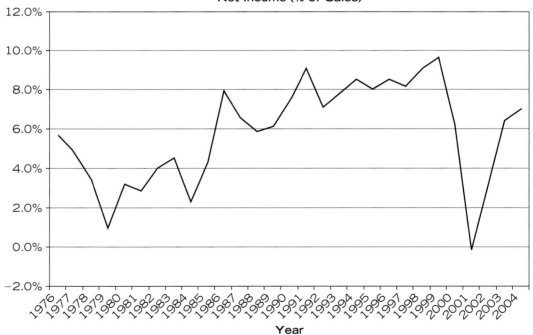

Source: Gap Inc. 1980, 1986, 1995, 1999, and 2004 Annual Reports.

INVENTORY TURN AND RETURN ON TOTAL ASSETS, 1976–2004

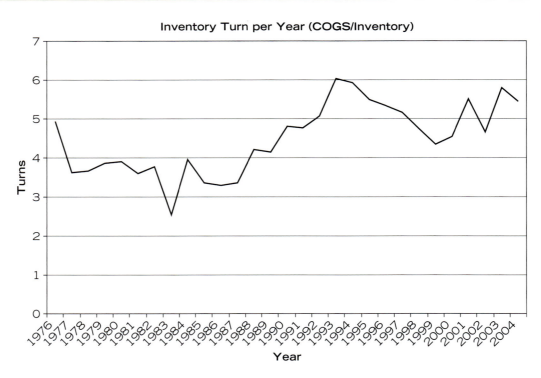

Source: Gap Inc. 1980, 1986, 1995, 1999, and 2004 Annual Reports.

RETURN ON EQUITY, 1976–2004, AND GAP INC. WEEKLY STOCK PRICE (ADJUSTED), 1983–2005

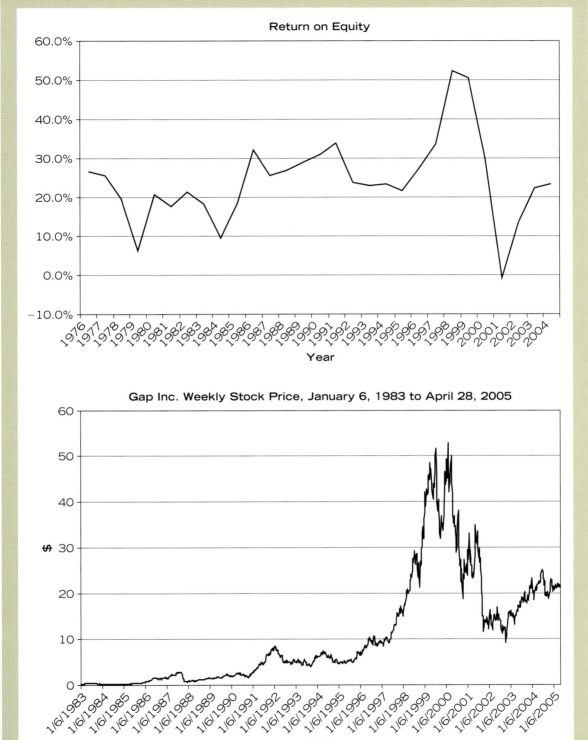

Source: Gap Inc. 1980, 1986, 1995, 1999, and 2004 Annual Reports; and Thomson Datastream, accessed June 2005.

GAP INC. MARKET CAPITALIZATION, JANUARY 6, 2003 TO APRIL 28, 2005

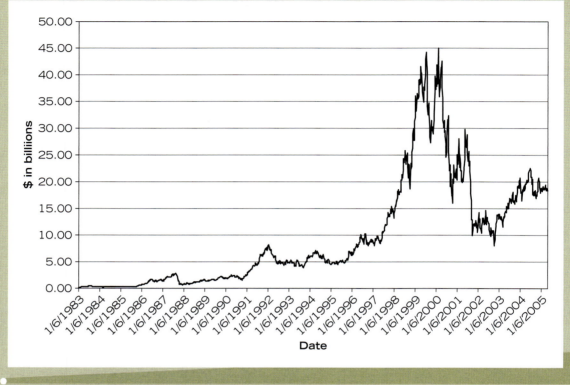

Source: Thomson Datastream, accessed June 2005.

Endnotes

1. Tracie Rozhon, "Designing a Brighter Future for The Gap," *The New York Times*, May 2, 2004, via Factiva, accessed March 3, 2005.
2. Ibid.
3. Teri Agins, "Wardrobe Malfunction: As Consumers Find Other Ways to Splurge, Apparel Hits a Snag," *The Wall Street Journal*, February 4, 2005, via Proquest/ABI Inform, www.proquest.com, accessed April 2005.
4. Gap Inc. "Gap Inc. Reports First Quarter Earnings," Gap Inc. Web site, www.gapinc.com, accessed June 2005.
5. Kimberly Greenberger and Corinna Freedman, Citigroup Smith Barney, "Gap Inc.," February 25, 2005, via Thomson Research/Investext, accessed March 2005.
6. Jenny Strasburg, "Gap 4th-Quarter Profit Higher Than Expected/Banana Republic Strong, but Gap, Old Navy Slip," *San Francisco Chronicle*, February 25, 2005, via Factiva, accessed March 2005.
7. Meredith Derby, "Gap's Five-Step Growth Plan," *Women's Wear Daily*, February 25, 2005, via Factiva, accessed March 2005.
8. Teri Agins, "Wardrobe Malfunction: As Consumers Find Other Ways to Splurge, Apparel Hits a Snag."
9. Michael Flanagan, "How Retailers Source Apparel," *Just-Style*, January 2005, via Proquest/ABI Inform, www.proquest.com, accessed April 2005.
10. The NPD Group, Inc., "The NPD Group Reports U.S. Retail Apparel Sales Up after Three Years of Decline," February 23, 2005, The NPD Group, Inc. Web site, http://www.npdfashionworld.com, accessed May 2005.
11. Arnold J. Karr, "Maintaining Men's Momentum; NPD's Marshall Cohen Believes Creativity and Promotion Can Keep The Men's Wear Bubble from Bursting," *DNR*, May 23, 2005, via Proquest/ABI Inform, accessed June 2005.
12. Sandra Jones, "Now Appearing at a Mall Near You: Men," *Crain's Chicago Business*, November 8, 2004, via Proquest/ABI Inform, accessed June 2005.

13. Gregory Melich, Morgan Stanley, "Wal-Mart," February 12, 2004, p. 41, via Thomson Research/Investext, accessed March 2005.

14. Valerie Seckler, "The Squeeze on Apparel's Sweet Spots," *Women's Wear Daily*, February 9, 2005, via Proquest/ABI Inform, www.proquest.com, accessed May 2005.

15. Cecily Hall and Meredith Derby, "The WWD List: Leaders of the Pack," *Women's Wear Daily*, May 12, 2005, via Proquest/ABI Inform, www.proquest.com, accessed June 2005.

16. Gregory Fowlkes and Michelle Clark, Morgan Stanley, "Retail, Apparel," September 20, 2004, p. 7, via Thomas Research/Investext, accessed May 2005.

17. Teri Agins, "Wardrobe Malfunction: As Consumers Find Other Ways to Splurge, Apparel Hits a Snag."

18. Ibid.

19. Kavita Daswani, "A Growing Market; After Adding Up the Benefits, Specialty Retailers Are Expanding into the Plus-Size Category," *Women's Wear Daily*, October 6, 2004, via the OneSource® Business Browser℠, an online business information product of OneSource Information Services, Inc. ("One Source"), accessed March 2005.

20. Rebecca Gardyn, "The Shape of Things to Come," *American Demographics* 25 (July, August 2003), via Proquest/ABI Inform, www.proquest.com, accessed May 2005.

21. Ibid.

22. Teri Agins, "Reshaping Boomer Fashion," *The Wall Street Journal*, April 15, 2005, via Proquest/ABI Inform, www.proquest.com, accessed April 2005.

23. Valerie Seckler, "Mothers of Fashion Reinvention," *Women's Wear Daily*, March 23, 2005, via Proquest/ABI Inform, www.proquest.com, accessed May 2005.

24. Ellen Israel Rosen, *Making Sweatshops: The Globalization of the U.S. Apparel Retail Industry* (Los Angeles: University of California Press, 2002), pp. 177–201.

25. Ibid., p. 179.

26. Jordan K. Speer, "Federated-May Merger Could Breathe New Life into Department Stores," *Apparel* 46 (April 2005), via Proquest/ABI Inform, www.proquest.com, accessed May 2005.

27. Ibid.

28. Federated Department Stores, Inc., 2004 Fact Book, (New York: Federated Department Stores, 2004), pp. 2, 11, www.federated-fds.com, accessed May 2005.

29. Gregory Fowlkes and Michelle Clark, p. 4.

30. Jack W. Plunkett, *Plunkett's Apparel & Textiles Industry Almanac* (Houston: Plunkett Research, Ltd., 2004) p. 14.

31. Gregory Fowlkes and Michelle Clark, p. 13.

32. Gregory Melich, p. 41.

33. Teri Agins, "The Lessons of Isaac," *The Wall Street Journal*, February 7, 2005, via Proquest/ABI Inform, www.proquest.com, accessed June 2005.

34. "Asda Top Clothing Retailer in U.K.," *Supermarket News*, September 6, 2004, via Proquest/ABI Inform, accessed June 2005.

35. Jack W. Plunkett, p. 16.

36. Sarah Raper Larenaudie, "Inside the H&M Fashion Machine," *Time*, Spring 2004, via Proquest/ABI Inform, www.proquest.com, accessed May 2005.

37. Kasra Ferdows, Michael A. Lewis, and Jose A.D. Machuca, "Rapid-Fire Fulfillment," *Harvard Business Review* 83 (November 2004).

38. Kasra Ferdows et al., p. 106.

39. Erin White, "For Retailer Mango, Frenzied 'Fast Fashion' Proves Sweet," *The Wall Street Journal*, May 28, 2004, via Proquest/ABI Inform, www.proquest.com, accessed May 2005.

40. Cate T. Corcoran, "How Star Retailers Turn Fast," *Women's Wear Daily*, November 10, 2004, via Proquest/ABI Inform, www.proquest.com, accessed May 2005.

41. Hoover's Inc., www.hoovers.com, accessed June 2005.

42. Kasra Ferdows et al.

43. Hoover's Inc., www.hoovers.com, accessed June 2005.

44. Sarah Raper Larenaudie.

45. Erin White.

46. Lauren Weber, "Termination of Trade Quota is Unlikely to Result in Lower Prices for 2005," *Knight Ridder Tribune Business News*, January 30, 2005, via Proquest/ABI Inform, www.proquest.com, accessed May 2005.

47. Ibid.

48. Gregory Fowlkes and Michelle Clark, p.17.

49. Lauren Weber.

50. "Gap Inc. Investor Update—Final," *Fair Disclosure Wire*, April 21, 2005, via Proquest/ABI Inform, www.proquest.com, accessed June 2005.

51. Teri Agins, "Plain Is Out; Vibrant Is In," *The Wall Street Journal*, November 22, 2004, via Proquest/ABI Inform, www.proquest.com, accessed May 2005.

52. The NPD Group, Inc.

53. Teri Agins, "Plain Is Out; Vibrant Is In."

54. Russell Mitchell, "The Gap," *BusinessWeek*, March 9, 1992, via Factiva, http://www.factiva.com, accessed March 14, 2005.

55. Ibid.

56. Ibid.

57. Ibid.

58. Susan Caminiti, "How the Gap Keeps Ahead of the Pack," *Fortune*, February 12, 1990, via Factiva, , accessed March 2005.

59. Nina Munk. "Gap Gets It," *Fortune*, August 3, 1998, via Proquest/ABI Inform, www.proquest.com, accessed March 2005.
60. Russell Mitchell, "The Gap."
61. Bridget O'Brian and Robert Berner, "As Jeans Stock Zips Up, Gap CEO Pockets Fortune," *The Wall Street Journal*, February 28, 1996, via Proquest/ABI Inform, www.proquest.com, accessed June 2005.
62. Nina Munk, "Gap Gets It."
63. Russell Mitchell, "The Gap."
64. Ibid.
65. Ibid.
66. Ibid.
67. Anne Kingston, "Bridging the Gap: The Clothes Are Boring. The Ads Are Fizzling. How Did a Retail Giant Wind Up on the Brink?" *National Post*, May 4, 2002, via Factiva, accessed June 2005.
68. Gap Inc., 1999 Annual Report (San Francisco: Gap Inc., 2000), p. 19, www.gapinc.com, accessed April 2005.
69. Hoover's, Inc., www.hoovers.com, accessed March 2005.
70. Anne Kingston.
71. Ibid.
72. Ibid.
73. Patricia Sellers, "Gap's New Guy Upstairs; Can Former Disney Hotshot Paul Pressler Make This Retail Wreck a Growth Company Again?" *Fortune*, April 14, 2003, via Factiva, accessed March 2005.
74. Neil Buckley, "Numbers Man Bridges the Gap," *Financial Times*, August 24, 2004, via Proquest/ABI Inform, www.proquest.com, accessed June 2005.
75. Cheryl Dahle, "Gap's New Look: The See-Through," *Fast Company* 86 (September 2004), via Proquest/ABI Inform, www.proquest.com, accessed June 2005.
76. Gap Inc., 2003 Annual Report (San Francisco: Gap Inc., 2004), p. 3, www.gapinc.com, accessed March 2005.
77. Jean Palmieri, "Using Intuition and Instinct to Turn Around Gap," *Women's Wear Daily*, November 17, 2004, via Proquest/ABI Inform, www.proquest.com, accessed March 2005.
78. "Gap Inc. Investor Update—Final."
79. Gap Inc., 2004 Annual Report (San Francisco: Gap Inc., 2005), p. 9, www.gapinc.com, accessed April 2005.
80. Valerie Seckler, "The Squeeze on Apparel's Sweet Spots."
81. Gap Inc., "Cynthia Harriss, President, Gap," Gap Inc. Web site, http://www.gapinc.com/public/About/abt_leader.shtml, accessed June 16, 2005.
82. Cat Callender, "How Gap Got Its Groove Back," *The Independent*, November 8, 2004, via Factiva, accessed June 2005.
83. Ibid.
84. Jean E. Palmieri, "Using Intuition and Instinct to Turn Around Gap."
85. David Moin, "Next Generation of Gap: Previewing the Prototype," *Women's Wear Daily*, via Proquest/ABI Inform, accessed X, 2005.
86. Ibid.
87. Ibid.
88. Gap Inc., "Gap Inc. Historical Net Sales by Division," Gap Inc. Web site, www.gapinc.com, accessed April 2005.
89. Dorothy S. Lakner and Roxanne Meyer, CIBC World Markets, "Gap," February 25, 2005, p. 4, via Thomson Research/Investext, accessed March 2005.
90. American Eagle Outfitters, Inc., "Corporate Profile," AE Web site, www.ae.com/corp; and Hoover's Inc., www.hoovers.com, accessed June 2005.
91. Robert Stockdill, "Gap Eyes Australian Foray," *Inside Retailing*, May 23, 2005, via Factiva, accessed June 2005.
92. "Gap Inc. Investor Update—Final."
93. Gap Inc., 2004 Annual Report, p. 6.
94. Samantha Conti, "Gap Inc. Taps Sunnucks for Europe Post, *Women's Wear Daily*, April 22, 2005, via Proquest/ABI Inform, www.proquest.com, accessed June 2005.
95. Louise Lee, "Yes, We Have a New Banana; The Casual Outfitter Is Moving Smartly from Khakis to High Fashion," *BusinessWeek*, May 31, 2004, via Proquest/ABI Inform, www.proquest.com, accessed March 2005.
96. Bridget Foley and Kristin Young, "Gap, Banana: The Big Makeover," *Women's Wear Daily*, April 20, 2004, via Factiva, accessed June 2005.
97. Jean E. Palmieri, "Gap's Banana Ripens; Banana Republic Sharpens Its Fashion Edge with Stylish Collection Approach," *DNR*, October 25, 2004, via Proquest/ABI Inform, www.proquest.com, accessed March 2005.
98. Louise Lee, "Yes, We Have a New Banana."
99. David Moin, "Banana Republic to Test Petites," *Women's Wear Daily*, January 28, 2005, via Proquest/ABI Inform, www.proquest.com, accessed March 2005.
100. Hoover's Inc., www.hoovers.com, accessed June 2004.
101. Valerie Seckler. "The Squeeze on Apparel's Sweet Spots."
102. Dorothy S. Lakner and Roxanne Meyer.
103. "Gap Inc. Investor Update—Final."
104. Patricia Sellers.

105. Joan Verdon, "Owners of West Nyack, N.Y., Store for Plus-Size Women Have Family Inspiration," *Knight Ridder Tribune Business News*, December 21, 2004, via Proquest/ABI Inform, www.proquest.com, accessed April 2005.

106. Gap Inc., 2004 Annual Report, pp. 6, 13.

107. Meredith Derby, "Old Navy Goes for the Perfect Fit," *Women's Wear Daily*, October 18, 2004, via Proquest/ABI Inform, www.proquest.com, accessed April 2005.

108. David Moin, "Gap Gets President, Old Navy Ships Out," *Women's Wear Daily*, April 19, 2005, via Proquest/ABI Inform, June 2005.

109. Amy Merrick, "Gap Plans Five Forth & Towne Stores for Fall," *The Wall Street Journal*, April 22, 2005, p. B1.

110. "Gap Inc. Investor Update—Final."

111. Ibid.

112. Ibid.

113. Amy Merrick.

114. "Gap Inc. Investor Update—Final."

115. Gap Inc., "Gap Inc. Introduces 'Forth & Towne,'" Gap Inc. Web site, April 21, 2005, www.gapinc.com, accessed April 2005.

116. Amy Merrick.

117. Hoover's Inc., accessed June 2005.

118. Gap Inc., "Gap Inc. Discusses Strategic Growth Initiatives at Investor Update Meeting," Gap Inc. Web site, April 21, 2005, www.gapinc.com, accessed April 2005.

119. Louise Lee, "Baby Boomer, Come Home," *BusinessWeek*, August 16, 2004, via Factiva, accessed March 2005.

120. Gap Inc., 2004 Annual Report, p. 50.

121. David Moin, "Old Navy Ads Get New Look," *Women's Wear Daily*, June 3, 2005, via Proquest/ABI Inform, http://www.proquest.com, accessed June 15, 2005.

122. Jean E. Palmieri, "Using Intuition and Instinct to Turn Around Gap."

123. Mercedes M. Cardona, "Differentiation Works for Banana Republic," *Advertising Age*, February 9, 2004, via Proquest/ABI Inform, www.proquest.com, accessed June 2005.

124. Roxanne Roberts, "40, but Sporting a $38 Million Figure," *The Washington Post*, March 23, 2005, p. C01.

125. Jeff Bercovici, "Ads Take a Wide Angle," *Women's Wear Daily*, May 26, 2005, via Proquest/ABI Inform, www.proquest.com, accessed June 2005.

126. Mercedes M. Cardona, "Old Navy to Keep It Quirky with Deutsch," *Advertising Age*, April 19, 2004, via Proquest/ABI Inform, www.proquest.com, accessed April 2005.

127. Ibid.

128. Cecily Hall, "The WWD List: Retail Ad Blitz," *Women's Wear Daily*, June 9, 2005, via Proquest/ABI Inform, www.proquest.com, accessed June 2005.

129. Mercedes M. Cardona, "Differentiation Works for Banana Republic."

130. Gap Inc., 2003 Social Responsibility Report (San Francisco: Gap Inc., 2004), p. 26, www.gapinc.com, accessed May 2005.

131. "Gap Inc. Investor Update—Final."

132. Ibid.

133. Meredith Derby, "Old Navy Goes for the Perfect Fit."

134. David Moin, "Gap Inc.'s Recovery Plan: New Format, Markets and Décor," *Women's Wear Daily*, April 22, 2005, via Factiva, accessed June 2005.

135. "Gap Inc." BusinessWeek Online, http://research.businessweek.com, accessed June 2005.

136. Samantha Conti, "Gap's Global Tech Strategy Is Slave to Fashion, Service," *Women's Wear Daily*, November 10, 2004, via Proquest/ABI Inform, www.proquest.com, accessed April 2005.

137. Ibid.

138. Ibid.

139. "Gap Inc. Investor Update—Final."

140. Ibid.

141. *hrSpectrum*, November-December 2003, p. 8, http://www.ilr.cornell.edu/depts/cahrs/downloads/PDFs/hrSpectrum/HRSpec03-12.pdf, accessed June 2005.

142. "National Association for Female Executives Honors Gap," *Display & Design Ideas*, March 22, 2005, via Factiva, accessed June 2005.

143. "GAP—Recruitment and Training Team," *Personnel Today,* October 29, 2002, via Factiva, accessed June 2005.

144. Ibid.

145. Gap Inc., "Store Management Opportunities," Gap Inc. Web site, www.gapinc.com, accessed June 2005.

146. *hrSpectrum*.

147. Gap Inc., 2004 Annual Report, p. 7.

148. Gap Inc., "Gap Inc. at a Glance, Summer 2005," Gap Inc. Web site, www.gapinc.com, accessed June 2005.

149. Meredith Derby.

1. Why do you think people are spending less on clothing, as this article suggests?
2. Why are the boomers such an important market segment?
3. How can communication between store managers and buyers affect a retail business?
4. What is cannibalism? How does this affect Gap Inc.?
5. Old Navy recently added plus sizes. How does appealing to this market niche improve sales?
6. Gap recently redesigned its stores. Do you think it will drive sales? Why or why not?
7. Do you think the concept of Forth and Towne is a good idea? Why or why not?
8. How can localizing merchandise by region be beneficial?
9. Do you think it is a good idea for Gap to use sales associates to hire or assess the skills of new employees? Why or why not?

>> case nine

ROCKET SCIENCE RETAILING IS ALMOST HERE... ARE YOU READY?

The holy grail of retailing—being able to offer the right product in the right place at the right time for the right price – remains frustratingly elusive. You would think we'd have captured it by now, particularly given the enormous amount of data that retailers and e-tailers can gather about points of purchase, buying patterns, and customers' tastes. But many retailers still have a long way to go.

Witness the much-publicized problems that e-tailers have had delivering the products that customers order on their Web sites. And who hasn't gone to a store only to find that it doesn't have the right item—even though the place is loaded with inventory, mostly discounted goods? Department store markdowns have grown from 8 percent of store sales in 1971 to 33 percent in 1995. These numbers include promotional markdowns as well as the forced markdowns that are the result of manufacturers' oversupply. But the increase is so large that most observers take it as a sign that retailers are having a hard time matching supply with demand.

That's not to say progress hasn't been made. Some retailers (we'll refer to retailers and e-tailers henceforth with the broader term) have dramatically improved their performance in ordering, distribution, and merchandising. But those companies are still a small, elite rank. The next step? An industrywide move toward something we call rocket science retailing – the act of blending traditional forecasting systems, which are largely based on the intuition of a handful of employees, with the prowess of information technology. Rocket science retailing fuses data and instinct with computer models and analysis to create a high-tech forecasting system supported by a flexible supply chain.

The model is not as far-fetched as you might think. Wall Street went through just such a transformation in the 1970s. And we've seen many retailers come quite close to achieving rocket science status during the past three years, as we've studied how they gather and process information, how they forecast demand, and how they manage their supplier relationships.

We recently completed an in-depth, multiyear survey of 32 generally cutting-edge companies in which we tracked their practices and progress in four areas critical to achieving rocket science retailing: forecasting, supply-chain speed, inventory planning, and gathering accurate, available data. In this article, we'll illustrate what some companies are doing best in these four areas, with the hope that other retailers can use their insights and practices to gain ground on the grail.

Forecasting

For many of the retailers in our study, forecasting product demand is a right-brain function that relies on the gut feel of a few individuals and not on the systematic use of sales data. But it's a big mistake to overlook the opportunity to mix art and science. Retailers can significantly improve forecast accuracy simply by updating their predictions based on early sales data, tracking the accuracy of their forecasts, getting product testing right, and using a variety of forecasting approaches. Let's discuss each of these practices.

› UPDATE FORECASTS BASED ON EARLY SALES DATA

Early product sales, appropriately adjusted for variations in price and availability, are an excellent predictor of overall sales. In fact, retailers that exploit these data for production and inventory planning can more than double their profits— especially retailers of products with short life cycles, such as clothing, consumer electronics, books, and music.

But despite the potentially high payoff—and a commonly accepted belief among retailers that early sales are a good indicator of future sales – many of the companies we surveyed had no systems in place to exploit early sales data. One retailer, for example, ordered garments and committed specific quantities of each stock-keeping unit (SKU) to each of its stores 11 months before the product was even available to the public. Even retailers that paid attention to their early sales data updated their forecasts in an ad hoc manner when sales greatly exceeded or fell far short of original predictions.

Several companies have retailing practices worth emulating, however. Japan-based World Company and Spain-based Zara are fashion retailers whose merchants systematically examine early sales data to estimate future demand for various products. They conduct this analysis for every product at predetermined periods in its sales cycle. And the merchants follow through, immediately reordering items that look as though they may end up in short supply. Not surprisingly, World Company has achieved a gross-margin return on inventory investments of more than 300 percent—a substantially higher return than any other retailer we are aware of.

Dallas-based CompUSA, which sells computers and associated merchandise, has found that even one or two days of early sales data can be very useful to predict sales and replenish its inventory for PCs. Buyers monitor the sales of a certain product line soon after it is launched and update their forecasts based on those observations. They expedite orders for PCs that are selling better than expected and, when possible, they decline items that have not been shipped. This process of reading and reacting to market signals has improved CompUSA's ability to match supply with demand.

Finally, book and music retailer Borders Group uses historical sales data to customize the product assortment in each of its stores. Borders tracks sales at each store by product category. It uses its merchandise planning system to automatically adjust the inventory at a store based on sales in each product category. Thus, a store in Anchorage, Alaska, would carry a wide assortment of books about small planes because sales for such books tend to be high at that outlet, while the Boston store might stock relatively few items in this category because demand is lower there. Why don't more retailers customize their inventories? The answer, as we explain later on, lies in slow supply chains, inadequate or inaccurate data, the inability to measure stockouts and forecast error, and planning software that is inappropriate for the retailer.

› TRACK AND PREDICT FORECAST ACCURACY

Only nine of the 32 retailers in our study said they analyzed the accuracy of their forecasts. And yet, tracking forecast errors, and understanding when and why they occur, is fundamental to improving accuracy. Even more important, knowing the margin of error on a forecast is vital to being able to react when the forecast is wrong. For example, if past forecasts for a certain product have been wrong by plus or minus 50 percent, when a merchant says you'll sell 10,000 of that item, that really means you'll sell between 5,000 and 15,000 units. Instead of buying 10,000, it might be smarter to buy 5,000 finished units and materials for an additional 10,000 units to be assembled quickly if early sales are strong.

World Company tracks and predicts forecast accuracy by item using the "Obermeyer method": new products are displayed in a room at corporate headquarters just as they would be in a retail store, and about 30 store employees, who are chosen to represent the company's target customers, estimate the likely success of each product. World has found that the products that generate greater disagreement among the employees are likely to have less-accurate forecasts.

› GET THE PRODUCT TESTING RIGHT

An impressive 78 percent of the retailers in our study test new products in a few stores before the actual product launch. But almost all the buyers said their test methods are highly unscientific and that any results that indicate that certain products will be *unsuccessful* are often ignored. Merchants often believe their products will sell well despite unfavorable test results; they blame the weather (bad or good), the poor choice of test sites, the inferior execution of tests, and other factors for suboptimal sales.

When a product testing method is developed with care and refined on a regular basis, the results can substantially improve forecasts. We helped develop a testing method at one apparel retailer that predicts the sales of a product based on the early sales at a few carefully selected test stores. We found that the selection of stores greatly affected the quality of the forecasts. By using historical sales data to pick a diverse group of test stores that matched varying customer preferences, we reduced forecast errors for each style and color from 30 to 9 percent.

› USE A VARIETY OF FORECASTING APPROACHES

Most companies we surveyed limit themselves to just one type of forecasting. Generally, a single forecast for each item is generated by the buyer or by a small group from merchandising. But generating multiple forecasts can be very valuable because in seeking to understand the differences in those forecasts, managers can explore the assumptions implicit in their forecasting techniques.

Take Old Navy, a division of the Gap. The company blends bottom-up and top-down forecasting approaches and then considers the results in a way worth emulating. Bottom-up forecasts are developed by merchandisers and planners who predict demand for each product based on factors such as current trends in the market, the product's "fit" with the target customer, and the complementary products that will also be offered. Top-down forecasts are developed by planners and occur independent of the bottom-up process. They are based on macroeconomic factors such as the economic growth rate and corporate growth objectives. The two approaches typically yield different results, which are reconciled during a meeting of managers from both groups. Old Navy finds that the different processes, and the ensuing discussion, lead to substantially better forecasts.

Supply-Chain Speed

Many products today have such long lead times that retailers can't call for a change in production—even if they have tracked early sales, have paid attention to product testing, and know without a doubt that a change is warranted. As one merchant told us, "We do pay attention to our tests. The problem is we already own the product; the test merely reveals that it will be a dog once it gets to the stores." Another retailer maintains an 11-month lead time from placing an order to receiving apparel at the distribution center—even for products with a life cycle of only three months. Consequently, buyers have to commit to ordering from a single vendor before any sales data are obtained. They must also specify how much of each product will be delivered to each store 11 months before the material is received at the distribution center.

Supply-chain speed is clearly a critical component of rocket science retailing, particularly for products that have short life cycles. A company that can observe early sales and respond quickly with any appropriate additional merchandise can obviously reduce the likelihood of selling out of hot items. It can also reduce markdowns because its ability to respond with more products during the season means the retailer can order less initially and cut its losses on products that turn out to be failures.

World and Zara use similar exemplary practices in this area. Consider how World manages its supply chain. It can manufacture and deliver an existing product to stores in two weeks. It can design a new product and supply it to stores in as little as three weeks. How does the company achieve such short response times? First, World does a considerable amount of work with supply chain partners before it even places an order. The company stores fabrics and findings (buckles, zippers, and so on) and reserves production capacity at factories in anticipation of demand. At the beginning of a sales season, World, like most retailers, finds it difficult to predict the sales of each product. It knows that carrying an inventory of finished products is risky. But the company does find it relatively safe to hold raw-material inventory and reserve production capacity, since forecasts for those materials tend to be more accurate than forecasts for finished products.

Second, World's factories troubleshoot production problems—separate from the main manufacturing area. The employees in the "debug area" work closely with designers at World's corporate office, changing the product design to enable easier manufacturing and, at times, replacing hard-to-find raw materials with more easily available materials.

Third, World has empowered its employees in product design, merchandising, operations, and its stores to make some decisions on their own, thus avoiding the bureaucratic delays that can accompany the decision-making process. For example, the decision to design, price, procure materials for, and manufacture a new product at World usually involves a meeting of five or six division managers who work in adjacent offices as a cross-functional team. At other retailers, such a meeting might involve convening managers located in different cities and might mean getting approval from executives at various levels in the organization – a more time-consuming process.

Why aren't other retailers as responsive as World? One common problem at many companies is an "efficiency mentality." The apparel retailer with the 11-month product lead time, for example, insisted on placing orders for individual stores instead of buying in bulk for all the stores and then strategically allocating goods to different stores once materials arrived at the distribution center. The retailer reduced its transportation costs and its inventory carrying costs at the warehouse, but it limited its ability to react quickly to market signals.

One distribution center manager told us about a video his company had produced illustrating how distribution efficiency could be improved. The video showed how fast warehouse personnel could gather garments for shipment if they collected and packed the reorders in the same mix of sizes – regardless of how many large, medium, and small items an individual store needed. The video also showed how much longer it took the warehouse staffers to collect the orders when the size mix for each store varied according to its need. The distribution manager and his peers were confident that the few-seconds-per-garment time savings would convince store managers that all reorders should be shipped in identical size mixes. Which begged our question to the manager: "How long does it take you to process garments that come back from the stores unsold because you haven't shipped what they need?"

Many retailers fall into a vicious cycle. Logistics and procurement officials argue that reducing lead times for products won't help the retailer because the company lacks good sales data and the tools to analyze that data. Merchandise-planning officials argue that being able to store and analyze sales data won't help the retailer since logistics and procurement can't respond fast enough to those signals. The problem is that companies can't quantify the value of a short lead time in reducing stockouts and markdowns. But as retailers adopt new software tools for forecasting and planning supply, they can use these tools to measure the impact of a shorter lead time and to better match supply with demand.

Inventory Planning

Inventory planning involves deciding when and how much to order, or how much to produce, of various raw materials, components, and finished goods. Inventory planning differs from forecasting because a planner might find it beneficial to stock more or less than predicted demand. In planning inventory for a household, for example, you might decide to stock far more medicine than you anticipate needing in case you become sick. Or you might buy certain items – batteries, for instance – many months' demand at a time while other items – bread and milk, for instance – might be ordered every week. Inventory planning at most retailers suffers from several shortcomings. One of the most glaring is that many retailers don't track stockouts and the resulting lost sales. Only 13 of the 32 companies in our study said they track stockouts, and 11 of the 13 used this information to estimate the resulting lost sales.

Lost sales are endemic among retailers, especially for products with short life cycles. Tracking stockouts could help retailers set optimal inventory levels and could help them see the value in improving supply-chain responsiveness. So why aren't these metrics studied carefully? One reason is that it's hard to know how much of a product would have sold if supply had been plentiful. The figure can be estimated using sophisticated statistical techniques, but retailers generally can't find such capabilities in commercial software, especially in the case of short-life-cycle products.

There is a way over that hurdle. We developed a method to estimate lost sales. Our procedure works in two steps. First, it calculates the underlying demand rate for a product based on the sales patterns that occurred when the product was in stock. Second, it combines the estimated demand rate with the duration of the product stockout at a particular store to derive the lost sales. To estimate demand rate and lost sales, the technique has to be modified for factors such as the variation of demand on different days and at different times within a day. In our experiments with real retail data, our technique estimated lost sales to within 2 percent at the store level and with higher accuracy at the chain level or for a category of products.

The benefits of tracking lost sales, and increasing inventory levels systematically to reduce those losses, can be substantial. One retailer found that sales could be improved by roughly 10 percent simply by increasing inventory at the stores, suggesting that lost sales – before the inventory boost—would have accounted for at least 10 percent of sales. At Rome-based jewelry manufacturer Bulgari, stockouts on a single item at one store had been high enough to reduce the store's revenue by 3.5 percent. As a result, Bulgari is seeking ways to improve its planning processes.

Accurate, Available Data

All the retailers in our study have point-of-sale (POS) systems and have used them to capture sales data electronically. But contrary to popular perception, most retailers have considerable difficulty capturing and maintaining sales data that are accurate and accessible to their employees.

First, let's consider the accuracy of the data that retailers collect. Store-level sales data are often inaccurate for several reasons. In the apparel industry, a common source of data inaccuracy arises from improper handling of returns. When a customer buys a medium sweater and then wants to exchange it for a small, the returned garment should be scanned into the register as a return, and the requested garment should be scanned in as a new purchase. In reality, the salesperson, trying not to inconvenience the customer, exchanges the medium garment for the small garment without scanning both items into the POS system. As a result, the inventory levels of both items are inaccurate.

In the grocery business, the sheer volume of transactions confounds the grocer's ability to maintain accurate sales and inventory information. Most consumers can recount a situation in which they bought multiple units with the same price (for example, a container of lemon yogurt and a container of vanilla yogurt, both the same brand) and the checkout clerk scanned one of these items multiple times. Clearly, this would cause the inventories of both the lemon and the vanilla yogurt to be inaccurate. One grocery chain found that sales of medium tomatoes have consistently been 25 percent higher than the actual shipment of medium tomatoes to their stores. Checkout clerks frequently entered into their registers the price lookup (PLU) code for "medium tomato" even if the customer was buying organic, vine-ripe, or other specialty tomatoes. "If it's red and soft, it's a medium tomato at the checkout counter," remarks the CIO at this supermarket chain. Most checkout clerks are reluctant to spend extra time to check the PLU code accurately and risk upsetting the customer and their manager, who, in many cases, is tracking the average rate at which the checkout clerks scan units.

Not all data inaccuracy is caused at the checkout register, of course. One retailer in our study found that inventory records were inaccurate for 29 percent of the items at a store that had been stocked but that had not yet opened for customers. The retailer traced the problem back to its distribution systems; warehouse employees often shipped the wrong item (for instance, sending small shirts instead of medium shirts, or sending one flavor of yogurt instead of another). Similarly, errors were caused when changes in vendor case-packs – the number of items shipped per box – weren't promptly entered in the retailer's merchandise replenishment system. In one instance, a vendor changed the dimensions of its case-pack from 144 units to 12 units; the merchandise replenishment system, unaware of the change, asked the warehouse to ship only one case-pack.

Many retailers don't know if their information is inaccurate because they don't track data accuracy. Other retailers track data accuracy, but the information discovered is not widely disseminated. At one apparel retailer, the merchandisers and planners had no idea their POS data were inaccurate even though the vice president of planning had, through periodic audits, concluded that the error in inventory data was close to 30 percent at the store level.

Some retailers have taken steps to ensure the accuracy of sales and inventory data. One interesting approach, the "zero balance walk," is practiced at office-supply superstore Staples. In this system, an employee walks through the store each day looking for SKUs that are out of stock. For each item that is out of stock, a stockout card is generated and a sticker is placed in the space reserved for the item. Other employees verify the events – sudden surges in consumer demand, computer data error, merchandise stocked in the wrong aisle, and so on—that caused the sellout. If the stockout was due to faulty data in the computer, the inventory level in the computer system is corrected. Performing the zero balance walk each day helps measure and improve data accuracy at Staples.

Now let's consider the availability of data. The retailers we surveyed varied in their ability to store and access their sales data. The median retailer in our study kept two years of sales data accessible online. One company kept only six weeks of data for its employees to use; at the other extreme, another company kept ten years of sales data accessible online.

People often wonder why it's valuable to keep a history of sales for so many years given how quickly trends change. In fact, the data contain some useful information about sales patterns that remain stable from year to year, such as seasonality, consumer reaction to a promotion, and differences in sales patterns at different stores. We have also found that the average forecast error tends to be reasonably similar from year to year, even if the products have changed almost entirely.

Forecasting product sales is much more difficult for the merchants at companies that lack sufficient online data. At the retailer with only six weeks' worth of online data, merchants referred to heavy stacks of paper copies of sales data from previous years when estimating future product sales. Given that the cost of computer storage space has fallen sharply, there's no reason for retailers not to store sales data electronically and make it easily accessible to their merchants. Those who don't either don't see how the data could be useful in their decision making or made the decision several years ago when computer storage space was extremely expensive.

Some retailers don't make even recent sales data available at the detailed level. For example, some apparel retailers track their sales according to style, color, and size (each has its own bar code) but they store only the data regarding style and color in the central computer. So a merchandiser might know how many red blouses in a certain style were sold at a particular store on a particular day but not if those units were sold in small, medium, or large. Is it any wonder that a recent survey found that one out of three consumers who enter a clothing store intending to buy something leave without buying because he or she can't find their size in stock?

Managers at these retailers claim there is little value in knowing sales by size since their vendors and distribution centers can ship only in standard size packs, which precludes customizing the size assortments by store or region. Meanwhile, it is difficult to justify changes to their transportation and warehousing systems that would let them customize their shipments, because they don't have the appropriate sales-by-size data that would tell them how to do that. It's the perfect example of the vicious cycle these retailers fall into: an inflexible supply chain justifies bad data, which justify an inflexible supply chain.

Costs, Customer Satisfaction, and Morale

We've outlined the current best practices—and the current best-case scenarios – for the four areas that are fundamental to achieving rocket science retailing. But there are other areas of improvement for retailers who seek to get closer to the grail.

Many of the issues we've touched on have dealt with metrics like forecast accuracy, stockouts, lost sales, gross margins, markdowns, and inventory carrying costs. But retailers also need to track the variables that drive those measures. For example, which products and market segments tend to have inaccurate forecasts, and how does forecast accuracy change over time? Only then will retailers have the information they need to get at the root cause of retail problems, solve them, and improve performance.

Some retailers also focus too much on the short term. The pressure to immediately improve profits can spur cost-cutting that leads to customer dissatisfaction and low employee morale. The senior managers at one retailer in our study were challenged by the board to achieve double-digit profit increases every year. Management achieved this goal by cutting costs through reducing the number of salespeople in the stores. The board was pleased with the short-term profit growth, but the reduced headcount pretty quickly created lower customer satisfaction, and employees were unhappy.

To prevent this kind of problem, retailers need to visibly and accurately track customer satisfaction and employee morale. At least one retailer in our study has engaged an outside audit firm to measure those factors, and the company is even considering reporting the results in its annual reports. That approach makes sense; without hard numbers on customer satisfaction and employee morale, those factors would take a backseat to cost reduction. In the long run the retailer would be worse off.

Marriage of Art and Science

It's useful to consider the long-standing conflict between left-brainers, the technical types who either produce or rely on information supplied through technology, and right-brainers, those who rely more on intuition. The core of rocket science retailing, as we've said, involves a marriage of the two. And many retail executives do acknowledge the need for blending left- and right-brain capabilities, particularly in planning.

Consistent with this view, their organizations have a left-brained planning organization to complement the traditionally right-brained buying or merchandising organizations. The planner typically looks at sales data—in the absence of software systems—to determine stocking quantities at the store and SKU levels. The buyer tries to look beyond numbers and history and focuses on right-brain tasks such as identifying changing patterns in consumer demand and developing new products.

The division of skills and responsibilities between buying and planning appears to work well at most retailers. But in other areas, there is vast room for improvement; a good example is the relationship between the management information systems group, which maintains computer systems at the company, and other departments such as merchandising. One retail CEO reports "The only time [the MIS managers] communicate with me is when they ask me for a $30 million write-off on some previous project that now has to be abandoned." Another CEO chastised us for not appreciating the MIS-merchandising divide: "You guys don't get it, the merchandising-MIS relationship is broken."

Most MIS specialists aren't experts in products or merchandising. They are experts in information technologies such as database management and computer networks. Prior to joining the retailer, they may have worked at nonretail companies. Consequently, they don't always understand the needs of the merchandising organization. In many cases, even the language is substantially different between the two groups. One MIS group at a leading retailer found, much to its surprise, that when merchants in the company say "always," as in "I always follow this procedure," they mean 75 percent of the time. This shocked the literal-minded MIS group for whom "always" means 100 percent. It is not clear how the relationship between MIS and merchandising will evolve. But we don't see how merchandising can become scientific without the two factions understanding each other.

The Systems at the Core

If rocket science retailing is ever to happen across the industry, retailers must pay more attention to the logic that is embedded in their planning systems.

Most retailers, for example, realize that inventory levels should be reduced toward the end of a product's life cycle and that forecasts should be updated based on early sales data after adjusting for product availability and price fluctuations. But most inventory-planning software is designed for products that have long life cycles and is thus inappropriate for products that have an economic life of just a few months.

Consider, for example, a catalog retailer that recently bought a new software package for planning inventories of short-life-cycle products. The company was advised to set the system's parameters to stock four weeks' worth of projected demand for each SKU. For these products, however, sales usually peaked in the first week and then declined exponentially. This meant that the four-week supply ordered by the system was based on inflated sales. It was inevitably too much inventory and often generated obsolete goods at the end of the products' life cycles.

What's more, most inventory planning systems typically require two or three years of demand history on which to model forecasting and stocking parameters. This is a problem for the many products whose life cycles are measured in months. Some software vendors are starting to address this problem, and we're confident an appropriate system will be developed soon.

Rocket science retailing will require the development and use of decision support tools. In the past, many retailers that have attempted to develop such systems in-house or purchase them from third-party vendors have been disappointed; the systems did not use the appropriate mathematical techniques and hence produced poor results. The mathematical techniques underlying such decision-support systems are not straightforward for a number of reasons.

Consider a task as simple as using early sales data to guide replenishment; see what's selling well and get more of it if you can. But implementing this concept requires careful attention to detail. For example, it's important to know not just how much has sold of a particular product but the conditions under which it sold, including price and inventory availability. This point is well illustrated by one retailer that had developed a replenishment model based on early sales data. The model showed that a product in one style and color was selling almost twice as well as had been originally forecast. Based on this, a large replenishment order was placed. The vice president of merchandising who had placed the order was dismayed to see sales in the next three weeks fall to 60 percent of what the model had predicted. She was convinced that the model was flawed. But careful examination revealed that sales were slow because a delivery of the product that had been expected at the time the order was placed, and that had been assumed by the model, was delayed by three weeks. Hence, stores were stocking out of many sizes. Once the fresh product arrived, sales rebounded to the level predicted by the model. The underlying principle is simple—you can't sell it if you don't have it in inventory. But retailers often overlook this principle when they interpret sales data.

Nature abhors a vacuum, and the retailing situation today is an economic vacuum that cannot persist. Retailers can't continue to suffer growing markdown losses yet disappoint a significant portion of their customers who can't find what they want. They can't continue to ignore billions of bytes of unused sales history that could help solve these problems. Somehow this vacuum will be filled.

Every decade sees a retailer that innovates so powerfully that it rewrites the rules for other retailers and for all companies in the retail supply chain. In the 1980s, it was Wal-Mart. In the 1990s, it was Amazon.com. We believe the next retail innovator will be the one that best combines access to consumer transaction data with the ability to turn that information into action.

QUESTIONS

1. What kind of data can be gathered via point of purchase? Are you comfortable, as a consumer, with this type of data gathering? Why or why not?

2. What are the advantages of early sales data? Are there disadvantages?

3. How does risk and uncertainty affect the fashion business? Discuss some ways in which risk and uncertainty can be minimized.

4. How can inventory planning in a retail store be improved?

Aaker, David; V. Kumar; and George Day. *Marketing Research*. 7th ed. New York: John Wiley and Sons, 2001.

Agins, Teri. *The End of Fashion: The Mass Marketing of Fashion*. New York: William Morrow and Company, 1999.

American Chemical Society. "Textile Chemistry." www.chemistry.org/portal/a/c/s/l/acsdisplay. html?DOC=vc2%5C3wk%5Cwk3_text.html (accessed September 15, 2004).

American Fiber Manufacturers Association. "Microfibers." www.fibersource.com/f-tutor/micro. htm (accessed August 25, 2004).

Bainbridge, Jane. "Baby-Boomers: A Generation Vexed." *Marketing*, May 7, 1998, Infotrac online database, article A20817420.

Baudot, Francois. *Fashion: The Twentieth Century*. New York: Universe Publishing, 1999.

Bellis, Mary. "Polyester." http://inventors.about. com/library/inventors/blpolyester.htm (accessed September 15, 2004).

Blumer, Herbert. *Symbolic Interactionism*. Berkeley: University of California Press, 1969.

Boone, Louis; and David Kurtz. *Contemporary Marketing*. 8th ed. Fort Worth: Dryden Press, 1995.

Buxbaum, Gerda. *The Icons of Fashion*. Munich, Germany: Prestel Publishing, 2000.

Cozzalio, Dawna. "Meet Generation Y." *Business-Week*, 1999.

Dychtwald, Maddy. "Marketplace 2000: Riding the Wave of Population Change." *Journal of Consumer Marketing* 14., no. 4 (1997).

Dychtwald, Maddy. *Cycles: How We Live, Work and Buy*. New York: Free Press, 2003.

Ehrenberg, Andrew; Neil Barnard; and Bryon Sharp. "Problems with Marketing Decision Models," *Visionary Marketing for the Twenty-First Century, Conference Proceedings,* 2000.

"Manufactured Fibers." www.fabrics.net/manufact. asp (accessed September 15, 2004).

Fernanzez, Jesus; and Dirk Krueger. "Consumption over the Life Cycle: Some Facts from Consumer Expenditure Survey Data." 2002. www.econ.upenn. edu/~jesusfv/empiricalpaper.pdf (accessed January 21, 2004).

Fernandex, Joao; Roberto de Oliveria; and Norberto Hochheim. "Application of Family Life Cycle Concept in Determining Potential Segment for Housing Projects." www.sinduscon-fpolis.org. br/artigoscientificos/application%20of%20family% life20.html (accessed January 21, 2004).

Finkelstein, Joanne. *After a Fashion*. Carlton South, Australia: Melbourne University Press, 1996.

Frings Stephens, Gini. *Fashion: From Concept to Consumer*. Upper Saddle River, NJ: Prentice Hall, 2002.

Gilly, Mary; and Ben Enis. "Recycling the Family Life Cycle: A Proposal for Redefinition." *Advances in Consumer Research*, 1982, pp 271–76.

Hicks, Rick; and Kathy Hicks. *Boomers, Xers and Other Strangers.*" Wheaton, IL: Tyndale House Publishers, 1999.

Howe, Neil; and William Strauss. *The Fourth Turning*. New York: Broadway Books, 1997.

Howe, Neil; and William Strauss. *Millennials Rising*. New York: Vintage Books, 2000.

Isaac, Stephen; and William Michael. *Handbook in Research and Evaluation*. San Diego: Education and Industrial Testing Services, 1997.

Kadolph, Sara; and Anna Langford. *Textiles*. Upper Saddle River, NJ: Prentice Hall, 1998.

Kaiser, Nagasawa; and Hutton. "Construction of an SI Theory of Fashion: Part One. Ambivalence and Change." *Clothing and Textiles Research Journal* 13, no. 3 (1995).

Kotler, Phillip; and Gary Armstrong. *Marketing: An Introduction.*" Upper Saddle River, NJ: Prentice Hall, 2003.

Kerin; Berkowitz; Hartley; and Rudelius. *Marketing*. 7th ed. Boston: McGraw-Hill, 2003.

Lauer, Jeanette; and Robert Lauer. *Fashion Power*. Englewood Cliffs, NJ: Prentice Hall, 1981.

McGuinness, Kevin. "Demography: Baby Boomers at Middle Youth." *The Futurist* 31, no. 3 (1997).

Maguire, Tom. "Conflicting Signals." *American Demographics*, November 1998.

Manolis, Chris; and James Roberts. "Baby Boomers and Busters: An Exploratory Investigation of Attitudes toward Marketing, Advertising and Consumerism." *Journal of Consumer Marketing* 17, no. 6 (2000), pp 481–99.

Murphy, Dallas. *The Fast Forward MBA in Marketing.*" New York: John Wiley and Sons, 1997.

Nickels, William. *Understanding Business*. New York: McGraw-Hill, 2001.

Portolese Dias, Laura. "Generational Buying Motivations for Fashion." *Journal of Fashion Marketing and Management* 7, no. 3 (2003).

Reda, Susan. "Reaching the Aging Boomers." *Stores*, March 1998. www.stores.org/archives/mar98cover.asp (accessed January 26, 2004).

Renyolds, Fred; and William Wells. *Consumer Behavior*. New York: McGraw-Hill, 1977.

Robertson, Thomas; and Harold Kassarjian. *Handbook of Consumer Behavior*. Upper Saddle River, NJ: Prentice Hall, 1998.

Rouncefield, "Diversity in Households and Families." 2004. www.rouncefield.homestead.cm/filesas_soc_family_3.html (accessed January 21, 2004).

Schewe, Charlies; and Geoffrey Meredith. *Defining Markets*, *Defining Moments*. New York: Hungry Minds, 2002.

Schiffman, Leon; and Kanuk Lazar, Leslie. *Consumer Behavior*. Englewood Cliffs, NJ: Prentice Hall, 1983.

Smith, J. Walker; and Ann Clurman. *Rocking the Ages.* New York: HarperBusiness, 1997.

Smith, J. Walker; and Ann Clurman. "Generational Marketing." *Inc.*, April 1997, Infotrac online database, article AI9257602.

Solomon, Michael. *Consumer Behavior*. Needleham Heights, MA: Paramount Publishing, 1994.

Solomon, Michael; and Nancy Rabolt. *Consumer Behavior in Fashion*. Upper Saddle River, NJ: Prentice Hall, 2004.

Smith, Joyce. "Rayon: The Multi-Faceted Fiber." January 15, 2002, http://ohioline.osu.edu/hyg-fact/5000/5538.html (accessed September 18, 2004).

Steele, Valerie. *Fifty Years of Fashion*. New Haven and London: Yale Publishing, 2000.

Stone, Elaine. *The Dynamics of Fashion*. New York: Fairchild Publications, 2004.

Strauss, William; and Neil Howe. *Generations*. New York: William Morrow and Company, 1991.

Textile Fabric Consultants. "Spandex: The Revolution and Return." www.fabrics.net/amyspandex.asp (accessed September 15, 2004).

Underhill, Paco. *Why We Buy: The Science of Shopping*. New York: Simon & Schuster Adult Publishing. 2000.

United States Customs. "Customs Quotas." 2004. www.cbp.gov/xp/cgov/import/textiles_and_quotas/archived/2003_year_rpt/ US Customs quotas (accessed October 20, 2004).

Weiss, Michael. *The Clustered World*. Boston: Little, Brown, 2000.

Wellner, Alison Stein. "Generational Divide: Are Traditional Methods of Classifying a Generation Still Meaningful in a Diverse and Changing Nation?" *American Demographics*, October 2000, pp. 52–58.

Wikipedia. "Nylon." http://en.wikipedia.org/wiki/Nylon (accessed September 15, 2004).

>> Credits

CHAPTER I

pp. 2–3, Hans Bjurling/Veer Inc; p. I7 (all), Amaryah Curnutt; p. I8, Amaryah Curnutt; p. I9, Amaryah Curnutt; p. 20, Amaryah Curnutt; p. 2I, Amaryah Curnett.

CHAPTER 2

p. 29, Mark Mainz/Getty Images; p. 34, Women's Wear Daily/AP Wide World; p. 35 (top), Stuart Ramson/AP Wide World; p. 35 (bottom), Tim Boyle/Getty Images; p. 36, Ryan McVay/Getty Images/DIL; p. 37, PhotoDisc/Getty Images/DIL; p. 38, Doug Menuz/Getty Images/DIL; p. 42, Pierre Verdy/Getty Images.

CHAPTER 3

pp. 46–47, Ryan McVay/Getty Images/ DIL; p. 49 (top left), Wang Leng/Asia Images/Getty Images; p. 49 (top middle), Chaloner Woods/Hulton Archive/ Getty Images; p. 49 (top right), White Cross Productions/The Image Bank/ Getty Images; p. 49 (bottom left), Mike Segar/Reuters/Corbis; p. 49 (bottom right), Selznick/MGM/The Kobal Collection; p. 50, Piotr Sikora/Photonica/ Getty Images; p. 52, Siede Presis/Getty Images/DIL; p. 53, S.Solumn/ PhotoLink/Getty Images/DIL; p. 54, C.Sherburne/PhotoLink/Getty Images/ DIL; p. 55 (top), Jan Suttle/LifeFile/Getty Images/DIL; p. 55 (bottom), Caterina Bernardi/Zefa/Corbis; pp. 57–58 (all), Courtesy Mohawk Industries; p. 60 (top), RF/Corbis; p. 60 (bottom left), Jose Luis Pelaez/Corbis; p. 60 (bottom right), RF/Corbis.

CHAPTER 4

p. 65, Bettmann/Corbis; p. 67 (top), Time/Life Pictures/Getty Images; p. 67 (bottom left), Kathy Willens/AP Wide World; p. 67 (bottom right), W. G. Phillips/Hulton Archive/Getty Images; p. 68 (top), Bettmann/Corbis; p. 68 (bottom left), Christel Gerstenberg/Corbis; p. 68 (bottom right), Mitchell Gerber/Corbis; p. 69, Seeberger Freres/Hulton Archive/Getty Images; p. 70 (top), Louis Lanzano/AP Wide World; p. 70 (bottom), Paramount Pictures/ Getty Images; p. 7I (top), 20th Century Fox/The Kobal Collection; p. 7I (bottom), Conde Nast Archive/Corbis; p. 72 (top), Hilton Archive/Getty Images; p. 72 (bottom), Bettmann/Corbis; p. 73 (top), Hulton Archive/Getty Images; p. 73 (bottom left), Gene Lester/Hulton Archive/Getty Images; p. 73 (bottom right), Reed Kaestner/Corbis; p. 74, AP photo; p. 75 (top), Bettmann/ Corbis; p. 75 (bottom left), Time Life Pictures/Pix Inc./Getty Images; p. 75 (bottom right), Bettmann/Corbis; p. 76, RF/Corbis/DIL; p. 77, MGM/The Kobal Collection; p. 78, Henry Diltz/Corbis.

CHAPTER 5

p. 85, Jack Hollingsworth/Getty Images/DIL; p. 87, Ian Tilton/Corbis; p. 90, Joshua Ets-Hokin/Getty Images/DIL; p. 9I, RetroAmerica/DIL; p. 92, RF/ Corbis/DIL; p. 96 (top), Nam Y. Huh/AP Wide World; p. 96 (bottom), Courtesy Gerber Technology; p. 97, Alexander Tamargo/Getty Images; p. 98, Courtesy The Tobe Report; p. 99, Courtesy Fashionsnoops.com; p. I00, Scott Gries/ Getty Images.

CHAPTER 6

pp. l04–05, RF/Corbis; p. l07, The McGraw-Hill Companies, Inc. Andrew Resek, photographer; p. llO (left), Reed Saxon/AP Wide World; p. llO (right), Sergio Puimatti; p. ll2 (left), Niki Mareschal/Getty Images; p. ll2 (right), Monica Lau/Getty Images/DIL; p. ll7, PhotoDisc/PunchStock/DIL.

CHAPTER 7

pp. l26–27, PhotoEdit; p. l3l (top), PhotoLink/Getty Images/DIL; p. l3l (bottom), Ryan McVay/Getty Images/DIL; p. l32, Rob Melnychuk/Getty Images/DIL; p. l34, Ted S. Warren/AP Wide World; p. l35, Michael Newman/Photoedit; p. l37, F. Schussler/PhotoLink/Getty Images/DIL; p. l39, Michael Newman/Photoedit; p. l4l, Susan Van Etten/Photoedit.

CHAPTER 8

pp. l50–5l, D.Normark/PhotoLink/Getty Images/DIL; p. l57, MNChan/Getty Images; p. l58, John Wang/Getty Images/DIL; p. l64, RF/Corbis/DIL; p. l65, Andrew Holbrooke/Corbis.

CHAPTER 9

pp. l70–7l, Rob Melnychuk/Getty Images/DIL; p. l73, The McGraw-Hill Companies, Inc. Jill Braaten, photographer; p. l75, PhotoLink/Getty Images/DIL; p. l79 (top), RF/Corbis; p. l79 (bottom), Mark Mainz/Getty Images; p. l80 (top left), Tom Wagner/Corbis SABA; p. l80 (top right), Dave Gatley/Bloomberg News/Landov; p. l80 (bottom left), Ralf-Finn Hestoft/Corbis; p. l80 (bottom right), James Leynse/Corbis; p. l8l (left), James Leynse/Corbis; p. l8l (right), The McGraw-Hill Companies, Inc. Lars Niki, photographer.

CHAPTER lO

p. l90, 200l Image lOOl Ltd/DIL
p. 2l2, Patagonik Works/Getty Images

APPENDIX

p. 2l6, The McGraw-Hill Companies, Inc. Lars Niki, photographer.